THE GENESIS AND EFFECT OF THE POPULAR FRONT IN FRANCE

Karl G. Harr, Jr.

UNIVERSITY
PRESS OF
AMERICA

LANHAM • NEW YORK • LONDON

Copyright © 1987 by

University Press of America,® Inc.

4720 Boston Way
Lanham, MD 20706

3 Henrietta Street
London WC2E 8LU England

All rights reserved

Printed in the United States of America

British Cataloging in Publication Information Available

Library of Congress Cataloging in Publication Data

Harr, Karl G., 1922-
The genesis and effect of the Popular Front in France.

Bibliography: p.
1. Front populaire. 2. France—Politics and government—1914-1940. 3. Fascism—France. I. Title.
DC396.H27 1987 944.081'5 86-28173
ISBN 0-8191-6056-3 (alk. paper)
ISBN 0-8191-6057-1 (pbk. : alk. paper)

All University Press of America books are produced on acid-free
paper which exceeds the minimum standards set by the National
Historical Publication and Records Commission.

To Cathy and Amy

TABLE OF CONTENTS

Introduction	i
PART ONE. The Luxury of Disunity:	1
I. The Development of Disunity	2
II. Hitler and the Problem of Common Defense	30
III. The Impact of Neo-Socialism	49
IV. Economic Crisis	76
PART TWO. The Challenge of Domestic Fascism:	95
V. The Paris Riots	96
VI. "Socialism or Fascism"	128
VII. Unity of Action and the Popular Front	146
VIII. Brussels - October 1934	166
IX. The Doriot Incident	183
PART THREE. The Crucial Congresses:	197
X. Mulhouse, June 1935	198
XI. The New Face of the Communist Party	230
XII. Conclusion	266
Bibliography	279
About the Author	316

INTRODUCTION

The salient feature of the period immediately after the 1914-1918 war for the French Left as well as for Socialists and liberals throughout Europe was the emergence of the new political phenomenon of the IIIrd International. The brooding omnipresence of Moscow, which made itself felt through the various national Communist parties, introduced a new factor into the calculations of the leaders of the non-Communist Left which required a major tactical and doctrinal adjustment. In the case of the French Left preoccupation with this adjustment was an important factor through the first post war decade, but by the end of that period the problems arising from this new intruder were presumably happily and successfully resolved. To only a slightly lesser extent than in England and the other western European democracies the bastions of nineteenth century Socialism and liberalism in France proved equal to the task of resisting the bolshevik onslaught. By the end of 1932 order was restored. The Socialists had recovered from the initial shock and again possessed virtually undisputed leadership of the proletarian forces of France.

But in January of 1933 a new and equally serious development imposed its effect upon the French Left. Fascism, the "Italian phenomenon", gained control of France's traditional enemy, and there were signs of its spread to other countries in Europe, even to France itself. As this danger grew the French Left felt itself increasingly forced into a choice of tyrannies. Effective resistance to one began to mean compromise with the other and, although both alternatives were extremely distasteful, the emotional predisposition of the Left and the relative seriousness of the threats presented in the 1933-1935 period made the ultimate choice inevitable.

Thus the primary purpose of the this book is to examine the metamorphosis of Socialist thought, and to a lesser extent Radical thought, as the danger from the Right, real and imagined, began to have its effect. The prejudices, irrationalities, miscalculations and fears which eventually led Socialist and Radical to bridge the broad emotional and doctrinal chasm between themselves and the Communists is, in my opinion, one of the most revealing and important aspects of modern French history.

However, there is also an important secondary purpose. The Popular Front was a Communist conception. Its introduction into Communist tactical and doctrinal thought marked a separation with the past policies of the Comintern to an extent often not fully appreciated. The impact of a rearming Germany upon the attitudes of the Soviet leaders, coinciding with internal developments within the Comintern hierarchy, served respectively to inspire and to permit this total revision. But the experience in France was decisive in shaping the new course of the Comintern. With Italy and then Germany controlled by facist and thus potentially hostile governments, and with the beginnings of disturbing developments in Austria and Spain, Comintern attention became focussed increasingly and somewhat desperately on that country which constituted its last substantial foothold in western Europe and also the last hope for an effective military ally for the Soviet Union. Thus it was in France that the experiment with the new and revolutionary tactic of the Comintern, the combined United Front-Popular Front tactic, was first introduced. Its success or failure was of the greatest importance to the Comintern. Constituting a move of considerable desperation -- consisting, in fact, of a last resort to stem the disastrous trend of developments throughout Europe -- the French experiment in the substitution of class and party collaboration for the class struggle and party isolation was to have a decisive effect upon Comintern policy. The secondary purpose of this book, then, is to examine in detail the interplay of cause and effect between the policies of the Comintern and the experience of its French section. Among other things this involves exploration of the extent to which the internal political factors in France determined the shape of the new Communist tactic.

Finally there is the question of the effect upon each of the parties of the French Left occasioned by their decision to embark on this new course. By this I mean the extent to which both their status within the French political scene and their theoretical and tactical outlook were altered in the course of accepting unity of action. Ostensibly the creation of the Popular Front and its electoral success constituted a significant victory for the entire Left over the alleged fascist threat. Underlying this overall victory, however, were more significant changes within the Left itself. To the lasting regret of the non-Communist Left the establishment of the Popular Front and the factors leading up to it served to resuscitate the decomposing and despised Parti Communiste Francais and clothe it with a "respectability" sufficient to give it a permanent foothold in France. The manner in which the French Communists, by playing on the exaggerated Socialist fears of the fascist danger in France, succeeded in making the Socialists the principal vehicle of their revivification, is the third main theme of this book.

These three main themes are manifestly closely interrelated and interdependent. Thus this book is primarily an intensive study of the relations between the parties of the French Left between January 1933 and August 1935, that is, between the date of Hitler's arrival to power and the VIIth World Congress of the Comintern. Within the period circumscribed by those two events occurred all of the drama, introspection, confusion, rationalization and change that went into the construction of the Popular Front.

A word about the work itself. The scholarly study of a subject as recent as the French Popular Front at the time this study was made had both advantages and disadvantages. The disadvantages -- lack of perspective, etc., -- are obvious. However, the compensating advantages were several. In the first place one had the unusual opportunity of choosing a subject of interest and importance without treading where others had been before. I needed waste no time distinguishing between this work and others for, despite the fact that every history of modern France (or of western Europe for that matter) must deal with the Popular Front in passing, there had not yet been any serious attempt at a detached and detailed study of the causes and effects of this phenomenon (see bibliographical note). Secondly, one had the incalculable advantage of an exceedingly broad range of "living" material the lack of control of which was, in my opinion, easily outweighed by its abundance and quality. Except for those documents destroyed during the German occupation, virtually all of the press reports, party committee and congress reports, pamphlets, speeches, etc., were well preserved and available in Paris. Where these documents were not available in France (either through destruction or for political reasons) most of them were available elsewhere, notably in Amsterdam. Furthermore, in this connection also, one had the added spice of the personal recollections of participants which, although dangerous as sources, provided intimate personal glimpses which are a luxury usually denied the researcher. Finally, and not least important, one had the opportunity of dealing with a subject the implications of which have not yet been fully realized, and the effects of which can be realistically related to contemporary events.

The day of the claim to absolute objectivity in modern historical or political writing is past, and I believe happily so. On the other hand the purpose of this thesis is to shed some light, through the use of original and comprehensive sources, on a political event of the first magnitude. I have endeavored to treat this subject in as scholarly a fashion as I am capable of doing and to let the conclusions arise from the assembly of material taken from the best sources I could obtain. To this extent I claim objectivity.

My debt of gratitude for aid in the preparation of this book is great indeed. Among those to whom I particularly wish to acknowledge my indebtedness for providing access to material are M. Rista of the Centre de Documentation du Conseil National, M. Joly, Archiviste en chef of the Chamber of Deputies, and M. Bourgin of the Service de Presse, Ministère de l'Interieur. I should also like to thank M. Jean Roux and other members of the staff of the Bibliothèque de Documentation Internationale Contemporaine for their great kindness during my long period of research there. I should like to express similar gratitude to the staff of the Internationaal Instituut voor Social Geschiedenis in Amsterdam for making available to me a comprehensive file of the records, reports, correspondence, etc., of the French Socialist party during this period, as well as some important documents of the Internationale Ouvrière Socialiste. In conclusion I cannot omit acknowledgement of my debt to the many Frenchmen who, through their personal knowledge of the event, have provided me with a valuable variety of firsthand impressions as well as filling in gaps in the psychological and emotional background of this period. In this connection, I am particularly indebted to M. Guy Jerram, former head of the national federation of the Association Républicaine des Anciens Combattants, and M. Émile Kahn, for years a leader of the Ligues des Droits de l'Homme.

The overwhelming portion of research for this book having necessarily been done from French sources, the question arose as to whether or not quotations and portions of documents used should be translated. I decided they should be for two reasons. The first of these was the positive one of hoping to improve the readability of a work in which virtually all of the quotations were in French. The second and more important reason stemmed from my belief that in a book on a political subject, where the content of quotations was infinitely more vital than style or phraseology, little or nothing would be lost by translation. I hasten to add that in those cases where nuances of meaning expressed in French were significant, and defied accurate translation, they have been presented in their original form.

PART ONE

THE LUXURY OF DISUNITY

Let us consider ourselves as friends momentarily separated, not as adversaries who must insult and fight one another. Perhaps one day a common foyer will reunite us.

> Léon Blum at the Congress of Tours, December, 1920.

The Communist party doesn't have to choose. It will use, if it can, the Radicals to beat the reactionaries, the reactionaries to beat the Radicals; it will beat them both when it is strong enough. That's all there is to it.

> L. O. Frossard, Secretary-General of the P.C.F.,
> 14 September, 1921

The Radical party has one goal; to organize society politically and socially according to the laws of reason, that is to say with a view to the complete development of the humane person in every human being, with a view to the full realization of justice in all the relationships between human beings.

> Léon Bourgeois, in a letter to Ferdinand Bouisson.

CHAPTER ONE

THE DEVELOPMENT OF DISUNITY

Until the scission at Tours in 1920 which separated the ranks of French Socialism into mutually hostile factions, the intrusion into French politics of the battle for and against collectivism had served to unify rather than separate the collectivists. From the quantity of widely disparate collectivist movements arising after 1848 there had gradually emerged an identity of interest and purpose leading to fusion in 1905. Furthermore, from their earliest origins the collectivists had found a community of interest, on the plane of political action, with the Republicans. For if the 1789 revolution only recognized the individual and not the working class, the effects of 1848 were not sufficiently significant to change this anachronism into conflict until the last decade of the century. In the middle and late 19th century the battle between Right and Left centered about issues which for the most part succeeded in suppressing the divergences within the Left and engaging all of its components in successive common causes. Thus a united Left against a Royalist and then a Bonapartist Right, a Left stretching from Gambetta to Clemenceau, a Left in common cause for the preservation of the Republic, a Left against the Church, a Left for Dreyfus, all preserved a history of unity of action up to the turn of the century which later served as a common tradition for extremist as well as moderate, for Marxist as well as Republican. The subsequent emergence of a unified workers party combining the influences of revolutionary syndicalism and 19th century Marxism did not immediately destroy this unity of action.[1] The task of resisting the formidable combination of Church and Conservative maintained the need for at least electoral collaboration on the Left, and collaboration toward this end had become a political axiom. Hence from 1902 to 1914 unity of action between Socialist worker and liberal bourgeois was preserved in the Bloc des Gauches.

If the 20th century collectivist could still find some identity of interests with the Republican, however, this identity grew exceedingly tenuous with the growth and development of workers movements after the turn of the century. Considerably before the 1914 war the spread of revolutionary trade unionism had pointed up the anachronism of a proletarian-Republican alliance and had posed one of the fundamental questions that was to dog the French Socialist from then on. Did his primary interest lie with the French Left within the national political sphere, or did it lie with the international proletariat? Until 1914 he was able to avoid decision, but the war forced a choice between national patriotism and international pacifism. In France as elsewhere in Europe the former proved the stronger bond. Not only would the Section Francaise de l'Internationale Ouvrière support this defensive war, it would permit its members to participate in the war government.[2]

The decision of the French Socialists -- and of international Socialism -- to "sanction" the war brought an end to unity within Socialist ranks. For the revolutionary, Socialism had been betrayed; the IInd International had failed. Rumblings from the ranks of the French Socialists which had been growing since unity was established in 1905 flared up into open defiance of both the International and the national party. In 1915 a French federation (Haute-Vienne) circulated a report to other federations asking for support in the condemnation of the position of the International.[3] In April 1916 three French Socialist deputies attended the international conference at Keinthal to support a resolution demanding the termination of Socialist participation in belligerent governments and an end to the voting of war credits.[4]

However it was the success of the Russian revolution which gave direction and purpose to the disillusioned revolutionaries. A surge of pro-bolshevik sympathy arose among French workers. Sympathetic mass strikes were held in Paris and St. Etienne. The extremists felt that there was now something positive to turn toward as well as something to turn away from. Revolutionary internationalism predominated over the reformist nationalism of the pre-war party. Following the national conference of the Parti Socialiste in 1918 Cachin the revolutionary replaced Renaudel the moderate Socialist as editor of L'HUMANITÉ. Bourgeois patriotism, social opportunism, peaceful development of the workers movement, social peace and the denial of revolution and illegal organization -- all the aspects of the IInd International which had permitted French Socialist and Radical to find a common basis for collaboration -- were disavowed by the revolutionaries. For them Leninism had become the sole guiding principle of revolutionary behavior.

At Strasbourg in February of 1920 disillusionment with the IInd International led to an almost unanimous vote to secede. But with this, unanimity ceased. A majority of the leaders who had constructed the unity of Socialist parties in 1905 refused to accept the conditions for entrance into the IIIrd International; however they succeeded in rallying the support of only a quarter of the delegates to the assembly at Tours in December.[5]

At Tours the French Socialists finally were faced with the decision which they had postponed for so long. The accumulated passions and doctrinal differences which had been developing within the party since well before the war, which had been inflamed by the war, and which had become crystallized by the creation of the IIIrd International reached their climax at this assembly. The IIIrd International had delivered an ultimatum in the form of 21 Conditions for adhesion.[6] One could either accept them absolutely or not at all, there was no room for equivocation. Blum and Longuet attempted to find a compromise, to patch up the divergences between bolshevik and Social-democratic doctrinal extremes as they had done so often in the past. But the Comintern had no interest in patching up.[7] As a result each delegate to the Tours assembly was made to realize that in voting for or against acceptance of the 21 Conditions he was not merely influencing the course the party as a whole would take, but was choosing his personal political future as well. For there was no doubt that scission would follow the vote whatever the outcome. The absoluteness of the alternatives presented to the French was not less than that presented to Socialists throughout Europe. Thus amid passionate appeals for the retention of unity, bitter recriminations and threats that were to echo through many years, the leaders of the French working class parted ways. Each claiming to be the heir of Jaurès (Jules Guesde being still alive to refute the Communist claim to his inheritance), the majority declared its allegiance to the new international and the minority retired to begin the reconstruction of the "Vieille Maison".[8]

The rupture of the proletarian political unity penetrated immediately to the trade unions. On Christmas day 1920, even before the adjournment of the Tours congress, a group within the C.G.T. convoked a meeting to demand that the confederation adhere to the revolutionary principles of the IIIrd International. In contrast to the decision on the party level the majority of the C.G.T. rejected this demand,

and it was the Communist-led minority that withdrew to form the C.G.T. "Unitaire". This new confederation shortly thereafter underwent a second scission over the question of affiliation with political organizations (specifically whether or not to adhere to the International of Red Trade Unions) in which the majority, led by the newly converted Communists Monmousseau, Dandicol and Sémard, voted to place the C.G.T.U. in affiliation with the Communist party.[9] From that moment the question of trade union unity in France passed from the control of the unions themselves into the realm of party politics. For, although Jouhaux had maintained the independence of the C.G.T., future reunification of the two confederations was dependent upon Communist desires concerning the C.G.T.U. Unity or unity of action between the confederations became a political question which, on the side of the C.G.T.U. at least, was to be decided frequently by considerations that had no relation to the trade union functions of that body.

The impact of the IIIrd International upon the French political scene caused a total reorganization of the relationships between the parties of the Left. The traditions and political demands of the 19th century which had kept Marxist and Republican allied in common action against the Right were now applicable to only a quarter of the former Marxists. The remainder constituted a new element in French politics which was as hostile to Socialist and Radical as it was to the Right. In contrast to the diluted revolutionism of the pre-war Socialist party, which by its behavior during the war had convinced most Radicals of its fundamental patriotism and revolutionary harmlessness, this new element cared nothing for the fate of the French nation. It was controlled by considerations external to France and dedicated to the overthrow of the Republic, Radical, Socialist, and all. It was the avowed enemy of unity of the working class except under its own banner, and of collaboration with other classes under any circumstances whatever. The extreme faction of the pre-war Bloc des Gauches was now an enemy. In the post-war Cartel des Gauches it made a gesture of retaining the pre-war electoral coalition but in 1928 withdrew entirely from cooperation with the Left.[10]

In regard to the national political scene the most significant aspect of the emergence of a Parti Communiste Francaise was that it destroyed the cause and effect relationship between events of a political and economic nature within France and the policies of a segment of the working class. Whereas syndicalism and revolutionary Socialism of all shades had been oriented toward internationalism and class warfare before the war, they had never been organized sufficiently to prevent individuals and groups from responding to national or local conditions within their respective countries. Those workers who adhered to the new international, however, sacrificed the freedom to develop their policies in relation to local events. Although the Comintern recognized that differences in the social and political structures of national societies required different application of revolutionary tactics, all tactical decisions were to be made by the Comintern and in the interest of International Communism rather than of the workers of a particular nation.[11] The extent to which this was true was not quite realized at Tours, but became immediately apparent upon the institution of the bolshevization of the French party.[12] In direct contrast to the situation that prevailed within the Socialist party, cause and effect on the national plane were completely subordinate to the considerations of the International, and where the interests of the French worker conflicted with the interests of the Comintern, the former became in effect irrelevant.

In relation to the genesis of the Popular Front, the tactics and doctrines which the P.C.F. inherited at Tours and immediately afterward exhibited purely negative aspects. For the embodiment of the theories of Marx, Engels, and Lenin into a code of tactical behavior for the new Communist parties produced that which was the exact antithesis of the Popular Front. The original Communist doctrine did not merely reject the combined United Front-Popular Front tactic, it virtually forbade it. In the 21 Conditions received at Tours, the THESES ON TACTICS and the THESES ON THE STRUCTURE AND ORGANIZATION OF COMMUNIST PARTIES received in 1921, and the communications that passed between Moscow and the French party in the early days of its existence, total emphasis was upon divorcing the new party from its Social-democratic traditions. In the words of Clara Zetkin at Tours, "You must divide in order to arrive at union". Riding the crest of international enthusiasm for the successful Russian revolution the bolsheviks were confident and uncompromising in 1921, and this attitude was reflected in the rules which they laid down as doctrinal guides for the new national sections.[13]

The extent to which the doctrinal inheritance of the P.C.F. was hostile to the idea of a Popular Front (a term which was not to be born for 14 years) is of importance in establishing the relationships of the French Socialist and Communist parties from Tours onward. It reveals to a considerable extent the nature of the rift that was created between them at that time. For although there was a half-hearted attempt at international unity of action in 1922, and although there were frequent attempts by the P.C.F. to engage the Socialists in joint action for limited objectives in the period from 1921 to 1928, according to the doctrines of the party in the early twenties there could be no establishment of a long range common program such as the Popular Front proved to be. That the Popular Front was not a part of Communist vocabulary in the twenties is not to be wondered at in view of the fact that such a concept was directly contrary to the policy which the Comintern was pursuing in France, and everywhere else, in the days of its early enthusiasm and doctrine worship.

The application of Communist doctrines to the new French party, to the accompaniment of multiple expulsions and resignations, served to verify the hostility of these doctrines to any but the most limited collaboration with the Socialists. The principal Comintern criticism of the leaders of the P.C.F. in the early twenties was their failure to make a complete rupture with the Parti Socialiste, their failure to include the Socialists as an enemy in the class struggle. It is true that Lenin, like the Bible, may be quoted to prove anything, and that when the front unique and front populaire were instituted in 1934 the French Communist leaders could find ample authority in the past writings of Marx, Engels, Lenin and Stalin to support the new course. It is also true, however, that from the origin of the P.C.F. until after the coming of Hitler the leaders of the P.C.F. and of the Comintern referred constantly to the teachings of Lenin in order to prove that no rapprochement with the reformists was possible. Moreover, it was during this period that Communist doctrine was established, both in its own eyes and in the eyes of the rest of French society, and, in turn, it was from this doctrine developed over a fourteen year period that the Communists had to withdraw when they inaugurated the Popular Front.

Not until the IXth Plenum and the VIth World Congress of the Comintern, seven years after Tours, was there a doctrinal change on the part of the Comintern that bore seriously on the relations of French Communists and Socialists. From the point of view of unity of action this change was for the worse, but it demands close examination since it established the position of the P.C.F. in regard to the Parti Socialiste for the ensuing seven years, that is, up until the formation of the Popular Front.

The change in the Comintern line first became evident to the French during the preparations for the legislative elections of May 1928. Acting in compliance with instructions from the Executive Committee of the Comintern, the Central Committee of the P.C.F. voted to reverse its electoral tactic of 1924. Instead of withdrawing its candidates on the second ballot where such withdrawal would aid a Socialist to defeat a reactionary candidate, it would henceforth cooperate electorally with the Parti Socialiste only upon the condition that the latter accepted a minimum "Workers and Peasants" platform prepared by the P.C.F. Since it was understood by the leaders of both parties that there was virtually no possibility of such acceptance, this step marked the end of the sole remaining phase of cooperation between the two parties.

The institution of this electoral change aroused violent protests from within the party as well as from the Socialists. Particularly among the regions outside of Paris was there strong resentment against this compulsion to renounce completely the previously profitable electoral collaboration with the Socialists. Despite the orders from the Comintern, 13 members of the Central Committee voted instead for a compromise proposal by Doriot calling for the support of at least left wing Socialists on the second ballot.[14] Renaud Jean, at the time a deputy as well as a member of the Central Committee, decried the change in tactics as a foolhardy measure which would cost the party dearly in terms of popular support as well as electoral benefits. Other prominent members of the Central Committee (including another deputy, Ramette) cautioned against a policy that would bring complete isolation from the Socialists. Finally the Executive Council of the Région du Nord, in defiance of the open letter issued by the Central Committee, voted instead merely to modify the 1924 electoral tactic within its region, and not to abandon it altogether.

Cachin, Thorez, Sémard and Monmousseau were successful in sustaining the position ordered by the Comintern, both before the Central Committee and the National Conference. But partly because of the demonstration of strong resistance within the P.C.F. over the electoral tactic, partly because of the serious loss of membership which that party had undergone since Tours, and partly through a desire to correct what was considered to be the dangerous misorientation of the leadership of the French party, the IXth Plenum of the Executive Committee of the Comintern was devoted largely to an examination of the "Question Francaise".[15]

All of the principals to the dispute were present at this meeting, at which the entire history and orientation of the French party were brought under review by the Executive Committee. Perhaps at no time, either previously or subsequently, has the wide disparity between the points of view of those who were primarily guided by the interests of the French worker and those who were blindly subservient to the Comintern been more strikingly illustrated than it was at this meeting. The argument which Renaud Jean had made before the French Central Committee was repeated.[16] France, it was argued, had regained its pre-war stability. The revolution was still far in the future. Hence an electoral policy cutting the Communists off completely from the Socialists, or even from the Radicals, was merely playing into the hands of an increasingly united Right for no immediate purpose. Worse, this policy was already having a disastrous effect within the ranks of the P.C.F. The decline in party morale and the falling off in numbers could be traced in a large measure to the application of this restrictive tactic which was so completely divorced from the realities of the French political scene. In a period such as that existing in 1928, with the forces of the Right and Center joining in a powerful National Union, accentuation of the division of proletarian forces was a folly which many of the French workers and militants would not sanction.

This line of argument, however, was that of the French practical tactician, not of the bolshevik. The Executive Committee reached precisely the opposite conclusion from a similar analysis of political trends.[17] If the forces of reaction were becoming stronger (and it held this to be true not only for France but for the rest of Europe as well) it was merely that much more essential that the Communists establish themselves as the only true defenders of the workers' interests. Moreover, resistance to the change of the electoral tactic was merely the external manifestation of the complete misorientation of the leaders of the P.C.F. The P.C.F. languished because it was still too closely tied to the methods of parliamentarianism; it lost sight of the fact that the essential role of the party was not to achieve parliamentary success, but was rather to present a rallying point for the revolutionary elements within the working class. Dengel, a member of the Executive Committee, declared:

> What is the basis of Doriot's error? It is that he, like the whole of the party in the past, exaggerates the importance of parliamentarianism in France ... It is not on parliamentary terrain that we will defeat the Social-democrats but rather in the battles which flow from the total situation in France, the economic struggles, the war question, the question of militarism, etc.
>
> Our line in the electoral battle must be such that the Communist party presents itself before the masses as a party which, from

the qualitative point of view, is entirely distinct from all other parties in France... In this electoral battle there must be a clear demarcation between ourselves and the Bloc des Gauches, between ourselves and the Parti Socialiste.[18]

Ercoli (Togliatti) added that the French preoccupation with parliamentarianism prevented the leaders of the P.C.F. from making a proper analysis of the changes that were taking place in France. France was no longer the petty bourgeoisie country of the immediate post-war period, but was in the process of becoming one of the strong points of world reaction. This particular change was related to a whole series of changes that were taking place in France involving a complete redisposition of the forces of the different classes, a fact which the French leaders seemed to fail to realize. Schuller's report elaborated upon this change:

> What Bukharin said for England is also true for France; there is a new fact. There is not only a new degree but there is a new form, a new manner of collaboration on the part of the C.G.T. and the Socialists with the bourgeoisie. **This new role of the C.G.T.** is indispensable to the bourgeoisie if it is to realize its plan of capitalist rationalization. We must realize that it is the program of the reformist trade unions that constitutes the present bridge between the political parties in France; it is this program that was accepted by the Radical party, then by Poincaré, then by the other parties which form the liaison between these diverse political groups which we call the reinforced National Union.[19]

There was absolutely no meeting of the minds between Doriot and Renaud Jean on the one hand and Thorez and the Executive Committee on the other. Whereas the former could and did make a persuasive demonstration of the extent to which the new tactic would injure the French party, the latter saw little importance in this fact when compared with the greater question of the international policies of the Comintern. Doriot made a final plea for the retention of the former electoral tactic before capitulating to the decision of the Executive:

> What was the danger we risked by an excessively radical application of the tactic advocated by the International? It was that in numerous cases our holding out on the second ballot against the Socialists when they were facing reactionaries ... meant having the capitalists win, and we feared that the workers

wouldn't understand our tactic and would turn away from us ... This truly risked bothering us at a moment when we needed to make a closer contact with the masses rather than to separate ourselves from them.[20]

Inevitably the position of the Executive Committee prevailed. Henceforth, the French Communists would not merely abstain from electoral collaboration with the Socialists but would also suppress all other tendencies toward acceptance of the lesser evil, i.e., the Socialists, as preferable "to any other bourgeois".[21] In the report ultimately adopted by the French Commission of the Plenum the analysis of the Executive Committee was propounded in full. Recognition was given to the change in the social and economic structure of post-war France and the embodiment of this change in the National Union government. The forces of capitalism were being concentrated. Finance capital was playing an increasingly important role. Workers were becoming more concentrated in industrial cities. Finally the petty bourgeoisie was playing a continuously less important role both politically and economically. In the course of these developments the C.G.T. and the Parti Socialiste were "accentuating their class collaboration and delivering the proletariat and its political organization to the bourgeoisie". Hence there could be no electoral cooperation with the Socialists.[22]

The effect of this new Communist attitude became dramatically apparent to the French Socialists in the legislative elections of 1928. Through the withdrawal of Communist support on the second ballot they lost between thirty and fifty seats in the Chamber that they would otherwise have won.[23] Blum raged against this new "treason" of the Comintern, appealing to the French Communist workers to "revolt against the ukases of Moscow ... this capitalism of a special kind that has ended by degrading the chiefs as the chiefs have degraded the men".[24]

However before the French Socialists had had long to contemplate the electoral perfidy of the P.C.F., this event was completely overshadowed by a development of considerably greater magnitude and import in the history of Communist-Socialist relations. In the summer of 1928 the VIth Congress of the IIIrd International met to declare all-out warfare upon International Social-democracy.[25] Social-democracy was elevated to the position of primary enemy of Communism. The theoretical basis for this change was the alleged threat to International Communism arising from imperialist preparations for war. Socialist and Social-democratic parties in all nations, the

Comintern charged, were supporting these imperialist war preparations and were thus either dividing or diverting the working class from its task of defending the "Fatherland". The PROGRAM OF THE COMINTERN, produced at this congress, contained the most vicious diatribes against the Socialists since the inauguration of the IIIrd International. "Social-fascist" became the official appellation for the Socialist, and the Comintern as a whole, as the P.C.F. had done a few months earlier, turned the full measure of its propaganda against the IInd International and its national sections.[26]

After the VIth World Congress any possibility of a rapprochement between the P.C.F. and the Parti Socialiste had vanished. As the French Communists intensified their attacks against the Socialist leaders, the latter responded in kind; and the C.G.T.U. and the C.G.T. engaged in identical recriminations.[27] The scission, emotionally as well as doctrinally, had become absolute.

A development during the 1920-1932 period second in importance only to the VIth World Congress was the disastrous effect of bolshevization on the size and morale of the P.C.F. Without embarking on a lengthy examination of the dominant influences in French politics during this period it may perhaps be hypothesized that there were three major traditions that opposed a strong resistance to the process of bolshevization; the nationalist tradition, the democratic tradition, and the traditions of 19th century Socialism. The Communists themselves recognized the unusual degree to which these traditions had been developed in France, and lingered even among the elements of the extreme Left.[28] But whereas a considerable loss of membership and the winnowing out of those leaders incapable of being bolshevized was a calculated price of bolshevization which the Comintern was willing to pay, the alarming degree to which nationalism and the devotion to democratic principles were prevailing over the rapidly dissipating appeal of the Russian revolution succeeded in both surprising and dismaying the leaders of the International by the late twenties.[29] The tendency in Germany, after national defeat, to turn with some enthusiasm toward internationalism found a striking contrast in France, where the post-war enthusiasm for international class alignment was tempered by the omnipresent attachment to the national tradition, a tradition enhanced rather than sullied by the war.[30] Rather than diminishing under the propaganda of the IIIrd International, this influence, closely linked to the desire for political autonomy, became increasingly apparent as the bolshevization process grew more severe.

The resistance encountered through the lingering devotion to the principles and patterns of 19th century Socialism was not particularly serious in the Paris environs, where membership consisted almost entirely of industrial workers a large percentage of whom were either first or second generation immigrants. But in the provinces, where membership was drawn largely from among men who had fought, or whose fathers has fought, to build the unity of 1905, the reluctance to separate completely from their Socialist colleagues was never entirely eliminated.[31]

By 1932 the tremendous decline in membership, the extreme biterness among an overwhelming number of Socialist or non-party workers against the P.C.F., and the flight of a majority of the original leaders to the Parti Socialiste or to splinter parties had reduced the French Communist party to a position of negligible influence. Piatnitski (who had replaced Manuilski as the Comintern's French "specialist") presented the figures showing the bankruptcy of the P.C.F. in his report to the XIIIth Executive.[32] It is certainly fair to accept these as presenting the best possible case for the French Communists.

According to Piatnitski the Parti Socialiste had dropped from 179,000 before the scission at Tours to 50,450 immediately afterward, but had subsequently increased steadily, reaching 130,000 in 1931 and 137,000 in 1932. The P.C.F., on the other hand, which had taken 110,000 from the Parti Socialiste at Tours, had dropped steadily until in 1931 it numbered but 29,415, and in the election year of 1932 increased only to 32,000. This decline permeated all aspects of the party's activities. L'HUMANITÉ'S sales had been halved between 1928 and 1932, whereas those of LE POPULAIRE had more than doubled in the same period. The P.C.F. lost 300,000 votes between the 1928 and 1932 elections and the Socialists gained 300,000. In the trade unions the C.G.T.U. lost 200,000 members between 1926 and August of 1933, and was 100,000 smaller than it had been in 1923.

If one considers separately the four unions of building, textiles, metallurgy and underground, it is seen that in 1924 they registered 184,000 members -- in 1932, 77,100. During that period we lost 107,000 members. Only the unitarian trade unions of railroad workers and state employees remained more or less stable, losing only 3,000 members in this period.

He compared this with the C.G.T.:

At the moment of the scission of the trade union movement the reformist trade unions registered almost 400,000 members, while today according to the reformist chiefs, who exaggerate surely, they number approximately 800,000, that is to say they have doubled their effectives.[33]

Piatnitski's report didn't include an account of the nadir of Communist fortunes in the mid-twenties, but in general it represented a fair picture of the enfeebled condition of the party at the end of 1932. Well before Hitler's advent to power the Comintern considered that the process of bolshevization of the P.C.F. had been completed. But this process had left the party small, isolated, despised by a major portion of the proletariat as well as by virtually the entire non-proletariat Left, and without substantial influence anywhere but in the industrial "Ceinture Rouge" around Paris.

A final consideration in the 1920-1932 period of Communist and Socialist relatons was the absence of any serious threat to the existence of either party. Despite the varied difficulties encountered in the post-war period, each party was relatively free to develop along whatever doctrinal lines it desired in France. In the Radicals and moderate Republicans there existed an effective buffer between the extreme Right and the proletarian parties which assured a considerable degree of political security to each.[34]

Similarly, after 1924 at least, the same relative security applied to the Comintern. Despite constant Communist clamoring that the "Fatherland" was in danger of attack from the imperialist powers, during this period there was no menace to the security of the Soviet Union in any way comparable to the threat created subsequently by the arrival of Hitler and the rearming of Germany. Regarding the security of the national sections of both Internationals, in none of the major European countries except Italy was there a government which was both in a position to and dedicated to the extermination of these parties. Furthermore the rise of Mussolini was dismissed by many Socialists and Communists alike as an "Italian phenomenon", so peculiarly Italian in nature that it did not represent a widespread tendency to be feared elsewhere.

On the international level this relative security meant that the Comintern could proceed with the second phase of its offensive without being hampered by defensive considerations. This in turn resulted in the initiation of the full fledged process of bolshevization of the national parties without regard for the quantitative losses or the alienation of non-Communist proletarians which this policy entailed. On the national level it allowed both Socialist and Communist to maintain their doctrinal and tactical intransigence vis-à-vis one another, and also permitted the French Socialists to indulge in a prolonged period of intra-party doctrinal quibbling without paying too severe a price. The relatively secure development of the Parti Socialiste, as well as that of the P.C.F., contributed to the widening of the rift between the two parties in the 1920-1932 period.

The slowly and painfully constructed unity of French Socialists, when shattered at Tours, left in its wake a Socialist party of uncertain doctrine. The bulk of that which had been the pre-war party having chosen the IIIrd International, the remnant was left without either international affiliation or established doctrine. Comprised of those who had formed the Center and Right of the pre-Tours Socialist party, the new party was no longer the most radical or revolutionary group in French politics. It now lay between the Communists and the Radicals, between those who while Marxist and proletarian had lost their independence, and those who while liberal and independent were neither proletarian, revolutionary nor Marxist. Blum, pulled toward closer collaboration with the Radicals by the parliamentary faction and at the same time anchored to the proletarian revolution by the Guesdist majority within the party, undertook the task of defining the doctrines of the new S.F.I.O. and of establishing its relationships with the Communist and Radical parties.[35] At its congress in October of 1921 the party reaffirmed its allegiance to the Charter of 1905 and engaged to restore workers' unity, and in May of 1922 at Hamburg it reestablished its affiliation with the IInd International. Steadily but surely a semblance of the form of the old party was reconstructed during the early twenties.

Nothing in the 1920-1932 period, however, tended toward a repair of the breach in proletarian unity. The nature of the development of the new Socialist party tended rather in the opposite direction. The legacy of bitterness from the Tours congress lent an emotional character to the doctrinal incompatibility of the parties, an incompatibility which was becoming increasingly evident to the Socialist leaders.[36] As bolshevization of the P.C.F. progressed and manifested itself in increasingly violent attacks upon the Parti Socialiste, the Socialist dream of a restored unity of the proletarian parties seemed to be postponed indefinitely. Blum, who at Tours had expressed the hope that the two factions would regard themselves as friends momentarily separated and not as adversaries who must combat and insult one another, later wrote in regard to the restoration of workers unity:

> It would be deplorable if the rapprochement were accomplished prematurely in the equivocation of and on the narrow level of national parties. It would be shameful and degrading if it were accomplished for interested reasons, for example for electoral expediency, without the real questions which separate us having been previously resolved.[37]

The Parti Socialiste was an amalgamation of the widest possible range of revolutionary and democratic thought -- "du rose pâle au rouge vif, du bulletin de vote à la guillotine". In the broad and somewhat equivocal definition of its doctrines every Socialist from Marceau-Pivert on the extreme Left to Renaudel on the extreme Right could find something of the doctrine in which he believed; none could find a complete expression of it. It was a doctrine calculated to protect the party against Communist accusations that it was neither Marxist nor revolutionary, and at the same time to dispel the fears of the Radicals.[38] Yet despite this internal doctrinal disparity there was considerable uniformity in the rejection of bolshevism and in the willingness of the party to accept Blum's leadership away from temporary and limited unity of action with the P.C.F.

Two features of the post-war decade made the problem of dealing with the P.C.F. considerably easier for the Socialist leaders. First, the absence of a serious external threat to the security of the party, in addition to permitting the continuation of internal doctrinal disagreement, allowed the party leaders to take an uncompromising stand in regard to the P.C.F. Secondly, the decline in Communist membership and the proportional rise in the membership of the Parti Socialiste did much to dispel the fear that the Communists might turn the left flank of the party. It was not difficult to discern what was happening to the bulk of the withdrawals from the P.C.F., for Socialist increases kept pace in almost exact ratio to Communist losses. Futhermore, supplementing this transfer of allegiance of the rank and file was the continuous procession of leaders of high or middle rank out of the P.C.F. and into the Parti Socialiste -- from Frossard in 1923 to André Ferrat after the formation of the Popular Front.

Until 1928 the Socialists went through the motions at least of declaring their dedication to the restoration of the pre-Tours unity. At the Congress of Lyons in 1927 they voted a resolution to this effect.

But after the Communist turning at the VIth World Congress in 1928, all hope for a rapprochement was abandoned. From the legislative elections of that year on, relatons between the parties worsened steadily. After 1928 Socialist propaganda against the P.C.F. almost matched the bitterness of the Communist attacks upon the Socialist leaders. Added to the "moral and sentimental" incompatibility of the parties there was from this time on an active campaign for mutual destruction.[39]

The history of relations between the opposing factions within the French proletariat was thus one of continuous degeneration from the time of the establishment of political unity in 1905 until 1932. Internal dissatisfaction with the moderate policies of the pre-war party broke into open defiance during the war, and after the war the majority rejected the leadership of the IInd International and formalized the disunity of the party by accepting the conditions of the IIIrd International at Tours. From Tours on the bolshevization of the French Communist party, and the Socialist reaction to this process, cemented the rift between them. Finally in 1928 the turning in the Comintern line changed mere doctrinal incompatibility into violent warfare between the parties. From 1928 until the coming of Hitler this warfare engendered within the Parti Socialiste hatred, suspicion and distrust of the Communists to an extent that, when coupled with the purposeful Communist campaign to separate the parties, made any rapprochement or unity of action between them inconceivable.

The focal point of bitterness between the two parties as they entered the early 1930's was the Communist tactic described as the **front unique en bas.** This tactic embodied all aspects of the P.C.F.'s campaign to undermine the Socialist party; it represented the tactical form of application of the change in Comintern line in 1928. Every phase of Communist activity vis-à-vis the Socialists from 1928 on was geared to this tactic. Simply stated it was the attempt to draw Socialist workers away from their leaders, to create a united front of the workers of all parties and to bring this front under control of the P.C.F.[40] In practice it involved incessant and violent denunciation of the Socialist leaders as betrayers of the workers and as the principal support of the bourgeoisie.[41] It involved constant efforts to embarrass the Socialist leaders in their relationships with the government and the non-proletarian parties. By cooperating with the Socialist worker on the lower level, by inviting him to take part in Communist-organized manifestations, by defending his grievances and by simultaneously continuing the polemics against the Socialist leaders, the P.C.F. sought to split the Socialist worker from his party and lead him into Communist ranks.

The fact that this tactic was proving strikingly unsuccessful did little to assuage the resentment which it caused within the Parti Socialiste. The **front unique en bas** tactic presented the very threat which the Socialist leaders most feared, that of having their left flank turned by the Communists.[42] This threat seriously hampered their attempts to find a modus operandi with the Radicals, forcing them constantly to reaffirm their revolutionary and proletarian nature at the expense of enjoying the fruits of a Socialist-Radical coalition. Of greater effect upon the growth of disunity, perhaps, was the direct impact of the Communist campaign. Four years of being labelled "Social-fascists", betrayers of the working class, principal support of the bourgeois and the like, had produced among the Socialist leaders an emotional hostility to the P.C.F. which belied the negligible effect of Communist propaganda upon the size or solidarity of the party itself.

When the arrival of Hitler in January of 1933 made Socialist and Communist throughout Europe pause to consider the price of disunity, relations between the French sections of these parties were at their lowest ebb. Disunity had advanced to bitter antagonism, and the problems, emotional as well as doctrinal, which stood in the way of a reestablishment of any sort of rapport whatsoever, appeared insuperable.

NOTES

1. For the early history of the development of the French trade union movement consult: Levine, Louis, SYNDICALISM IN FRANCE, Columbia University, N.Y. 1914; Dollèans, Edouard, HISTOIRE DU MOUVEMENT OUVRIER, 1871-1936, Librairie Armand Colin, Paris, 1939; Paul Louis, HISTOIRE DU SOCIALISME EN FRANCE DE LA REVOLUTION À NOS JOURS, 1789-1936, Marcel Rivière, Paris, 1936.

2. When Guesde and Sembat accepted the offer of Viviani to participate in the war government, the then Socialist HUMANITÉ permitted itself the chauvinism of declaring, "Victory will mark the beginning of a new civilization". L'HUMANITÉ, 18 August, 1914.

3. An excellent account of the dissatisfaction of the French Socialists at the war policy of the party and the International is to be found in A. Spire, LE DECLIN DU MARXISME DANS LES TENDANCES SOCIALISTES DE LA FRANCE CONTEMPORAINE, These pour le doctorat, Faculté de Droit, Nancy, Imprimerie A. Tollard, presented 1937. Also worth consulting, although of a more general nature, are G. Pirou, LES DOCTRINES ECONOMIQUES EN FRANCE DUPUIS 1871, Armand Colin, Paris, 1934; and A Zevaes, HISTOIRE DU SOCIALISME ET DU COMMUNISME EN FRANCE DE 1871 A 1947, Editions France-Empire, Paris, 1947.

4. Maxe, J. DE ZIMMERWALD AU BOLCHEVISME, Editions Bossard, Paris 1920. Aftalion, A. LES FONDEMENTS DU SOCIALISME, ÉTUDE CRITIQUE, Rivière, Paris, 1923.

5. Blum, Paul Faure, Longuet and Renaudel, four of the foremost among the leaders of the Parti Socialiste, sought in vain to maintain the discipline of their followers for the rejection of the 21 Conditions posed by the Comintern. Cachin and Frossard, in their campaign for acceptance, were able to exploit the unsettled and disillusioned attitude of the majority. More than six weeks before the assembly at Tours the pro-bolshevik faction

published its resolution to adhere to the Comintern. "Résolution d'adhesion a la IIIe Internationale, redigé et adoptée par le Comité de la IIIe Internationale et la fraction Cachin-Frossard", BULLETIN COMMUNISTE, 4 November 1920. The vote at Tours was 3,028 for adhesion, 1,022 against.

6. LES VINGT ET UNE CONDITIONS D'ADHÉSION A L'INTERNATIONALE COMMUNISTE, Paris, Bureau d'éditions, 1922. Those portions of the Conditions relevant to the question of unity include:

Condition 7: "... a complete rupture with reformism and centrist policies, and the advancement of that rupture among the members of the organization. Consistent Communist action is only possible at this price. The International demands that this rupture be accomplished without the least discussion or delay."

Condition 10: demanding a campaign against the Amsterdam International of "yellow" trade unions.

Condition 15: "The parties that still maintain the old Social-democratic programs must revise them without delay and create a new Communist program adapted to the special circumstances of their country, and in the spirit of the Communist International."

And in the last sentence of Condition 1: "In the columns of the press, in public meetings, in the trade unions, in cooperatives, everywhere that the followers of the IIIrd Internationale have access, they will attack not only the bourgeoisie but also their accomplices, reformists of all shades."

7. Walter, Gérard, HISTOIRE DU PARTI COMMUNISTE FRANCAIS, Somogy, Paris, 1948, pp. 39-52.

8. The position taken by Blum at Tours is reproduced, along with the arguments of the minority leaders immediately after the scission, in Blum, POUR LA VIEILLE MAISON, Librairie Populaire, Paris, 1936.

9. The minority which rejected affiliation with any political party was led by Lecoin, Weber, Colomer and Barthe (the first two syndicalists and the other two anarchists), and subsequently became merged in the C.G.T.

10. The abortive and short-lived attempt of the Executive Committee of the Comintern to institute the front unique in France in early 1922 did not have sufficient bearing upon Socialist-Communist relations to make its inclusion worth while. Blocked by the P.C.F. itself, this decision by the Executive Committee

never reached the point of a proposal to the Socialists, and the project was dropped after six weeks discussion between party and International. The account of these negotiations is also contained in Walter, **op.cit.**, pp. 77-89.

11. Lenin's insistence that: - "the definite peculiar features which this struggle assumes and must assume in each separate country in accordance with the peculiar features of its economics, politics, culture, national composition, colonies, religious divisions, etc., must be taken into account quite consciously by the Communists of every country" -- Lénine, LA MALADIE INFANTILE DU COMMUNISME, Imprimerie Centrale, 1930, was reproduced in the "Thèses sur la structure et organisation des Partis Communistes", printed in the BULLETIN COMMUNISTE, 8 September, 1921:

    "The conditions of the proletarian battle of the classes transforms itself ceaselessly and, conforming to these transformations the organization of the advance guard of the proletariat must also seek constantly new and more suitable forms. The historical peculiarities of each country also determine the special forms of organizations for the different parties." Thèse 2; p. 631.

    "The tactic of Communist parties will be inspired by the particular conditions of each country." Thèse 8; p. 632.

12. The attempt by Frossard to retain a measure of autonomy for the French party, which resulted in his exclusion, dramatically illustrated for the French Communists the significance of membership in the International. cf. Frossard, DE JAURÈS A LÉNINE, NOTES ET SOUVENIRS, Paris 1930, pp. 181-192.

13. See Lebas, SUR L'ORDRE DE MOSCOU COMMENT LES COMMUNISTES ONT BRISÉ L'UNITE, Imprimerie Ouvrier, Lille, 1921; Souvarine, "Le Congres de Tours", BULLETIN COMMUNISTE, 30 December 1920.

14. Report of the Meeting of the Central Committee, 10-11 January 1928, L'HUMANITÉ, 12 January 1928. 21 members of the Committee voted for the change, 13 for the Doriot proposal.

15. CLASSE CONTRE CLASSE, LA QUESTION FRANCAISE AU IXe EXECUTIF ET AU VIe CONGRÈS DE L'INTERNATIONALE COMMUNISTE, Courbevoie, Societé Ouvrière d'imprimerie, Paris, 1929.

16. The argument made by Renaud Jean before the National conference of the P.C.F. and the Central Committee meeting in January

was taken up by Doriot at the IXth Plenum. Schuller undertook to reply to Renaud Jean.

"He tells us that in France there is no substantial change in the situation in comparison with the situation in 1924, and even with the pre-war situation. Obviously comrades there is a point of departure quite different from our own, and one which must lead inevitably to completely false conclusions in the coming tactic. He says that we have before us a more or less long period which gives no possibilities for the class battle, that we are facing a stagnant situation which will remain for a long time as it is at present. As for the peasants, he denies that there is a serious change in political point of view among them. . . He advises us in our tactic toward the Parti Socialiste and the Parti Radical first of all to take into consideration the backward state of mind of the peasants, and not only of the peasants but also the other backward working groups. . . He asks that we desist on the second ballot for the Radicals when they are facing reactionaries, and do even more for the Socialists.

"To follow that line would be to damage our tactic of front unique considerably. . . If the Socialist workers know that, despite the fact that the Parti Socialiste has rejected the offer of a front unique the Communists vote for Socialists just the same, it would appear to them like an insincere maneuver on our part. The front unique is a serious class maneuver that we undertake in order to bring us closer to the masses at the same time as we turn them away from their chiefs." Discours de Schuller, CLASSE CONTRE CLASSE, **op cit.**, p. 43.

17. Schuller dismissed the argument that the tactical change would cost the P.C.F. a further membership loss:

"... it is clear that if we accepted the proposal of the Region du Nord perhaps thousands of Socialist workers would be with us, but also thousands of revolutionary workers would be against us just because we applied this tactic. . . they would not understand and would consider our tactic as treason if we accepted the tactic advocated by the Region du Nord." CLASSE CONTRE CLASSE, **op.cit.**, p. 44.

18. Rapport du Dengel au IXe Plenum, CLASSE CONTRE CLASSE, **op. cit.**, p. 48.

19. Rapport du Schuller au IXe Plenum, CLASSE CONTRE CLASSE, **op.cit.**, p. 36.

20. Discours de Doriot au IXe Plenum, CLASSE CONTRE CLASSE, **op. cit.**, p. 76. Doriot's discussion at this time was neither of a rebellious nature nor long lived. He accepted the decision of the Executive and of the National Conference of the P.C.F. rather mildly. Professing to recognize, as did the Comintern, a growing concentration and unification of the forces of the Right, his dissidence was based on the principle that the most effective mode of combatting this was by the coalition of the forces of the Left. Hence his attempts to urge upon the Executive the conclusion that "at the present hour we live under the sign of class collaboration".

21. At every subsequent conference or congress of the P.C.F. the need for ceaseless attack upon the leaders of the Parti Socialiste was included in the form of a resolution. RÉSOLUTIONS ADOPTÉES PAR LA CONFÉRENCE NATIONALE DU P.C.F., 9-12 MARS, 1930, Bourges, Imprimerie Ouvrier du Centre, 1930; THÈSES, RESOLUTIONS, ET DECISIONS À LA Xe SESSION PLENIÈRE DU COMITÉ EXÉCUTIF DE L'I.C., JULY 1929, Paris, Bureau d'editoins, 1930; AU PAS DE CHARGES, CAMARADES, résolutions du Comité Central du Jeunesses Communiste (April 1931), Paris, Bureau d'éditions, 1931; VIe CONGRÈS NATIONAL DU P.C.F. (St. Denis, March and April 1929), Paris, 1929.

22. Report of the French Commission to the Plenum, reporter Sémard, CLASSE CONTRE CLASSE, **op. cit.**, p. 90.

23. See Lebas, CRITIQUE SOCIALISTE DU PARTI COMMUNISTE, Lille, Imprimerie Ouvrier, 1933, pp. 27-29. Lebas was among those displaced as a result of the Communist tactic in the 1928 elections.

24. LE POPULAIRE, 29 April 1928.

25. THÈSES ET RÉSOLUTIONS DU VIe CONGRÈS MONDIALE DE L'I.C., Paris, Bureau d'éditions (no date).

26. "The essential role of Social-democracy now is to sap the indispensable unity of the proletarian struggle against imperialism. Splitting and dividing the united red front of the proletarian battle against capital, Social-democracy is the principal support of imperialism in the working class. International Social-democrats of all nuances, the IInd International and its trade union affiliate of Amsterdam have become the reserves of bourgeois society -- its surest rampart." PROGRAMME DE L'INTERNATIONALE COMMUNISTE, Paris, 1936, edition, p. 20.

". . .Social reformism constitutes the commercial, cynical, laic and imperialist aspect of the ideological submission of the proletariat to bourgeois influence."

The Social-democrats were condemned for having participated in the imperialist war under the banner of national defense, for supporting the colonial policies and the expansion of the imperialist state, of sanctioning the counter-revolutionary "Holy Alliance" of imperialist powers under the aegis of the League of Nations, and for mobilizing the masses under pseudo-fascist slogans. Most seriously they were accused of active support for the preparation and the waging of war against the Soviet Union. They had denied Marx and diluted the "ardent theory of the battle of the classes into a banal predication of class peace".

"For the revolution it substitutes evolution; for the destruction of the bourgeois state, the active participation in its edification; for the doctrine of dictatorship of the proletariat, the theory of coalition with the bourgeois; for the doctrine of international proletarian solidarity, it has substituted that of imperialist national defense; for the dialectic materialism of Marx, an idealist philosophy in harmony with the religious offals of the bourgeois." PROGRAMME DE l'I.C., **op. cit.**, pp. 64, 65, 66.

27. Blum explained his position in regard to the Communists in his brochure BOLCHEVISME ET SOCIALISME, and maintained a running editorial account in LE POPULAIRE, particularly after 1928, which served to redefine the incompatibilities of the two parties. In part these stemmed from the fact that,

"Communism aims only at introducing in men a spirit of audacity and of attack as on the eve of an assault. Its propaganda doesn't instruct, doesn't elevate; it overexcites, overheats. It tends to create a sort of intoxication, a kind of fanaticism for violence and suspicion and hate -- violence, suspicion and hate which, as we have cruelly learned, are not directed solely against the class enemy, but of which it seems at times as if Socialism has had the almost exclusive benefit."

and in part from the fact that the P.C.F.

". . .systematically gives birth to division of the workers, not only because its shock troops had to be recruited from among the ranks of existing organizations, but because a party such as it conceives itself to be cannot endure a minority." BOLCHEVISME ET SOCIALISME, Librairie Populaire (9th edition), Paris, 1937, p. 15.

28. In his report to the IXth Plenum, Thorez included among the reasons for the failure of the P.C.F.:

"The third cause is that up until recent times we have remained very closely linked to democracy, we have not succeeded in disengaging ourselves, we have not succeeded in loosening the grasp which grips our party.

"Our party developed in a country that for 57 years has been infested with democracy; this party has not yet waged revolutionary battles, serious campaigns." CLASSE CONTRE CLASSE, **op. cit.**, p. 64.

29. At the XIth Plenum of the Executive in 1931 Manuilski classed the failure of the P.C.F. with that of the Communist parties in the U.S. and England, analyzing the failure in sweeping terms:

"The fundamental defects of the Communist parties are their feeble recruiting power, the weakness of industrial cells, the very great fluctuation of members attaining 50% in France; ... But it is in the trade union domain that the Communist parties have been neglectful in orienting themselves toward the primary grievances of the masses. And this negligence has resulted today in the diminution of the trade union effectives in France, in a stagnation of the trade unions in Czechoslovakia." LE P.C.F. DEVANT L'INTERNATIONALE, Bureau d'éditions, Paris, 1931, p. 33.

L'HUMANITÉ of 18 November 1928 admitted that "Nothing is more alarming in the present situation than the decrease in the number of effectives in the P.C.F. and the C.G.T.U."

At the XIth Plenum Thorez confessed to "... the crying insufficiency of the party, ... its retarded state in the presence of the acceleration of the crisis on the international scale, and above all in the presence of the growing threat to the Soviet Union." LE P.C.F. DEVANT L'INTERNATIONALE, **op. cit.**, p. 36.

30. "In France where the chauvinist poison of 'national defense' and the subsequent intoxication with victory was stronger than anywhere else, reaction against the war has developed more slowly than in other countries. . . The potential advantages of this situation will be realized by the P.C.F. to the extent that it categorically liquidates within itself -- above all among its leaders -- the remnants of the ideologies of national pacifism and parliamentary reformism." "Theses on Tactics, BULLETIN COMMUNISTE, 1 September 1921, p. 600.

31. It was always the provincial departments that displayed the greatest resistance to bolshevization, and as the size of the party diminished during the twenties it was in the provinces that the greatest number of withdrawals occurred until the "Ceinture rouge" around Paris contained, in 1931, approximately half of the party membership. Writing in 1930, André Siegfried presented an excellent analysis of the effect of Socialist tradition upon the contemporary worker:

    "The transformation of the working-man was less marked in France, without doubt, than in any of the other great Western nations, for our craftsman lingered on long after the Industrial Revolution. He was a fine type, imbued with professional honor, his very being bound up in his work, according to true French tradition. Behind his barricade it was he who was mainly responsible for the revolutions of the past century, which drew their inspiration not from class hatred or revolutionary doctrine, but from a democratic ideal. He later became a Socialist, and it was he who originated the Socialist party and the C.G.T. His Socialism was always true to the ideals of the 19th century, and therefore, he is not and never will be a Marxian."

    Siegfried, "The Psychology of French Politics", ATLANTIC MONTHLY, January 1936, p. 89.

32. Report of Piatnitski to XIII Plenum, C.B. 1 February 1934, p. 140 ff.

33. Report of Piatnitski to XIII Plenum, C.B. 1 February 1934, p. 141. Cf. Paul Louis, **op. cit.**, p. 279 and Zevaes, **op. cit.**, p. 384 as to growth of Parti Socialiste and decline of P.C.F.

34. A fact which Déat recognized in his attempts to get the Parti Socialiste to maintain close relations with the Radicals:

    "It is only in France that there exists a buffer party; the Parti Radical between the reactionaries and the Socialists; that is a fact which one should not forget when one would outline the policy of the groups." L'OEUVRE, 3 April 1933.

35. After his description of the scission in POUR LE VIEILLE MAISON, Blum wrote a positive exposé of the program of the reconstituted S.F.I.O entitled L'IDEAL SOCIALISTE, which appeared first in article form in LA REVUE DE PARIS of 1 May 1924.

    Blum emerged as a leader in the vein of Louis Blanc and later Jaurès, repudiating violence and seeking to stay in the tradition of the St. Simoniens, Fourierists and Proudhons:

    "The battle of classes is one of the essential formulae of Socialism. It means that the present regime of property creates an inevitable opposition of interests between those who draw from production and those who draw only from their personal working strength, that is to say between the capitalists and the proletarians. It signifies that the new regime, that one which we want to install will not be handed to us as a gracious gift, but that the proletariat must conquer it by its own action, its class action.

"Professing a doctrine of human fraternity, we ardently wish that this evolution be amiable and pacific. More than any other party Socialism has a horror of violence and blood. We wish that the social transformation could be accomplished by legal processes, by a victory of universal suffrage, but in this regard the lessons of history render us a trifle skeptical." L'IDEAL SOCIALISTE, **op. cit.**, p. 28.

And in LE POPULAIRE of 5 and 9 February 1927:

"We refuse to erect a dictatorship and terror as a systematic and lasting method of government. We want ... the temporary dictatorship to be exercized not by a cast, not in the exclusive interest of a class -- since classes must specifically disappear -- but in the name and interest of all of collective humanity."

36. "As a direct and necessary consequence of this doctrinal opposition, we find ourselves in disaccord today with bolshevism on questions such as the recruitment and the organic life of the parties, the revolutionary effectiveness of reforms, the attitude to take in relation to economic or political crises of the Capitalist society, the action to exercise in favor of peace or war. . . These divergences have not only created, between bolshvism and us, an extreme difficulty of common action, but they have provoked between the parties a sort of sentimental and moral incompatability." Blum, BOLCHEVISME ET SOCIALISME, **op. cit.**, p. 22.

37. Blum, BOLCHEVISME ET SOCIALISME, **op. cit.**, preface, p. I.

38. The wide disparity between the conceptions of the right and left wings of the party itself did nothing to clarify popular confusion as to the nature of Socialist doctrine. Hence in the Paul Faure motion voted at the Congress of Lyons, 20 April 1927, was the statement:

"Certainly there exists between the bolshevists and ourselves an incontestable community of doctrinal ends. That is why we have never ceased to believe and to say that the near or distant destinies of the Parti Socialiste and the Parti Communiste were to rejoin amid the reconquered unity of the working class, a prerequisite to the victory of the international proletariat." COMPTE RENDU STÉNOGRAPHIQUE DU XXIV CONGRÈS NATIONAL, Lyons, 17-20 April, 1927, p. 16.

And eight days later in LE POPULAIRE appeared a declaration by Renaudel to which few Radicals would have objected:

"Socialism remains placed on these bases; that of democracy, which is the common ground of the battle of the classes in the nation; that of national defense, which is th common ground of the individuals of the nation; and that international peace which is the common ground of peoples in humanity." LE POPULAIRE, 28 April 1927.

39. On the part of the Socialists this took the traditional form of a heated denial that bolshevism had any relation to the principles of Socialism:

"It is not an attempt at the construction of Socialism which is being effectuated in the Soviet Union; whether it succeeds or not will not bear witness for or against Socialism because it is being effectuated to the detriment of the working class. With slaves one can always build pyramids." Blum, LE POPULAIRE, 25 May 1931.

40. The front unique had only one goal, to battle against the Social-democrats:

"The front unique (en bas) tactic, the most effective means of ... demasking and of isolating the reformist chiefs, is one of the primary elements of the tactics of Communist parties during the pre-revolutionary period." PROGRAMME DE L'INTERNATIONALE COMMUNISTE, **op. cit.**, pp. 76-77.

41. Report of Manuilski:

"The class against class tactic doesn't mean that maneuvering be renounced. If the adversary still has a strong position within the working class, it is necessary that the Communists maneuver in order to undermine his position by continually demasking it. Since the Xth Plenary session our maneuvers have been poor. It isn't we who have maneuvered, but Social-democracy which has maneuvered against us. Many Communists, starting from the idea that Social-democracy has achieved the cycle of its fascist development, don't expect any capacity on its part to maneuver. They have been taken unaware ... as can be seen particularly in France in the question of the unity of the trade union movement." LE P.C.F. DEVANT L'INTERNATIONALE, **op. cit.**, p. 31.

42. The most destructive aspect of this from the Socialist point of view was the perversion of the class struggle to divide the proletariat parties. For the Communists, the Socialists declared:

"Class against class translates itself, in practice, into proletariat against proletariat, to the great satisfaction of the reactionary bourgeoisie." L'UNITÉ, EST ELLE POSSIBLE? Raymond Gernez, Paris, 1946, p. 13.

CHAPTER TWO

HITLER AND THE PROBLEM OF COMMON DEFENSE

The dramatic implications of Hitler's appointment to the Chancellorship in January of 1933 have obscured some of the facts of the immediate impact of this event upon Marxist and liberal thought. Nazism presented a double-edge threat to both the French Left and the Soviet Union, a military threat and an ideological threat. Since Hitler had never masked his antipathy to bolshevism and the Versailles Treaty, his arrival to power obviously constituted a potential military threat to both countries. Moreover, the traditional sensitivity of both countries to a militarily strong and hostile Germany cannot, of course, be exaggerated. Yet in 1933 the German military threat was still very much of potentiality; it was not a present fact. The French army, in the eyes of the vast majority of Frenchmen and other Europeans as well, was a more than adequate safeguard as long as a careful watch over German rearmament was maintained. In 1933 then it was not the military threat caused by the establishment of the Third Reich that constituted the immediate and principal concern of the French Left, it was rather the ideological threat.

The primary source of alarm for Socialist, Communist and Radical France was the evidence presented by events in Germany that fascism was no longer an Italian phenomenon. Blum's complacency concerning the possibility of a Nazi success, a complacency that had been maintained virtually until the moment of the event, was utterly shattered. The warnings of Renaudel and others since 1930 had been well founded. Hitler's victory in a nation containing 11 million Marxists (of one form or another) had exploded the total and uncritical faith of Blum in the ability of the German Social-democrats to prevent such an occurrence. In view of the German experience other events took on a new and more sinister aspect. If Hitler could succeed against such formidable opposition what did that indicate for the future of France, in which the organized forces of the Left were puny by comparison, and in which the nuclei for a fascist movement were only too evident?

Underlying this fear was a gnawing sense of guilt and frustration concerning the events in Germany. It was undeniable that a principal reason for the defeat of the left in Germany had been its internal disunity. Even in the face of the Nazi threat Social-democrats and Communists in Germany had been unable to find a common ground for defensive action. Failing in this they had been routed "to be reconciled only in concentration camps". This fact, above all others, impressed itself on the minds of the French Socialist leaders. To an even greater extent it impressed itself on the rank and file of both Socialist and Communist parties, as well as non-party antifascists of all shades. Among the latter the slogan "No Hitler in France" tended to overbalance all other considerations. For many in the lower echelons of both the P.C.F. and the Parti Socialiste the legacy of thirteen years of disunity and hostility was forgotten overnight.

Any sort of reconciliation for common defense on the level of the party leadership, however, was an entirely different matter. Despite the shock to the French Socialist leaders occasioned by the success of Nazism they were powerless, and it may be said disinclined, to seek unity of action in the face of undiminished Communist attacks. The identical factors which had kept Social-democrat and Communist apart in Germany still existed in France. As long as the Communists persisted in their attacks upon Socialist leadership and their attempts to undermine the loyalty of the party members, in short as long as they adhered to the tactic of **front unique en bas,** there could be no common action. And the P.C.F. showed no intention of relaxing this campaign. Quite the contrary, in fact, for the Communists now added to the sins of which they accused Social-democracy that of leading the German working class to disaster.

The effect of the coming of Hitler, as distinguished from the effect of the subsequent rearmament and aggression of the Third Reich, was merely to illustrate dramatically to the French Left the price of disunity and inaction. While this was sufficient to cause the leaders of the Parti Socialiste to modify their reservations against joining with the Communists in common defense, it was not sufficient, by itself, to cause the Comintern to abandon its campaign to undermine the French Socialists.

Socialist reaction to the advent of Hitler produced a flurry of negotiations for common defense immediately following that event. The Internationale Ouvrière Socialiste (the IInd International) issued an "Appeal to the workers of the whole world" on February 19th which appeared in LE POPULAIRE the follow day. This constituted a declaration by the leaders of the IInd International to the effect that the dangers of fascism were too great for either party to permit doctrinal obstacles to divide the proletariat, and that a common ground must be found upon which the two parties could unite their forces in the struggle against these dangers. It declared the principal barrier to such unity to be the mutual attacks and recriminations to which an end must be made before positive steps toward this common action could be undertaken. Not addressed specifically to the Comintern but merely to "all the workers" this appeal dealt primarily with the German sections of the two parties. However it also embraced the proletarians of all countries and extended an unmistakable invitation to the IIIrd International:

> The I.O.S. has always been ready to negotiate with the Comintern upon the subject of such a common struggle whenever the latter declared itself ready to do the same.[1]

Shortly after this the president of the IInd International, Émile Vandervelde, published L'ALTERNATIVE in Paris, in which he posed the question of the need for common defense:

> It is not that there aren't men in the two camps who understand that, at least in the face of common perils, common defense is necessary.
>
> Trotsky himself, in spite of his execration for all that touches upon Social-democracy, has recently uttered some words of good common sense on this subject.
>
> Otto Bauer, Léon Blum, Friedrich Adler and how many others have always refused, even at the worst moments, to despair of workers' unity.
>
> There is also no doubt that, in spite of the IIIrd International directives to the contrary, the mass of German workers, Communist as well as Social-democrats, felt deeply the need to lock elbows.
>
> Under these circumstances how does it happen that in spite of everything the obstacles persist?

The answer that he gave was that, despite the histories of the two parties since the war, the Communists clung to the stubborn conviction that they could and would destroy Social-democracy.

> If, despite all the evidence to the contrary, they did not still believe in the possibility of annihilating Social-democracy and

of rebuilding proletarian unity under the sign of Communism, they would not practice that mad policy which humors their worst enemies, which compounds with them to wage an implacable war on those who, despite all, will be alongside the U.S.S.R. the day when an imperialist and capitalist offensive puts it in danger.

Will the moment nevertheless come when, on both sides, a more exact realization of the true interest of the proletariat will be reached? One can hope. The important thing is that it not be too late.[2]

These overtures, vague and indefinite as they were, were unprecedented in the post-war history of the I.O.S. Constituting a desperate and somewhat wistful plea to the Comintern to abandon its hostility in the face of the fascist threat, they came to nought. In fact in France they succeeded merely in embarrassing Blum, for the P.C.F. used them as a pretext to submit proposals for unity of action which the Socialists could not accept, and which required all of Blum's artistry to decline without having it appear that the Socialists were the barrier to unity. When Blum referred to the I.O.S. for instructions concerning the Communist proposals the International withdrew from its earlier position and warned the national sections not to engage in common manifestations with the Communists until the policy of the International had been established.[3]

The ideological threat of the coming of Hitler, that is the indication afforded by that event of the possibility of the spread of fascism, was of course no less serious to the Comintern than it was to the national Socialist parties throughout Europe. The failure of the Comintern to respond in the same manner as the Socialists cannot be explained on that ground. Communist unwillingness to accept the alternative proposed by Vandervelde on the international level and Blum within France, stemmed rather from the fundamental nature of the change that would be required to do so. In order to achieve unity of action with Socialists, i.e. create a common defense in France, the P.C.F. would have had to cease its polemics against the leaders of the Parti Socialiste, cease its attempts to divorce the Socialist workers from the party. To do this would mean to abandon the whole policy established at the VIth World Congress. It would, in their view, constitute an admission of defeat in the new course, a renunciation of all of the dogma that had been constructed on the framework of the VIth World Congress, perhaps even a compromise of their entire concept of the revolutionary struggle.[4] These were the considerations which the Comintern weighed against the unassessable danger of the rise of fascism in France. Unlike the Socialists the question of common defense for the Comintern was not merely that of forgetting former antagonisms or overlooking doctrinal divergences in a greater cause, the very act of entering into unity of action constituted renunciation of established policy.

If in 1933 the Communists were not yet willing to make the concessions necessary to unity of action with the Socialists, they were nevertheless impressed with the need to find an improved method of combatting the potentially dangerous Rightist Leagues which were appearing in France. To this end they tried every conceivable device short of unity of action. The P.C.F., as we have seen, was exceedingly weak in 1933; it was a party which Paul Faure might find to be "a mass of ruins" and of which Vandervelde could say "today its decline and the rapidity of its decline, or rather of its decomposition, strikes everyone", without evoking as much as a denial.[5] Frustration in the attempts to enlarge the party and the C.G.T.U. caused it to turn elsewhere for a means of extending its future. For the French Communists the year 1933 saw a large scale search for a means to circumvent the need for unity of action and at the same time to increase its defensive strength.

The principal attempt made by the P.C.F. in this direction was the establishment of the so-called Amsterdam-Pleyel Movement. Through the medium of Henri Barbusse, leader of the Association Républicaine des Anciens Combattants (A.R.A.C.), and some of the lesser leaders of this veterans organization, an international rally against war had been held in Amsterdam in the summer of 1932.[6] After the coming of Hitler a second congress was held at the Salle Pleyel in Paris in the summer of 1933, and the slogan of the Movement was broadened to "anti-war and anti-fascism". In order to add the appearance of intellectual sponsorship to the two congresses, Romain Rolland was chosen as co-sponsor. Ostensibly the function of the Movement was to join intellectuals, veterans and miscellaneous sympathizers in an international and non-party block against the preparations for war and against the rise of fascism. André Gide was but one among many French and non-French intellectuals to lend wholehearted support to the cause.[7] Not so the leaders of the Parti Socialiste, whose detection of the ill-concealed Communist sponsorhsip was sufficient to evoke a formal prohibition to party members against joining the Movement, and the expulsion of those who did.[8]

Nevertheless the Amsterdam-Pleyel Movement became an invaluable adjunct to the P.C.F.'s campaign for a **front unique en bas**. Having failed to develop a substantially large Communist-dominated trade union movement by which it might maneuver large numbers with only a minority P.C.F. representation, the P.C.F. relied increasingly on the Comités d'Amsterdam-Pleyel which were organized throughout France.[9] Socialist denunciation of the Movement provided the P.C.F. with an excellent propaganda weapon in its campaign to identify the Communists as the only true defenders of antifascism and peace. Furthermore the Movement, unlike the C.G.T.U., provided an extremely useful means of indirect action. As the Comintern maintained its firm doctrinal opposition to unity of action with the Socialists, and the **front unique en bass** tactic failed to penetrate the fabric of Socialist allegiance, the opportunity for indirect action thus afforded became important.

Amsterdam-Pleyel was merely an attempt to achieve the same ends that would be afforded by unity of action with the Socialists without paying the price of such action. As a tactical device by which the P.C.F. could participate unofficially in (and frequently initiate) joint action with the Socialists the Movement served its purposes well. But, as both the Socialists and the leader of the **Croix de Feu** pointed out, it represented an admission by the Comintern that the P.C.F. was no longer an adequate Communist weapon in France. In a brochure published in 1935 attacking the "Communist-Socialist plot" de la Rocque described the Movement as the manifestation of a new Moscow tactic born of the realization that it was impossible to create a powerful Communist party in France solely by direct recruitment.[10] According to de la Rocque, Moscow decided in 1932 that the number of cardholders wasn't important if their quality was certain. Taking these as a nucleus it would broaden its base by integrating organizations which were not strictly Communist but were linked to the party and controlled by it. All were agreed that the Movement represented merely an extension of the traditional **front unique en bas** tactic by less direct means. Nor did the P.C.F. make any serious attempt to conceal this, Thorez declaring a month before the riots of February 1934:

> According to the directives formulated in the last resolution of the Central Committee, we must work for a united front of battle with the Socialist workers. . . We must submit to them precise proposals for action, invite them to prepare organs of preparation and direction for these actions and collaborate with them actively therein. We must ask them to adhere to

the large non-party organizations. We must multiply the links with those who follow the Action Socialiste and who fight at our side in the Amsterdam Movement. Naturally such a united front does not exclude, but demands, an incessant battle against Social-democracy.[11]

In conjunction with the Amsterdam-Pleyel Movement the Communists also initiated a program for more direct short-range methods of "self-defense". The need for this, they asserted, had been demonstrated by the German experience. In contrast to the Rightist leagues, however, the P.C.F. rejected the concept of paramilitary organizations. In place of these or of an elite guard it instructed each of its front organizations to train its own members in the techniques of street fighting and in the defense of its manifestations.[12]

The final means by which the P.C.F. sought to expand its influence and create a base broad enough to resist aggression from the Right was by intensifying its campaign to identify the party with the defense of the immediate grievances of the working class. As the economic crisis in France worsened through 1932 and 1933, this took the form of a "battle for the beefsteak".[13] The XIIth Plenum of the Executive had established this as the primary task of the P.C.F. in September of 1932:

> The P.C.F. must turn towards the defense of the daily interests of the worker and peasant masses, against the reduction of salaries, in favor of social insurance, and in favor of immediate aid to the unemployed...[14]

Duclos amplified the task in July 1933:

> Our tasks must be concentrated in three directions:
> (a) Economic grievances.
> (b) The battle against war.
> (c) The battle against fascism.
>
> Concentrating our efforts on grievance struggles, in particular among the railroad workers, the miners, the metallurgists and the textile workers; entering into the factories, developing our work in the factories, consolidating it in the direction of the mass movement, these are the immediate questions.[15]

All this presumed an increased attack against the Socialists. Each of the Executive meetings of the Comintern, Central Committee meetings of the P.C.F. and speeches and articles of the leaders of both, emphasized throughout 1933 and until February 1934, that the primary task of the P.C.F. was to broaden its proletarian base by a closer identification of the party as the champion of workers and peasant grievances, and the the **front unique en bas** was to be applied with an intensity surpassing anything in the past.

The fact that Communist intransigence barred unity of action between the parties, however, did not dispel the uneasiness among the leaders of both parties concerning the effects of disunity in Germany. This uneasiness manifested itself in attempts by each party to place the blame on the other for the German defeat. As part of its **front unique en bas** tactic the P.C.F. unleashed a vicious attack against the "lesser evil" policies of the German Social-democrats which, it alleged, had prepared the way for Nazism. But in May the French Communists were placed on the defensive by the renewal at Berlin of the protocol of amity between Germany and the Soviet Union. Rosenfeld wrote in LE POPULAIRE:

> The bolshevik party is persecuted in Germany as the German section of the Comintern, whose seat is in Moscow... The Soviets then choose this precise moment to sign a pact of amity with Hitler. The 'government of Russian workers and peasants' is linked by a 'protocol of amity' with the persecutor of the German workers.[16]

Secondly there was a fervent desire on the part of each party to demonstrate that the other was the obstacle to unity in France. In this the Communists completely outmaneuvered the Parti Socialiste. On the 5th of March the P.C.F. received instructions from the Comintern, presumably in response to the February overtures of the I.O.S., directing that proposals be made to the leadership of the Socialist parties with a view to common action against "fascism and the capitalist offensive".[17] Acting on these instructions the Bureau politique of the P.C.F. proposed to the Permanent Administrative Commission (the C.A.P.) of the Parti Socialiste the establishment of joint committees for the purpose of holding manifestations and strikes in common. These proposals differed from the usual pattern of such offers from the P.C.F. in the important respect that they offered the hitherto denied temptation of an agreement to cease propaganda attacks against the Socialist leaders in the course of the common action. Despite the fact that the wording of the proposals themselves gave ample justification for the Socialist belief that this was merely a maneuver on the part of the P.C.F., the inclusion of the offer to cease criticism made it difficult for the Socialists to refuse.

Also despite the fact that they could point to the past futility of dealings with the P.C.F and the ill-concealed evidences of continued attempts by the P.C.F. to undermine the Socialist leaders, there was no doubt that the Communist offer received great sympathy among the rank and file of both parties. Blum assumed the challenging task of preventing the acceptance of the P.C.F. offers and at the same time parrying the propaganda which the Communists were making out of this rejection. During the week following receipt of the Bureau politique's letter he published a series of articles in LE POPULAIRE explaining the inability of the Socialists to accept the Communist offer, and simultaneously asserting the faith of the Socialists in the ultimate reestablishment of unity of action. Meanwhile the Communist leaders exploited Socialist reticence. In L'HUMANITÉ, in the regional press, and at large manifestations held in the name of proletarian unity, the Communists invited the Socialist workers to observe the hypocrisy of their chiefs who, they pointed out, professed a desire for unity only until the opportunity for it was presented to them. Thorez wrote:

> Not only does Paul Faure no longer pronounce the 'five letters' but he excels in demagogic phrases. He is 'unitarian, violently, passionately', just like his confreres Severac and Zyromski. Of course he dismisses Socialist workers who effectively realize the united front, but he does not cease to proclaim his love for unity. He places only one little condition on that unity, to know that the Communists cease to be Communists, that they renounce troubling the tranquility of the bourgeoisie and of their valets the Socialists chiefs with the revolutionary struggle.[18]

The stigma of being the cause of continued disunity, a stigma which rightly belonged almost entirely to the Communists, was thus passed in some measure to the Socialist leaders, and the growing dissatisfaction with party policy among the lower ranks of the P.C.F. began to find its counterpart within the Parti Socialiste.

For it was among the workers themselves and the lower echelons of both parties that the greatest effect of the coming of Hitler was felt. Removed from the doctrinal considerations that prevented the attainment of an accord at the leadership level, the rank and file could and did regard the event in its simplest terms and react in the most direct manner, i.e. by seeking to prevent the occurrence in France of the disunity which had led to defeat in Germany. Within the trade unions, within the regional federations and sections of the parties, and even within the Amsterdam-Pleyel committees and l'A.R.A.C., the growth of pro-unity sentiment severely taxed the ability of party leaders to retain discipline. Throughout France there was a tendency on the part of the militants of each party to combine with one another on the lower levels in spite of the official policies of the parties. Duclos noted this growing tendency in his report to the Central Committee of the P.C.F. in July of 1933:

> Let us examine the case of Bourges. At Bourges the comrades of the regional leadership voted a joint resolution with citizen Lazurick, secretary of the Fédération Socialiste of Cher. Together they declared the following:
>
> 'The representatives of the Region Communiste of the Centre and the Fédération Socialiste, etc. ... proceeded to exchange views on the situations of their two parties and they found themselves in accord in regretting the division of the working class.'
>
> Now we have just demonstrated with sufficient facts that the division of the working class is the work of the Social-democrats.
>
> 'They agreed that each menace of fascism and of war would find them united in action. They will meet to examine how organic unity of the working class can be realized.'
>
> You see comrades how the maneuvers of Social-democracy have been able to sow a certain amount of trouble in our ranks. I know that the comrades of Bourges realize the error they have committed. They have corrected it.[19]

Similar "errors" were noted at Cahors, Troyes, Levry-Gargan and other places, and the Central Committee was kept busy correcting regional and local organizations which tended to lose sight of the position of the party in their search for workers unity. In condemnation of these practices Thorez expressed the attitude of the Communists toward unity of action:

> The fact that these comrades commit errors many times condemned by the party and the International, that they continue to believe in the effectiveness of controversies and that they are constantly favoring the sending of proposals for a united front to the leadership of the Socialist party, demands the attention of the party. For such an orientation hinders the realization of our true policy of front unique and doesn't permit the rapid and convincing correction of errors which the Central Committee has the duty of relieving and preventing. Instead of devoting themselves patiently and systematically to the work of the

> front unique en bas, to the realization of class and trade union unity by seeking and initiating contacts with Socialist workers and reformist workers, some comrades are tending in the direction of the least effort. They conceive of, or even realize, compromises at the top of the party, notably with the leaders of the Blum-Paul Faure faction. That is a capitulation in the face of the difficulties of bolshevik work, a capitulation before Social-democracy.[20]

Despite the widespread effect upon the rank and file of both proletarian parties, and despite the initial attempts at unity of action, within six months after Hitler's arrival to power he was being used by all parties of the Left to a large extent merely as a tool to further the same political ends that had been pursued before his arrival. He had become a weapon for the Left as a whole against the Right, an extremely useful bogeyman with which to arouse the emotions of all antifascist elements. He had also become an important factor in the three sided inter-party fight within the Leftist group. The method in which the Comintern used the German defeat was illustrated in the Theses of the XIIIth Plenum (based on the report by Kuusinen):

> In the battle against Social-democracy the Communists must show to the workers that the new failure of the Social-democrats and the IInd International (the Nazi success) was historically inevitable. By conscientiously demasking and by refuting, before the masses, the hypocritical and treacherous sophisms of Social-democracy the Communists can attract the Social-democratic workers to the active and revolutionary battle under the direction of the Communist party.[21]

The Socialists made use of the rise of Hitler against both the intransigence of the Comintern and the conservative policies of the Radicals. The latter on the whole were concerned less with the success of German fascism as an ideological threat than as a military threat, and as it was primarily the former thoughout 1933 they manifested little of the panic of the proletarian parties.

This apparent willingness to reduce the threat posed by Hitler to the level of party politics, puzzling in retrospect, is more easily understood in the light of the manner in which each party regarded the threat in 1933. The Communists would have had the world believe by their creation and support of the Amsterdam-Pleyel Movement that they regarded the Hitler accession principally as a threat to peace and international Socialism. In view of the absence of a serious threat to the Soviet Union at that time in all probability they did so regard it. Bergery and those who, with him, conceived of the Common Front in March of 1933 also professed the same motives.[22] The French Socialists, perhaps more sensitive to the problem of domestic fascism than to that of international fascism, were concerned principally with the danger of its appearance in France. Finally the Radicals, preoccupied with the problems of government during a series of financial crises, tried to lessen as much as possible the effect upon internal affairs of the coming of Hitler.

Each of these attitudes can be explained only in terms of that which was lacking from the Hitler threat in 1933, i.e. the military threat to France or the Soviet Union. The absence of such a threat permitted the Radicals to remain reasonably complacent about their primary concern, the security of the Republic. It permitted the Socialists to continue to wage their campaign on the familiar double fronts of economic affairs and the defense against internal fascism. Finally it allowed the Comintern, and hence the P.C.F., to continue its offensive against Social-democracy without being hampered unduly by considerations of the defense of the Soviet Union.

NOTES

1. LE POPULAIRE, 20 February 1933.
2. Vandervelde, L'ALTERNATIVE, l'Eglantine, Paris, 1933, p. 239.
3. According to the official Socialist version, contained in the COMPTE RENDU STÉNOGRAPHIQUE DU XXX CONGRÈS NATIONAL, RAPPORT ADMINISTRATIF, there had been other overtures by the Parti Socialiste and the Parti de l'Unité Proletarienne in February and March 1933. Finally at its meeting in Zurich on May 18th and 19th the I.O.S. decided that further attempts were hopeless and forbade its national sections to make individual pacts with the Communist parties. FRONT UNIQUE INTERNATIONALE, TEXTES ET DOCUMENTS, Bureau d'éditions, Paris, 1935.
4. When, after unity of action had been decided upon, the P.C.F. agreed to the cessation of its attacks upon the Socialist leaders, Bela Kun wrote: "We declare openly and categorically that to stop polemicising with the Social-democratic parties, to stop attacking their policy of collaboration with the bourgeoisie for the duration of our common action against the offensive of capital ... is **a concession** on our part." Bela Kun, "La lutte pour l'unite d'action", INTERNATIONAL COMMUNISTE, 5 July 1934.

    In his speech before the Conference National at Ivry in June 1934, Thorez expressed the difficulties that such a change would entail for the Communists: "... We are Communists. We have a doctrine, a program and a tactic which have proved themselves, which have permitted the workers of the Soviet Union to liberate themselves from capitalist exploitation, from the Tsarist yoke, and to construct Socialism in their country. We have a program, a doctrine, a tactic forged by the Dmitrovs, the Thaelmanns, the best among the combatants of the anti-fascist battle.

    "Can anyone believe that we are now ready to alienate this capital so precious to the working class? Can anyone believe that we are ready now to renounce to the slightest degree that which is dearer than our own life?" Thorez, "L'Organization du front unique de lutte", C.B., 1 July 1934, p. 777.

5. Vandervelde, **op. cit.**, p. 236.

6. l'A.R.A.C., which was the basic organization of Communist "self-defense", was founded in 1917 in conformity with the law of July 1, 1901, as an affiliate of the Internationale des Anciens Combattants et Victimes de Guerre. Governed by a federal committee elected at its national congresses, it was divided into twenty regions each grouping four or five departments. Its resources were derived from dues -- 9 francs a year in 1933 -- and from the sale of its journal LE REVEIL DU COMBATTANT, a monthly, which averaged about 15,000 copies a month in 1933-34. Its founder and chief spokesman was Henri Barbusse, author of FEU, who became a Communist in 1923. In 1933 the organization numbered approximately 20,000 members, of whom only 5,000 were in the Paris region. Originally a non-party organization, with the conversion of its leader it came increasingly under Communist domination. See AUDITION DU PERRIER AU COMMISSION D'ENQUÊTE, **op. cit.**, p. 2242.

7. See Naville, Claude, ANDRÉ GIDE ET LE COMMUNISME, Paris, LIbrairie du Travail, Paris, 1936.

8. In the Rapport Moral presented by Paul Faure to the XXXth Congrès National of the Parti Socialiste in July 1933, he declared: "In June of 1932 we had to face a new maneuver of the Parti Communiste in relation to a front unique in the form of a world congress against war, better known under the name Congress of Amsterdam.

    "The numerous documents and letters exchanged ... leave absolutely no doubt as to the character of the bolshevik maneuver directed against our party. They demonstrate in the most undeniable manner that the end pursued is to raise trouble in our groups, sections and federations, and to dislocate our action while seeking to rupture and destroy unity itself." COMPTE RENDU DU XXXe CONGRÈS NATIONAL, Rapport Moral, p. 2.

    On the 19th of June, 1932, Fellicien Challaye, on behalf of Romain Rolland, addressed a letter to Paul Faure, which was answered by the Parti Socialiste in an article entitled "La Vie du Parti" in LE POPULAIRE of July 11th: "The Secretariat brings to the attention of the Sections and Federations of the party that, at its meeting of 29 June last, the C.A.P., possessed of an invitation by Romain Rolland and Henri Barbusse, decided that the Parti Socialiste would not take part.

"Our action against war will not be to act outside of the framework of the international to which our party and the C.G.T. belong, that is to say the Internationale Ouvrière Socialiste and the Fédération Syndicale Internationale."

At the same time the secretary of the I.O.S., Friedrich Adler, entered into the negotiations with Rolland Barbusse in order to determine the nature of the Movement, and found it to be a purely Communist organization, directed more against the Socialists than against war. Adler approved of the decision of the Parti Ouvrier Belge and the Parti Ouvrier Socialdémocratique of Denmark, as well as that of the French party, not to enter that manifestation.

"All of these congresses are directed not merely at the tasks which their title proclaim, but above all against the Socialist parties. The battle against the Socialists is considered the supreme task not only by the Communists in general, but by Henri Barbusse in particular." Adler's report, printed in LE POPULAIRE, 20 July 1932.

"Louis Gibarti has been named International Secretary of the world congress against war. His name suffices to make obvious the relationship existing with the other front unique maneuvers of the bolshevists. He was a disciple of Munzenberg in the Secours Rouge International, and Munzenberg detached him to the congress against colonial repression as secretary. Now he is charged with putting under way the tasks of the world congress against war in the direction wished by the bolshevists."

Ibid.

Finally on January 26th, 1933, the Parti Socialiste issued a circular to its federations warning them to stay out of the Amsterdam group: "We have the satisfaction of noting that with very rare exceptions the Sections and Federations have replied to (the Communist) proposals with the responses inspired by the decisions of our congress. They have thus thwarted the old bolshevik maneuver, called front unique, which -- although presented under a new guise -- is nonetheless directed against our party." COMPTE RENDU DU XXXe CONGRES NATIONAL, Rapport Administratif p. 61.

9. Through the Movement the P.C.F. organized a Comité Central d'Unité d"action, comprised of 57 regional organizations and, according to Communist claims, 300,000 adherents throughout France. G. Cogniot, PAIX ET LIBERTÉ, Editions du Mouvement Amsterdam-Pleyel, speech delivered to the Congrès Populaire of the P.C.F., 28 January 1936. Cogniot also claimed that the

slogan of the Popular Front, "Pain, Paix et Liberte", originated June 28th, 1932, at Amsterdam.

Piatnitski asserted before the XIIIth Plenum that 122 organizations containing Socialists as well as Communists adhered to the movement, C.B. 1 February 1934, p. 148, and despite this exaggeration the list of affiliated organizations which appeared in the RÉVUE HEBDOMAIRE of September 1934, was impressively long. The variety in the nature of these affiliates was rivalled only by the obscurity of a large number of them, bearing such names as Cercle des emigrés Bessarabiens en France, or Amateurs photographes ouvriers. Nevertheless l'A.R.A.C., the Jeunesses Communistes, the C.G.T.U., the Fédération Sportive du Travail and others, lent considerable substance to the list.

10. De la Rocque, LE COMPLOT COMMUNO-SOCIALISTE -- L'INSURRECTION ARMÉE DANS L'UNITÉ D'ACTION, Edited by Croix de Feu, Grasset, Paris, 1935. Despite de la Rocque's extreme and obvious prejudice, his analysis of the tactics of his enemy was both perspicacious and comprehensive.

11. Speech to Central Committee in January 1934, C.B. 15 January 1934, p. 83.

12. The VIth World Congress had established: "In no case can one lose sight of the fact that in imperialist countries the existence of proletarian militia or of a garde rouge in the framework of the bourgeois state in time of general peace is inadmissible and impossible." PROGRAMME DE L'INTERNATIONALE COMMUNISTE, **op. cit.**, p. 66.

Drawing from its direction from this citation the P.C.F. rejected special organizations such as the Groupes de defense anti-fasciste and the Jeunes gardes antifascistes which had been formed within l'A.R.A.C. On the other hand the Comintern had declared in August of 1931, at a time when Chiappe was being particularly effective in his suppression of the P.C.F.: "To preach now the renunciation of resistance to the workers provoked by the police and the fascists, that would be to abandon the terrain of the class battle. Proletarian self-defense against armed aggression on the part of the columns of official and volunteer assassins of the bourgeoisie must be organized in a careful and conscientious fashion." INTERNATIONALE COMMUNISTE, 15 August 1931, p. 37.

Thus in an article in the CAHIERS DU BOLCHEVISME in early 1934 Gaston Mornet issued the instructions for self-defense: "... each of the revolutionary organizations must form its own proletarian self-defense group. The Communist party, the C.G.T.U., the Secours Rouge Internationale, the Comite de defense de l'Huma, the Locataires, the Amsterdam and antifascist movement, the Fédération Sportive du Travail, the unemployed workers, the Coopé, etc., each of these organizations has contact with a part of the workers and peasant masses, each needs its own self-defense; therefore each must train its adherents and sympathizers in the defense of its manifestations, meetings, sale of journals, defense of orators ..." C.B., 15 February 1934, p. 246.

13. Gitton, reporting to the Central Committee meeting in July 1933, argued: "In the state of the present economic crisis the battle for the relief of immediate grievances constitutes the principal task, because the attention of the masses is monopolized by the problems of their existence.

"The battle for the beefsteak constitutes the link which must permit us to rally the masses, to orient them toward our class objectives. We must never believe that the battle for immediate claims, however small they may be, is of inferior importance." L'ACTION DU PROLETARIAT ET LE FRONT UNIQUE, Reports of Duclos and Gitton to the Central Committee, July 1933, Publications Revolutionnaires, Paris, 1934, p. 31.

14. Report of XIIth Plenum, **op. cit.**, p. 27.

15. Reports of Duclos and Gitton to Central Committee, July 1933, **op. cit.**, p. 20.

16. LE POPULAIRE, 11 May 1933. In the same issue Blum wrote: "How do the French Communists intend to make the working masses understand the government of the Soviets in view of the fact that, 'when the German brother is reduced to illegality by fascism, when its chiefs are threatened with death by Hitler and by Goering', it rushes to sign a pact of confidence and amity with fascism?"

In response to L'HUMANITÉ'S claim that the protocol was merely being ratified by Hitler at this time, that its renewal had been ratified by Stalin in 1931, Rosenfeld wrote: "Let us assume for an instant that this is true ... But how is it that the commentators in Pravda and Izvestia **saluted** this ratification as an international act of the highest importance and congratulated themselves upon it?

"No L'HUMANITÉ will have to find another way to calm its readers, who are more and more uneasy." LE POPULAIRE, 23 May 1933.

17. Text:
    "The Executive Committee of the Comintern, before the offensive of capitalism against the German working class, demands that all of its Communist parties make another attempt to establish the front unique of combat with the Social-democratic working masses through the Social-democratic parties. The Executive Committee makes this proposal in the firm conviction that the front unique of the working class will repulse the offensive of capitalism and will be able to hasten the inevitable end of all capitalist exploitation.

    "Since as a result of special conditions ... which are posed differently before the working classes of the different countries an accord between the Communist and Socialist parties can be realized most effectively within the framework of the different countries, the Executive Committee of the Comintern recommends to the Communist parties of the different countries that they address to the Central Committees of the Social-democratic parties belonging to the I.O.S. proposals for common action against fascism and the offensive of capitalism." L'HUMANITÉ, March 6, 1933.

18. Thorez, "Contre l'opportunisme", C.B., 1 February 1934, p. 138.

19. Reports of Duclos and Gitton to the Central Committee, July 1933, **op. cit.**, p. 18.

20. Thorez, C.B., 15 January 1934, p. 80.

21. C.B., 15 January 1934, p. 118: "The party does not progress enough in either influence or numbers because it is not yet active enough, because all of its members, all of its organizations are not turned toward the work of the masses; it doesn't intervene in each event, whether minute or substantial, to alert, to mobilize the masses and orient them toward action.

    "... because it does not wage the battle against Social-democracy in a resolute and systematic manner.

    "Because there exists a tendency to consider the front unique as an alliance, a block with the Parti Socialiste and reformist trade unions, or at best as a maneuver at the top vis-a-vis the Social fascist leaders.

    "... the faults are the expression of deviations of an opportunist rightist or sectarian character, or of conciliation in regard to these deviations in the interior of our own ranks. That prevents the mobilization of all our forces for the battle against the external enemy, capitalism and Social-democracy." Thorez, Report to the Bureau politique to the meeting of the Central Committee of the P.C.F. of 24 January 1934. LA LUTTE POUR L'ISSUE REVOLUTIONNAIRE A LA CRISE, Publications Revolutionnaires, Paris, 1934, pp. 14-15.

22. Langevin, Bernard Lecache, Georges Monnet and Bergery shared in the conception of the Common Front in March of 1933 as a response to the arrival of Hitler. Bergery explained in LE MOND 10 June 1933, that the movement was distinct from Amsterdam-Pleyel but there was "no divergence of goal or principle", since both movements "look upon fascism as the highest form of capitalism, when the latter has lost faith in **its** parliament and **its** democracy". Bergery believed there was an identity of interest between the two movements in that they both considered that "the maintenance of bourgeois 'democracy' could never be an end in itself and that we must defend what is left of the so-called democratic liberties, not to maintain the regime but to overthrow it".

CHAPTER THREE

THE IMPACT OF NEO-SOCIALISM

The first substantial and positive response among the parties of the Left either to the worsening economic situation or to the rise of fascism was the revolt of the Neo-Socialists against the traditional doctrines of the Parti Socialiste. Essentially this was a revolt against the revolutionary aspects of 19th century Marxism. Before the arrival of Hitler, the Marxist doctrines were attacked as being obsolete, having been contradicted by events and shown up as theoretically unsound in the light of contemporary developments. After the arrival of Hitler, however, these doctrines were attacked not on the theoretical level alone but rather as actual, and dangerous, impediments in the battle against fascism. Tactical exigencies now demanded a renunciation -- or at least a suspension -- of the application of Marxist principles and an end to the isolation of the proletariat from the middle classes.

But neither before nor after the coming of Hitler could the Neo-Socialists enlist widespread support within the Parti Socialiste. When in November 1933 the parliamentary group, of which a majority were Neo-Socialists, voted to support a Radical government in defiance of party orders, the Neos were expelled and their limited influence on party affairs was at an end. Despite their expulsion and the rejection of their program, however, the Neo-Socialists incident established a valuable precedent for the future course of the Socialist party. The Neos were the first to argue for a united front with the Radicals, or, more broadly, for the substitution of class collaboration in place of the class struggle as a means of parrying the double threat of fascism and economic crisis.

There were two principal sources of Neo-Socialist thought; (1) the lingering tendency toward participationism which Jaurès had allegedly sanctioned, and (2) the planism of Henri de Man which Déat adapted to fit the French situation. The participationists, among whom were Compére-Morel and that fervent disciple of Jaurès, Renaudel, had no quarrel with Socialist theory as such. However, like Jaurès, this group thought that no doctrinal violation was committed by the participation of Socialists in the government of a non-Socialist State. Believing Jaurès' hypothesis that "In fact the State does not express a class, but rather expresses the relationship of classes, that is, the relationship of their strengths", and that the role of the State was to "open to the class that is rising paths proportional to its real power, to the force and to the extent of its movement of ascension", the participationists regarded Blum's refusal to take part in a Radical government as a tactical error for which there was no doctrinal justification.[1] Speaking before the Congrès extraordinaire at Avignon in April 1933, Renaudel declared:

> Of what is it a question? Not of casting doubt on the essential principles of Socialism but rather of pronouncing on **the tactic**. It is a question of knowing whether at the present moment the party is for or against Social-democracy. The risks which this democracy is running have been revealed sufficiently by events abroad. In order to defend the country against these risks what will we offer it?
>
> Does the country await our bringing it as a tactic descent into the streets, tumultuous manifestations, threats of violence which fascism has used everywhere as the pretext for crushing Socialist parties? Our answer to ourselves is clear; we have confidence in democratic methods."[2]

The second group, on the other hand, led by Marcel Déat, Barthelemy Montagnon and Adrien Marquet, took the extreme Neo-Socialist position and advocated a complete revision of Socialist doctrine. In its view Blum's refusal to sanction participation was not merely a tactical error but also demonstrated an absurd retention of a doctrine which the development of events had made obsolete and dangerous. Addressing the Congrès extraordinaire of the party in January 1930, Déat had declared:

> On the day when you accept for the first time the idea of the taking of power in a capitalist regime you will have accomplished the true revision of the Charter. From that time on you will be situated on firm ground of fact.[3]

Revision of the Charter of 1905, escape from the hamstringing effects of the class struggle doctrine, reinspection of the tenets of Socialist theory in light of the need for an intermediary regime during this period of transition, these then were the goals of the Déat faction of the Neo-Socialists. For doctrinal guidance and inspiration they borrowed heavily from the teachings of the Belgian, Henri de Man.

De Man's principal theoretical exposition, AU DELA DU MARXISME, was first published in Paris in 1927 and again in 1929.[4] Thus its appearance coincided with the beginnings of dissident thought among the Right wing group of the Parti Socialiste. His basic thesis, envisaging a coalition of the forces of the Left for the purpose of establishing the intermediary regime, was bound to be attractive to the French dissidents. His plan of partial nationalization, which he claimed would combat the economic crisis in a manner impossible for either the liberal or Marxist doctrines, also held considerable appeal for the Déat-Montagnon-Marquet faction.

Opposing the formula of Adler and Vandervelde of "passage to nonviolence by means of violence" de Man rejected the use of violent methods either to effect a change in the social order or as a means of arriving at power. He believed the orthodox argument to be as self-contradicting as that of combatting war by war, and he pointed out that the doctrine calling for dictatorship of the proletariat as a means of transition overlooked the fact that a dictatorship required a dictator who would be reluctant to relinquish his power. The Neos could accept and interpret de Man's thesis as the rejection of the traditional concept of the class struggle, which in fact it was, and it thus served them as a precedent for liberation from the political limitations imposed by that concept.

De Man's contribution to Socialist thought consisted essentially of a re-evaluation, in economic terms, of the vestiges of Marxist principles that still served as the basic tenets of Socialist doctrine. His analysis of the trends leading to the economic crisis was not dissimilar to that of the Communists as stated in the report of the IXth Plenum. He found the three main causes to be the growing predominance of finance capital, the substitution of monopolies for freely competing enterprises, and economic nationalism. Hence an institutional or structural reform was indeed necessary, particularly to combat unemployment. He believed, however, that only those enterprises that had become monopolistic in nature need be nationalized, and even in these it was the removal of authority rather than the dispossession of property which was considered to be the essential characteristic of nationalization. The remainder of the economy would be submitted merely to such control as was necessary to prevent the above-mentioned abuses from taking place.[5]

However de Man's impact on the French Socialists was primarily of a political rather than an economic nature. It was the political conclusions arising from his economic propositions that held the greatest appeal for the participationists as well as the Neos. Renunciation of the exclusively proletarian point of view, acceptance of the role of national sentiment, recognition of the need for a conciliation between the interests of the workers and those of the middle classes, and rejection of the materialistic dialectic, could be translated into political terms coinciding to a great degree with the desires of the Déat faction.[6]

Déat's chief work, PERSPECTIVES SOCIALISTES, published in 1930, appeared to many to be merely an extrapolation of the theories contained in AU DELÀ DU MARXISME.[7] However, in its adaptation to the peculiarities of the problems of the French Socialists as well as to the ambitions of its author, it assumed a character of its own. According to Déat the mission of Socialism in a transitional situation such as that existing in France was not to remain aloof from the sources of power but rather to adapt itself to an intermediary regime in which the Socialists could possess or share power during the transition to a Socialist state. To this end the positions conquered by Socialism within a non-Socialist state were not precarious occupations in an enemy country. On the contrary, each municipality under Socialist control, each departmental assembly under its influence, was a fraction of the state conquered for the working class.[8]

In taking this position Déat aligned against himself not only the Guesdists but also those more prudent militants who, foreseeing an eventual equilibrium within the state between the forces of capitalism and Socialism, argued that political power and influence should not get too far ahead of power within the economic and social order. Waging too rapid an offensive within the state, delegating militants to advanced posts when the mass of anti-capitalist forces was too far behind them to give adequate support, they argued, was risking that these militants be encircled by their adversaries and thus that the gradual but well-supported advance of Socialism be delayed.[9] But Déat steadfastly maintained that the primary function of the Socialists was the assumption of power. As early as October 1929 he had written:

> The historic task of trade-unionism is to remove economic authority from capitalism, bit by bit. That of Socialism is primarily to relieve capitalism of its political power, to realize what I have called the separation of capitalism and the State. Of

course the C.G.T. cannot remain aloof from this preliminary operation, and the Socialist party will have to rely on it in order to succeed.[10]

Since at this time, 1928-1931, the world economic crisis had had no noticeable effect upon France's domestic economy, the recession, which was to play such an important part in the future development of the Neos, can have influenced them but little if at all. The same may be said of the as yet embryonic fascist threat. The personal ambition of Déat and some of the others, plus their chronic lukewarmness toward Marxism, helps explain their readiness to lead or adopt a new school of Socialist thought but does not disprove their dedication to these new principles. Like the Bernsteinists in Germany and the Millerands in France a generation before him Déat found the predictions of Marx being contradicted by events. The traditional concept of the manner in which Socialism would come to power was obsolete according to the Neos.

It was at the Congrès extraordinaire of January 1930 that the Déat group and the participationists joined forces. Déat and Renaudel both delivered speeches advocating Socialist participation in the government. Renaudel, asking for a modification of the party position on national defense and anti-militarism in order that a rapprochement with the Radicals might be tactically feasible, appeared in a role similar to that of Renaud Jean and Doriot before the Central Committee of the P.C.F. in 1928. He presented, as had Doriot, not a rebellion against party doctrine, but merely a strong request for qualification of doctrine to allow the pursuit of a more reasonable tactical policy.[11]

The Neos received support in the early stages from several prominent party members such as Ramadier, Salengro, Spinasse and Emile Kahn who felt that the party must place itself in a position to act more effectively in order to hasten the improvement of workers conditions. However the Blum-led majority was successful in overcoming a motion favoring participation.[12] The question was shelved during the succeeding congresses until after the legislative elections of 1932, partly in order not to reveal the growing discord within the party before the elections and partly because there was no single new issue upon which the participationists could pin the justification of a revival.[13]

After the elections of 1932, however, the participationist and Neo-Socialist coalition within the parliamentary group was resumed. Now there were three additional bases upon which to predicate a new attempt. The sweeping electoral victory indicated a popular mandate for governmental as well as electoral collaboration between Socialist and Radical which could not be ignored. The fruits of the Socialist share in this victory must be gathered; the parity in electoral strength between the Socialists and the Radicals must reflect itself in a parity of influence.[14] There was the tardy but now full-fledged economic recession as another argument for Socialist assumption of power. Finally there was the rise of German fascism as a goad to unity among the parties of the Left. This was the time for Socialist participation to assure alleviation of the economic and political crises, not for an attitude of aloofness toward the governmental problems which beset the country. Montagnon declared at the Congress at Montrouge a few days after the election:

> The world is a boiling cauldron ... It is not true, even for the revolutionaries, that Socialism will benefit from an aggravated crisis.[15]

Growing uneasiness in Socialist ranks coupled with restlessness at being unable to make full use of the electoral mandate caused a trend within the party in favor of the translation of electoral power into political power.[16] This trend led in turn to the preparation of the Cahiers de Huyghens and their unsuccessful submission to the Radicals. With the failure of the Huyghens negotiations the beliefs of the anti-participationists were confirmed and negotiations ceased, but both minority factions continued their campaigns.[17]

It is undoubtedly of more than coincidental significance that Déat and Renaudel, like Doriot and Renaud Jean within the P.C.F., were representatives of their party in the Chamber.[18] It is also worth while to compare the manner in which the opposition of each pair to its respective party changed both in nature and in intensity as the rise of Nazism became more pronounced and then culminated finally in the arrival of Hitler to power. The relatively mild dissidence of Doriot and Renaud Jean over the proposed change of Communist electoral tactics in 1928 was based entirely upon the tactical misfortunes that such a change would incur both within Parliament and before the electorate. There was no criticism of the underlying doctrine and even the tactical dissension was not adhered to with rebellious insistence. With the coming of Hitler, however, all this was changed. If we accept the divisibility of Communist doctrine from Communist tactic, which Doriot would do but the Comintern would not, it will be seen that the tactical importance of class collaboration became so crucial for Doriot that no doctrinal considerations could stand against it.

As in the case of the dissident Communists the imminence and then the arrival of Hitler also caused a profound change in the nature of Neo-Socialist opposition. Before 1932 the pressure exerted by the Neos took the form of doctrinal argument, based on an analytical disagreement with the traditional Marxist principles which served as the party creed. In late 1932, however, and from the beginning of 1933 on, the Neos were no longer primarily concerned with their theoretical economic inheritance from de Man but rather with those political implications of de Man's theses which would provide an effective tactical barrier to fascism in France.[19] Pressure for the party to assume authority and to undertake a rapprochement with the middle classes stemmed increasingly from the desire to block fascism and only to a rapidly diminishing degree from a wish to impose the positive measures of planism. Free of the doctrinal worship indulged in by the Marxists the Neos responded much more actively and unreservedly to the stimulus of rising fascism. It was this fact that caused them, as it did Doriot, to become irretrievably separated from their party when the doctrinaire majority refused to make either an adjustment or a compromise of its doctrines.[20] From their beginning the Neos had been vehement against "those who reject the principle of participation in power out of a desire to keep the Socialist idea pure of any compromise", but after the coming of Hitler the need for assumption of authority took on an urgency that altered its original character. The emphasis shifted from authority for the installation of planism to authority for the defense of the nation. Max Bonnafous wrote in 1933:

Let's have the courage to say it, the ideology of liberty is no longer any safeguard in the circumstances presented (in 1933). All the 'intermediary forms' that we see developing under our eyes have the common characteristic of being an effort for order. Whether we wish it or not our country will be constrained, tomorrow, to an effort of the same kind.[21]

Closely allied to this concept of the need for authority and order was the demand for some measure of action by the Socialists. This demand met widespread sympathy within the party. Before the advent of Hitler it had taken a form not dissimilar to the old Jauressist position and as such had attracted to it the participationists and all others who were restless under the inactivity of Blum.[22] But after the arrival of Hitler, the need for action, like the need for authority, was more than merely an attractive route to power. It had become a defensive necessity. Speaking at a banquet of the VIE SOCIALISTE on June 8, 1933, Déat declared:

The Parti Socialiste must say whether it is for a policy of action in defense of the Republic, of pressure in favor of the working class, or whether it is for a policy of opposition ... the latter being a 'policy of suicide'.[23]

The experience of the German Social-Democrats had a profound effect upon the Neos as it had upon the Communist dissidents. It was also one of their strongest points of argument. In NEO-SOCIALISME? Bonnafous wrote:

We don't want, like some of our German comrades, to die without having fought, nor to wait to unleash the battle until reduced to a condition of desperate resistance.[24]

And in June of 1933 Marquet wrote:

To immobilize French Socialism, to impose upon it a rigid doctrinal corset which renders it at once incapable of revolutionary action and of reformative action, that is too much.
... Between those who seem to want to abandon themselves without a battle to the fascism that they declare is inevitable and ourselves the points of view are far apart indeed. Neither injuries nor threats can bring them together.[25]

Authority and action thus became the two major tenets of the Neo-Socialist position after Hitler's arrival. In addition, however, it was now more necessary than ever to refrain from alienating the middle classes. Déat, like de Man, had argued that the workers as a class could not stand alone if they cut themselves off from and alienated the middle classes. By doing that they would arrive at the situation existing in Italy and Germany. For in time of economic crisis it was the little merchants, the minor civil servants and intellectuals who were often reduced to misery by monetary devaluation. Furthermore, Déat argued, the sentiments of irritation and revolt that were thus produced among this class did not necessarily lead them to accept Socialism. It was more likely that they would tend toward fascism out of disillusionment with the democratic forces that had failed them. Furthermore the unemployed often were tempted in the same direction out of similar emotions. The attitude most certain to alienate the middle classes and thus drive them into the fascist camp, was the insistence upon the Marxist characteristics of Socialism and the renunciation of class collaboration.[26]

Speaking to the Congress of the Fédération Socialiste de la Seine in June of 1933 Déat said:

> The problem is to lead the middle classes to us. That is why I don't want to cut Socialism off from democracy.[27]

And three weeks later he attacked the policy of the leaders of the left wing, Zyromski and Pivert.

> Above all they want unity with the Communists, unity in which they see the simultaneous remedy to all the evils of fascism and war. Therefore they want to accentuate the proletarian character of Socialism, its dictatorial and violent allure, and its internationalist affirmation. I am not ignorant of the appeal that this impassioned reflex can have in the present crisis. But a party doesn't live on reflexes and passion. All that will lead us to a rupture with the middle classes, with democracy, with the Nation. In other words to the three fallacious maneuvers on which our adversaries rely.[28]

Here was the argument made by Bergery's Frontists and in a different but corresponding form by Doriot. The defense against fascism demanded the emphasis of those characteristics of the doctrine of each party most favorable to, or in any case least incompatible with, class collaboration. And this class collaboration did not mean merely the removal of the obstacles to unity of the proletariat, but removal of the barrier between the proletariat, whose full potential after all comprised less than a quarter of the population of France, and the vast and crucial lower middle class, the peasants, small merchants, craftsmen, etc. It was from the latter that the danger of fascism sprang.[29]

The most difficult barrier for the Socialists, as for the Communists, lay in the acceptance of the concept of the Nation. The doctrines of both parties, although the Socialist position in France was rather a confused one, rejected the principle of national fealty. Class struggle and national allegiance were considered to be mutually exclusive. Both groups of dissidents, however, maintained that this attitude must be qualified if a successful barrier were to be opposed to fascism. The acceptance of the Nation had been part of the positive doctrine of the Neos before the fascist threat emerged. Déat wrote in PERSPECTIVES SOCIALISTES:

> Today the Nation is undergoing a crisis. Monopolized by capital-

ism, it has been denied violently by the proletariat. Capitalism has been denationalizing itself, at least partially. We don't say that by an inverse formula anti-capitalism is going to renationalize itself. This only occurs in the case where a Socialist nation is isolated in the middle of capitalist nations, which explains ... the very nationalist character of Russian policy. But anti-capitalism today relies on the Nation, as a heritage promised to it, as a framework in which its victory will be attained, and where its constructive efforts will be unfolded.[30]

Yet another source of the Neo-Socialist belief in the value of the national concept as opposed to the internationalism of the Marxists, was that, whereas the failure of Socialism to withstand patriotic sentiment in the 1914-1918 war had led many former members of the IInd International to seek stronger Socialist bonds by joining the IIIrd, this same event had merely confirmed the conviction of others that Socialism must make peace with nationalism if it was to be successful in countries such as France. Among the latter were many of the more prominent Neos. At the first congress of the Neo-Socialists after they had split with the parent party Marquet declared:

> Until 1914 I believed with a complete and sincere faith that in relying solely on the notion of class, that in organizing the working class internationally, one could overthrow the capitalist regime. But on August 2, 1914, the notion of class collapsed before the concept of the Nation.

Declaring that it was thus necessary to find another point of support, he continued:

> This support can only be found in the national instinct. It is only thus that we will be able to ... win the popular masses and transform the regime.[31]

This, the Neos alleged, was the position held by Jaurès. There need be no rejection of national defense nor refusal to vote military credits for bourgeois governments. Particularly was this so in view of the rising threat of fascism which had assumed a national rather than an international form. The internal as well as the external danger had to be met and fought on the grounds where it existed. To behave otherwise would be to default in the face of fascism. It was Blum's inactivity, his constant indecision, that was the source of the greatest danger facing the French Socialists.[32] Action, for authority, within the nation, was the only formula that was feasible in this period of crisis.

Occupying the right wing of the S.F.I.O. the Neos were closer to the Radicals, in many respects, than they were to large segments of their own party. Certainly the bitterness that passed between the Neos and the Socialist left wing was more acute than any feeling that existed between Neo and Radical. As early as January 1931, after the participationists and Neos had inaugurated their campaign for middle class allies, the running battle between Right and Left wing of the party had begun. Severac published an article in BATAILLE SOCIALISTE denouncing middle class allies as doubtful and unreliable, floating uncertainly between capitalism and Socialism.[33] Déat answered later in the month in VIE SOCIALISTE defending a rapprochement with the middle classes and attacking the doctrinal rigidity of the left wing.[34] There was a lull in the participationist left wing battle after the failure of the Huyghens negotiations, but the subsequent offer by Daladier to the Socialists to participate in his government revived factional feeling. The parliamentary group, comprising mostly Neos and participationists, was publicly reprimanded at the Conseil National held in early February of 1933.[35] Paul Faure stated that he had been present at a meeting of the parliamentary group and was horrified to find that there was a majority within the group prepared to flaunt the legal prescriptions of the party. Zyromski called for a rejection of the policy advocated by the parliamentary group, declaring:

> There is no common policy between the republican parties of the bourgeoisie and ourselves.[36]

The anti-participationist motion was carried and a Congrès extraordinaire called at Avignon in April in order to discuss the question before the whole party.[37]

In its preparation for the Avignon congress the Neos rallied all of their arguments behind the slogan "bar the route to fascism". No longer was there merely theoretical dissension over the best method by which to bring about the planned state. The entire Left must rally to the defense of the nation. The Neos sought to convince party militants of the gravity of political and social events in France and the inadequacy of the existing "rules for daily group action" to cope with them. Marquet declared in a speech at Bordeaux that participation was the only means of bringing the necessary authority to the party, and that the policy of support merely brought the responsibilities of action without its advantages.[38] Déat traced the activities of the parliamentary group since the opening of the legislature with a warning as to the importance of an understanding with the Radicals:

> They (the parliamentary group) have made efforts toward negotiations with the Radicals which are more important than that which is at the base of the conflict between the party and the parliamentary group.
>
> ... It is only in France that there exists a buffer party, the Parti Radical, between the reactionaries and the Socialists; that is a fact which should not be forgotten when the policy of the group is defined.[39]

The congress at Avignon opened in an atmosphere as far from cordiality as had that at Tours in 1920. This was again a meeting of two incompatible doctrines one of which must be repudiated. Was the party to follow the path of orthodox Socialism or that of the "Socialisme democratique" of the Neos and participationists? Renaudel moved for participation and parliamentary cooperation, but the anti-participationist motion of Blum, Paul Faure and Pivert was voted by an overwhelming majority.[40] Portions of the successful motion reveal the confusing mixture of doctrinal purity and tactical equivocation that marked the majority position:

> The Congress reminds again that the Socialist party is a party of class struggle, that it is not a party of reform, and that the elected representatives of the party form in parliament a single group facing all the bourgeois political factions.
>
> Neither a Bloc des Gauches, nor ministerialism will find the slightest chance of success in the ranks of the Socialist party.
>
> The Socialist party will not dream of a policy of organic collaboration with other parties, either on the parliamentary or the governmental level.
>
> ... The Congress reaffirms also that there be no confusion between the concept of fundamental class opposition vis-a-vis the capitalist regime and the parliamentary tactic of systematic opposition to all governments. Such systematic opposition, far from serving the working class, would only serve, in present conditions, to favor the designs of the most aggressive capitalism against the working class.
>
> The Congress proclaims therefore that the duty of the Socialist

party, and therefore of its parliamentary group, is to assure the policy most favorable to the preservation and development of civic liberties as well as of workers liberties.

The National Council has recognized the necessity under the circumstances in which the parliamentary group now finds itself, to entertain occasional relationships with the representatives of other political parties.[41]

Despite this pronouncement the parliamentary group continued its policy of party cooperation in parliament and voted to support the 1933 budget in direct contradiction to the will of the party majority. Blum accused the group of having wilfully misinterpreted the resolution of Avignon "in its text and in its spirit".[42] Paul Faure and Zyromski launched a bitter attack against this flagrant breach of party discipline, the former declaring that the time had come to choose between those who had remained faithful to the law of the party and those who, once elected,

... sought to place themselves beyond the rules which they had accepted. Men are nothing, the party is everything. Men will bend and the party will pursue its path ... All resistance will be broken.[43]

As the parliamentarians refused to desist from their policy of collaboration the schism between them and the party leaders continued to widen. Blum had resigned from the leadership of the parliamentary group as far back as March in disagreement over its policies. Auriol followed him. When, at Avignon, Frossard and Severac's attempts to dissuade Marquet and the others proved futile, Severac declared himself resigned to the loss of that faction to the party:

We don't use the same words and if by chance we pronounce the same words they no longer have the same meaning. We don't attribute the same significance to them. Today we no longer have the same ideas in common. Therefore the best thing is for us to separate... I no longer consider you as Socialists. Scission is inevitable. I don't say that it will be produced at this congress, nor tomorrow, nor in three months time, but it will happen, it cannot fail to happen.[44]

The XXXth National Congress of the Parti Socialiste meeting in Paris July 14-17, 1933, saw the culmination of the battle between the parliamentary group and the rest of the party. Vandervelde opened the Congress with an assertion that the minority must bow before the majority on the question of participation, that the Belgian party was divided by the same tendencies but disagreement had not led to scission. The effect of this plea for harmony, if any, was soon lost in the heat of the debate over the behavior of the parliamentary group. Marquet and Renaudel attempted to defend this behavior, and did so eloquently, nevertheless the Bräcke motion calling for a "blame" against the parliamentary group won a convincing victory.[45]

However the voting of the condemnation of the actions of the parliamentary group served merely to accentuate the temper of the session. The Neos were far from being subdued. Montagnon challenged the validity of the orthodox doctrine and cited the loss of faith in that doctrine:

> Doctrinal crisis? Yes. Why? Capitalism is dying; we say it, we know it, it is known outside of our ranks. Well then, according to our formulae, according to our propaganda, we should be happy at this crumbling of capitalism, at the end of this system which we always condemn. Nevertheless we are not happy; we are worried; and it is precisely this worry which constitutes the full extent of the Socialist drama.
>
> You see there is a great law which dominates us all, a historic law upon which not enough insistence is laid; that is that one class can only replace another in power if it is capable of assuring to the country a life at least equal to that which it had before. And the drama of the present time is that we wonder if that condition can be fulfilled today; it is because in our souls we doubt this, that we have these worries.[46]

Paul Faure in turn attacked the Neos as standing for the do nothing position of the Radicals and other moderates, of using the excuse of the financial crisis to postpone reforms. He cited the examples of the social experiments being undertaken in America and even Germany and contrasted them with the conservatism and lack of initiative in France. Furthermore, he argued, even as reformists the Neos had failed.[47]

Marquet returned to the attack. Since Paul Faure admitted that at present the revolution was impossible, he argued, what course of action remained to the party? What was it to do to satisfy the growing need for some action to improve conditions? How far away the revolution was became painfully apparent when one regarded the slow rate of increase of the party. In 1914 it had had 100,000 members and 104 representatives in the Chamber, in 1932 it had grown to only 120,000 members and 130 seats in the Chamber. Meanwhile the economic crisis was injuring the cause of Socialism while the party stood by and refused to taken any active part in the struggle against it. He warned against the belief that unemployment could bring anything but harm to the party. Unemployment, he said, saps and enervates, it does not create a high revolutionary morale. In Germany unemployment aided Hitler precisely in that manner. For these reasons the party must take an active part in the solution of the national problems and undertake a share in national responsibility, if it did not wish to drive its members and the rest of the proletariat to seek this leadership somewhere else:

> If we are incapable of progressing in the milieu of international and national difficulties, in our own country as in others, the workers themselves will seek elsewhere the solutions which we have not know how to find and will applaud the acts accomplished by others, from which we have recoiled.[48]

Subsequently Renaudel made a long and moving plea for the lesser evil in this time of crisis. Socialists must join a coalition government and vote military credits. They must keep Daladier in power in order to keep Tardieu and Flandin out.[49] Blum, however, would accept none of these arguments as a satisfactory excuse for the actions of the parliamentary group, which were not only contrary to the doctrine of the party but were a flagrant violation of the decisions taken at Avignon as well. It was evident that in the case of Blum as of Paul Faure, the arrival of Hitler, for all the anxiety it may have caused him, had not yet led to any willingness to compromise party doctrine.[50] Blum concluded by remarking to Renaudel

> You invoke the tradition of Jaurès in support of certain ideas which have been enunciated here and of which traces are found in that document (of Renaudel's). If only he were here he would receive that text with supreme indignation.[51]

Although the extent of the incompatibility between the Neos and the remainder of the party became obvious at this Congress, the breaking point was not reached until the Neos held a factional conference at Angoulême and issued a manifesto defying the majority ruling on participation. The inevitable scission came in November. Exclusion was based on indiscipline, and to the motion of exclusion was appended a warning to those members of the party who were wavering or who had been occasional supporters of the participationists. The motion read:

1. The elected representatives who participated in the manifestation of Angoulême are placed outside the party, plus those who expressly and publicly supported them, and further, those who belonged to the minority of undisciplined in the Chamber in the voting of Article 37 on the project of financial redressment. These are citizens Déat, Marquet, Cayrel, Renaudel, Deschizeaux, Lafont, Montagnon.

2. A last warning is given to the disobedient members of the parliamentary group.

3. Written renewal of the undertaking of fidelity to the decisions of the Party is demanded from all legislative electives, to be communicated to the secretariat of the Party before November 20th.

Any electives who have not performed the above by that date will be considered as being placed outside of the Party. -- 6 November 1933.[52]

Although this exclusion was the first official consummation of the rift between Neo-Socialist and the party, the separation was no less involuntary for the Neo-Socialists than was Doriot's subsequent self-removal from the control of the P.C.F. The reason that the scission was inevitable lay not in the fact that either faction changed its doctrines, but in the fact that the growing political and economic crises of 1932 and 1933 revealed the full extent of the incompatibility of these doctrines. The illusion of a true doctrinal synthesis that had been adequate in times of peace and plenty was shattered by the impact of fascism and economic distress. The Neos, who were later to describe themselves as "anti-Marxist and anti-Blumest", were of an entirely different political breed than the doctrinaires and always had been.[53] Whether they were, as they claimed, the true disciples of Jaurès, whether they were, as some others claimed, embryonic French fascists, they had never had anything but the most tenuous relationship to Marxist principles. Indeed they shared much more common political ground with the Radicals, differing from them on only one important issue, the question of a directed economy.

Within a month after their exclusion the Neos held their first independent congress, as the Parti Socialiste de France (union Jean Jaurès), with Déat presiding.[54] The manifesto of the new party was issued in March of 1934 under the motto of a revolution to make France French, Republican and Socialist. French, "that is to say national without being nationalist"; Republican, "that is to say conforming to the will of the people freely expressed"; and Socialist, "that is to say resolved to apply economic forces to the law of collective interest". Fascism, the manifesto warned, was the alternative to electoral reforms. Only the Parti Socialiste de France "bears the solutions conforming to the interests of all workers and all Frenchmen".[55]

With their divorce from the S.F.I.O. the Neos became all but devoid of further direct influence upon the course of Socialist policies. Amalgamated two years later into the more or less homogeneous Union Socialiste et République under the presidency of the Independent Socialist Paul-Boncour, their impact on the S.F.I.O. and their important factional significance had disappeared.[56] As the rift between Neo and orthodox widened to the point of scission, Communist propaganda sought to capitalize on it in the application of the P.C.F.'s tactic of **front unique en bas.** The Communist line was to emphasize the fascistic characteristics of the Neo-Socialist doctrines and then to identify these with the doctrines of the entire party. Reporting to the Central Committee of the P.C.F. in January of 1934, Thorez declared:

> Scissions are being produced. In France the rupture between the 'hards' and the 'softs' does not in any way express a fundamental divergence between them. Each faction is firmly convinced of the support which it owes to the bourgeoisie. The rupture between the Renaudel-Déat team and the Blum-Paul Faure team merely reflects the divergences in the bourgeois camp on the methods, the forms, and the allure of the process of fascisation. Renaudel-Marquet believe, along with certain bourgeois groups, that it is already time to employ the methods of brutality, of authority, which are those of avowed fascism, and to proclaim the nationalist and counter-revolutionary ends of Social-democracy. Blum-Paul Faure, expressing the point of view of other capitalist groupings, believe it useful to dupe the workers as long as possible by means of methods called 'democratic' while accentuating the demagogic and pseudo-revolutionary phase.[57]

Neo-Socialism was labelled by the Communists as "simply fascism in a leftist mask". The task of the P.C.F. in regard to the Neos was to:

> ... reveal it in its double aspect as defender of bourgeois democracy and sergeant-major of fascism.

But while doing this we must also demonstrate that this applies equally to the whole of Social-democracy. The policy of the Neo-Socialists is identical **at the base** to that of the S.F.I.O. and the C.G.T.[58]

In early 1934 Lucien Constant wrote a series of articles in the CAHIERS DU BOLCHEVISME upon the crisis in the Socialist party. The theme was ever the same -- the Neos were now openly manifesting the pro-bourgeois aspects not only of their own faction but of the Socialist party as a whole. In this connection the influence of Henri de Man upon the entire party was a favorite point of attack:

> It is necessary to change Socialist strategy -- declare the new strategists of reformism. The battle for the reform of assessments, in other words for the augmentation of salaries, for the raising of the share of the proletariat in the social revenue, must be abandoned. The period of battles for reform is completed -- proclaim simultaneously the "leftist" Paul Faure and the representative of the most extreme right wing of Social-democracy, the revisionist in chief Henri de Man, who has succeeded in Belgium in realizing the union of all Socialist groups around his "Plan du Travail".[59]

In fact, however, the scission weakened Communist opportunities for effective propaganda against the Socialist party. Stripped now of its extreme right wing the Socialist party no longer presented all the targets that had previously enabled the Communists to point to the bourgeois character of the S.F.I.O. By rejecting the Neos and participationists the S.F.I.O. could once more lay claim to being an exclusively proletarian party, a claim which Paul Faure and Blum wished at all costs to be able to make. If it would be an exaggeration to aver that in ridding itself of the Neos the party took a pronounced step to the Left, it could not be denied that it had rejected unequivocally those elements seeking to pull it closer to the parties of the Center. Thus as an unintentional but nevertheless important result of the scission the S.F.I.O. was in a better position to effect unity of action with the P.C.F. With the scission, membership of the S.F.I.O. dropped from 130,000 to 110,000, most of the 20,000 withdrawals representing those who followed Déat and Renaudel into their new party. Thus those elements in the prescission S.F.I.O. who would have opposed unity of action with the bolsheviks most violently were no longer present in the party.

But it was in the positive effect on Socialist thinking that the greatest contribution of the Neos was made. They were the first within the party to comprehend the inadequacy of the old electoral and parliamentary tactics to combat the political crises of the early thirties. If the remedies which they proposed possessed too much of the flavor of the fascism they were designed to combat, nevertheless they had made a scoring point when they warned that the proletariat must not cut itself off from the middle classes if it was to avoid a catastrophe such as that which had befallen the German Social-democrats.

Stripped of the emotionalism that attended the scission and of the suspicion of excessive authoritarianism in some of its leaders, the fundamental arguments of the Neo-Socialists after the arrival of Hitler were: (1) the combined economic and political crises made support an obsolete form of action; the party must either share power or take it all by revolution. Since revolution was impossible the only remaining course was to share power. (2) Extreme care must be taken not to alienate the middle classes as they constituted the most fertile breeding ground for fascism. (3) The party must be prepared to accept and support the nationalist concept if it were to provide either an effective domestic barrier to fascism, or to allow France to be able to withstand external fascist pressure. (4) The route of fascism could be barred only by cooperation between the parties of the Left; the proletarian parties must stand shoulder to shoulder with all available allies among the middle classes. It is not of merely negligible significance that the program of the Neos was so nearly identical to that of Bergery's Frontists, that the plan of the C.G.T. in 1935 bore such obvious evidences of Neo-Socialist influence, and that, ultimately, the program of the Popular Front drafted by all parties and groups of the Left included the major principles of Neo-Socialist doctrine.[60]

Like Bergery for the Radicals and Doriot for the Communists, the Renaudel-Déat faction split with the Socialist party in the course of defending those principles which the party was later, and not very much later, to adopt almost in their entirety. The impatient tacticians of the three parties of the Left were to see their ideas prevail over those of the doctrinaires, but not until they had departed from the fold in the most diverse and peculiar directions.

NOTES

1. Jean Jaurès, L'ARMÉE NOUVELLE, Paris, 1910, pp. 357-358.
2. L'OEUVRE, 18 April 1933.
3. L'OEUVRE, 26 January 1930.
4. Paris, Alcan, 1927, 1929; the French edition of PSYCHOLOGIE DU SOCIALISME, Iena, appeared 1926.
5. De Man's PLAN DU TRAVAIL received its full exposition only after the French Neo-Socialists were expelled from the Parti Socialiste. Although he presented the plan before the Parti Ouvrier Belge at its Congrès de Noel in 1933, it was not until the International Conference at Pontigny in September of 1934 that he expounded those of his theses which he believed to have universal application, and not until December 10th, 1934, that he presented these theses to the New School of Peace in Paris. Thus it was not from his PLAN DU TRAVAIL but rather from his earlier works that the French Neo-Socialists derived their theoretical guidance. The development of de Man's planism and the French Neo-Socialism after 1933 tended to become increasingly separate and distinct.
6. The disillusionment of the Neos with the Marxist traditions is expressed in the compilation NEO-SOCIALISME?, Grasset, Paris, 1933: "(Socialism foresaw) -- the great international pitched battle, in lines, between a proletariat more and more conscious of itself, more and more organized into a homogeneous class over and above frontiers, and a capitalism itself more and more concentrated, more and more internationalized. Then the troops of Social-democracy, armed and prepared for this combat, arrived on the field of battle where they no longer met the enemy they had expected, where the banners no longer had the same color, where the language that was spoken was no longer the same as that to which they were accustomed, where the slogans had changed. It was felt that something in Socialism had been perverted, that something of its spirit, of its program, had been stolen from it by its very adversary." p. 80.

7. PERSPECTIVES SOCIALISTES, Librairie Valois, Paris, 1930.

8. Déat, PARTI SOCIALISTE, S.F.I.O., Rapport du groupe socialiste au Parlement, rapport du groupe au Congrès Nationale Extraordinaire, Avignon 16 et 17 Avril, 1933, p. 7.

9. This over-cautiousness was one of the chief points of attack by the Neos. Marquet issued an open letter to Blum in July of 1933: "Installed in capitalism you condemn it in the name of your immutable doctrine, and yet you benefit from the advantages which it accords its privileged ones. That has lasted for fifteen years and if nothing changes will last for a long time to come. For those who know you, it is more than evident that action is precisely your antithesis." L'OEUVRE, 27 July 1933.

10. "Problèmes Confédéraux et Problèmes Socialistes", VIE SOCIALISTE, 12 October 1929.

11. Renaudel's influence and prestige within the Parti Socialiste was almost on a par with that of Doriot within the P.C.F. As in the case of Doriot, when it became evident to the leaders of the Parti Socialiste that Renaudel would carry his disagreement to the point of scission if necessary, there was considerable concern as to how much of the party would follow him. Thus at the XXXth Congress in July 1933, Longuet made an impassioned plea to Renaudel not to destroy the unity which he had helped to create in 1905: "At the Congress of Amsterdam it was you, Renaudel, who, after the speeches of the brutally hostile factions, brought a thought of union, a thought of unity, in which we all shared. It was just a bit after your speech that Kautsky, Bebel, Victor Adler and Vandervelde introduced that magnificent motion which has remained the bases of our united action." COMPTE RENDU STÉNOGRAPHIQUE DU XXX CONGRÈS NATIONAL, op. cit., p. 339.

Similarly after the expulsion in November of 1933, Frossard in his request to the IInd International to use its offices to heal the scission, warned of the prestige possessed by Renaudel among the workers and of the possible magnitude of the scission. RAPPORTS DU XXXI CONGRÈS NATIONAL, RAPPORT ADMINISTRATIF.

12. However only by the small majority of 450 votes. Following this decision Déat read the minority report announcing the refusal of the participationists to accept the decision as final: "As to the problem of sharing power, the solution given it depends much more on events than on the wishes of men... We will

continue our propaganda efforts and our persuasion. We claim absolute freedom to express our thoughts and we claim our fair share of the leadership of the party itself."

Paul Faure thought this to be sufficient manifestation of rebellion to jump to the platform and shout: "We leave here with fists clenched. This is war!" L'OEUVRE, 27 January 1930.

13. Despite the smallness of the majority, the rejection of participation in 1930 had been as definite as the party leaders could make it: "Concerning the eventuality of participation in the government, the idea is rejected for the present and will be re-entertained only in case of well recognized exceptional circumstances." LE POPULAIRE, 27 January 1930.

14. The popular vote had been 1,970,000 for the Radicals and 1,957,00 for the Socialists. LE TEMPS, 15 May 1932.

15. L'OEUVRE, 16 May 1932.

16. On May 15, Renaudel declared in a speech at Toulon: "The parties of the Left have nothing to fear but themselves, and if they fail to reach an understanding it will be a cruel deception for the country." L'OEUVRE, 16 may 1932.

17. At the Conseil National of the Parti Socialiste in November 1932, Marquet resumed the challenge of the participationists: "Support is an obsolete form of parliamentary action. The policy of support doesn't permit any beneficial initiative. The truth is that one must choose; either power or revolution." **Ibid.**, 7 November 1932.

18. The tendency of those members of each party who were deputies; the entire Neo-Socialist faction; Doriot, Renaud Jean and even Ramette for the Communists; Bergery, and later Daladier for the Radicals; to be more favorably inclined toward party collaboration than were their non-parliamentary colleagues, is not particularly surprising in that they, unlike the latter, were constantly faced with the tasks of the practical solution of parliamentary problems. Its importance stems from the fact that in each case (even in the case of the Communists, due to Doriot's peculiar position in the P.C.F.) the parliamentary representatives possessed considerable influence over their respective parties. With the exception of Bergery each held a position of leadership within his party. As a result this tendency toward collaboration, born in the Chamber, necessarily played a substantial role in the party congresses of each party.

19. De Man had condemned Marxism as obsolete with the statement: "It didn't wish enough because it didn't comprehend enough." AU DELÀ DU MARXISME, **op. cit.**, preface p. XIV.
    Déat applied the implications of this position to the anti-fascist struggle, responding to Blum's defense of the Marxist traditions: "Do you believe that the dialectic would console those who are being martyrized today by Hitler and fascism?" COMPTE RENDU DU XXX CONGRÈS NATIONAL, **op. cit.**, p. 373.

20. Blum refused to accept the de Man plan as possessing anything new or different from the traditional Socialist position. In LE POPULAIRE of 17 January 1934 he wrote: "Nothing in all this presents anything novel. The portion extracted from the program (i.e. the socialization of credit) became a **plan** by its very isolation and by the privileged study of which it was the object; but it figures classically in all Socialist programs."

21. NEO-SOCIALISME?, **op. cit.**, p. 124.

22. Montagnon expressed the Neo-Socialist interpretation of Jaurès' attitude in a letter to President Flandin three weeks before the arrival of Hitler: "You know that we are anti-statist. In the trade union or corporate system which we advocate, the State should be merely an animator, a controller, an arbiter guiding private interests in the general interest. But in the period of transition, of the installation of the system, we are convinced that the State will be forced to intervene directly." appearing in article by Montagnon, "Pour faire tourner l'usine" L'OEUVRE, 9 January 1933.

23. VIE SOCIALISTE, 9 June 1933.

24. NEO-SOCIALISME?, **op. cit.**, p. 130.

25. L'OEUVRE, 3 June 1933.

26. PERSPECTIVES SOCIALISTES, **op. cit.**, p. 80.

27. Congrès du Fédération Socialiste de la Seine, salle des fêtes du Pré St. Gervais, compte rendu in L'OEUVRE, 26 June 1933.

28. L'OEUVRE, 11 July 1933.

29. Jacques Grumbach stated at XXXth National Congress: "The fascist danger does not lie with Tardieu or Flandin, it is in the middle classes, in the working classes, who, deceived tomorrow, will no longer have confidence in democracy, and will join with the most violent reactionaries in order to take power by force and violence." COMPTE RENDU STÉNOGRAPHIQUE DU XXX CONGRÈS NATIONAL, **op. cit.**, p. 431.

30. PERSPECTIVES SOCIALISTES, **op. cit.**, p. 179.
31. L'OEUVRE, 4 December 1931.
32. Thus Montagnon: "What do you want Léon Blum, one cannot have everything; you are the man of the microscope, you cannot also be him of the long view. You have everything of the great revolutionary except the most essential quality, that instinct which pushes him to act at the decisive moment, that sense of great human forces which permits of a comprehension not to follow but to lead." L'OEUVRE, 18 September 1933.
33. BATAILLE SOCIALISTE, 10 January 1931.
34. VIE SOCIALISTE, 31 January 1931.
35. L'OEUVRE, 6 February 1933.
36. To which Compère-Morel replied: "Never will we have total power if we have not previously entered into a coalition ministry." **Ibid.**
37. At this meeting of the Conseil National, 5 February 1933, the party also rejected a Radical offer to form a permanent delegation of the Left. Rapports du XXX Congrès National, **op. cit.**, Rapport Administratif, p. 47.
38. L'OEUVRE, 7 April 1933.
39. **Ibid.**, 3 April 1933.
40. 2,807 votes for the Blum motion to 925 votes for that of Renaudel.
41. LE POPULAIRE, 2 June 1933.
42. Rapports du XXX Congrès National, **op. cit.**, Rapport administratif.
43. L'OEUVRE, 2 June 1933.
44. L'OEUVRE, 18 April 1933.
45. By a vote of 3377 to 22, with 662 abstentions. Renaudel declared of the blâme: "This decision truly threatens to lead to a sort of moral scission capable of shattering the unity of the party. The threat of exclusion which from now on accompanies this decision leaves no doubt as to the results that were intended to be given to it." COMPTE RENDU STÉNOGRAPHIQUE XXX CONGRÈS, **op. cit.**, p. 179.

46. COMPTE RENDU STÉNOGRAPHIQUE, XXX CONGRÈS, **op. cit.**, pp. 251-252. Blum rose angrily and shouted: "But no!"

47. "**Paul Faure:** -- You substitute reformism for the revolutionary conception, but in your parliament of today, with a deficit budget, with the total disequilibrium of the finances of this country, the deficit of 12 billions, a budget not dealing with the reforms, even cut off of it a part of the credits which went to social work, to hygiene, to the sick, -- you speak of reforms! You are reformists without reforms!"

    "**Grumbach** -- "And you, you are revolutionaries without a revolution."

    Paul Faure: -- "I beg your pardon, the promise of reforms is short term, that is why your failure is so evident (laughter), while we never said that we would make a revolution during the Daladier legislature."
    COMPTE RENDU STÉNOGRAPHIQUE, XXX CONGRÈS, **op. cit.**, pp. 299-301.

48. COMPTE RENDU STÉNOGRAPHIQUE, XXX CONGRÈS, **op. cit.**, p. 315. In his appeal for the party to recognize the Nation, Marquet said: "Hitler has succeeded only once, to my knowledge, in achieving great eloquence. That was when ... replying to citizen Wells, who in the tribune expressed regrets that Social-democracy had perhaps remained too aloof from the national terrain, Hitler began with these words: 'I do not accept your tardy regrets sir ...'"
    "I hope that no one will be able to speak to us in that manner tomorrow." **Ibid.**, p. 313.

49. **Ibid.**, pp. 344-353.

50. Blum rejected all of the Neo-Socialist proposals: "Renaudel has said that we must revise the articles of the charter which refer to ministerial collaboration, voting against budgets and military credits.

    "... I reply in my own name: I do not accept the revision of the statutory text on ministerial collaboration.

    "I also do not accept revision concerning the question of the budget. The same for military credits ... to go back on our rules, on our traditions concerning military credits, that would be the act most dangerous to peace that we could commit.

    "They said that our propaganda needs simpler and more striking slogans. Let us not go too far in that direction. There would be danger in so doing. Simple 'elementary slogans' have never been given by Socialism."

Finally: "I do not know what the intermediary forms of power will be able to insert between the present forms and those which we have always considered to be the forms of Socialist power. But it is not for us, Marquet, to take the leadership of intermediary movements between Socialism and capitalism should we suffer for some years. We must remain faithful to our traditional concepts." VIE SOCIALISTE, n. 333, pp. 51, 52, 53.

51. COMPTE RENDU DU XXX CONGRÈS NATIONAL, op. cit., p. 506.

52. RAPPORTS DU XXXI CONGRÈS NATIONAL, RAPPORT ADMINISTRATIF, 1934, p. 47.

53. Marquet at Congress of Parti Socialiste de France, May 1934, L'OEUVRE, 21 May 1934.

54. 3 December 1933.

55. MANIFESTO DU PARTI SOCIALISTE DE FRANCE, L'Appel, March 6, 1934.

56. The union of the Parti Socialiste de France, the Parti Socialiste Francais, and the Parti Republicain Socialiste, took place November 3rd, 1935, at Pantin, the presidency being confided in Paul-Boncour.

57. Rapport du Bureau politique par Thorez, 24 January 1934, LA LUTTE POUR L'ISSUE RÉVOLUTIONAIRE À LA CRISE, Publications Revolutionaires, Paris, 1934, p. 10.

58. C.B., 15 April 1934, p. 470.

59. Lucien Constant, "Les réformistes et la crise", C.B. 1 April 1934, p. 413. Attacking de Man's thesis that a smaller cake means smaller portions for all Constant continued: "Thus the first chapter of this evangelic neo-reformism consists of abandoning the struggle for partial claims, under the absurd pretext that the bourgeoisie cannot give more." **Ibid.**

60. The PROGRAMME ÉCONOMIQUE ET FINANCIER DU FRONT POPULAIRE, issued in early October 1935 described the Popular Front thus: "What does the Popular Front represent? A movement which coordinates the forces of the **middle classes, agricultural workers and the proletariat** against the feudalism of money which seeks to defend itself by fascism."

This was precisely the counsel offered by the Neos in 1933. The Parti Socialiste found itself accepting in 1935-36 the four major tenets of the Neo-Socialist platform, the propriety of participation in power as well as its ideas on internationalism, national defense, and collaboration with the middle classes.

CHAPTER FOUR

ECONOMIC CRISIS

As the world economic crisis finally spread to France in 1932 the illusive nature of the traditional Socialist-Radical entente became increasingly evident to both parties. The measure to be taken to combat the combined economic and financial crises divided Socialist and Radical almost as completely as they divided the Socialists from the Right by placing the greatest emphasis on that aspect of Socialist-Radical relations in which their doctrines were most incompatible.

Anti-clericalism had pervaded Radical thought up until the end of the war. For want of any indications that a positive social program had replaced it, the Radicals were not unjustly described as being dominated by this concept in the post-war period as well.[1] However anti-clericalism was hardly a basis upon which to build a program fitted to the problems of post-war France, and when the anti-clerics turned to face social problems they found a wide range of social philosophy in their own ranks. Among the few positive tenets detectable in their social program were the belief that merely to take care of labor in bad times was not sufficient, and that while not condemning monopolistic practices as such, the consumer must be protected from the evils of these practices. This was not nearly enough to appease a Socialist party that was becoming increasingly convinced of the need for positive and drastic measures to combat the crisis. The tendency toward social conservatism, retrenchment in the face of the financial deficit, dedication to the balancing of the budget and a policy which the Socialists considered to be one of "doing nothing" in regard to relieving the burden of the workers accentuated the gulf between the parties that had been growing since the war.[2]

Moreover the Radicals also exhibited an increased caution in relation to the Socialists in the post-war period. After the war the relatively tight Bloc des Gauches was supplanted by the looser Cartel des

Gauches. The Radical slogan, "Pas d'ennemi à gauche" which had served so well in the anti-clerical battle was becoming a trifle heavy with two Marxist and revolutionary parties "à gauche" now that the political issues in France centered largely about economic problems. Radical abhorrence of the deprivation of private ownership of property, a directed economy, and the "general strike, direct action and insurrection" of Socialism was no longer obscured by greater considerations.[3]

Nevertheless the Cartel des Gauches persisted throughout the twenties and early thirties. The Radical passion for governmental power demanded an ally, and the Socialist policy of lesser evil led that party to support the moderates against the Right. Thus in 1924 and again in 1932 the Socialist electoral contribution to the success of the Radicals gave the former a "mortgage" on the resulting government. In 1924 the creation of Poincaré's Union National precluded the extension of this mortgage to participation, and although the Cartel continued in the Chamber for two more years, Socialists wouldn't join the ministry.[4] The party retired to its former position of "soutien à éclipses".

After the elections of May 1932, however, neither party could escape the implications of this sweeping electoral victory for the Left in which each had played an equal part. The Parisian press of all political inclination recognized the magnitude of the Left's victory and also the decisive part played in it by the Socialists. On the Right the conservative LE TEMPS cautioned the Radicals:

"And now? ... We warned the Radical party against the dangerous tactic which it has followed, that of the electoral cartel. It risked, indeed, not responding to the sentiment of the country; it risked having a heavy Socialist mortgage weigh on the next legislature. In order to 'break' as their chiefs say, a pretended 'cartel des droits' which existed only in their imagination, the Radicals have practiced what they call by way of euphemism 'la discipline républicaine'. Today the Socialist mortgage is perhaps heavier than the Radical party would have wished. It will be difficult if not impossible for the latter to carry it, or for the government to disengage itself from it even if it so desired.[5]

Similarly Emile Buré in the moderate Republican L'ORDRE:

The Radicals could not triumph without the concurrence of

the Socialists who trailed them by only a small margin, and the latter will not fail to claim their reward from their allies. What dreaded results therefore were hidden in the events of yesterday?[6]

On the Left, however, the possible difficulties between Radical and Socialist in the arrangement of an equitable division of power that had been won were ignored in the elation over the victory. The orthodox Radical organ L'ÈRE NOUVELLE announced:

> The country has gone to the Left where it saw reason and wisdom, where it felt a will toward Republican conciliation affirming itself and felt a true desire to realize the unity of the Republicans.[7]

Paul Faure merely exulted in LE POPULAIRE, but the organ of the C.G.T., LE PEUPLE, interposed a word of caution:

> In spite of the orientation of the new Chamber to the Left, it would be a dangerous error to base upon this too many illusions as to the renderings of the next legislature.
>
> It will be at grips with serious difficulties proceeding from the unfavorable budgetary situation, and perhaps also with the maneuvers of high finance. It will have to face the economic crisis whose formidable effects will continue to make themselves felt heavily if nothing is changed in the mechanism of our economy.
>
> It will also have to solve the wretched and pressing problem of unemployment.
>
> Finally, it will face the necessity of taking a clear position on the question of disarmament at Geneva, and its responsibility will be charged profoundly in international policy, where it will have to choose between the route that leads to peace, and that which leads to the abyss of war.[8]

When the Socialist party met at the Salle de Huyghens on the 28th of May popular elation over the electoral victory plus the growing pressure from within the party created a mood favorable to a new attempt at participation. With such a definite electoral mandate the party must "extract from the Left majority all that the popular will placed in it", including participation in the government if asked. On the 22nd of May various departmental federations of the S.F.I.O. had declared themselves favorable to participation. Even the left wing Fédération de la Seine, although it passed a resolution opposing ministerial participation, authorized its delegation to the National Congress to permit negotiations with the Radicals if the latter asked for them.[9] On May 30th the Socialists, by the overwhelming vote of 3,862 to 154, adopted a resolution to the effect that the gravity of both the foreign and domestic situations "did not permit the Parti Socialiste to oppose the reception of any offers of governmental collaboration that it might receive from the Parti Radical."[10] Paul Faure sent this motion to Herriot and advised him that a delegation had already been named from the Socialist Party to enter into negotiations with Radical representatives. Armed with the conditions of participation, the so-called Cahiers de Huyghens, Auriol, Lebas, Renaudel and Blum called on the Radical delegation composed of Herriot, Caillaux, Sarraut and René Renoult. The latter promised to take the conditions under consideration at their executive committee meeting, to be held that night (May 30). At this meeting Herriot advocated rejection of the Socialist proposals and the Executive Committee supported him. Herriot sent a letter to the Socialist delegation informing it of this decision and on June 1st the Socialist party unanimously adopted a motion to the effect that the negotiations with the Radicals were closed.[11]

There was disappointment in some elements of both parties at the failure of the Cahiers de Huyghens, but there can hardly have been any great surprise. Neither party could seriously have expected the other to accept the conditions offered. A member of the Executive Committee of the Radical party who represented the faction most sympathetic to governmental collaboration with the Socialists wrote in early June:

> All would be different if, to the cordial Socialist proposal to discuss their program of action, the Radicals had replied with a no less cordial proposal to negotiate on the basis of the Radical program of action. I who believe that nothing in the Socialist offers is unacceptable in principle to the Radicals, am absolutely convinced that we could offer them at the same time a more precise and more adequate program under the circumstances.
>
> Certain statements of doctrine relating to nationalization, which contains nothing that could frighten a Radical since the Radicals have always been avowed partisans of national control over the economy and of the organization by the state of truly large monopolies, would have appeared in the Radical program not as a symbolic manifestation but as a logical consequence

of the battle to insure budgetary equilibrium and to parry the aggravation of the economic crisis.

Instead of a positive response the Radicals addressed a negative response to the Socialists.[12]

However despite these expressions of regret at the time, it was not until four years later, after the formation of the Popular Front, that each side deemed it important to place the blame on the other for the failure. In 1932 both accepted the fact of doctrinal incompatibility, but looking back in 1936 each party claimed that there had been nothing in its position that was doctrinally unacceptable to the other. Socialist headquarters issued a pamphlet claiming that the Cahiers de Huyghens had contained only conditions which the Radicals had subsequently endorsed.

The program of the Rassemblement populaire of January 1936 contained all of the points of the Socialist Cahiers de Huyghens of 1932 which Herriot rejected. The preamble states 'The program of immediate claims published by the Rassemblement populaire resulted from a unanimous accord between the ten great organizations which constitute the Conseil Nationale of the Rassemblement', which include the Radical and the Socialist parties. The acceptance by the Parti Radical, if it had been given to such a program in 1932, **would have assured the governmental collaboration offered by the Socialists and would have totally transformed the history of the present legislature.**[13]

Herriot then published a brochure entitled LES NEGOTIATIONS DE MAI-JUIN 1932 ENTRE LES SOCIALISTES ET RADICAUX,[14] in which he presented his version of the Huyghens negotiations. A few weeks later Blum issued the brochure LES RADICAUX ET NOUS, 1932-34,[15] describing the history of attempts at participation from Huyghens to the riot in February 1934.

Point by point the Socialists demonstrated the identity between the Cahiers de Huyghens and the program of the Rassemblement populaire. The Socialists proposed in 1932 "Immediate control of the commerce in weapons of war and nationalization of the factories making them" -- Herriot was silent on control and said nationalization of war factories depended on international accord -- the Rassemblement program included "Nationalization of war industries and suppression of private commerce in arms".

Socialists in 1932 demanded "Defense of agricultural production against speculation or a slump by the establishment of public offices of wheat and fertilizer" -- Herriot was silent on this point -- the Rassemblement platform included the statement "In order to suppress the tithe levied upon producers and consumers by speculation, creation of a national inter-professional office of cereals; delivery of fertilizers at cost price by the national offfices of nitrate and potash, control of the sale of superphosphates and other fertilizers".

The Socialist program required "Application of the 40 hour week without loss of pay, conforming to the program of the C.G.T." -- Herriot responded: "It can only be realized by way of international accord" -- the program of the Rassemblement included, "reduction of the work week without reduction of weekly salary".

The Cahiers de Huyghens required "control of the banks" -- Herriot didn't mention this -- the Rassemblement stood for "Regulation of the banking profession, regulation of the accounting of banks and societes anonymes. In order to withdraw credit and savings from the domination of the economic oligarchy make of the Bank of France, today a private bank, truly the Bank of France".

The Socialists demanded that the budget be balanced "by means other than the contraction of educational and agricultural expenses, the reduction of salaries, or the diminution of the claims of veterans or war victims" -- Herriot replied: "It is necessary to economize in all possible ways" -- the program of the Rassemblement stated "While awaiting the complete and rapid abolition of the many injustices introduced by the decree-laws, immediate repression of the measures falling upon those whose existence has been most affected by these decrees."

Finally the Cahiers de Huyghens sought "the return to the nation of the private monopoly of insurance" and "the dissolution of the railroad companies with a view to the organization of a single nationalized network" -- Herriot refused on the grounds that nationalization would oblige the State to reimburse fully the capital of the insurance and railroad companies -- the Rassemblement urged prosecution of the "most fundamental measures in order to rescue the State from industrial and financial feudalism".[16]

Identification of the Cahiers de Huyghens with the program of the Popular Front, although it might tend to show that the Radicals had made a greater doctrinal compromise than the Socialists in adhering to the Popular Front, had little relevance to the situation existing between the parties in 1932. At that time the Socialists were well aware that their programs would find little sympathy within the ranks of the Radical party. The Cahiers can be regarded more as an indication of doctrinal intransigence on the part of the Socialists, as a victory of the doctrinaires within the party, rather than as a serious attempt at participation.[17]

After the failure of the Huyghens negotiations the Socialists drew steadily away from cooperation with the Radicals. As we have seen, the fate of the Neo-Socialists in November of 1933 settled the question of participation which had plagued the Socialist party since the war. However it was not merely participation that was at an end, but the parliamentary support of Radical governments was also drawing to a close. The Neos, with their protestations that support was an obsolete policy, which they used as an argument to induce the party to participate in power, were finding an unlooked for response. The argument that support was obsolete was leading the majority of the party not toward participation, but toward an abandonment of support altogether. The fundamental divergence over the means of dealing with the economic crisis was serving to poison all aspects of Socialist-Radical relations.[18]

Thus when Herriot was defeated over the question of the American debt his successor (the Independent-Socialist Paul-Boncour) sought Socialist collaboration in vain, as he conditioned it upon the acceptance of a balanced budget policy requiring deflationary financing. This was a question on which the Socialists would not compromise, and the negotiations were as brief as they were unsuccessful. Subsequent negotiations with the Daladier government in 1933 were also blocked by the question of the budget; Daladier's proposal for Socialist participation in January was rejected on that basis, and his initiation of the 6% cut in the salaries of civil servants in October resulted in the withdrawal of Socialist support altogether. Daladier pleaded for support in the Chamber:

> You have accomplished an admirable effort. You have, in 1932, put an end to the progression of expenses which was uninterrupted until then. You have also reduced the expenses of State by 10 billions; the hardest effort remains to be done. I have chosen the hardest route. If you are not in agreement with the Government, you will upset it.[19]

But Blum replied that the Socialists could not "frapper les fonctionnaires".[20] Socialist support was withdrawn and Daladier fell. After this neither Sarraut, Chautemps nor Daladier again made any attempt to secure direct or indirect participation of the Socialists.

Perhaps the most notable characteristic of the growing Socialist tendency to separate completely from the Radicals was the total absence of a sense of urgency in 1933. The Socialist party was motivated, it is true, by a sense of extreme urgency in regard to the fascist threat and the economic crisis, but it related neither of these to its association with the Radicals. Except for the Neo-Socialist faction the party could see no solution to either problem through closer ties with the Radicals. Thus it was but a week after the coming of Hitler that the Conseil National of the Parti Socialiste rejected a Radical offer for the establishment of a Délégation des Gauches, and but a few days after Germany withdrew from the League of Nations that they caused the Daladier government to fall.[21] Also when they forbad their militants to join Bergery's Common Front a resolution was voted by the C.A.P. placing strict limitations on the relations which the party might undertake with other parties.

This tendency on the part of the Socialists to regard the usefulness of a coalition with the Radicals as being at an end was, as we have seen, principally a result of the attitude of the latter toward the economic crisis. This was not the only aspect of the post-war era that the worsening economic situation brought to a close.

The delayed impact of the economic crisis, like the coming of Hitler, was a factor which, while it in no way served to bridge the doctrinal gap between the leaders of all three parties of the Left, tended to accentuate the feeling among the workers in both proletarian parties that they shared a common cause. In addition it provided an added incentive to positive action and an end to the toleration of the unlicensed financial activity which had marked the twenties:

> The end of the post-war era, of that period of moral relaxation, of nervous relaxation, of feverish delight, of economic illusions and of intellectual disorder. The end of an era during which the liquidation of stocks, industrial reconstruction, payments in kind, repair of war damage, starting of new industries, financing of international loans, rationalization, stock speculation, the miracles of credit, flashy publicity, permitted the pushy businessmen of every country, of every shade, to swarm dragging behind them their cortege of courtiers, of beauty queens, of speculators, of stars and of unlicensed agents.[22]

In comparison with the severity of the depression elsewhere, its effects in France, from the point of view of unemployment, were not only late but were also mild. Despite the fact that the number of unemployed was popularly presumed to be approximately a million (and the Communists claimed three million), official sources record fewer than a quarter of a million unemployed in January of 1932 and approximately a third of a million in January of 1934.[23] Furthermore in all probability even a million unemployed would not have brought about economic misery proportional to that of a like percentage in Germany, England or other more highly industrialized nations. For in France the large percentage of industrial workers who had the cushion of personal connections with rural and agricultural families was an important factor in absorbing the distress of unemployment. On the other hand the French had been in a position to watch the world-wide development of disastrous unemployment over a three year period and the first signs of a substantial increase in unemployment in France produced a strong emotional reaction even though that increase hadn't attained, and never did attain, catastrophic proportions. In their propaganda the leaders of the P.C.F. and the Parti Socialiste of course made full use of the extreme examples outside of France as portents of the developments that lay ahead.[24]

But if the unemployment aspect of the French crisis had greater emotional than actual effect upon the workers, the successive financial crises were both real and severe and their effects were felt at all levels of society. It was these effects that came between Socialist and Radical.[25] It was also these effects that received such dramatic illumination by the Stavisky scandal. Had this affair been brought to light at any time earlier in the post-war history of France there might well have been merely a flurry of temporary excitement; but coming at a time when concern over the growing economic crisis had already reached an emotional pitch that made it the primary political issue, the scandal evoked an explosive response among all elements of French society. Whereas it was unquestionably true that French society as a whole was responsible for the existence of a situation in which operatons such as those of Stavisky could endure for as long as they did, politics take little notice of absolute standards of guilt and innocence. It was enough for the parties both to the Right and the Left of them that the Radicals comprised the government in power, and that those government officials who were implicated with Stavisky were Radicals. The scandal provided the Communists with an unexpected propaganda windfall which they were not slow to recognize. The P.C.F. began a systematic exploitation of it in the traditional style. Pierre Darnar, a party propagandist, asked Chautemps rhetorically if there was nothing that he felt would soil him, nothing to which he wouldn't stoop.[26] Nor did the Socialists, who were quick to point out their dissociation from the Chautemps government, lag far behind the Communists in the tirade against the "government of thieves". For the first three weeks in January of 1934 every lead article in LE POPULAIRE followed the same theme as L'HUMANITÉ -- and of course the conservative organs -- in raising the chorus against corruption in high places. But there was an important difference between the way in which the Socialists and Communists approached the scandal. Unlike the P.C.F. propaganda, Socialist vehemence was tempered from the start by the fear that the Right might find in the scandal a pretext for overthrowing the government and installing a sample of the authoritarianism for which it had already begun to clamour.

The Stavisky affair was not the only development in early 1934 that helped to pull the Socialists in two directions simultaneously. For if they felt they had an interest in defending the government against an attempted coup from the Right, they were nonetheless anxious that one official of that government, the Prefect of Police M. Chiappe, be removed and removed quickly. Socialist antipathy toward Chiappe, although real enough, was mainly derivative, for it was principally against the Communists that he had exerted his effective measures of maintaining order in Paris. "Chiappe au poteau" had been a cry of the Parisian Communists since 1930 when "the Prefect" and " the Premier" (Tardieu) had devised and put into execution new and extremely effective techniques for countering Communist tactics.[27] The period when Chiappe had been most active against the Communists was at a time when the relations between Communists and Socialists were as bad as they had ever been. But, for all their delight at seeing the discomfiture of the Communists, even in 1929 and 1930 the Socialists could not dispel a certain uneasiness that once the Communists had been disposed of their turn would come next. Renaudel had at that time succeeded in having a resolution adopted by the Socialist parliamentary group to the effect that while the tactics of the P.C.F. were to be deplored, this did not warrant the "outrageous" repressions committed by the government in the name of combatting bolshevism. Paul Faure had noted with anxiety that whereas the suppression of the Communists was commendable, it marked the entry of France into a period of reaction. Similarly in January of 1934, when the prefecture was kept busy minimizing the violence between rightist and leftist groups on the streets of Paris, the Parti Socialiste delivered a vigorous protest against Chiappe's methods.[28]

Thus it was that when Daladier finally removed Chiappe from the prefecture the Right was convinced, or at least claimed, that the removal of Chiappe was the price of Socialist support for the Radical government, without which it would not hav a parliamentary majority. LE PETIT PARISIEN of February 4 wrote:

> From the parliamentary point of view it cannot be ignored that the 'head of M. Chiappe' was claimed by a part of the extreme elements of the Chamber. Can one believe that the measure which struck down the Prefect of Police was executed merely to facilitate an arithmetic operation of the majority?[29]

Blum of course denied all assertions that the Parti Socialiste had used the lever of parliamentary support for the removal of Chiappe. On the 4th of February, speaking at the Fédération Socialiste of Puy-de-Dome at Clermont-Ferrand, he asserted:

> Only this can I say, that none of us, no person qualified to speak in the name of the parliamentary group has had the dealings stated by the press, with M. Daladier or with any member of the government whatever.[30]

But the impression to the contrary lingered in the minds of many besides the extreme Right. The Socialists again found themselves in a paradoxical position, a position of indecision, through the pursuit of their lesser evil policy. Their support (albeit faltering) of the government at the same time as they attacked the Stavisky scandal and the excesses of Chiappe began to appear to many of the leaders as a policy which brought the worst rather than the best of two worlds. Inclined to protect the workers against police officers such as Chiappe even though to do so meant to benefit the Communists; and inclined to protect the Republic against attacks from the Right even though to do so meant to support a discredited government, they were finding little compensation in the policies of either of their beneficiaries. But they could do little else. For even before the riots of February 6th, the Socialists realized that all the advantages of the sensational developments in January and their effect on national opinion would accrue to the Right, and that the principal loser would in all probability be themselves.

This attitude was sharply in contrast to that of the Communists, who were to all intents united with the extreme Right in the attack upon and denunciaton of the "government of crooks". Consistent with the tactics laid down at its Central Committee meeting in

January, and in fact at the instructions of the Comintern, the P.C.F. was riding the scandal for all it was worth.[31] Despite the German experience the Communists apparently remained unconcerned about the possibility of an overthrow of the Republic by the Right. Appeals by Parisian Socialists to the P.C.F. up until the morning of the day of the great riot to join in the defense against the Rightist leagues were sneered at by the Communists. Not so by a large portion of the Communist rank and file, however, who could see a substantial difference between a Radical or coalition government functioning within the republican forms and a government supported by a complement of the Action Francaise, Solidarité Francaise, or Jeunesses Patriotes governing with the authority which these organizations claimed to be necessary. A situation similar to that which had existed in the P.C.F. over the question of the change in electoral tactic in 1928, and the coming of Hitler, again existed within the party. Comintern policy, which seemed to take little account of the problems of a Communist who was also a Frenchman, sought to blow on the fire, to capitalize on the chaos and turn it to advantage against the Republic, the Right and the Socialists all at once; many of the French militants, however, saw in the chaos a danger of fascism, a danger that the Right might destroy the Republic, the Socialists and the Communists all at once, and this spectre tended to become the all important consideration for them.

* * *

By February 1934 almost all of the elements that subsequently led to unity of action between the parties of the Left were already present on the French political scene. Germany had withdrawn from the League of Nations and the fact that she had commenced rearmament was no longer a secret to the French. This development along with the economic crisis had destroyed the illusions of security and plenty that had persisted through the 1920-1932 period. All of France, although Paris in particular, was restive from the effect of successive political sensations, Stavisky, Chiappe, government corruption and the like. In addition the steadily increasing frequency and size of the Rightist demonstrations served as a constant reminder to the Left of the potential fascist threat in France. Finally the groundwork for unity of action had been laid among the workers and others who made up the rank and file of the proletarian parties. Pro-unity sentiment among the majority of each party had reached the point at which the leaders would have had to do little more than to allow such unity to come to pass.

But among the leaders of the parties there was no tendency toward unity of action. Despite the brief and vain attempts at unity of action immediately after the arrival of Hitler, the P.C.F. and the Parti Socialiste were as far from unity of action as they had ever been, and the vituperations of each had in no way diminished. The parliamentary entente between the Parti Socialiste and the Parti Radical had been badly upset as a result of the conflicting views on treatment of the economic crisis. Finally Radical and Communist were, as ever, as far apart as the poles.

It would be delusive to argue that the leaders of these parties failed to recognize or were insensitive to the external and internal pressures that indicated the need for some measure of unity. Such a position is flatly contradicted by the public statements of these men during 1933. Continued disunity was caused primarily by the confusion, most notable perhaps within the Parti Socialiste, as to the relationship of the developments of 1933 to the position and security of the respective parties. In the case of the P.C.F., of course, the decision was not for the national party to make, and the question of unity of action within France was related to the overall tactics of the Comintern. However, from all evidences, the Executive Committee of the Comintern was no less confused in the early weeks of 1934 than were the French Socialists and Radicals.

In the face of an uncertain and rapidly changing international situation, a worsening economic situation, and increased political tension within France, the tendency on the part of the leaders of all three parties was to cling tenaciously to the policies of the past 14 years, even as the merits of these policies became increasingly doubtful. This resulted in unusually violent suppression of the voices within each party urging positive measures or a new course. The collaborationists, the participationists, the activists, were rejected utterly and completely. On the eve of the February 6th riots the leaders of all three parties exhibited tendencies that could only be described as defensive, negative, confused, conservative and frightened. Their political initiative had all but vanished.

It is not germane to this thesis to describe in detail the history of the Rightist manifestations that took place in Paris in January.[32] The effect of any one of them or even of the sum total of them all upon the thinking of the Left, while it might have been important under other circumstances, was totally eclipsed by and engulfed in the events of February 6th.

NOTES

1. Corcos, CATÉCHISME DES PARTIS POLITIQUES, Editions Montaigne, Paris 1932. Perhaps the best single piece of writing on the doctrines of the Radical party is Maurice, Gaston, LE PARTI RADICAL, doctorate thesis presented in 1929 at the Faculté de Droit, Paris; Librairie des Sciences Politiques et Sociales, 1929.

   The similar attitude of the Parti Socialiste toward anticlericalism was summarized in a resolution voted at its Congress at Nancy in 1929: "The Parti Socialiste is anticlerical ... in as much as it encounters the Church in all enterprises of reactionary politics and social conservatism. Anticlericalism for it, far from being merely scorn or sectarian persecution, signifies on the contrary the defense of liberty for all, assured protection for all against the various forms of restraint, and becomes a part of the class struggle.

   In consequence the Parti Socialiste, without ever lending itself to the maneuvers of those who would seek in anticlericalism a front for the diversion from social problems, considers on the contrary that the laic battle is inseparable from the social battle ..." Résolution du Parti Socialiste, 13 June 1929, LE POPULAIRE 14 June 1929.

2. Paul Faure pointed to the "do nothing" attitude of the successive governments in his argument for rejection of the Neos at the Congrès National in Paris, July 1933. COMPTE RENDU DU XXX CONGRÈS NATIONAL, **op. cit.,** p. 247. In a pamphlet published just before the 1936 elections, he repeated his plea: "In all other countries there have been experiments. In Belgium it is the plan du travail. In the United States it is Roosevelt; in the Republics of South America, to some extent everywhere, experiments are being made, often full of audacity, which to me, a modest Socialist, will not resolve the problem; but nevertheless one can recognize that they represent an effort, and often a rupture with the old prejudices and the old traditions.

"In France nothing! Speeches before the microphone! Then nothing more! Current affairs are despatched, evil is left to fester." Paul Faure, SOCIALISME DANS LE BATAILLE ELECTORALE, Librairie POPULAIRE, Paris, 1936, p. 7.

3. The traditional Radical attitude on this subject was expressed by Sarraut as early as 1908: "The Congrès of Dijon confirms the resolutions of the Congress of Nancy imposing on all its adherents the duty to refuse their votes to any candidates who advocate the disorganization of the armies of the Republic ...

   "It affirms also the will of the Parti Radical et Radical-Socialiste, while remaining completely faithful to the policy of the Bloc des Gauches against all reactionaries, to fight with all the force of its propaganda against the propaganda and the propagandists of the general strike, direct action and insurrection." RÉSOLUTION DU CONGRÈS NATIONAL DU PARTI RADICAL À DIJON, Brochure editée par le centre de propagande Republicains, Paris, 1909, p. 17.

4. André Chaumeis wrote: "The possesion of power did not appear to the Socialists either so enviable or so useful that it should impose on them the slightest sacrifice of their principles." Chaumeis, "La Nouvelle Chambre", LA RÉVUE DE PARIS, 1 June 1924. The Socialists voted to adopt the policy of support but no participation in their XXI Congrès National at Marseilles January 30-February 3, 1924.

5. LE TEMPS, 9 May 1932.

6. L'ORDRE, 9 May 1932.

7. l'Ère Nouvelle, 9 May 1932. L'OEUVRE of the same date declared: "In adding those elected on the two ballots one finds 151 Radicals, 130 Socialists (S.F.I.O.), 44 Republican Socialists, Independent Socialists, and Socialistes Francais, without even taking into account the numerous independent Radicals elected against the candidates of M. Tardieu. The former opposition possesses an absolute majority in the new Chamber."

8. LE PEUPLE, 10 May 1932.

9. RAPPORT ADMINISTRATIF AU XXIX CONGRÈS NATIONAL, 29 May 1932, Librairie Populaire, Paris, 1932.

10. Blum, LES RADICAUX ET NOUS (1932-1934), Librairie Populaire, 1936, p. 16.

11. COMPTE RENDU DU XXIX CONGRÈS NATIONAL, **op. cit.**, RÉSOLUTIONS, p. 97.
12. Jacques Kayser, RÉPUBLIQUE DE L'OISE, 4 June 1932.
13. RADICAUX ET SOCIALISTES, 1932-1936, Editions du Parti Socialiste, Librairie Populaire, Paris, 1936, p. 23.
14. Brochures du Parti Radical et Radical Socialiste, 1936.
15. SUPRA
16. RADICAUX ET SOCIALISTES, **op. cit.**, pp. 16-22. See also PROGRAMME DU RASSEMBLEMENT POPULAIRE, Editions du Comité du Rassemblement, January 1936.
17. Herriot accepted only two points in the Cahiers, international arbitration and the protection of savings. In his rejection of the rest before the Executive Committee of the Radical party, he stated: "The Radical party also wants organization of peace through arbitration, protection of savings, international understanding, and compulsory arbitration. I am for aid to the unemployed having had more than 180 days of unemployment. I am for the prolongation of scholarships and free secondary education."

    However he could not agree with the Socialist "a priori" formula for the limitation of military expenses, declaring: "Who can eliminate the terrible unknowns posed by very recent events?

    "The program which must dominate all others at present is that which would permit us with a balanced budget to establish political relaxation internally and economic understanding abroad." L'ÈRE NOUVELLE, 3 June 1932.
18. Auriol denounced the Radicals, in the Chamber on December 8th, 1933, for having included texts in Chautemps' financial program which they knew that the Socialists couldn't accept. He concluded: "We don't wish to participate in this powerlessness. From now on it is to the country that our voices will be addressed. But when it pleases you to return to a Republican program then the unanimous Parti Socialiste will follow you and support you." JOURNAL OFFICIEL, 9 December 1933, p. 2378.
19. RAPPORT DU GROUPE PARLEMENTAIRE AU XXXI CONGRÈS NATIONAL, Librairie Populaire, Paris, 1934, p. 78.
20. **Ibid.**
21. Report of the meeting of the Conseil National, 5 February 1933, RAPPORT ADMINISTRATIF AU XXX CONGRÈS NATIONAL, **op. cit.**

22. Paul Elbel, REVUE DES VIVANTS, April 1934.
23. According to the figures published in Peel, THE ECONOMIC POLICY OF FRANCE, Macmillan & Co., London, 1937, p. 16:
Jan. 1932 - 241,000 unemployed
" . 1933 - 316,000   "
    1934 - 332,000   "
    1935 - 479,000   "
24. The Communists established a Central Committee of the Unemployed which was instructed to coordinate its work with the action of the factory workers. In preparation for a "Hunger March" on December 5, 1933 before the Chamber, tracts were distributed which read:

    "You who have worked for 10, 20, 30 years, the crisis throws you out on the street. With the draconian regulation which is in force at the depths of unemployment if you draw your allocation it is unsufficient or it is reduced because you are a war, labor or unemployable pensionee ..."
25. Reporting to the Commission d'enquête upon the causes for the February 6 riots, Marc Rucart said of the financial crisis: "The crisis had already begun to become more severe, and in 1932 public receipts were 8 billion less than in 1929.

    "In order to cover budgetary deficits thus created governments had recourse to resources accumulated in the treasury before 1929.

    "Finally, in June 1932, the budget had a deficit of 15 billions and the treasury didn't posses more than 70 millions of available funds. Thus the governments that followed after June of 1932 were to find themselves in a difficult position, faced with accomplishing a particularly unpleasant task because of the sacrifices which were imposed on all citizens." Commission d'enquête, Rapport General, **op. cit.**, p. 22.
26. Pierre Darnar was also the author of one of the most pernicious pieces of propaganda capitalizing on the Stavisky scandal. In MON CAMARADE, the P.C.F.'s organ for the propagandization of children, he wrote a "Story of Capitalist Thieves":

    "Stavisky was one of those men, one of those thieves, one of your enemies. He had five or six magnificent automobiles. Mme. Stavisky carried off the prize for elegance at Nice. With the Ministers, with Chiappe, with all the chic people who do nothing and who live off the work of your parents, Stavisky lived the 'grand life'.

"Stavisky the thief of labor, refused himself nothing; fat, flourishing, gay and happy, while in your homes you go without. With you if someone is sick there is the greatest misery. And one is often sick while eating little and without going to breathe the good air.

"The parents were sick and they could only scrape together a few sous with great difficulty.

"But Stavisky the financier said to himself,'That money is pretty, it pleases me. I'm going to take it'. With the complicity of the Ministers he extracted the money from the workers. He took the money and left a paper in its place. The judges said 'Chut! he is a thief, but he is rich, he is a financier, he is right'. The police said 'He is a thief, but he is an employer. We will cudgel the workers if they go on strike, but him, he is an employer, he is right'.

"And when the workers got angry the friends of Stavisky had him killed in order that he not denounce those who had aided him.

"Such is the story of Stavisky, and there will always be such as long as there are employers and financiers, because their life is to steal.

"When the workers take power as in Soviet Russia, only then will **this be finished.**"

Pierre Darnar, MON CAMARADE, March, 1934.

27. Ranging from the withdrawal of licenses from striking cab drivers to the use of an airplane hovering over Paris to spot any Communist concentrations. See report of the Paris correspondent of the NEW YORK TIMES, 7 March 1930.

28. JOURNAL OFFICIEL, 14 January 1934.

29. L'INTRANSIGEANT commented on the same day: "M. Chiappe has refused this high post rightly guessing that the compensation offered him hid a certain scorn. In fact it is not M. Daladier who was scornful of him. It was the extreme Left who wouldn't pardon him for having assured and maintained order for so many years."

And L'AMI DU PEUPLE, 5 February 1934

"The bargain is concluded. "After hours of negotiations similar to those of horsedealers at a fair, M. Daladier ceded to Socialist pressure.

"M. Jean Chiappe leaves the Prefecture of Police."

Finally Tardieu wrote in LA LIBERTÉ, 4 February 1934, under the title "The Cartel of Horsedealers":

"Minister Daladier has shown his true face.

"He has said fast and strong; he is only a hypocrite.

"He announces himself as a nationalist. He is merely a cartellist.

"He proclaims himself a judge. He is only a contriver.

"... Never has horsedealing been pushed so far nor displayed so impudently. After having offered the head of M. Chiappe to the S.F.I.O., which at first refused to engage itself, and then having offered his support to the gentlemen of the Center, the minister has returned cynically to the first solution; this is his way of having equity reign.

"He has thus paid the Socialist vote. He will no longer be able to say to M. Léon Blum that he no longer has capital or capitalists to defend.

"We will see Tuesday how this bargain, as dishonourable for the seller as for the buyer, is executed."

30. LE POPULAIRE, February 5. Compère-Morel wrote, in the Neo-Socialist journal, L'APPEL of 6 February:

"The Parti Socialiste de France has not entered into any operation, any warnings, any negotiation, any bargaining either or in the course of easily arranged meetings in the halls of the Palais-Bourbon."

31. LA LUTTE POUR L'ISSUE RÉVOLUTIONNAIRE À LA CRISE, report of the Bureau politique pronounced by Thorez to the meeting of the Central Committee of the P.C.F., 24 January 1934, Publications révolutionnaires, Paris, 1934. The P.C.F. sought to implicate the Parti Socialiste in the scandal as much as possible. In its criticism of the regional press it stated: "But we must repeat that the essential and almost general weakness is the absence of denunciation of the role of the Parti Socialiste in the affair ... etc."

C.B., 1 February 1934, p. 188.

32. For these details consult, Arqué and Dantun, UNE ÉMEUTE - ÉTUDE HISTORIQUE SUR LE 6 FEVRIER, Editions des documents du Siècle, Paris, 1934.

PART TWO

THE CHALLENGE OF DOMESTIC FASCISM

"Paris no longer governs France, but it animates it always.

"When a movement rises there one doesn't know if it will last a day, the instant of an anger or the lifetime of a civilization. All depends on the echo. Should the provincial horizons remain mute the spirit of the capital will subside. Should the countryside respond, a regime is born, society casts off its previous form. Paris proposes, France disposes....

"Without Paris nothing is done. Without the provinces nothing lasts."

Henry de Jouvenel, VU, 16 June 1934.

"But what was the determining factor in the realization of the common front was the great popular uprising of February 6th, on that day patriotic Paris became conscious of its force ... and its force terrified the revolutionary parties. On February 12th they organized, with the aid of the trade unions, a 24 hour strike. For the first time in 14 years, one could see parading along the Cours de VIncennes the troops of M. Cachin and of M. Blum united in the same fear."

Jean Legendre, LE FRONT COMMUN, Imprimerie du Centre de Propagande Républicaine, p. 21.

"Paris, in its entirety, is either for reaction or revolution.

"The people of France, harmonious and measured like the soil of their country want neither the one nor the other.

"Also Paris which, for most foreigners, is the luminous representation of France, has completely lost its role of leadership in French policy.

"It is in the interior of our provinces that we others, the provincial deputies, are able to be the force that prevents it from deviating from the straight line."

Deputé de Finistère, 16 March 1934.

CHAPTER FIVE

THE PARIS RIOTS

On February 6th, 1934, the restless Parisian political volcano suddenly erupted in the Place de la Concorde in a riot which, both in size and violence, surpassed anything that Paris had seen since before the turn of the century. Although many thousands of Parisians of no particular political affiliation constituted the bulk of the rioters, the initiative and the leadership for this **émeute** belonged to the various rightist leagues. Manifesting against corruption in government and the refusal of either the Chamber or the Ministry to take strong measures to punish and remedy this state of affairs, the rioters were motivated principally by disgust and disillusionment, and their rather vague aim was to throw the deputies into the Seine, a goal which they only narrowly failed to achieve.

In the eyes of the Left, inevitably, this minor revolution indicated something much more sinister than merely the wholesale expression of disgust. Unprepared for anything of this magnitude the Left in general was thrown into a temporary panic by what it considered an attempt, and a dangerously powerful attempt, to effect a coup. As a result, during the week following the **émeute** the various groups of the Left in Paris were plunged into action which contrasted strongly to their previous paralysis.

There have been several studies devoted specifically to the **émeute** (including one in English),[1] and of course every historian or political analyst of modern France has had to give an interpretation to the effects of this crucial event. In all of these, however, the extremely complicated problems that this event posed to the parties of the Left seem to have been disregarded.

We have seen that all three parties of the Left had their advocates of renovation and that all three also had leaders determined not to sacrifice the essence of doctrine to the passions or temptations of the moment. Doriot, Déat, and less directly Bergery pulled against Thorez, Blum and Herriot. We have also seen that thus far the anchor of sacred tradition had proved effective against the tugging current of a demand for action at any cost. The advocates of tactical realism and doctrinal evaluation had been persuasive when their arguments were considered in the light of the rapid and unfavorable developments both at home and across the Rhine. But the strong devotion to tradition was combined with another factor that prompted the party leaders to resist these arguments. Each of the party leaders concerned owed his position to a record of absolute devotion to party doctrine, and had done so for a long time.

The factors for and against some compromise of traditional doctrine for the sake of tactical expediencey in this time of crisis were so nearly balanced in all three parties that their leaders paused. With this pause the initiative passed from the Left. When the **émeute** established beyond all doubt that the Right was, temporarily at least, the dynamic force in French politics, indecision had so paralyzed the Left that it could act only by reflex. This reflex action manifested itself in a week of counter-demonstrations culminating in a general strike, which were executed with a mutuality and spontaneity by the lower echelons that belied the traditional difficulties in attaining common action. But as the panic of the moment passed and the Left became reassured as to its security the party leaders reasserted their control over the rank and file and the old barriers between parties were restored. Nevertheless the balance within both the P.C.F. and the Parti Socialiste had been badly upset, and when in the ensuing months the leaders of each party considered the lessons to be learned from the week of February 6-12, this balance began to swing heavily in favor of tactical expediency.

In order to avoid the irrelevancies that would necessarily attend a narrative of these events, a selection of those salient facts germane to this thesis has been made. In addition to the documents and publications of the Socialist and Communist parties there is a further important source of enlightenment upon the occurrences of this eventful week which, because of its peculiar nature, is of great value. This is the voluminous report of the Commission appointed by Doumergue to investigate the events and causes of the riot.[2] Every shade of political opinion within the Chamber was represented on this Commission. As a result there is a considerable divergence of conclusions both as to the facts and their causes. But this wide range of political opinion also provides an invaluable insight into the reactions and attitudes of all parties of the Left.

1. **Although the extent of the émeute had not been anticipated, both Communists and Socialists were aware, well in advance, of the impending demonstration by the Right.** Ample publicity had attended the preparations of the Leagues of the Right. Paris was indulged with appeals, communiques, tracts, posters, etc., of the Action Francaise, Solidarité Francaise, Jeunesses Patriotes, Croix de Feu, Fédération des Contribuables, and assorted veterans organizations.[3] Tableaux of the times and places of meeting of the various groups were published in their organs and even in some of the large newspapers. Furthermore, the Parti Socialiste and the P.C.F both issued mobilization orders on the morning of the 6th calling in general terms for the workers to defend their organizations.[4]

2. **Fear of the impending demonstration led the Socialists to seek common defense with the Communists.** For the first time since Tours (if one excepts the vague and subsequently withdrawn "Appeal to all workers" made by the I.O.S. in February of 1933) a group of Socialists, impressed by the demonstrations of the Right throughout January and increasingly uneasy about the coming demonstration, sought to initiate negotiations with the P.C.F. for common action.[5] It must be noted that this offer was not the action of the Socialist party itself but merely of the federations of the Seine and Seine-et-Oise, the two federations within the party chronically most inclined toward unity of action with the Communists. Nevertheless, despite the comparatively large degree of regional autonomy within the Parti Socialiste, it is virtually inconceivable that the Paris federations would have undertaken these overtures against the wishes or even without the approval of the party. The letter of invitation of the 6th was followed that evening by a visit of a delegation from the two federations to the offices of L'HUMANITÉ to propose a joint manifestation on the 8th.

3. **The P.C.F. rejected all efforts by the Socialists to arrange joint manifestations or common defense.** The letter from the Socialists of Seine and Seine-et-Oise was ignored, and when a delegation from these two federations called on the P.C.F. it was put off with a promise to refer its proposal to the Bureau Politique, from which nothing materialized. On the morning of the 7th L'HUMANITE published an article entitled "Une question, une réponse":

> ... We want a **front unique** between all the federated and Socialist workers and functionaries for the battle against fascism. But how can we realize unity of action with those who support governments that decrease salaries? With those who torpedo

strikes? With those who abandon class terrain to collaborate in the defense of the capitalist regime and who thus prepare the bed of fascism in France as they did in Germany?

From now on we ask all unitarian and Communist organizations without delay to enter into rapport with the lower echelons of the federated and Socialist groups, to prepare immediately, manifestations, strikes and all other action necessary for the safeguarding of the proletariat.

Socialist and federated workers, hear our appeal! Realize the **front unique** against fascism with your unitarian and Communist fellow workers! -- (signed by the C.G.T.U., P.C.F. and Jeunesses Communistes).

In other words the Communists made it clear immediately that there was no tendency on the part of the P.C.F. to modify its tactics either in the face of the impending émeute or after the unexpected extent of it had become evident. When, on the 8th, the Socialists again requested the P.C.F. and the C.G.T.U. manifest with them that evening, both of the latter again refused. A headline in L'HUMANITÉ on the 7th lashed out at the Socialists in traditional style, declaring:

While the bullets of the Gardes Mobiles lay low 12 dead and almost 200 wounded, the Parti Socialiste gives its confidence to the government.

And Frachon wrote in the article below this headline:

The leaders of the C.G.T. not only work to prevent the hour of battle but are the best artisans of defeat.

On the previous day, before the émeute, André Marty had declared in L'HUMANITÉ that the Commmunist battle against the fascists was indistinguishable and inseparable from its battle against the Socialists. These anti-Socialist attacks continued through the entire week following the émeute as well. The P.C.F. left no doubt that whatever the extent of the riot's impact upon the Communists, it had not been sufficient to force an alteration in the **front unique en bas** tactic.[6]

4. The P.C.F. participated actively and positively in the riot at the Place de la Concorde. Communists participated, in negligible numbers, in many of the anti-government manifestations initiated by the Right during January; a group of approximately 50 of them was observed on the night of the largest of these, January 28th, singing the Internationale and chanting "Up with the Soviets".[7] However on the occasion of the February 6th riots the Communists went a step further, and l'A.R.A.C. was ordered by the Comintern to join in the manifestation and aid in its avowed purpose of throwing the deputies into the Seine. As a result of this the Socialists accused the Communist leaders of having given to their adherents and sympathizers on February 6th "orders which were equivalent in practice to a front unique with the troops of the fascist organizations" (Bernard).[8] This positive participation by the P.C.F., small though it was, was quite significant as an indication of Communist attitude toward the political crisis in France. Far from despairing at the threat which the Right was presenting to the government, the Communists sought to add to it, and, above all, to see that the Communist party was officially represented in these attacks on the discredited government. The total lack of concern for possibly serious political harm that might befall the P.C.F. as a result of its participation indicates the presence of Comintern leadership rather than merely a local decision by the P.C.F., for the latter might well have been exceedingly hesitant to take this unpopular position.[9] In any case subsequent references to Communist participation by the leaders of the P.C.F. always sought to explain that this participation was not in aid of the forces of the Right but a counter-manifestation against both the Right and the government. Thus Doriot, when questioned before the Commission d'enquête about the extent of and reason for Communist participation, replied:

> You know that the veterans organizations, the A.R.A.C.s, had invited their members and sympathizers to participate at the manifestation, or rather to the counter-manifest, the evening of February 6. A certain number of Communist organizations responded to this appeal. In particular the organizations of St. Denis launched an appeal to the working class asking it to come to the Rond-point des Champs Elysées on the 6th in order to counter-manifest against the organizations of the Right, who had prepared the manifestations of the Place de la Concorde.... That is to say that there was not on the 6th of February, as has wrongly been asserted, a conjunction of the efforts of Communists and nationalist organizations, but two perfectly distinct manifestations, both as to aim and as to the geographical location of the manifestation.[10]

Duclos' explanation was couched in terms more in harmony with the line and vocabulary of party propaganda:

Doubtless it was believed among certain sections of the bourgeois that this event was the expression of divergent interests or opinions between certain classes of the bourgeois, that the working class should hold itself aloof from all that, should remain with its arms crossed, and participate in none of these manifestations.

We considered that it was absolutely essential that the working class enter upon the scene of events, not as reinforcements of the troops of the Republic, nor as reinforcements of the police agents and Gardes mobiles, but to combat simultaneously the fascist bands and the governmental form of power, that is to say the government which was then constituted.[11]

Despite these protestations the fact that the Communists had ordered certain of their militants to take part and that these militants had participated in a manner indistinguishable from that of the Rightist manifestants, was of course known and in many cases bitterly resented by large segments of their own party as well as by the Socialists.

5. The Socialists believed that the émeute constituted a threat to the Republic. The Communists did not. Either the riot of February 6th constituted a serious threat to the Republic or it did not. Its size, the violence on both sides, and the declared objective of throwing the deputies into the Seine, lent strength to the belief that it did. On the other hand the heterogeneous composition of the mob which participated in it, the weak and disorganized character of the organizations which led it, and the very obvious and non-revolutionary reasons for its spontaneous appeal, would have assured anyone who could have reflected calmly, that it did not constitute a revolution against Republican institutions. But February 1934 was not a time for calm reflection, particularly among the parties of the Left. Hitler and the Reichstag fire were all too recent events for the Left to regard a manifestation of the scope and violence of this one as anything but a powerful attempt at a fascist coup. Some neutrals were hardly less inclined to so regard it. The moderate Paris journal LE PETIT BLEU, which specialized in parliamentary news, reported:

They (the deputies) didn't understand.

One can be sure that there was not, among all those who were enclosed in the besieged Chamber on the historic night of 6-7 February, one deputy in twenty who had a clear picture of the events. It is beyond doubt that, if the Garde Mobile had not fired, the barriers would have been breached. The Palais-Bourbon would have been taken by assault and its occupants, parliamentarians or not, lynched without distinction as to opinion, and that the fire which would have followed would have made even Van der Lubbe's fire jealous.[12]

If it is somewhat idle conjecture to speculate as to what would have happened had the Garde Mobile not held, it is important to determine what the official reaction of the leaders of the Parti Socialiste and the Comintern was to this threat. From their actions and words at the time it must be concluded that whereas the Socialist leaders saw a real threat in this riot, the Communists, at the time at least, did not so regard it. It has been noted that the Socialists both before and after the **émeute** took the unprecedented step of initiating overtures to the P.C.F. seeking common action. They also sought common action with the Radicals, Blum making an offer of support to the Daladier government surpassing in firmness any hitherto made by the Socialists. On the morning of the 7th he read the declaration of the Socialist parliamentary group before the excited Chamber:

The attitude of the group is dictated by circumstances.

The vote which it is going to make is not a vote of confidence but a vote of combat.

The parties of reaction, vanquished for two years, and who sought their revenge alternately in financial and moral panic, today held a coup de force.

It is no longer dissolution that they want; it is the seizure of public liberties which the working people have conquered, which they paid for with their blood, which are their own, which remain the ultimate gauge of their deliverance.

If the government wages the battle with sufficient energy, with sufficient faith in the popular will, it can rely on us. If it fails in its duty, it is we who throughout the country will launch an appeal to the republican forces simultaneously with an appeal to the workers and peasants.

. . . In the battle from now on we claim our place in the foremost ranks.

Fascist reaction will not pass.[13]

Both of these offers for common action represented departures from the traditional Socialist tactic. Each of them involved an implicit or expressed affirmation that the emergency was considered sufficiently serious by the Socialists to warrant their abandonment of the reservations which had hitherto prevented common action. Blum was subsequently fond of attributing the formation of the Popular Front to the events of February 6th (although many of such statements by him may be regarded as merely an exploitation of the myth appeal of the riot).[14] In the final analysis of course it is to the actions of the party during the week of February 6-12 rather than to subsequent statements that one must look for signs of its actual attitude. And it is here that the most convincing evidence can be found of real panic among the Socialist leaders.

On the other hand it is virtually inconceivable that the Communists could have acted as they did if they had believed the émeute to represent an attempt to overthrow the Republic. For while the P.C.F. could perhaps profit from embarrassment of the government from increased disorder, and even from forcing the government to resign, it was in a position to lose as much or more than the Socialists from a rightist coup. Yet the Communists continued to aggravate the situations leading to the riot, participated in the riot, and afterwards refused to accept Socialist proposals for common defense. It was one thing for the Comintern to order l'A.R.A.C. to participate in a demonstration calculated merely to embarrass, frighten, and perhaps cause the dissolution of the Daladier government. However in view of the Communist concern at the turn of events in Germany, it would have been quite another for it to have done this if it foresaw any serious possibility of a successful Rightist coup.

6. There was no interparty unity of action at any time in the course of the week of February 6-12. Once the Communist counter-proposals to the Socialist overtures for a joint manifestation on the 8th had proved unacceptable to the latter, each party prepared distinct and separate actions. The Communists held a counter-manifestation on the 9th and the Socialists, or rather the C.G.T., initiated the general strike on the 12th. The demonstration on the 9th was a purely Communist affair, organized and led principally by Doriot and held despite the specific prohibition of the new Prefect of Police, M. Bonnefoy-Sibour (who had called Doriot to the prefecture on that afternoon to try to persuade him to call off the manifestation). The Socialists ordered their militants to abstain from the demonstration. On the morning of the 9th L'HUMANITÉ issued an appeal calling "all of the working class" to rally at 8 o'clock in the evening at the Place de la République:

The C.G.T.U. invites you to effect your mass united front in order to undertake strikes and manifestations.

We must break the mounting fascist wave.

Socialist and Communist workers, let us fight together for the dissolution of the fascist leagues, and for their disarmament; let us fight together for the defense of liberties and of the workers' press, for the liberty of manifestations and reunions, for our immediate grievances.[15]

The general strike on the 12th was initiated solely by the C.G.T., the Parti Socialiste calling a rally in conjunction with it, to be held at the Cours de Vincennes.[16] The C.G.T.U. also ordered its affiliates to join in the strike. Both the strike and the manifestation were overwhelming successes from the Socialist point of view. It is worth noting that the decision of the C.G.T. to call a general strike was not at the behest of the Parti Socialiste nor did it represent a new change of tactic on the part of the C.G.T. It was an independent decision of the confederation itself (although of course made in consultation with the Socialist leaders) and had been decided upon by Jouhaux as the course of action to be used by that body in an emergency since immediately after the arrival of Hitler.[17] The idea of the general strike was attractive to the leaders of the Socialist party, particularly to Blum, because it seemed to provide a method by which they could oppose the maneuvers of the Right effectively without having to resort to the doctrinal compromise necessitated by joint action. Jouhaux testified to the effectiveness of the strike in response to the sympathetic interrogation of M. Petrus Faure (who was at the time a deputy of the P.U.P., a party which had also joined in the strike):

M. Petrus Faure - The witness is an old trade unionist. Would he like to tell me how long it has been since a movement of such amplitude has been seen in France?

M. Jouhaux - I have no recollection of a movement of equal amplitude. Can the movement of May 1, 1906 approach that of February 12th? I don't think so. I don't believe that in 1906 the movement of May 1st assumed the proportions of those which attended the movement of 12 February last.

M. Petrus Faure -	The general strike in the provinces and in the large cities, was almost complete in France that day.
M. Jouhaux -	Almost total.
M. Petrus Faure -	If events such as those of February 6th were repeated, would the C.G.T. have any hesitation even for an instant to do what it did, even to accentuate it?
M. Jouhaux -	Not the least in the world.[18]

In addition to the C.G.T.U., many other organizations adhered to the C.G.T.'s strike order. The P.C.F., the Parti de l'unité proletarienne (P.U.P.), the Parti Socialiste de France (Neos), the Union anarchiste, the Fédération ouvrière et paysanne, the Combattants républicains, the Anciens Combattants pacifistes, all invited their members to participate in the general strike. The Parti Socialiste issued its appeal for the rally at the Cours de Vincennes in LE POPULAIRE of February 10th and 11th, calling "all of the French proletariat" to rally against "the real dangers with which fascist forces are menacing public liberties, workers' rights and the Republican regime itself by their attempted coups, of which Paris is the theatre". Those same organizations which joined the general strike also appealed to their members to take part in the manifestation at the Cours de Vincennes. However the C.G.T. itself took no part in the manifestation, by agreement leaving that part of the day to the party administration. The P.C.F. tried to make a propaganda point of the C.G.T.'s absence, which under the circumstances was about as meaningless an attempt to usurp some of the credit for its success as could possibly have been made.[19] Paul Faure clarified the Socialist attitude toward the manifestation and also the part each party played in it when he appeared before the Commission d'enquête:

M. le president -	What are the reasons which led to your attitude and your decision to participate en masse at that manifestation?
Paul Faure -	These reasons were publicly exposed by us. We considered that the manifestation of February 6th was clothed in a character of fascism and violence. It appeared to us that public liberty was at stake and that it was necessary to have popular manifestations, not only by the C.G.T. and the Parti Socialiste, but by all the groups that wanted to defend democratic liberties.

	Manifestations in the street, in Paris and in the provinces and the general strike ordered by the C.G.T. appeared to us to be the effective means of popular protestation.
M. le president -	What results did you have, from the point of view of the number of manifestants belonging to these organizations, in Paris and in the provinces?
Paul Faure -	It is difficult to say exactly. I myself was at the manifestation at the Cours de Vincennes. An enormous crowd left the Place de la Nation and went as far as the Cours de Vincennes. Our friends have estimated the number of manifestants at between 150,000 and 200,000, but I decline to affirm that this is an exact figure.
	For the provinces I have no figures, but everywhere that I went my friends told me that they had never been present at more complete or more numerous manifestations.[20]

Paul Faure then denied any knowledge of, or relation to, Bergery's Common Front. The deputy M. de Tinguy du Pouët continued the audition:

M. de Tinguy	What point of contact did you have with the Communist organizations?
Paul Faure	None.
M. de Tinguy	They also took part in the manifestations.
Paul Faure	The Communists participated in the manifestations that is true. However the cortêges were distinct.
M. de Tinguy	I know that they were distinct. That is why I asked if there had been a previous understanding.
Paul Faure	If my recollections are correct it was the Parti Socialiste that took the initiative for the manifestation. The Parti Communiste, it should be noted, was invited.[21]

In his explanation of the part played by the Communists in the manifestation and general strike Paul Faure called attention to the wide range of political opinion that it represented:

M. Jean Longuet	Over and above the manifestants, those who participated in the general strike were much more numerous?
Paul Faure	Certainly, for our influence, by our press, is exercised over the two million electors which we obtained in the last elections.
Longuet	In Paris the Central Committee (of the P.C.F.) participated in the manifestation?
Paul Faure	Also in the provinces. There were even Republicans.
Longuet	You said that the future leaders of the National Union participated in the deliberations for the general strike?
Paul Faure	At least one, M. Adrien Marquet, who adhered to the order for the general strike.[22]

7. **Despite the absence of official unity of action, the week of February 6-12 provided a striking demonstration of the pro-unity sentiment of the rank and file of each party.** If the intransigence of the Communists and the resultant reaction of the Parti Socialiste prevented the parties themselves from cooperating, the lower echelons of the parties, trade unions members, and thousands of non-party leftist sympathizers saw in the February 6th riot a danger which would no longer permit the luxury of disunity. As Doriot reported to the Commission, the workers organizations had sought counter-manifestations since before the *émeute*, and had wished these to be not exclusively organizational affairs but to include all of the working forces of Paris. ALthough this desire had received only a negligible response before the 6th of February, "by February 7th the riot in the Place de la Concorde had created so great an emotion in the Parisian population and in the working masses" that, despite the fact that the parties and their affiliated labor unions could not reach an accord, from the time of the common manifestation at the Bastille on the 8th the lower organizations of each party were in evidence in each manifestation regardless of the initiating party.[23] Even on the evening of the 9th when the Socialists had specifically forbidden their organizations to take part in the Communist manifestation, the local Parisian sections of the Jeunesses Socialistes joined with the Communists.[24] In regard to the general strike of the 12th, Doriot said:

Everyone saw there the way to react in mass against the manifestation of the 6th and the extremely brutal acts of the 9th. What did this produce in the Paris region, or in all of France for that matter? A spontaneous union between the lower organizations of the different parties and the different trade unions that wanted to participate in the strike of the 12th. Therefore even where we have the majority of the working class, as at St. Denis, we were able to come to an agreement on this point with the Parti Socialiste, and in the centers where this party found itself to have a majority it could come to agreement with the lower organizations of the Communist party in order to organize a great manifestation.[25]

In addition to this demonstration of the strength of pro-unity sentiment among the ranks of the two parties, there was another revelation to the party leaders in the events of the second week of February. This was the marked success of appeals based on the defense of the Republic, in fact upon defense of the French nation, from fascist attacks. The popular strength gained by broadening the appeal beyond the limits of the class struggle into the realm of democratic liberties, of identifying it with the traditions of 1789 and the subsequent actions of the populace in defense of that tradition, was a phenomenon of great interest to two parties searching for a formula, hitherto unfound, by which to resist the fascist epidemic.[26]

From their respective behavior it would appear that the events of February 6-12 produced a marked effect on the attitude of the Parti Socialiste and no visible effect on the Communist attitude. The Comintern's most recent Executive Committee meeting had been the XIIIth Plenum in December of 1933. Since then the P.C.F. had had only one Central Committee meeting. At both the international and national meetings the necessity for intensifying the campaign against the Socialists had been reaffirmed. Both meetings had recognized the fact that "the bourgeoisie has greater and greater recourse to the methods of fascism", but saw in this merely further reasons for uniting the workers under the Communist banner.[27] This interpretation meant that the zeal of the lower echelon militant was as far removed from and as alien to the official decisions of the International as it had been at any time since Tours. The Comintern Executive was far from ready to endorse the wholesale coordination of the lower echelons of the two parties. Moscow held back, and without new instructions the leaders of the P.C.F. continued in the pre-riot vein. The Socialists as "defenders of the Republic" were no less to be attacked after the riot than they had been previously as "principal supporters of the bourgeois state". Duclos wrote:

The Parti Socialiste which has sabotaged the united front of action and boycotted the committees of battle against war and fascism, which has made the working class believe that it could have confidence in the bourgeois Left, today associated with Tardieu in a government preparing for fascism, speaks of 'defending the Republic'.

We are the party that can mobilize the masses for the battle against fascism, and when today the Parti Socialiste takes on an anti-fascist mask in order better to deceive the workers, it is our duty to make it clear that the Social-democratic policy of lesser evil, of weakening of the class front and of capitulation before the bourgeoisie, aids the development of fascism. The Austrian workers, who with their immense majority remained under the influence of the Austro-Marxist Social-democratic Left, today have the cruel experience of defeat. They effected unity within the ranks of the Parti Socialiste which, by retreat after retreat, led them to an impasse and defeat.[28]

The pattern established during the February days continued through the spring. The Socialists maintained the conciliatory attitude toward the P.C.F. that they had adopted the day before the émeute. The Communists retained their attitude of aloofness to Socialist offers, and refused to recognize the Socialist argument that the answer to the fascist threat lay in common action between the parties. A few days after the general strike the C.A.P. of the Part Socialiste authorized the federations of the Seine and the Seine-et-Oise to send a delegation to the funeral services of the Communists killed in the manifestation of the 9th. For this gesture they were repaid by a vicious attack against the Socialist leaders calling attention to the fact that the Socialists had supported the government whose bullets had killed these rioters.[29] Throughout the spring Socialist efforts to create a formidable antidote to the threat from the Right continued. The sole condition which they imposed upon the offers of common action made to the P.C.F. was the cessation of anti-Socialist propaganda. They established Committees of Vigilance immediately after the February 6th riot and later in the month centralised the control of these in an Anti-fascist Liaison Center. They sought to induce the P.C.F. to join with them in a combined antifascist committee in early March. All of the organizations affiliated to the Parti Socialiste were united in the demand for security against the Right, and they were looking to any available means to attain this security. The Doumergue government, although at the same time under attack from the Socialists for its decree laws, was warned and beseeched to provide an adequate safeguard. The C.G.T., meeting in Paris in the first week of April, issued a document entitled LA RÉORGANIZATION ÉCONOMIQUE DE LA C.G.T. in which claims for the 40 hour week, the initiation of large public works, an end to deflation and fiscal fraud, and the reform of the system of duties were combined with a caution to the government to remember the gravity of the events of February 6th:

> Having decided to fight against all coups de force and to prevent the forfeiture of democratic liberties, the États-Generaux du Travail demands that preventive measures be taken to avoid civil war.[30]

Farinet and Pivert, the leaders of the Paris federations, became increasingly violent in their attestation of the need for a revolutionary approach to the defense of the workers' rights. Pivert, commenting on the motion to be supported by the BATAILLE SOCIALISTE faction of the Parti Socialiste at the Congress of Toulouse, stated:

> Should not the proletariat prepare itself carefully and methodically for its own defense as well as for its revolutionary offensive? ... to retreat, to refuse to give the attack order at the proper moment, always to apply the brakes, ceaselessly to compromise, stubbornly to cling to an impossible hope for a peaceful solution ... this leads only to defeat. The program of action of the party must involve a chapter bearing on the taking of power.[31]

In conjunction with this acentuation of the need for the whole party to swing to the Left, Pivert and Farinet led their own federations into joint participation with the Paris P.C.F. groups, participating in the Communist manifestation of April 20, and that at Vincennes two weeks later. Doumergue gave way to the pressure of the Left to the extent of taking action against the Rightist Leagues and ordering the inquiry into the February riots. But this was not enough of a guarantee for the majority of the Parti Socialiste. At the party congress at Toulouse (May 20-23) the Blum-Paul Faure motion (which was voted by the overwhelming majority of 3,600 to 237) contained the following statement:

> Since the fascist émeute of February 6th, and in the face of the prospects of new attempts, the party must consider itself in a state of permanent mobilization ...
> Organize defense against all that fascism menaces; civil liberties, personal liberties, workers' liberties and peace ...

In this battle the Parti Socialiste is not alone, but it is in the role of being the animator of it.

It emerges intact from the scandals which shaped the cultural milieu of the émeute of February 6th, as well as from the capitulations which allowed its success.

It is the party around which is grouped the resistance of the popular masses disgusted with parliamentary ways and corruptions, but passionately faithful to Republican liberties.[32]

It is next to impossible to ascertain with any accuracy at what point if ever Socialist use of the February riot as a rallying cry changed from sincere concern to exploitation of a myth. It now seems that surely, when coupled with the Communist manifestation on the 9th, the rally at the Cours de Vincennes on the 12th must have convinced Parisians, and the general strike that day must have demonstrated to all of France that the great preponderance of organized power in the country lay with the Left. Surely these must have constituted an assurance to the leaders of the Left that they had overwhelming forces at their disposal. One hears Socialists today state that the fascist menace ended with the general strike. But no such remarks were passed in either the documents or press of the parties at any time up to the formation of the Popular Front. Obviously they would not have been, since the value of the myth of a fascist menace, if such it was, depended upon the maintenance of an impression of danger. On the other hand, it would be imprudent indeed to overlook the tremendous impact upon the French Socialists of the experience in Germany and also of events in Austria, which reached a climax disastrous for the Left at precisely the time of the February disturbances in Paris.[33]

Furthermore the actions of the Socialists in the spring of 1934 violently contradict any hypothesis that, by that time at least, the party had regained its pre-February complacency and was using the émeute wholly or even principally as a myth. Nor is the evidence afforded by these actions in any way refuted by the fact that the party was simultaneously waging an intensified campaign against the economic and other policies of the government in the name of the fascist threat.[34] There was a certain aspect of desperation to the Socialist search outside the party for a means of strengthening the leftist front. For the month following the riots the party was apparently ready to move in either direction, or perhaps more accurately in both directions at once, in order to find allies. When Blum called for proletarian unity at Toulouse in May, he appended a declaration that the party had been, at the time of the riots, ready to give its support to the Radicals:

> If Daladier had wished to resist, there would have been a unanimous movement within the Parti Socialiste to confer on its militants such a mandate in the government.

This apparent desire to seek allies everywhere was somewhat self-defeating in that it gave the Communists, who had no notion of responding to Socialist overtures, ample material with which to link the Parti Socialiste to the moderates; and on the other hand the revival of revolutionary noise which this policy demanded scared a majority of the Radicals. Nevertheless, inadvertently perhaps, as the impact of the events of early February became clearer the Socialists found that they had pursued the policy best calculated to win popularity among the masses. By taking a position of defending the "whole" Republic, by making frequent and well-publicized attempts to achieve unity of the proletariat, and by indicating a willingness to make the doctrinal sacrifices or modifications necessary for unity, the Parti Socialiste emerged as the most attractive rallying point for leftists of all nuances who were repelled by Communist intransigence and Radical inaction. The attitude of the Socialists toward the general strike of the 12th was the keynote to the Socialist position in the months following the émeute. As Jouhaux declared:

> . . . The general strike was neither a revolution nor a riot ... We never wished to make of it either a revolution or a riot. We wished to signify by a powerful unanimous gesture, made in an orderly fashion, that the working world did not intend to let the democratic regime or established liberties be tampered with. It was a warning, only a warning.[36]

In this role of defenders of the Republic as well as the workers the Parti Socialiste fell heir to the allegiance of all those, and they were many, to whom the émeute had meant that both the Republic and the rights of the workers were in danger. The Comintern failed to recognize how widespread an attachment to both of these causes existed in France. But of course even if it had, the weight of a doctrine born of Lenin and nurtured and developed through fifteen years of experience would, the argument runs, have blocked any change in its policy.[37]

The P.C.F. flatly rejected all Socialist proposals for common action during the February days. It continued this policy throughout the spring. When in March the Socialists sought to form a joint Communist-Socialist committee composed of all the anti-fascist organizations affiliated with either party, the Communists agreed in principle but attached patently unacceptable conditions to their participation. At one time only in this period did the P.C.F. initiate negotiations with the Parti Socialiste. This was an appeal to the C.A.P. in June to join the Communists in common action to save Thaelmann, chief of the German Communist party, whose sentence was impending. Even for this cause the Communists would not agree to the cessation of attacks against the Socialists and the negotiations were fruitless.

But the P.C.F., however contemptuous it might be of the role of defender of the Republic, nevertheless had to take the lead in the defense against fascism and in the defense of the workers' interests if it was to prevent complete usurpation of that role by the Parti Socialiste. Blocked by Comintern policy from common action, the only way in which the P.C.F. could do this was by countenancing the joint action of the lower echelons with those of the Parti Socialiste, and then trying to gain the leadership of this joint action. The line which resulted was a peculiar paradox combining obedience to the as yet unaltered line of the Comintern with recognition of the fact that inter-party cooperation at the base was both an accomplished fact and a necessity.[38] The unity of workers and others that had been created during and after the week of the riots had proved its effectiveness. Neither the P.C.F. nor the Socialists wished to destroy it, but rather each was striving to secure its leadership. Thus Gitton, attempting to clarify the fine line being drawn by the P.C.F., revealed the confusion existing at all levels of the party as to what was occurring in the streets of Paris:

... Our comrades and our organizations, in the face of the immediate danger which menaced the working class, were concerned primarily with the uniting of all the workers. That is good. The greatest fault would have been inaction, passivity. But as it happens this uniting is often done in confusion and at the sacrifice of the essential principles of our tactic. All criticism in regard to the Parti Socialiste was literally abandoned.

... At the same moment as hundreds of thousands of workers adopt our slogans, and fight on this basis, it is occurring that in the name of the tactic of united front at any price they forget the decisive role of the party, they ignore the class difference between it and Social-democracy.

> ... it is not a question of destroying (this unity). That which has been created is primarily our work. We wish to improve it.[39]

Throughout the spring of 1934 the Communists could observe the phenomenon of the **front unique en bas**, so strongly sought after by the P.C.F., being brought about by the workers and others of all leftist political affiliation. But this had not been effected through any efforts of the leaders of the P.C.F.; on the contrary it had resulted directly from the events in early February and in spite of the attitude of the Communist leaders. Therefore it had an aspect which considerably cooled the ardor of the Communist leaders; it was neither a Communist controlled nor even Communist dominated united front. It was rather an anti-fascist front stretching across party lines to include large numbers of people some of whom were well to the Right of the Socialists and even of the Radicals. To the extent that any party exerted superior influence over this united front it was the Socialists, with the P.C.F. and the C.G.T.U., because of the numerical inferiority and unwillingness to unite in common action, playing a distinctly minor role.

Moscow made no change in policy during the early months of 1934.[40] Thorez could but adhere to the old line. The advocates of cooperation with the Socialists within the party must be denounced as opportunists. The expansion and consolidation of the Communist controlled **front unique en bas**, a tactic now completely obsolete, was retained as the only positive line. Hence the tirade against the Socialists showed no sign of abatement.[41]

The resolution of the Central Committee of March 15th upon the tasks of the French Communists included:

> ... The organizations of the party, while exerting their efforts to realize the united front of action, will reject all policies having as a consequence the realization of a bloc with the Parti Socialiste and will correct all their deviations from party principles and their tendencies in the direction of Social-democracy.[42]

Pressure for unity of action with the Socialist chiefs was resisted not only in the name of the traditional doctrines of the party, but in addition as a tactic that was demonstrably unwise:

> We cannot accept the constitution of a bloc with Social-democ-

racy, such a revision of the tactic of the party would place it at the tail of the masses and in the tow of Social-fascism.[43]

And:

> The tactic of **front unique** whose principal goal established by the International is the **unity of all the workers in their battle** against capitalism, union in their common struggle, is a tactic of **unrelenting war** against the principal obstacle of that battle -- Social-democracy.
>
> The Communists in employing that tactic reserve the unreserved right to demask the Social-democratic chiefs even during the common action and above all while pursuing a tactic of **front unique en bas**.
>
> The IInd International (must be fought against) as being the principal culprit in the scission of the workers' movement, and the principal enemy of the proletarian revolution in the ranks of the working class.[44]

Having the Socialists receive credit for being the motivating force behind a united front of the Left was intolerable to the leaders of the P.C.F. Blocked by Moscow from taking the lead in this movement they screamed that the "pretended attitude" of the Parti Socialiste was mere hypocrisy and a trap for the workers. They pointed to the election of Frossard and Evrard to the C.A.P. (on March 11th), calling them both notorious anti-Communists, as evidence of the bad faith behind Socialist offers for unity of action. They made repeated reference to the prohibition against Socialists joining the Amsterdam-Pleyel group, and the refusal of the Parti Socialiste to send a delegation of Socialists workers to Moscow.[45] The offer of the Parti Socialiste to cease its propaganda against the P.C.F. was labelled a "stringy maneuver". It was the left wing of the Parti Socialiste that received the brunt of the Communist attack. For Severac, Paul Faure, Zyromski, Pivert et al, by defending the revolutionary position within the Parti Socialiste, could offer a leadership to the united front based on principles closely akin to those offered by the Communists. Lucien Constant wrote:

> The tragedy of the Austrian workers consists of the fact that they had at their head not an organized revolutionary party seeking victory over the bourgeoisie, but agents of the enemy class all of whose action was dominated by the wish to avoid battle and at best defend itself, a policy which can only lead

to defeat and capitulation. The sophistry of Paul Faure and Severac, the French Otto Bauer, will not suffice to dispel this fundamental lesson of the Austrian insurrection.[46]

After February this left wing of the Parti Socialiste concentrated on a vigorous campaign for broad popular support for the creation of "total and integrated socialism" in contrast to the "intermediary regime" policies advocated by the moderates, to which the P.C.F. responded:

> The faction of the BATAILLE SOCIALISTE is at present the principal obstacle to the realization of class unity of the proletariat against the bourgeoisie, the most effective instrument of the bourgeoisie for deceiving and betraying the workers.[47]

The C.G.T.U. followed the line of the party, declaring in its resolution of 12 April:

> This principle being accepted and the collaboration of classes being condemned, not only in theory but in fact, the unitarian trade unions will work toward trade union unity at the base as a means of hastening the realization of a united class battle under Communist leadership.[48]

The unwillingness of the Communists to share leadership of the ever growing body of anti-fascist sentiment with the Socialists caused the period from the February riots until the middle of June to be characterized by a bitter battle between the two parties for a predominant position in this as yet largely unpledged group. The events of February had created a unity at the base of all parties of the Left despite the inability of the two parties to get together. Those who were Socialists were satisfied that the failure of the two parties to get together was not the fault of their own chiefs, but those who were Communists were becoming increasingly dissatisfied with the policies of their party, policies which created an absolute barrier to effective joint action on the party level.

Restlessness among the rank and file of the P.C.F. was crystallized behind the leadership of Doriot. Always an advocate of unity of action with the Socialists, Doriot's mild dissidence over the electoral tactic in 1928 became open rebellion after the February riots. Demonstrable proof of both the need for and efficacy of this unity had been amply provided in the events of February. Armed with sympathetic sentiment far in excess of the widespread but rebellious support he had had in 1928, Doriot felt he had both a cause and the support needed for a test of strength with the P.C.F. Between the riot and May "le cas Doriot" moved toward its inevitable climax. Underlying this conflict of personalities was the omnipresent greater issue. Must the class struggle be abandoned, or at least put in abeyance, in order that substantial Communist influence survive in France? The most significant effect of the February events was to raise this doubt in the minds of the Communist leaders.

NOTES

1. See Arqué and Dantun, op. cit.; Bonnevay, Laurent, LES JOURNÉES SANGLANTES DE FÉVRIER 1934, Flammarion, Paris, 1935; Chalouveine, Marc, ÉTUDE HISTORIQUE DU 6 FÉVRIER 1934, Figuiere, Paris, 1935; LE COUP DE MAIN FASCISTE ET LA RIPOSTE RÉPUBLICAINE, Imprimerie de l'union Ngruyen-van-Cua, Saigon, 1934. The only work in English that treats the riot in any detail is the pro-Left, somewhat journalistic book by Alexander Werth, FRANCE IN FERMENT, Jarrolds Publishers, London, 1935.

2. COMMISSION D'ENQUÊTE CHARGÉE DE RÉCHERCHES LES CAUSES ET LES ORIGINES DES ÉVÉNEMENTS DU FÉVRIER 1934 ET JOURS SUIVANTS, AINSI QUE TOUTES LES ENCOURISES. RAPPORT GÉNÉRAL PAR MARC RUCART. Imprimerie de la Chambre des Députés, Paris, 1934.

3. The incitation of the Fédération des Contribuables had started as early as January 23. It was in many respects typical of all appeals of the groups of the Right: "To bring an end:

   "To statism, fraud, demagogy, bureaucracy, nepotism, disorder, lies, calumnies, theft, slavery.

   "On the day of rallying indicated in the press, all contribuables, rally at the Place de la Concorde in order to go to the Chamber.

   "Let us march, good folk, beware your skin is in danger.

   "Come all, we count on you, the mass will save us."

4. On the 6th LE POPULAIRE called for "all citizens and comrades to defend themselves against an attempted seizure of power".

5. The Paris federation of the Parti Socialiste sent the following letter to the Communists on the afternoon of February 6th, addressed to both the P.C.F. and the C.G.T.U.:

   "Comrades;

   "The fascist associations hold the street and their audacity grows each day. The liberties of the working class are menaced.

There is no longer time for divisions. All organizations of the proletariat must join hands to form an unbreakable barrier to the fascist peril.

"We request an interview with you in order to fix the bases for a loyal accord and to realize unity of action of the workers.

"We beg you to reply as soon as possible. We will be at our headquarters until midnight."

The Federal Secretary
Émile Farinet

Commission d'enquete, **op. cit.**
De Frammond report, p. 4.

6. L'HUMANITÉ, 6 February 1934.

7. Arqué and Dantun, **op. cit.**, p. 67.

8. LES JOURNÉES OUVRIERES DU 9 ET 12 FÉVRIER, Paris, 1934. See also report by MM. Dormann and Salette, on "The participation of the veterans associations in the manifestation of 6 February", COMMISSION D'ENQUÊTE, **op. cit.**, p. 377 ff.

9. It is impossible to verify claims by ex-Communists that the orders for A.R.A.C.'s participation came directly from Moscow, and even that the Comintern had one of its principal troubleshooters, Fried, in France to observe the events of January and early February. There is no reason to doubt either of these assertions, but neither are they of particularly great importance to the thread of this thesis.

   What is important is that the order to participate alongside the rightist forces was resisted fiercely by many members of l'A.R.A.C., who thought that the Communists must defend against the threat rather than aid in it, if they were to prevent the emergence of a "French Hitler". Hence the National Association of l'A.R.A.C. refused to obey Moscow's dictates, and its leader and many of its members split with the P.C.F. in the ensuing months over this very issue. The A.R.A.C. group which did participate in the riot was the local A.R.A.C. of the federation de la Seine. - (Information supplied by M. Guy Jerram, leader of the national organization at the time of the riot. M. Jerram split with the party later in 1934 principally as a result of this dispute.)

10. COMMISSION D'ENQUÊTE, **op. cit.**, p. 2298.

11. Audition de Duclos, COMMISSION D'ENQUÊTE, **op. cit.**, p. 2163.

12. LE PETIT BLEU, 11 February 1934.

13. LE POPULAIRE, 8 February 1934, under the headline -- "Le Coup de Force Fasciste à Echoué".

14. For instance in the Senate in February, 1937, Blum parried attacks by various Senators of the Right upon the role of the P.C.F. in the Popular Front, with the statement:

    "One has the right to regret it gentlemen. However men of politics cannot ignore the (fact that sovereignty belongs to universal suffrage) they cannot not take this into account. Moreover, I gladly permit myself to remind those who regret it to take this up with M. Gautherot and his friends rather than with me, for the birth of the Popular Front has an authentic date, a certain date; February 6, 1934."

    JOURNAL OFFICIEL, 3 February 1937, p. 80.

15. L'HUMANITÉ, 9 February 1934 and Doriot described the reason behind the Communist demonstration of the 9th at the hearing of the Commission d'enquête:

    "The idea of organizing a counter-manifestation in Paris was very popular. Whatever organization took the initiative for it, it would have been very successful.

    "The meetings which we were able to hold between the 6th and the 9th -- and they were many -- all acclaimed the idea of the counter-manifestation. It appeared intolerable to the Parisian working class to see those whom we designated under the name 'fascists' take possession of the streets without there being a popular counter-offensive. In this period, each proposal for a counter-manifestation was received with enthusiasm."

    AUDITION DE DORIOT, COMMISSION D'ENQUÊTE, **op. cit.**, p. 2297.

    See also the conclusions adapted from the report of M. de Frammond on the "Communist day of 9 February 1934":

    "1. The manifestation of the 9th was an exclusively Communist manifestation. It had been forbidden by special arrest.

    "2. It was wished, organized and directed by the Communist party. According to general reports, the number of manifestants was about 4,000.

    "3. The paper L'HUMANITÉ published all the appeals.

    "4. The manifestations consisted of partial and disseminated engagements, more or less violent, which unfolded over a large area from the Place de la République to beyond the Gares de

Nord and l'Est, along the canal St. Martin, Boulevard du Temple, Boulevard de Strasbourg, rue St. Maur, to the neighborhoods of Charonne, Belleville and Menilmontant:

"6. At no time were the manifestants in possession of the street." Rapport de M. Framond, COMMISSION D'ENQUÊTE, op. cit., p. 5.

In the audition of Paul Faure:

M. le president (Bonnevay) "Didn't the Communists seek to enroll your support on the 9th and didn't they reproach you afterwards for not having taken part?

Paul Faure "Not to my knowledge." (op. cit., p. 2282)

M. le president "Your organizations took part in no prior manifestations in January and February?

Paul Faure "No.

M. le president "It is only on the 12th that the Parti Socialiste officially took part?

Paul Faure "Yes. (op. cit., p. 2283)

16. According to the RAPPORT ADMINISTRATIF AU XXXI CONGRÈS NATIONAL, Librairie Populaire, Paris, 1934, on the morning of the 7th of February the C.A.P., the Executive Delegation of the parliamentary group, and the Executive Commission of the Federations of the Seine and Seine-et-Oise, formed a Permanent Vigilance Committee composed of Blum, Evrard, Auriol, Farinet, Paul Faure, Lebac, Zyromski, Descourtieux, and Marceau Pivert which went that evening to the C.G.T. and signed the C.G.T.'s proposal for a general strike on the 12th.

17. Jouhaux declared at the meeting of the Comité Confederal National of 30, 31 March 1933:

"I ask you to believe that there is only one way to repulse these attacks, to bring a stop to the reactionary coup d'etat; that is the general cessation of activity, the general strike of all without exception."
COMPTE RENDU STÉNOGRAPHIQUE DU C.C.N., 30-31 MARCH 1933, LIBRAIRIE DU TRAVAILLEURES, Paris, 1933.

At this same meeting the C.G.T. voted the following resolution unanimously:

"The Comité Confédéral National;

"In the presence of the development of fascism in Europe and specifically of its triumph in Germany, where the violence of Hitler's forces knows no limit and exercises veritable terror:...

"For its part the C.G.T. from now on will take all measures to provoke a strong reaction within the country with a view to the defense of public liberties and the workers' conquests.

"If the baiting tendency progresses and if the defection of the forces on which the working world believes itself to have the right to rely becomes critical, the C.G.T., in order to safeguard the framework indispensable to all social progress, avows itself resolved to undertake all means, including the general strike in the public services as well as in private industry."

Ibid.

On the 31st of January 1934, the C.G.T. published the following manifesto in its organ, LE PEUPLE:

"The administrative commission of the C.G.T. in face of the dangers created by reaction **will not let the established liberties be touched.**

"**It does not intend to let the need for purification transform itself into a vehicle of war against the democratic regime. It declares that public liberties will be defended, if necessary by the general strike.**

Finally, on the morning of the riot, the same journal published this declaration:

"We have had enough.

"Each day sees a renewal of the manifestations of the supports of dictatorship and royalty.

"... We are not in Germany.

"The workers and the people of Paris had defended democracy and liberty at other times.

"They will know how to defend them again.

"Let everyone be ready to respond to the call of the C.G.T."

LE PEUPLE, 6 February 1934.

18. Audition de Jouhaux, COMMISSION D'ENQUÊTE, **op. cit.,** p. 2417.

19. Ramette, a Communist deputy on the Commission of Inquiry, sought to embarrass Jouhaux as to the failure of the railroad workers to join in the general strike.

Ramette	"It seems thus that the decision of the Fédération des cheminots (i.e. not to strike) should have extended to all the public services following the orders of the C.G.T.
Jouhaux	"The decision, I repeat, was a decision for a general strike. It was taken by the C.G.T. but it could only be translated by the organizations which make up the C.G.T. It was these organizations which examined by what means and in what measure they could apply the decision of the C.G.T."

Op. cit., p. 2416.

20. Audition de Paul Faure, COMMISSION D'ENQUÊTE, **op. cit.**, p. 2281.
21. **Ibid.** p. 2282.
22. Audition de Paul Faure, COMMISSION D'ENQUÊTE, **op. cit.**, p. 2282.
23. Audition de Doriot, COMMISSION D'ENQUÊTE, **op. cit.**, p. 2292.
24. Their arrival, according to Walter, **op. cit.**, p. 255, was acclaimed by shouts of "Unité d'action" by the demonstrating Communists.
25. Audition de Doriot, COMMISSION D'ENQUÊTE, **op. cit.**, p. 2293.
26. In its appeal for the manifestation of February 12th, for instance, LE POPULAIRE said:

    "35 years ago the people of the capital rallied in the same place for the triumph of the Republic.

    "Today it is for the defense of the Republic.

    RALLY MONDAY

    "Against corrupt government.

    "Against royalist and fascist groups.

    "In favour of public liberties.

    "In favour of workers' liberties."

    LE POPULAIRE, 11 February 1934.
27. LA LUTTE POUR L'ISSUE REVOLUTIONNAIRE A LA CRISE, **op. cit.**, p. 15; Theses of the XIII Plenum, **op. cit.**

28. Duclos, "Contre le gouvernement Tardieu, contre le fascisme", C.B., 15 February 1934, p. 200.
29. "Qui a payé les balles", Vaillant-Couturier, L'HUMANITÉ, 15 February.
30. LE PEUPLE, 7 April 1934.
31. BATAILLE SOCIALISTE, 15 April 1934.
32. COMPTE RENDU DU XXXI CONGRÈS NATIONAL, op. cit., p. 147. One section of the party at least made a literal interpretation of the party's call to arms. In the statutes of the Jeunes Gardes Socialistes which appeared in the JOURNAL DE TOULOUSE, 10 June 1934, the following appeared:

    Article 1: - There is constituted in the core of the Fédération des Jeunesses Socialistes of the Haute-Garonne, an organization of Jeunes Gardes complying with the necessities of the times, which must function as a living reply to the fascist organizations.

    Article 2: - The Jeunes Gardes are the elite of the Jeunesse Ouvrière. Their aim is to ensure order at meetings, to make the Socialist word respected everywhere, to battle against the fascist organizations, and when the time comes, to act in such a way as to ensure the victory of the proletariat, even by armed insurrection.

    Article 3: - Uniform. Red shirt, black tie, elastic belt, must always be neat, etc.

    See also Legendre, op. cit., pp. 93-96.
33. The Karl Marx apartments in Vienna were fired upon on the same day as the general strike, February 12th.
34. The resolution voted at Toulouse, for instance, declared the program of the party to include the following: dissolution of the Chamber which was tainted with corruption; no increase in military expenditures or length of service; a concentrated attack against unemployment and the under-consumption policies of the government; the establishment of agricultural security in the form of national offices controlling such commodities as wheat and fertilizer; the socialization of large industries such as railroads, mines and electricity; and the democratic organization of the press, radio and all means of expression. It concluded with the statement:

    "Here is the undertaking that the Parti Socialiste contracts before the country:

"To act for the conquest of power by intensifying its educative propaganda, by imbuing it with a character of agitation and ordered protestation, by promoting around the slogans of the party great mass rallies like those of February 12th whose power must be broadened ever further, by working for proletarian unity of action and for the close coordination of efforts between corporative political organizations of the working class, by giving a revolutionary effectiveness to the general strike by these same means."

COMPTE RENDU DU XXXI CONGRÈS NATIONAL, **op. cit.**, p. 475.

35. Blum, LE POPULAIRE, 20 May 1934. And see the party pamphlet, RADICAUX ET SOCIALISTES:

    "After the fascist riot of February 6, the Socialists were ready, on the next day, to participate in the government without any condition except that of relying on the people and on the legal representatives of the nation in order to resist these factions, then Daladier moved to put Parliament in vacation, which was the first concession to the rioters, and at noon he resigned."

    Op. cit., p. 14.

36. COMMISSION D'ENQUÊTE, **op. cit.**, p. 2415.

37. "In 1934 they ask us to renounce the tactics of the **front unique en bas** and to propose to the leadership of the Socialist party a united front of action.

    "But the opportunist character of the proposal which is made to us is affirmed in the fact that it is the conclusion of a pessimistic appreciation and in no way conforms to the reality of our revolutionary movement, and that it is based on an opinion which breaks away with the point of view of the party and the Comintern on Social-democracy and the battle against the agent of capitalism.

    "The proposal to address ourselves now to the leadership of the Socialist party could only facilitate the demagogy of Blum and of Paul Faure, and consolidate their influence over those of the Socialist workers who still follow them and who believe in the redressing of the party of **'durs'**."

    Thorez, "Contre l'opportunisme", C.G., 1 February 1934, p. 135.

38. Hence Michel Marty, writing in February after the riot, started with an attack upon the Parti Socialiste in the old language of a 1933 resolution of the Central Committee as "the principal

obstacle to the realization of unity of action of the proletariat against the bourgeois class", and then concluded:

"... Our department will continue to offer to them the united front of common action concerning specific and concrete objectives: defense of all the immediate claims of the workers of industry, battle against fascism and war, and battle in favor of the defense of the U.S.S.R. in the committees of Amsterdam and Pleyel."

M. Marty, C.B., 15 February 1934, p. 224.

39. Gitton, "Contre le fascisme, pour le dictature du proletariat", C.B., 1 March 1934, pp. 263-264. And in the press criticism in the CAHIERS DU BOLCHEVISME:

"Congratulations to ROUGE-MIDI which didn't satisfy itself with rejoicing in the realization of the front unique as if it were spontaneous, but underlined that these results were obtained thanks to the wisdom of the decisions of the Central Committee of the party and their correct application. That is an argument to use widely: that the front unique grows thanks to the work of the P.C. and in spite of the sabotage of the Parti Socialiste."

C.B., 15 March 1934, p. 383.

40. See Deutscher, Isaac, STALIN, Oxford University Press, 1949, p. 414.

41. "... The P.C.F. must strengthen its battle against the Parti Socialiste and against the C.G.T., which attempt by repeated maneuvers to create obstacles to the front unique and to hinder the battles of the masses against capital and its fascist bands.

"... The Central Committee, while approving the line followed in the course of those February days, condemns vigorously the opportunist suggestions to revise the policy of the party and of the International, suggestions the result of which would be a bloc with Social-democracy.

"... the entire party is indignant against the opportunists who ... say that **in Italy and Germany the defeat of the proletariat was caused by a lack of unity of action, that the working class was defeated because it did not have unity of action,** and who remain silent deliberately as to the responsibility of Social-democracy while directing their attacks against the P.C. and its Central Committee.

"Social-democracy and Social-democracy **alone** bears the responsibility for the coming of Hitler to power in Germany, just as Social-Democracy **alone** led the Austrian proletariat to the Dolfuss dictatorship.

"... The Central Committee has condemned as a manifestation of weakness that affirmation that an accord is possible with the Parti Socialiste for the taking of power as well as the battle against fascism. That is a repetition of the Brandlerian error. That is a revision of the entire Leninist concept of the role of Social-democracy, the principal support of the bourgeoisie, the moderate wing of **fascism**."
Thorez, "Accelerons la cadence", C.B., 1 April 1934, p. 392.

42. L'HUMANITÉ, 16 March 1934.

43. GItton, C.B., 15 April 1934, p. 464.

44. Theses of the Agit-prop section of the Executive Committee of the Comintern for the 15th Anniversary of the Comintern, Bureau d'éditions, Paris, 1934, p. 7.

45. Gitton, C.B., 15 April 1934, p. 463.

46. Lucien Constant, "La crise du Parti Socialiste", C.B., 15 May 1934, p. 597.

47. **Ibid.**, p. 604.

48. VIE OUVRIÈRE, 13 April 1934.

CHAPTER SIX

"SOCIALISM OR FASCISM"

Despite the general willingness of the Socialists at the time of the riots and for a short time thereafter to make the concessions necessary in order to secure allies on either side, the cause of unity between Radical and Socialist was not served by the events surrounding the fall of the Daladier government and the installation of Doumergue as Premier. Doumergue, perhaps, represented political opinion substantially to the Right of that of the series of Radical governments that had been in power since 1932. But it became evident immediately that the new government was not prepared to exclude Radical influence, or even the Radical leaders themselves, from a share in the National Union. Indeed it could not.[1] Thus the passions aroused by the émeute had not even begun to die down before the Radicals were faced with the problem of whether to support the new government or look to the Left for allies against the Rightist threat. The corollary problem for the Socialists, whether or not they could find an effective ally in the Radicals, was necessarily largely contingent upon the decision made by the latter. In May each party held a national congress, that of the Socialists following the Radicals by two weeks. In the respective decisiosns made at these two congresses the rift between the parties which had been growing since 1932 was widened considerably and the possibility of a rapprochement, despite or perhaps because of the events in February, virtually ended.

The dilemma in which the Radicals found themselves stemmed in large part from the stigma which had been cast upon the party by the Stavisky affair. It would be extremely inaccurate to hypothesize that the majority of the Radicals had been unmoved by the threat to the Republic in February. Unlike the Socialists the Radicals could throw the full measure of their enthusiasm into the defense of the Republic without the slightest suspicion of a dilution of doctrine. In fact Radical political philosophy found in the threat posed by the events of February the first opportunity for positive action absolutely consistent with its conception of the traditional role of the party since the war. However France, in the eyes of patriots and politicians on both the Right and the Left, needed defending not only against the threat of a coup but also against the corruption in government that had given the February riots such widespread support. As the party which had held the predominant position in the government during the years of its suspected corruption, and as the party in which were found the majority of those officials implicated with Stavisky, the Radicals needed an internal cleansing of a sweeping and convincing nature before they could emerge as the defenders of the Republic. As a result the months following February were a period of recoupment for the Radicals, a period devoted to the redefinition of their position and a period for the purging of those elements that had brought the taint of corruption upon the whole party. Garat, Bonnaure and Bonardi, among others, were expelled for their association with the Stavisky affair.

Preoccupied to a large extent with these affairs the Parti Radical was both less inclined and less able to take a strong position in regard to the Rightist threat. Moreover the tendency toward strengthening its ties with the Socialists was checked to some extent by the considerable resentment within the party against the Socialists for their self-righteousness in regard to the Stavisky scandal. Finally, there was a growing conviction among the Radicals that Socialist support was unreliable. Blum had played his cat and mouse game with support and participation too long. His offers of support on the 6th and 7th had come too late.

When the Radical Congress convened May 9th at Clermont-Ferrand there were evidences of a real split within the party. The Daladier faction among the leaders of the party and the Ligues des Droits de l'Homme among the major affiliated non-political organizations opposed the principle of support of the National Union.[2] But Daladier's position was weakened by the fact that it was he who was receiving the brunt of the criticism for the Radical surrender to the forces of the Right on February 7th, and he found himself obliged to explain and to some extent apologize to the congress for his actions. Moreover Herriot, favoring support, could capitalize on the party's traditional inclination to pursue that course best calculated to bring it a share in governmental power. In view of Doumergue's attitude this course was obviously that of cooperation with the National Union rather than with the Socialists.

The divergence in points of view between Daladier and Herriot, however, was neither the only nor the most significant split in the party that first became evident at Clermont-Ferrand. Like the "Young Turks" in Spain who had followed Barrio away from Lerroux's moderate policies to join in the Spanish common front, there was a similar tendency of the younger elements in the French Radical party to rebel against Herriot's support of the National Union government.[3] At Clermont-Ferrand this rebellion reached its climax and at the close of the congress a group led by Cudenet and LeBrun resigned from the party in protest. They subsequently convened at Royat to inaugurate a new party dedicated to the principles of the Charter of 1901 and taking the title of Parti Radical-Socialiste Camille Pelletan.

Thus the elements that opposed Herriot's policy were either neutralized to a considerable extent or else separated from the party entirely. Under the leadership of Herriot the majority turned toward the establishment of a modus vivendi with, and within the framework of, the National Union government.[4] By so doing they turned their backs upon the Socialists and took one big step away from unity of action. Throughout 1934 there was little indication that if a unified Left were to be created the Parti Republicain Radical et Radical-Socialiste, officially at least, would be numbered in its ranks.

We have seen how the events of February had aroused the Socialists to seek unity of action with both the Radicals and the Communists. We have also seen how Communist intransigence prevented any rapprochement on the party level between those two parties. When the majority of Radicals demonstrated at Clermont-Ferrand that they would adhere to the National Union bloc, Socialist desires for unity of action were frustrated in both directions. In their search for a guarantee against seizure of power by the extreme Right they were forced to rely almost entirely on their own strength and to shape their post-February policies to conform to this isolation.

In the spring of 1934 the Parti Socialiste was of a substantially different composition than it had been in 1933. With the expulsion of the Neo-Socialists the most moderate elements of the party were no longer present.[5] On the other hand, however, certain of the extreme left wing party members had also been expelled, for disobedience of the prohibition against joining the Amsterdam-Pleyel movement.[6] As a result, Blum, Paul Faure, Severac and Auriol found themselves in more undisputed possession of the party leadership than at any time since the beginning of the Neo rebellion. Also although there was still a large and vociferous left wing, composed mainly of the delegates from the Parisian federations, there was a considerably greater degree of uniformity in party thought after the loss of these extreme factions.

With its character altered to this extent and faced with the combination of factors resulting from the émeute and the refusal of either the Radicals or Communists to accept unity of action, the Socialists spent the weeks from the middle of February until the middle of May in a careful examination of the merits of the various courses of action that lay open to them. Blum, and others, wrote numerous articles in LE POPULAIRE during that period posing the problems which lay before the party and proposing solutions to them. At the meetings of the regional federations as well there was extensive and often heated argument about the extent of the fascist threat and the best means by which the party could oppose it. A **congrès extraordinaire** had been planned for rhe 10th and 11th of February at Lille, but with the riot and the ensuing excitement this had been cancelled and the party-wide discussion of the effect of these events postponed until the regular congress to be held in May. Thus the party members, and to only a slightly lesser extent the leaders as well, remained uncertain during this period as to the effect of these events upon the party as a whole.

In January, and thus before the émeute, there had been an attempt by the P.U.P. to bring the proletarian parties together to discuss organic unity. Paul Louis, the leader of the P.U.P., had requested both the Socialists and the P.C.F. to send delegates to a common meeting in order to determine the best means by which the proletarian parties could defend themselves against the Right. Communist intransigence and bullying prevented the meeting from materializing, but the Socialists also were not altogether free from blame for its failure. The C.A.P. wrote to Paul Louis on January 11th asserting that it agreed in principle with the plan for a common meeting and that it would send its delegates, but it also insisted that the basis for any such discussion be the Charter of Unity of 1905.[7] Thus the C.A.P. of the Parti Socialiste established a precedent to the effect that its willingness to attempt reunification of the parties was conditioned upon the acceptance of the 1905 Pact, just as it had previously imposed the condition that the Communists cease all criticism against its leaders before it would consider unity of action.

These two conditions constituted the only definite aspects of Socialist policy in regard to the other parties in the early months of 1934.

Despite the experience in February the C.A.P. was unwilling to alter them until after a national congress had been held and the opinions of the entire party had been expressed and examined. Thus at its meeting on April 4th the C.A.P. rejected the request of the Amsterdam-Pleyel Committee for the Socialists to join in its projected rallies of May 20th and 31st, stating:

> The Parti Socialiste must hold to the resolution of its Conseil National of March 11 which 'calls to the attention of the federations and sections of the party that joint rallies of all proletarian parties against fascism must not extend beyond the local plane'.[8]

Also at this meeting the "Rapport Moral" which the C.A.P. would submit to the national congress in May was approved. This report, prepared by Paul Faure, indicated both the uncertainty and the caution with which the party leaders approached the question of the effects of the February riots upon party policy. Listing those developments since the last congress that would have a profound influence on party policy, the report warned the party against being led to dangerous extremes:

> The study and projection of 'plans' must not lead (the party) to follow that chimerous folly of the partial and progressive realization of Socialism by stages within the framework of capitalism.
>
> Also the legitimate desire for unity, which so animates its militants, must not lead it in the path of imprudences and disorder from which nothing will emerge but an increased unbridling of discord and fraternal quarrels.[9]

The XXXIe Congrès National of the Parti Socialiste opened at the Theâtre du Capitale in Toulouse on the morning of May 20, 1934. This was to be the congress that would settle the many questions arising from the grave developments that had taken place since the previous national congress ten months before. Paul Faure opened the business of the congress with the reading of the Rapport Moral. In the discussion that followed it immediately became evident that this report had received infinitely greater attention by the provincial federations than was usually the case. Delegates from outlying federations such as those of Puy-de-Dome, Vosges, and Meurthe-et-Moselle rose to announce that after considerable and often heated discussion withing their federations they had been charged to vote against acceptance of the Rapport Moral since it lacked the essential revolutionary aspects that should be present in the declaration of a revolutionary party. These attacks upon the report along with those of the veteran left wing leaders were the first indication of the turning in party opinion toward the Left.

As the debate over the Rapport Moral developed, this tendency toward the Left became increasingly evident. It manifested itself primarily in bitterness toward the Radicals. The majority of the delegates to the congress exhibited a more embittered attitude toward the Radicals than they had at any time since 1926 or perhaps before. There was almost uniform agreement that the Radicals had failed absolutely in the crisis; that they had failed to follow the proper policies for relief of the economic crisis; that they had surrendered unnecessarily before the attempted coup of the Right; that in both of these actions they had deserted the interests of the Left as a whole and of the workers in particular; finally, that they had added insult to injury by their declarations at Clermont-Ferrand earlier in the month, and that as a result of the decisions taken there, there remained nothing to choose between the Radicals and the rest of the parties that made up the National Union government.

In the course of this repudiation of the Radicals there were violent denunciations of the departed Neos. Pierre Renaudel was treated in absentia to vilifications far surpassing anything that had been said even at the most acrid moments of the Avignon and Paris congresses in 1933. Quite justifiably the Neos were accused of having been the principal promoters of closer collaboration between the Socialists and Radicals. Much less justifiably but with equal vehemence they were accused of having betrayed the party to the Radicals, which had become synonymous with having betrayed it to the interests of the bourgeoisie. Recriminations became so violent, and were frequently so absurd, that Blum felt constrained to make a mollifying speech to end them.[10]

Repudiation of the Radicals was accompanied by an attempt to dissociate the Parti Socialiste from the past and future activities of that party. Fervent demands were made by the left wing delegates that support of the Radicals in the future should not even be allowed to become a subject for discussion, and these demands were met with only the mildest of protests by the more moderate elements. However dissociating the Parti Socialiste from the past activities of the Radicals, particularly just before and during the period of the riots, was not quite so simple. By supporting the Daladier government in the Chamber on the 6th the Socialists had put themselves in a position which allowed the Communists and the Right as well to link them to the Radical policies; conversely by advising Daladier to resign on the 7th the Socialists brought upon themselves a share in the blame for this capitulation for which they denounced the Radicals.

Blum explained to the congress, in a speech calculated to reach well beyond the walls of the Theâtre du Capitale, that the Socialist parliamentary group had given its support to the Daladier government, not as a vote of confidence but as one of combat. The party, he claimed, had not been endorsing the behavior of the Daladier government any more than it had that of the previous Radical governments, but had given its support merely on the basis of opposing the increasingly violent pressure from the Right.[11] The seriousness of the **émeute** on the 6th helped to justify this move on the part of the Socialists, but whether that had been the true motivation of it or not the popular notion persisted that the Parti Socialiste had pledged its support previously in exchange for the removal of Chiape. The **émeute** and the subsequent resignation of Daladier relieved the Socialists from having to reveal at that time the extent to which they were prepared to support the Radicals. But popular speculation about this, fanned by L'HUMANITÉ as well as the rightist press, served to create the suspicion that the Socialists had been willing to support the policies of the Daladier government, a suspicion which the party felt it necessary to try to dispel at Toulouse.

The question of Socialist approval of the Daladier resignation was more complicated. It was common knowledge that Daladier had consulted Blum and Frossard, among others, when making up his mind to resign on the 7th. At the Toulouse congress several delegates demanded an accounting of this, charging that the advice to Daladier to resign had aided in the capitulation before the Right and had laid the Parti Socialiste open to attacks from all sides. Quite naturally Frossard and not Blum was made the whipping-boy.[12] Frossard defended himself eloquently, saying that he and Blum had had no other course. He denied that he had actually suggested to Daladier to retire. But Isnal (Puy-de-Dome) pressed the point, declaring that this wasn't the version given by Daladier -- that Daladier had told the Radical congress at Clermont-Ferrand that "Frossard himself told me to depart", and that "I pretty well had to leave since the Socialists came and told me that it was necessary that I do so". Now the Radicals, continued Isnal, were alleging that the Socialists were to blame for their defection in the face of pressure from the Right on the 7th of February.[13] Coming to the defense of Frossard Blum then read extracts to the congress from the stenographic account of Frossard's contacts with the government on the 7th. To the extent that this document is an accurate account it sheds important light on the Socialist position on the morning after the riot.

Frossard - I was called to the Ministry of the Interior and went there the next morning (the 7th) at 10 o'clock. I met Hèrard, P. Cot, and Frot.

Hèrard told me as soon as I arrived that the situation was serious and that they could not be sure of anything. We discussed the possible courses of actions.

I asked whether it had been thought possible to mobilize the provinces and to try to bring some thousands of the militants that could have been found in those federations densely populated with workers. I told them: 'If you act in time we could gather them rapidly by sending out some of our comrades'. They replied; 'It is too late, we are not even sure of today'.

Frot then said: 'I have reflected since two o'clock last night. The Prefect of Police told me that he is not sure of the police. I am not even sure of the regiments of the Guard. I believe that today's manifestation risks being more violent than that yesterday evening. To overcome it we would have to use tanks and machine guns, in other words kill several hundreds this evening, without any assurance that it will not recommence tomorrow. I don't want to do it. I consider at the present time, the best thing in a situation such as this is for the government to resign quickly in order to give way to a National Union combination'.

Blum continued that Frot told Frossard that he would so advise Daladier and that it was only then that Frossard told Daladier to put up a fight or get out.

Frossard - I will add that since yesterday evening I have felt that the battle was lost. I told this to Blum. It is not possible to win a battle with men who will not fight.[14]

On the basis of Blum's defense the congress was satisfied that its desire to purge the party of any association with Radical activities in February had been accomplished. The report of the parliamentary group was accepted unanimously.

The positive aspect of this shift away from the Radicals was to be found in the slogan "Socialism or Fascism" which Blum, supported by Bräcke and Paul Faure, urged upon the congress. The French people, Blum declared with considerable vehemence, would have to choose "either them or us", there would be no middle way.[15] Translated into a statement of policy this meant the abandonment of all the intermediary quasi-Socialist policies which the party had pursued in its attempts to find a modus vivendi with the Radicals, or during the period when it had been to some extent under the influence of the Neos. It meant that the planists would no longer be tolerated. It also meant that the past concessions that had been made in order to secure the allegiance or at least the sympathy of the non-Socialist petty bourgeoisie were at an end. Whereas it did not necessarily mean closer collaboration with the Communists, it did mean that this was now more possible.

There was considerable resistance within the party to the adoption of the "Socialism or Fascism" **mot d'ordre.** It was argued that to take such a position would mean the unnecessary alienation of many of those who would otherwise be with the Socialists in the battle against fascism. The arguments against presenting the people of France with such absolute alternatives were in many cases persuasive. Maurice Paz (Deux-Sevres) declared that the party had demonstrated that it was aware of the commencement of a new era for it with the events of February 6th. It must be admitted, he argued, that the party as a whole had been taken by surprise on that day, presumably because it hadn't been oriented properly to the state of events within France. After the émeute everyone, both inside and outside of the party, looked to the Parti Socialiste for something positive. It was generally agreed that immediate action was essential. But the implications of the slogan "Socialism or Fascism", by divorcing the party completely from the Radicals and non-party moderates, excluded the only means which offered an opportunity for immediate action. By its denial of all forms except "pure and integral Socialism" it relegated the party to a negative role not dissimilar to that played by the P.C.F., precisely at a time when the need was most urgent for a policy that would permit positive steps within the realities of the French political scene, realities which indicated that the moderate Left as a whole was a long way from accepting the full Socialist program.[16]

There were others who, like Naegelen (Bas-Rhin), were willing to accept the renunciation of all relations with the Radical party but who didn't believe it necessarily followed from this that the persons or classes upon which the Radicals most depended for support need be included in that rejection. Naegelen turned Blum's own words against him in the defense of that position:

> Léon Blum said in the meeting of the Conseil National that on February 12th we saw men manifesting against fascism, behind our red flag, who considered themselves to be moderate Republicans; because these moderate Republicans were not merely moderately attached to our liberties, to all that makes a citizen's dignity, a man's dignity. Even under this title they can join with us in this combat.
>
> Let us therefore not push them too far from our party by our intransigence. In this battle against fascism all those who want to remain free citizens seek to and must be allowed to unite themselves.[17]

Some of the minority factions opposed this absolute formula for a variety of reasons. The planists reiterated their lingering plea for the reconsideration of the merits of a partial plan, a plea in which Jacques Grumbach, Deixonne and even Jules Moch participated. This, however, was virtually howled down by the congress. Frossard warned of the dangers involved, from the electoral point of view, in making too violent a rupture with the Radicals. He called attention to the large number of Socialist deputies who wouldn't hold their seats if it weren't for the withdrawal of Radical candidates on the second ballot. Even Severac gave only limited approval to the new slogan and its implications:

> When I hear it argued that we should 'take power by revolution or propaganda', propaganda being interpreted to mean the rejection of all intermediary forms, I reply that this choice appears false to me also, and that its adoption as the basis of our action would result in the renunciation of a large part of the means that might otherwise facilitate our task.[18]

Despite this opposition Blum was successful in securing the adoption of his position. The Parti Socialiste would return to its traditional task so long neglected in the vain and illusory attempt to adapt the pattern of party policies to national politics rather than vice versa. The former method had not prevented the Right from causing the overthrow of the government. This had demonstrated the fallacy of relying on the moderates or on moderate policies to oppose an effective barrier to fascism. The creation of such a barrier was now the chief aim of the Socialists. Thus the Parti Socialiste henceforth would rely on its own methods and its own strength to combat fascism. The people of France would soon learn that there was only one effective force in opposition to fascism, the Parti Socialiste, and they would have to make their choice between the two alternatives.

The acceptance of the slogan "Socialism or Fascism" raised the question of whether or not the party was now more prepared to seek unity or unity of action with the Communists. There was considerable pressure in favor of this from the left wing, and the left wing was, to a substantial degree, setting the tone of the Toulouse congress. The delegates from the Vosges and Meurthe-et-Moselle had been given mandates by their federations to vote in support of a motion to send a Socialist delegation to undertake discussions with the Comintern concerning the possible bases for unity of action. Left extremists such as Just and Farinet and other leaders of the Paris federations also argued in favor of sending a delegation to Moscow, Farinet adding an appeal for the continuation and extension of the "loyal common action" established between Socialists and Communists of the Paris region after February 6th.[19] In addition to the proposals to send a delegation to the Comintern and to tighten the collaboration of the Socialist and Communist groups in the Paris region, the pro-unity faction sought the relaxation of the party's attitude toward the Amsterdam-Pleyel Committees although, unlike the first two propsals, this was never placed in the form of a motion.

However leadership of the party failed to display the same enthusiasm for these plans to bring the P.C.F. and the Parti Socialiste closer together that it had shown toward a complete rupture with the Radicals. The caution which Paul Faure had exhibited in the drafting of the Rapport Moral manifested itself in the attitudes of the party chiefs toward the proposals of the left wing. Moreover, the residual hatred and mistrust of the Communists had by no means been completely submerged by the greater considerations arising out of the events in February. Bräcke, among others, called attention to the ill will and faithlessness of the Communists in the history, and particularly the recent history, of Socialist-Communist relations. He delivered a passionate denunciation of the behavior of the Communists in Germany toward the Socialists even after the arrival of Hitler:

> ... If I were to tell you that even at the present time our comrades (in Germany) have to face bolshevik attacks.[20]

In addition to the leaders many of the provincial federations which had favored breaking away completely from the Radicals nevertheless resisted violently the idea of closer collaboration with the Communists. Vielle (Gironde) received heavy applause for his denunciation of the P.C.F.:

> I must say that I was quite surprised yesterday evening to hear

certain comrades speak of the Communist party as if it were one of our friends and not a political adversary.

In our department through the years we have come to know the Communist party.

On every occasion, in all of our work, the Communists have opposed us, often being the sole opponents.

As resolute partisans of workers unity we refuse to confuse the working class and the Communist party. Community action calls for the mutual respect of participants. It is intolerable that the violent attacks and insults against our party by the Communists should continue. By these the P.C.F. has taken the responsibility for perpetuating the spirit of division amongst the workers.[21]

When at the end of the congress the various motions were voted upon, the leaders were successful in imposing their wishes in all the major issues. However the results of the voting also constituted a considerable victory for the left wing. If the party would not abandon its prohibitions against joining in the Amsterdam-Pleyel Committees it nevertheless modified its tone considerably in the reply which it voted to send to the latest invitation of that organization.[22] Similarly although the party rejected the motion to send a delegation to the Comintern it voted unanimously to:

Charge our delegates to the Executive to ask the I.O.S. to renew those proposals which it has already made to the Comintern on the subject of common action against fascism.[23]

Thus Toulouse marked an important turning in the attitude of the Parti Socialiste. An analysis of the policies decided upon at that congress and an inspection of the trends in party thought that were demonstrated there reveals that the party had left open to itself only one course of action. By its unequivocal affirmation of its intention to wage the battle against fascism under the banner of revolutionary Socialism, and by its violent denunciation of collaboration with the Radicals it had rendered impossible the reconstitution of anything resembling a Bloc des Gauches or even a Cartel des Gauches. The only direction in which it could turn for allies in the fight against fascism was toward the other proletarian parties.

We have seen that at Toulouse the decisions taken imposed both reservations and strict limitations upon the nature and extent of unity of action with the Communists. We have also seen, in the preceding chapter, the manner in which Socialist attempts to achieve unity of action with the Communists immediately following the émeute resulted in utter frustration for the Socialists, and how this frustration led to both bitterness and resignation on their part in regard to unity of action. Thus it cannot be said, despite the marked swing to the Left, that the Parti Socialiste embarked on a course at Toulouse which was consciously directed at effecting unity of action with the P.C.F. On the contrary the policies established at Toulouse were merely an attempt to solve, quite independently, the problems which faced the party itself, principally the problems posed by the events surrounding the February riots and the emergence of a strong rightist-moderate coalition. However at the Toulouse congress the Socialists erected a barrier between themselves and the Radicals which effectively terminated any possibility of joint action between those two parties. By virtue of this act alone they necessarily eliminated some of the barriers between themselves and the Communists. A more important development perhaps was the less tangible but quite general emotional orientation of the majority of the party toward the other proletarian parties and away from the moderates. This emotional trend meant in fact that in May of 1934 the party as a whole was more prepared to look favorably upon unity of action with the Communists than it had been at any time since the scission at Tours almost fourteen years earlier. But who could have believed at that time, and least of all the Socialists, that there was any possibility of the Communists allowing such unity of action to come to pass?

NOTES

1. The dilemma facing the Doumergue government in regard to the inclusion of Radical ministers is well described in Werth, FRANCE IN FERMENT, **op. cit.**, and from the Radical point of view in Bonnet, G., LE PARTI RADICAL DEVANT LES PROBLÈMES DU TEMPS PRESENT, Paris, 1936.

2. Immediately after the congress the Ligue des Droits de l'Homme expelled Herriot because of his presence in the Doumergue ministry. However on the 21st of June the Central Committee of the Ligue annulled his expulsion and he was reinstated.

3. The striking parallels between political developments in Spain and France in the period 1930-1934 were noted by Legendre, for one, in his pamphlet attacking the Common (i.e. Popular) Front.

    In 1930 there was joint action between the Radicals and the extreme Left in both countries.

    In 1931 the Spanish Radicals and Socialists won power after the municipal elections. In 1932 the French Radicals and Socialists won power through electoral collaboration.

    In 1933 (October) after two years of the "dictatorship" of the proletariat the Radical and Socialist combination was defeated at the polls. In February of 1934 the corresponding French combination was overthrown by popular indignation.

    In each country this was succeeded by a government of Radicals and moderates.

    In Spain after the constitution of the Lerroux government the Socialists entered a common front with the Communists. The same thing happened in France after the constitution of the Doumergue government.

    In Spain the "Young Turks" of Lerroux, under Barrio, joined the common front. In France the "Young Turks" of Barriot did the same under the name of one of the earlier Radical leaders, Camille Pelletan.

    Legendre, **op. cit.**, pp. 104 ff.

4. The following motion was presented by the Fédérations de l'Est, de l'Ouest, de l'Aude, and de Ardeche, and accepted by the congress:

The Congress approves (the action) of President Herriot, remaining faithful to the word given in the name of the party, and renews its expression of its indefeasible attachment to him. He suffered under the campaigns which were waged against him as much as against Presidents Daladier and Chautemps and the other members of the party whose honor remains intact despite the audacity of their calumnifiers.

It places complete confidence in the Radical ministers and will maintain its support of the government of truce, which must:

1) Assure the respect of those principles which prevailed at its constitution.

2) Demand loyalty from all equal to that which the Radicals have demonstrated in respect to the truce.

3) Use its authority impartially in order to repress the action of seditious organizations and of all factions, and to put an end to the propaganda pursued against the men of the Left.

4) Be inspired, in the work of financial redressment and reestablishment of the authority of State as well as in foreign relations, by the democratic principles which Republican France cannot renounce without falling.

On the proposal of Caillaux a paragraph was added demanding the continuation of the "peace policy" followed by the Herriot, PaulBoncour, Daladier, Sarraut and Chautemps governments.

LE PARTI RADICAL ET RADICAL-SOCIALISTE, comptes rendus des congres, le Comite Executif, Paris, 1936, pp. 277.

5. In addition to the drop in membership from 130,000 to 110,000 with the expulsion of the Neos, the party also lost 28 deputies and 7 senators. The list of expellees and those who followed them out of the party is impressive in quality as well as quantity.

Senators: Auray, Dherbécourt, Fourment, Giraud, Laudier, Reboul, Voilin;

Deputies: Barthe, Bérenger, Camboulives, Carmagnole, Cayrel, Cazalet, Chommeton, Compère-Morel, Déat, Deschizeaux, Gounin, Hymans, Lafaye, Ernest Lafont, Lagrosillière, Lasserre, Lebret, Luquot, Marquet, Paul Perrin, Pringolliet, Ramadier, Renaudel, Auguste Raynaud, Maxence, Roldes, Simounet, and Varenne.

6. The same meeting of the Conseil National that expelled the Neos, that of November 4th and 5th 1933, also expelled Etcheverry, Thurotte, Poupy, Mallarte and Caillet for participation in both rallies of the Amsterdam-Pleyel Movement. When ordered not to join in the original rally this group had defied the party with the statement, "We are at Amsterdam and we will stay here" - Rapport du Conseil National, LE POPULAIRE, 6 November 1933.

7. Paul Louis replied on the 23rd of January to the effect that he had had no reply from the P.C.F., and no further negotiations were undertaken before the February riots. RAPPORT ADMINISTRATIF AU XXXI CONGRÈS NATIONAL, **op. cit.** p. 206.

8. RAPPORT ADMINISTRATIF AU XXXI CONGRÈS NATIONAL, **op. cit.** The Conseil National held on March 11th, however, declared the party to be in favor of as intimate as possible a coordination with the corporative organizations of the working class as a response to the "men of February 6th".

    It is interesting to compare the language of the resolution of March 11th, quoted in the text, with that of the Conseil National in November 1933 when it rejected the invitation by Bergery to join in his common front. The latter said, in part:

    "In application of the decisions of the congresses at Lille and Clermont-Ferrand forbidding members of the party from entering other organizations created for political action, and considering that the group known as the 'Common Front against Fascism' has the characteristics of a political formation, the C.A.P. decides that the members of the party must abstain from it."

    Rapport de Severac sur le Conseil National, 5 November 1933.

9. COMPTE RENDU DU XXXI CONGRÈS NATIONAL, RAPPORT MORAL, p. 5. The salient developments selected by Paul Faure included the departure of the Neo-Socialists, the great modification of the parliamentary policy of the party, the growth of the economic crisis, the **émeute,** the general strike and manifestation on the 12th, and the creation of the Committees of Vigilance.

10. One delegate went as far as to accuse Renaudel of having secretly sabotaged the party and of having once declared that LE POPULAIRE was in the hands of "corrupt jews". COMPTE RENDU DU XXXI CONGRÈS NATIONAL, **op. cit.**, p. 91.

11. Which was corroborated by his declaration in the Chamber on February 6th, see LE POPULAIRE, 7 February 1934.

12. Frossard's career was a remarkable example of steady transition from Left to Right. Starting in 1921 as the Secretary-general of the P.C.F. he left the party in 1923 and joined the Parti Socialiste in which he passed from its left wing to its right wing in an amazingly short time. In late 1934 he resigned from the Socialist party in order to serve in a National Union government. At the time of the Toulouse Congress he was already fair game for attacks from the left wing, in contrast to Blum whose position within the party was virtually sacrosanct.

13. COMPTE RENDU DU XXXI CONGRÈS NATIONAL, **op. cit.**, p. 122.

14. COMPTE RENDU DU XXXI CONGRÈS NATIONAL, **op. cit.**, pp. 124, 125.

15. COMPTE RENDU DU XXXI CONGRÈS NATIONAL, **op. cit.**, p. 357. It was in this speech that Blum stated baldly for the first time that the central theme of all of the Parti Socialiste's activities was and must be the battle against fascism.

16. COMPTE RENDU DU XXXI CONGRÈS NATIONAL, **op. cit.**, pp. 304, 305. Compare this with the arguments of the Neos presented in Chapter III.

17. COMPTE RENDU DU XXXI CONGRÈS NATIONAL, **op. cit.**, p. 148.

18. COMPTE RENDU DU XXXI CONGRÈS NATIONAL, **op. cit.**, p. 178.

19. Intermittent articles to this effect by Farinet, Just, Zyromski and Pivert, had appeared in BATAILLE SOCIALISTE throughout March and April.

20. COMPTE RENDU DU XXXI CONGRÈS NATIONAL, **op. cit.**, p. 347.

21. COMPTE RENDU DU XXXI CONGRÈS NATIONAL, **op. cit.**, pp. 268-269.

22. The following telegram was sent to the Amsterdam-Pleyel Committee:

"To the proposal which you have addressed to us fraternally about the form in which collaboration against war and fascism could be established between your organization and the Parti Socialiste, S.F.I.O., we are constrained to reply that:

"1. The rules formulated by our party make it a law not to form a permanent organization for that action.

"2. But we are decided more than ever, as we have proved, to work cordially for unity of action between the proletarians, we are and always remain ready to undertake actions with you which are determined as to time and space and are for definite objectives, while hoping that these contacts will be increasingly frequent and effective.

"The citizens affected by party sanctions because of their participation in the Amsterdam-Pleyel Movement, may secure reinstatement by engaging to observe the discipline of the party henceforth."

LE POPULAIRE, 23 May 1934.

This motion prevailed over one moved by Andre Philip which called for the C.A.P. to send immediately a delegation to discuss unity with Amsterdam-Pleyel. Philip's motion was killed in the Committee on Resolutions by a vote of 22 to 11.

23. COMPTE RENDU DU XXXI CONGRÈS NATIONAL, **op. cit.**, p. 372. Just's motion to send a delegation to Moscow was rejected by the congress by a vote of 2,324 to 1,301. Similarly Lebas' motion calling for caution in the question of unity of action with the Communists was successful over that of Zyromski calling for the immediate initiation of steps in that direction by a vote of 2,502 to 1,280. The large minority in each case illustrated the extent to which the position of the left wing of the party was succeeding in gaining substantial support.

CHAPTER SEVEN

UNITY OF ACTION AND THE POPULAR FRONT

On the 19th of June the C.A.P. of the Parti Socialiste passed a resolution to the effect that further negotiations with the P.C.F. were useless.[1] On the 21st Paul Faure addressed a letter to the Central Committee of the P.C.F. stating the reasons why the Parti Socialiste felt this to be so.[2] This apparently marked the end of the series of vain attempts by the Socialists to find an acceptable ground of unity of action with the P.C.F. The latter's adhesion to its policy of violent denunciation of the Socialist leaders had proved an insuperable barrier to any collaboration between the parties.

Two days later the P.C.F. inaugurated its national conference at Ivry, and Thorez, reading the report of the Central Committee, indicated that the entire policy of the P.C.F. had changed. There had been no warning that this change was impending. Up until the eve of the conference the traditional line of bitter attacks upon the Socialist leaders, of rigid adhesion to the principles of the class struggle, of the refusal to share leadership of the **front unique** had been maintained in all the party organs and speeches. Now all of this was swept away. Thorez declared that the Central Committee, in convoking the national conference of the party, had inscribed as its order of the day the single question of the organization of the **front unique** for the anti-fascist battle. Unity must be secured at any price. The new tasks of the party were to work for unity of action with the Socialists, organic unity of the trade unions, and the assurance that the middle classes were not won over to fascism. All that hitherto had been regarded as inviolable doctrine was to be subordinated to this end.

> Each worker, each Communist will agree that there is no task more pressing. Each worker, each Communist will agree that this heavy task is not beyond the forces of our Communist party, as we have been able to prove, notably, before, during and after the February days.

> The aim of the National Conference specifically is to arm the whole party with a view to the accomplishment of its unitary mission, a mission heavy with honor and responsibility.[3]

In a France that it considered to be nationalist and democratic the P.C.F. was now emerging as the defender of the nation (but not of national defense) and of democratic liberties. The essential change in its policy was that instead of waging an independent campaign in the name of anti-fascism and denouncing all other parties of the Left as betrayers of the anti-fascist battle, it sought to join with these other anti-fascist forces and, implicitly, lead them in this battle. For this certain concessions would have to be made. Democratic liberties could no longer be scorned:

> Non-Communist workers and elements of the petty bourgeoisie wish to protect their democratic liberties, liberty of the press, liberty of thought, liberty of opinion. They still have some illusions as to the possibilities of bourgeois democracy. Very well, we Communists vow that it is not the intent of the revolutionary proletariat to ignore the defense of democratic liberties. It is the fascists, it is finance capital which progressively limits these democratic liberties.[4]

Nor could the nation be spurned:

> In order to combat the penetration of chauvinist ideology into the petty bourgeoisie we have said openly 'We love our country'. That has been said at other times by us in a debate in the Chamber of Deputies when we proclaimed the right of free disposition of the peoples of Alsace-Lorraine. It was said by the Central Committee of the German Communist party in its recent manifesto on the question of the Saar. We truly have at heart the interests of the workers of France; we wish to safeguard the interests of the working classes of the country.[5]

But the **sine qua non** of a rapprochement with the Socialists was the cessation by the Communists of their attacks upon the Socialist leaders. This was the important concession announced at Ivry:

> We have said and we repeat: **'We the P.C.F. are ready to renounce criticism of the Parti Socialiste during the common action'**. If we organize the battle together against fascism, against the decree laws, against war, neither from the pens of any of our editors, in L'HUMANITÉ, in the CAHIERS DU BOLCHEVISME,

or in any of our press, nor from the mouths of any of our propagandists will there be the slightest attack against the organizations and leaders of the Socialist party faithful to the agreement which they make with our party.

At any price we want action. **At any price** we want unity of action.[6]

With this pronouncement the most important barrier to unity of action was removed. But Thorez went further:

We wish, in addition to the proletariat ..., to enroll the middle classes and rescue them from the demagogy of fascism. We wish to prevent the employees in large cities, the civil servants, the middle classes -- little shopkeepers, artisans -- and the mass of peasant workers from being won by fascism.[7]

Here was an analysis similar if not identical to that argued by Déat within the Parti Socialiste and Bergery among the Radicals. It went beyond the aims of the Socialists who were looking for proletarian unity rather than a sweeping unification of all groups of the lower middle class. It should be noted that the Communist analysis, at this time at least, did not lead to the conclusion of a Popular Front. Despite the similarity in analysis, the manner in which the middle classes were to be prevented from following fascism was not to be that of the Neo-Socialists and the frontists but rather by the application of a familiar Communist tactic to these classes:

Other indications have underscored how we should win elements of the urban and rural petty bourgeoisie. First by concerning ourselves with their grievances, by not regarding all their grievances as hostile to the interests of the working class. On the contrary we must ourselves undertake the defense of each grievance of the middle classes at the instant that it does not oppose the interests of the proletariat.

Secondly we must take a positive position on the question of democratic liberties.[8]

The Bureau politique of the P.C.F. was charged by the conference to offer proposals for unity of action to the Socialists. This was done in a manner which made it virtually impossible for the Socialists to refuse, for the Communists embodied in their proposals the very conditions which had appeared in a suggested "non-aggression pact" published in LE POPULAIRE on the 23rd of June. The P.C.F. proposals for unity of action were in the hands of the C.A.P. on the 25th, a day before the Ivry conference had closed. From that moment on the Parti Socialiste was thrown into considerable confusion.

The doubts and hesitation with which the Socialists greeted this offer centered about a single question. Was this a sincere positive desire on the part of the P.C.F. to achieve long range unity of action with the Socialists, or was it merely a maneuver which would be reversed, to the disadvantage of the Socialists, when it suited the P.C.F.? There was no other substantial question in the way of immediate acceptance. At Toulouse the Socialist party had made a strong affirmation of its proletarian and revolutionary character, and had renounced all moderate policies designed to maintain amity with the Radicals. It had gone further than that and resolved to devote its efforts to the unification of the proletarian forces. Ever since February 6th it had sought unity of action with the Communists, imposing the single condition that the latter cease their attacks upon the party. Now this condition had been fulfilled. But the question of good faith remained.

The Communist offer quite naturally was greeted with great enthusiasm by the left wing of the Parti Socialiste, particularly by the Paris federations, which interpreted this change on the part of the P.C.F. as meaning that unity of action was as good as accomplished and organic unity but one step away. Pivert, Zyromski, Farinet and Just hailed what they called the reunion of the proletariat with displays of emotion beyond anything seen since Tours. Dating from the close of the Ivry conference they conducted the affairs of the Paris federations as though unity were an accomplished fact. On July 2nd at Bulliers the two federations held a joint rally with the Paris Communists in celebration of the event. On the 10th the Fédération Socialiste de la Seine passed a resolution anticipating the national party's acceptance by almost a week.[9]

There were other elements within the party, including the majority of its leaders, who approached the question with considerable caution. The moderate wing, composed of Grumbach, Frossard and Dormoy, opposed it as a maneuver by men whom the Socialists had learned could not be trusted. Paul Faure, Severac and Lebas were in favor of acceptance but only after taking every possible precaution that the party was not being led into a trap.[10] The burden of decision, however, rested most heavily on the shoulders of Blum. That sensitive man whose dominating passion was the restoration of proletarian unity and to whom the destruction of that unity at Tours had been a personal tragedy, was sorely perplexed by this sensational change in Communist policy. During the week preceding the meeting of the Conseil National he exposed the basis of his dilemma in a brilliantly written series of articles in LE POPULAIRE. What lay behind the Communist move? Obviously the Comintern had given instructions to the P.C.F. which were directly contrary to its former policy. But how could one penetrate the motives of the International? The united front which it now offered was a long way indeed from the 21 Conditions. Had the Comintern actually abandoned that aim which was as old as the Communist party itself, the destruction of Social-democracy? Or was this new move merely a maneuver designed to fulfill that aim in an indirect fashion the full implications of which were not yet clear to the Parti Socialiste? Nowhere else in the world did such a united front exist; the Comintern had never before made such an offer anywhere.[11] The responsibility in the decision which the Conseil National would have to make was very great indeed.

Blum's ultimate decision resulted from his evaluation of the effect of recent world events upon the position of the Comintern. The Comintern leaders, he believed, had seen the necessity of a change of policy every since the advent of Hitler, for Hitler presented a threat to the Russian Revolution far in excess of any other since 1920. This threat was accentuated in the minds of the Communist leaders by the fear that Hitler and Pilsudski were preparing a German-Polish coalition for an attack on Russia.[12] It was as a result of this fear, according to Blum's analysis, that Russia sought entry into the League of Nations and that Litvinov was travelling all over Europe in a search for non-aggression pacts. France offered the best guarantee of security against Germany, and attempts were being made to conclude such a pact with the French government. As the same time the émeute of February 6th had given the Comintern an excuse to change its policy in France in the name of domestic anti-fascism and thus secure an ally among the French masses for the active support of a Franco-Soviet military pact.

There were probably few men in Europe who comprehended the interrelation of these factors and the underlying motives of the Comintern as clearly as did Blum. Yet his analysis did not lead to a decision to reject the offers of the P.C.F. On the contrary, if his analysis were correct it removed any possibility that the offer of common action was merely a narrow maneuver. If protection of the Soviet Union was the motivation behind it, this move by the P.C.F. was part of an overall plan which, in contrast to previous policy, did not have as its purpose the destruction of the Parti Socialiste in France. Thus it was not a maneuver which could be discarded lightly by the P.C.F. Blum was primarily interested in the motives behind this Communist move, not in order to pass upon its morality, but rather in order to determine its durability. Once convinced that he had discovered the key to this move he was reassured rather than dismayed, for a French Communist party embarked upon a more or less permanent course of action in the direction of unity was infinitely more valuable to the anti-fascist cause and infinitely less dangerous to the Parti Socialiste, whatever the motivation behind the Communist move, than it had been when pursuing its former tactic or than it would be if the cause, and hence the duration, of its change of tactic were unknown.

The outstanding feature of the direct negotiations between the Central Committee and the C.A.P. on the establishment of a program for unity of action was the uncustomary meekness of the former. The Communists accepted without protest the rejection by the Parti Socialiste of their request to send a delegation to the meeting of the Conseil National, and were satisfied with a visit to Social headquarters on the day before the meeting. Secondly when the delegations of the two parties did meet on the 14th of July the docility with which the Communists accepted Socialist conditions and relinquished their own was sufficient to evoke expressions of astonishment from the Socialist leaders. This attitude served to demonstrate at least that the Communists had been serious when they said they wished unity of action "at any price".

On the 15th the Conseil National met to issue a decision on the Communist proposal. Again there were questions within the Conseil National as to the motivation behind this move, but finally, over the vigorous protest of Frossard and Dormoy, a motion presented by Paul Faure was adopted. It was broken up into the following three parts:

Motion I

The Conseil National accepts the offer of the P.C.F. for common action against war and fascism.

It delegates to the C.A.P. the task of specifying the terms of the pact and signing it.

It decides as of this moment to propose to the Communist party the organization of common manifestations on the 20th Anniversary of the declaration of war.

It is happy to see realized the unity of action to which the popular masses aspire and which must oppose an unsurmountable barrier to the fascist menace. etc.

Motion II

Conditions: 1. **Reciprocal good faith.** During the duration of the pact, and even outside the field of common action, the propaganda and action of each party excludes insult and outrage.

As for the manifestations of common action themselves, they must be devoted exclusively to the common aim and exclude controversies touching on the doctrine and tactic of the two parties.

2. **Character of the Common Action.** The battle against fascism which we are going to wage with the Communist party necessarily implies the defense of democratic liberties. Also it must embrace those who should be called to participate in such action, all those who want to defend these liberties.

It excludes systematic recourse to violence.

It must also, lest it enervate the militant vigor of the working class, not multiply its manifestations to such a point as to engender lassitude or indifference among the working masses.

3. **Control of the Common Action.** Control belongs to each of the two parties...[13]

Motion III demanded that there be no slackening of Socialist activity and propaganda. The three motions were considered as one and received 3,742 votes to 365 for the Frossard-Dormoy motion. After this decision a stenographic account of the interview between the French Communist and Socialist chiefs was sent to the Secretariat of the I.O.S., along with a request to the latter to apprise the IIIrd International of the decisions taken by the Conseil National and to inquire whether the IIIrd International was prepared to do on the international plane that which had just been done in France. The Conseil National closed with a warning to its members not to let themselves be swallowed up, in the name of unity of action, by Amsterdam-Pleyel, the Secours Ouvrier, the Secours Rouge, or other organizations to which they had been forbidden to belong. Zyromski, jubilant at the acceptance, launched a parting shot to the effect that although the Socialists still couldn't join the Amsterdam-Pleyel movement they could now collaborate with it to the fullest extent.[14]

Thus on the 16th of July the Socialists notified the P.C.F. that they had accepted unity of action, the initiative for which, at the last moment, had come from the Communists. On the 27th the pact was signed by delegations of both parties. Each occasion was saluted in the press of the two parties as the beginning of a new era. It was true that there now existed a concrete program for unity of action. Committees of coordination consisting of seven delegates from each party had been established to handle the arrangements for common manifestations and to settle any conflicts or misunderstandings that might arise in the course of common action. The common aims had been agreed upon; (1) the disarmament and dissolution of the fascist leagues, (2) an end to the preparations for war, (3) the defense of democratic liberties and an end to the decree-laws, (4) an end to the fascist terror in Germany and Austria and the liberation of all those anti-fascists now in prison. But there existed a fundamental divergence in the attitude with which each of the parties approached unity of action. For each it was a step toward something else, but these ultimate goals were quite different.

Socialist enthusiasm for unity of action was based largely on the belief that it was the first important step toward organic unity, a return to the pre-Tours situation. That organic unity on something approaching the terms of the 1904 Charter was the ultimate aim of the majority of the Parti Socialiste had been demonstrated conclusively even before its Toulouse congress. Moreover Blum, in his analysis of what lay behind the Communist move, expressed the hope that the same fears which had led the Comintern to seek united action might ultimately lead it to sanction organic unity. But the Communist plan, and this was made obvious as early as the Ivry conference, did not envisage the extension of unity of action with the Socialists to organic unity with them, but rather to unity of action with all other anti-fascist groups. Thorez had said this in so many words at Ivry, and in the articles which he and Duclos wrote in the next and subsequent issues of the CAHIERS DU BOLCHEVISME this theme was fully developed. From the moment of the initiation of unity of action, then, the two parties were working toward different ends.

The Communists waited more than two months before initiating the next step of their program. In the meanwhile the sky of Socialist-Communist relations was by no means cloudless.[15] Many of the provincial federations of the Parti Socialiste, never having had the enthusiasm for common action possessed by their Parisian colleagues, found confirmation of their distaste and distrust of the Communists in the attempts to put the new pact into practice.[16] There were also occasional lapses in the "no criticism" policy on the part of the leaders of both parties. The principal source of conflict, however, came from the Communist attempts to represent the Parti Socialiste as having been forced into unity of action, against the will of the leaders, by the pressure of the masses. These attempts were kept sufficiently reserved so as not to constitute flagrant breaches of the pact, but they served to put the Socialists on notice that the essential character of their partner had not changed, whatever the change in tactics.[17]

There also arose disputes over concrete issues. The question of strikes as a part of the projected common action had created difficulty from the start. The Socialists had objected to incorporating the use of strike action in the pact because they considered that to be the affair of the C.G.T. which ran its own affairs and whose actions the Parti Socialiste would not and could not dictate.[18] There was also a complete split on the question of the disposition of Alsace-Lorraine which led to a running fight between Georges Weill and Thorez in the Chamber of Deputies and in the party press.[19]

In early October however the Communists unleashed the second phase of their new approach to anti-fascism. This was the Popular Front. In his report to the VII World Congress Thorez later credited Duclos with the initiation of this appeal, but it was Thorez himself who, on October 9th at a rally at Bulliers, first made public the Communist project for a "Popular Front of work, peace and liberty". An appeal was submitted immediately to the Socialists to seek an acceptable program for such a front. In the November 1st issue of the CAHIERS DU BOLCHEVISME articles by Thorez and Duclos elaborated upon the Popular Front concept, and the Central Committee, meeting on the 1st and 2nd of November, received a report from the Bureau politique upon the urgent need for a Popular Front programme. At that meeting the Central Committee unanimously adopted a manifesto which revealed the breadth of the projected front:

> The Communists want to institute every measure to bar the route to reaction and to fascism, to lighten the misery of the working population, to raise up the workers of the cities and the fields against the parasites, those who starve the people and the tyrants.
>
> To all enemies of tyranny and oppression we make the appeal that they join to act in common.

Act to obtain the disarmament of the factions and the dissolution of all fascist leagues;

Act so that the rights of popular representation are enlarged, in order that proportional representation be established in all the elected assemblies, in order that youth and women have the right to vote;

Act so that royalists and fascists be chased from the army and from high administrative posts.

... then:

To all the victims of speculators, of profiteers, of exploiters, we ask that they fight together to defend themselves;

Fight together against the decree-law despoilers, for the defense of salaries, wages and pensions.

Fight together to insure something to eat for the unemployed.

Fight together to defend the peasant workers, the small businessmen and the artisans.

Fight together to defend youth, assure it work and open to it the paths to the future.

Fight together to prevent the robbers of public savings and the destroyers of the franc from pursuing their criminal work, to give work to the unemployed and relieve those who are suffering.

The triumph of fascism would accelerate the way to war. The Doumergue government, protector of the factions and organizer of civil war, leads us straight to foreign war.

Peace is menaced. We must defend it and we Communists are proud to state that **the Soviet Union is the rampart of peace in the world.**

Let us unite in the cities and in the country in order to repulse the abettors of war who swallow billions in the manufacture of armaments and fortifications;

Let us unite to impose the general disarmament which the Soviet Union proposed at Geneva;

Let us unite to impose control of the manufacture and commerce of arms.

Finally:

The Communist party in realizing unity of action with the Parti Socialiste has already opened the way for a union of all the popular forces in France.

We want to unite in the common action not only those who wish to transform the present social order, but also all those who cry 'Halt' to the insolence of reaction.

Hand in hand with all the trade union organizations whose unity of action, a prelude to organic unity, will give the working class the possibility of fighting victoriously, and of eventually replying to the attacks of the enemy by a general strike;

Hand in hand with the workers and peasants organizations that want to defend the grievances of the workers;

Hand in hand with the veterans associations who want an end to the decree-laws;

Hand in hand with the Radical workers who don't want to let the factions pursue their miserable work.

We the sons of those whose work, battles and sufferings built France have facing us enemies who are the descendants and the disciples of those who, for all time, have plundered, martyrized and betrayed the people of France.

Let that France which works, which suffers, and which will rid itself of the parasites which gnaw at it rally together.

FORWARD WITH THE POPULAR FRONT OF LIBERTY, WORK AND PEACE.[20]

Here was the official appeal. On the 13th in the Chamber of Deputies Thorez supplemented this with a long speech in which the call for a Popular Front was repeated and in addition several rather startling claims were made about the Communist party.[21] This was the famous "We love our country" speech which was to give the Communists the appearance of having a common interest with all other groups in France that were dedicated to the protection of the nation against both internal and external fascist threats. By including all such groups the Popular Front necessarily transcended the proletariat and invaded the middle classes, and by so doing became almost indistinguishable in composition from the Social Front advocated by Bergery.

Following this speech by Thorez the program voted by the Central Committee was submitted to the Parti Socialiste. Discussion of this program constituted the principal business of its Conseil National which convened on the 24th of November. Thus far the projects of the P.C.F. had contained little or no mention of the organic unity desired by the Socialists. There had been articles in the CAHIERS DU BOLCHEVISME and L'HUMANITÉ proclaiming that organic unity must be centered about the "democratic centralism" which prevailed in the Communist party. Other than this there had only been mention of the need for trade union unity. But the letter which the P.C.F. addressed to the Conseil National on the 24th included the following:

> In order to fight more effectively against its enemies the working class needs to realize its own unity, to build a single party of the proletariat, a party unfalteringly waging an intransigent class battle and rejecting any class collaboration; a party repudiating national defense within the capitalist regime; a party fighting for the dictatorship of the proletariat; a party united ideologically and, which is the true measure of its revolutionary capacity, a party imposing strict discipline on its adherents.[22]

Here was the affirmation of a desire for the organic unity wanted by the Socialists. But it contained two conditions unacceptable to them; (1) the absolute repudiation of national defense, and (2) the imposition of the strict discipline practised in the Communist party. The Conseil National approached the Communist offer with the same reservations that had persisted since the initiation of the Popular Front. Organic unity, not a Popular Front, was the desired goal. Lebas declared:

> That (organic unity) responds to the deepest instincts of the working class. We are on the path which leads to it. Whatever happens ... let us stay with it and follow through to the end.[23]

And, he added, unity of action was the prelude to such organic unity. But the Popular Front was not necessarily a step in that direction, in fact it might well constitute a Communist attempt to evade organic unity. In addition questions such as the attitude toward national defense presented a barrier. Speaking before the Conseil National, Weill said:

> Since unity of action has been decided upon it has taken an organic character within the Committees of Coordination. It is necessary to determine under what conditions we can continue in this manner.
> First it is necessary that a party congress redefine its position

on national defense. That which it has taken is equivocal. That of the Communists has, at least, the merit of being clear. Clear but unacceptable.[24]

After a lengthy debate the Conseil National charged the C.A.P. to reply to the Communist proposals. The Socialist party did not reject the Popular Front, but it emphasized that its chief concern was with steps leading to organic unity. Hence it was pleased to see the expression of the desire for such unity contained in the Central Committee's letter. It voted to send the following letter to the P.C.F.:

To Citizen Maurice Thorez,
Secretary of the P.C.F.

Dear comrade,

The Conseil National of the Parti Socialiste has taken cognizance of the letter published in L'HUMANITE and which you addressed to it on the subject of a possible program of common action and of the perspectives which such action could open.

It has charged the C.A.P. to prepare and to place in your hands a response of which it has defined the spirit.

It insists on declaring to you immediately that the Parti Socialiste -- which has never ceased wishing the reconstitution of political unity of the proletariet, nor working for it -- welcomes with the greatest satisfaction this letter by which the Communist party, entering into its views, speaks in its turn of this unity, which must always be possible.

Associate Secretary
J.B. Severac

Secretary General
    Paul Faure

Paris, 25 November 1934.[25]

In addition it voted unanimously in favor of a motion by Pivert which expressed an acceptance of the spirit of the Popular Front, if nothing more:

The Parti Socialiste:
Addresses to all the victims of the fascist repression its fraternal

salute and the expression of its complete solidarity.

It particularly denounces Hitlerian barbarism exercised in regard to the 25 militants of the Socialist Workers party (S.A.P.) whose trial begins November 26th in Berlin ...

... The Conseil National resumes its challenge and appeals to all popular forces in order that a powerful reproof arise from universal opinion against the fascist hangmen.[26]

With this expression of the unanimity of its anti-fascist sentiment the Conseil National closed. Neither the cause of the Popular Front nor that of organic unity had been measurably advanced. The barriers which each party placed in the path of the other's proposals continued.

However the unity of action pact had gained for the Communists most of what they desired of the Socialists. The aim of the Popular Front, although it of course envisaged Socialist participation, was primarily to link the Radicals and other more moderate groups to the Communist plan. Thus even before the official launching of the Popular Front the P.C.F. started making overtures to the Radicals, in the form of speeches by Thorez and Duclos, to the effect that the Communists sought an alliance with the middle classes. A few days before the Radical Congress at Nantes, in the last week of October, Thorez proposed to the "Radical groups hostile to reaction" a program which was to serve as the basis for joint action between the Communists and Radicals.

* * *

It is impossible in such a naked factual account to give full effect to the magnitude of the change that had been brought about by the complete reversal of position by the P.C.F. Within little more than a month, from June 23rd to July 27th, the entire history of Socialist-Communist relations in France had been reversed. Everything that the Comintern had professed to stand for and all that it had proclaimed to be its fundamental doctrine seemed to have been abandoned in France. Similarly the bitterness toward and distrust of the Communists that had been developing within the Parti Socialiste for fourteen years appeared, superficially at least, to have been swept away before the enthusiasm for proletarian unity. Nor was this all. The Communists were looking well beyond mere collaboration of the two principal proletarian parties and were seeking to enlist as allies all of liberal and moderate Republican France. The bolshevik who had recognized no friend for fourteen years, who had sabotaged Socialist and Radical with equal or perhaps greater vigor than he had devoted to his capitalist enemy was now the champion of all their claims and a friend to all. This necessarily altered completely the inter-party relationships of the entire French Left.

Few within any of the other parties, and none of the leaders, were duped by the new face worn by the P.C.F. However it was not a question merely of not being duped. Unity of action with the Communists was one of the alternatives offered the Radicals and Socialists as a solution to the threat of domestic fascism, and the Communists were doing everything in their power to make it as attractive an alternative as possible. Since a choice of one of the available alternatives was being forced upon the non-Communist Left with increasing urgency, and as other alternatives proved inadequate or unobtainable, acceptance of the course proposed by the P.C.F. became, as the Communists had intended that it should, inevitable.

NOTES

1. At its meeting of June 5th, the first since the Toulouse Congress, the C.A.P. considered letters of May 30th and June 5th from the P.C.F. seeking a joint demonstration in favor of the release of Thaelmann. The C.A.P. replied that it was always ready to discuss united action for such projects but that the P.C.F must cease its attacks against the Socialist leaders. Failure of the P.C.F. to comply with this condition led to the decision of the C.A.P. on the 19th to cease negotiations. RAPPORT ADMINISTRATIF AU XXXII CONGRÈS NATIONAL, Librairie Populaire, Paris, 1935, p. 27.
2. Printed in LE POPULAIRE, 21 June 1934.
3. Thorez' report to the Conférence National at Ivry. See LA CONFÉRENCE NATIONALE D'IVRY AUX ASSIZES DE LA PAIX ET LIBERTÉ, Bureau d'editions, Paris 1935, p. 4.
4. Speech by Thorez to the Conférence Nationale at Ivry. "L'Organization du front unique de lutte", C.B., 1 July 1934, p. 773.
5. **Ibid**
6. Speech by Thorez to the Conférence National at Ivry. "L'Organization du front unique de lutte", C.B., 1 July 1934, p. 776.
7. **Ibid.**, p. 772.
8. Speech by Thorez to the Conférence National at Ivry. "L'Organization du front unique de lutte", C.B., 1 July 1934, p. 773.
9. At this meeting the Conseil Fédéral of the federation received three motions concerning the attitude it should take before the Conseil National scheduled for the 15th. A small minority (including the Trotskyists) advocated extreme caution; a slightly larger group took an extreme leftist position, and led by Just advocated incorporation of the bolshevik line; the majority voted to advocate the extension of the local negotiations with the P.C.F. to all other federations and then to the national plane. -- Report printed in BATAILLE SOCIALISTE, 11 July 1934.

10. See Walter, **op. cit.**, pp. 280-281.

11. Blum's articles on this subject appeared in LE POPULAIRE from July 7th to 13th. Blum did not consider the attempts made in 1922, at the conference in Berlin, as a serious effort on the part of the Comintern to establish a **front unique.**

12. cf. Deutscher, **op. cit.**, p. 416.

13. RAPPORT ADMINISTRATIF AU XXXII CONGRÈS NATIONAL, **op. cit..** p. 20.

14. RAPPORT ADMINISTRATIF AU XXXII CONGRÈS NATIONAL, **op. cit.**, p. 20. The account of this meeting was also printed in the supplement to LE POPULAIRE of 16 July 1934, entitled "La Vie du Parti".

15. Blum summarized the difficulties experienced by the Socialists in understanding the Communist position:

    "(The Communists) affirm that they are simultaneously partisans of the defense of democratic liberties and of the dictatorship of the proletariat as a permanent system of government; of an immense body grouping no matter what social category and the most severe theories of the class struggle; of avoiding all reforms affecting the structure of the bourgeois state and of the necessary destruction of the organisms of that state; of the general position of the U.S.S.R. now more than ever hostile to the Hitlerian group and its allies and favorable to a rapprochement with France, and of the repudiation of national defense in a capitalist regime." LE POPULAIRE, 26 November 1934.

16. The Pas-de-Calais Socialist federation, for instance, announced that common action would be suspended there from September 1st to October 15th. Marx Dormoy, as deputy from and Mayor of Montlucon, is reported to have told the Montlucon Communists, "Perhaps the front unique will be made in all of France. Of what you may be certain is that it will not exist in Montlucon". C.B., 1 September 1934, p. 996.

17. Thorez stated in his report to the Central Committee meeting of 2 November 1934:

    "One cannot forget that the pact was accepted by the Parti Socialiste under the pressure of the masses, in spite of the many refusals of earlier proposals for a united front ..." L'HUMANITÉ, 7 November 1934.

This caused Paul Faure to include in his Rapport Moral to the XXXII Congres National the following:

"The latter (the P.C.F.) has tried to give the false impression that our party, after long years of refusal and of resistance, has finally ceded to Communist pressure and given a belated adherence to the **front unique.**"

The truth is quite different and there is not a militant who could not bear witness to that fact."

RAPPORT MORAL AU XXXII CONGRES NATIONAL, **op. cit.**, p. 3.

18. On the 7th of November Duclos wrote a pointed article in L'HUMANITÉ regretting the Socialist refusal to participate in a projected strike. Lebas answered on the 12th in LE POPULAIRE:

"It is true that in the course of the meeting where the unity of action pact was discussed and adopted, when the Communist delegation proposed its plan for the preparation of strikes to combat the decree laws, the Socialists made the objection that the strike is, for our party, the business of the trade unions, and that we refuse to exercise any pressure whatever upon them; it is only if they decide freely themselves that we will be at their side to defend them."

Blum repeated this at a meeting of the C.A.P. on November 26th:

"As far as the trade union problem is concerned we must remember that, if we are ready to support a strike movement, we possess no qualifications to decide it."

LE POPULAIRE, 26 November, 1934.

19. JOURNAL OFFICIEL, 16 November 1934, p. 2342. Thorez:

"Without restating all the reasons of an economic, linguistic, political and historical nature which require that Alsace-Lorraine be considered as a national minority, we rise once more against slavery and subjection, against the moral and intellectual assassination of a whole people. Once more after having noted the urgent needs of the people of Alsace-Lorraine ... the Communists have defended its fundamental grievance: the right to free disposition."

L'HUMANITÉ, 17 November 1934. To which Weill replied:

"Alsatian Socialists and Simonists unanimously refuse to allow the question of the return of Alsace-Lorraine to France to be raised again.

"On this point the Parti Communiste maintains its own attitude and its own vocabulary. It pretends to combat fascism and French 'oppression' simultaneously.

"No unity of action will be possible if that extreme antinomy persists."

Report to Conseil National on 25 November, LE POPULAIRE, 26 November 1934.

20. LA CONFÉRENCE NATIONALE D'IVRY AUX ASSIZES DE LA PAIX ET LIBERTE, **op. cit.**, p. 37.

21. Thorez said, in part:

"... We Communists, who love their country, are firmly attached to the revolutionary traditions of the people of France.

"For many who have not followed the debates in this Chamber that declaration may appear new. But those who were present at the discussion of the budget of Alsace-Lorraine know that I previously made such a declaration almost two years ago.

"We are proud of being the descendants and the disciples of the giants of 1793, of the heroes of February and June 1848, of the glorious Communards of 1871.

"We claim the spiritual heritage of the great French encyclopedists of the Eighteenth Century, who prepared the revolution by their writings and whose materialism deepened, developed and is at the base of historic materialism, at the base of the genial doctrine of Marx and Lenin.

"We claim the heritage of the Jacobins, as Lenin wrote, 'the best examples of the democratic revolution and of resistance to the counter-revolutionary coalition of the monarchies'...

"It is because we love our country that we fight with all our heart, with all our strength, in order to spare it the barbary and shame of fascism, in order to spare it the horrors of a new war.

"... But to act we must tie ever more tightly the links of unity of action.

"In order to act we must overcome rapidly those obstacles which retard the reconstitution of trade union unity.

"In order to act we must seal the fraternal alliance of the working class and the workers of the middle classes.

"In order to act we must rally in the workers faubourgs and in the villages around committees elected democratically by popular assemblies.

"In order to act effectively and victoriously, we must develop the organization of a broad popular front of work, liberty and peace."

LE FRONT POPULAIRE, EN MARCHE, speech by Thorez in the Chamber of Deputies, 13 November 1934, Bureau d'editions, 1934.

22. Legendre, FRONT COMMON, **op. cit.**, p. 32.
23. Bräcke:

    "But there is another thing, that is that unity of action must lead to organic unity and that unity must be extended to the International."

    And Zyromski:

    "In the same manner as unity of action was willed by the working mass, in that same manner will organic unity be imposed by it."

    Legendre, FRONT COMMON, **op. cit.**, p. 35.
24. LE POPULAIRE, 26 November 1934.
25. RAPPORT ADMINISTRATIF AU XXXII CONGRÈS NATIONAL, **op. cit** , p. 42.
26. **Ibid.**, p. 53.

CHAPTER EIGHT

BRUSSELS, OCTOBER 1934

The extent to which it was the internal fascist threat that influenced the French Socialists in the direction of unity of action with the P.C.F. is best illustrated perhaps by the inability of the I.O.S. to bring itself to accept unity of action on the international plane. At the National Congress of the Parti Socialiste at Toulouse in May of 1934, as we have seen, a motion to send a delegation to Moscow received one third of the total votes. When, in July, unity of action with the P.C.F. was accepted the Parti Socialiste urged the I.O.S. to make overtures to the Comintern toward creating international unity of action. However there was little corresponding enthusiasm for unity of action among the majority of the national delegates to the I.O.S., and the leaders themselves, like Blum prior to July, combined a strong desire for some "real" unity of action with the conviction that Communist untrustworthiness and insincerity made it impossible of achievement.[1] Thus as in February and March of 1933 the I.O.S. limited itself to vague and tentative appeals for workers' unity which were somewhat timidly withdrawn when the Communists seized upon them for propaganda purposes. On the tenth anniversary of Mateotti's death, May 28th, the I.O.S. issued an appeal to all workers calling for a "fight under the red flag" against fascism. A similar appeal, directed specifically against the terror in Italy, issued from its meeting of August 3rd and 4th. These constituted the sum of its expression of the need for proletarian unity before October 1934.[2]

In October the Comintern attempted to extend unity of action to the international plane. The dramatic about face that had taken place in France three months earlier was repeated on the international level. On the 10th, less than a week after the revolt of the Asturian miners, the Comintern issued an appeal to the workers of all countries to organize common action in support of the Spanish workers. The following day it sent a letter to Vandervelde and Adler, as president and secretary of the I.O.S., proposing a conference of the two Internationals to discuss the possibilities of an agreement between them toward this same end.[3] The leaders of the I.O.S. were not given the time that Blum had had to ponder on the inner workings of the collective Communist mind, for under the pressure of Comintern insistence as to the urgency of this question a meeting was arranged for the 15th at the new I.O.S. headquarters in Brussels.

In the attempt to discover the underlying thought and motivations of both the Socialist and Communist leaders in relation to unity of action the discussion which took place at the Hotel Metropole in Brussels must rank in importance with the VIIth World Congress of the Comintern and the National Congress of the Parti Socialiste at Mulhouse (July, 1935). For despite the developments in France the Socialist leaders could not have been more surprised by this Comintern move. Relations between the two Internationals were as bad as they had ever been. What communications there were between them were confined to occasional letters, usually of protest, or use of the party organs of the national sections as in February and March of 1933. Not since 1928 at least and in all probability not since the conference at Berlin in 1922 had there been an official meeting of delegates.[4] The only aspect of the Communist overture that was not surprising was the appointment of Cachin and Thorez as the Communist representatives. In view of the establishment of unity of action in France they were an obvious choice, but this also had some significance as it was the first public and official benediction given by the Comintern to the developments in France, and presaged to some extent a desire on its part to create a rapport between the Internationals similar to that which had been established there.

In contrast to the situation in France where the tendency toward unity of action had been growing steadily within the lower echelons of both parties since the February 'emeute, there had been no such internal preparation for the leaders of the IInd International. Quite the contrary in fact, for the majority of its lower echelons, the national delegations, were opposed to such common action. As far as the I.O.S. was concerned the French Socialists had undertaken unity of action on their own responsibility, and whereas the International had not disapproved of this step, had in fact even favored it in this case, the opposition in other countries and within the International itself to common action was strong indeed.[5] Thus, prior to the meeting, the I.O.S. leaders prepared a strongly worded response to the Comintern letter which in effect rejected the latter's proposals. However this was not sent pending the results of the discussion.[6]

Here again we see how in 1934 the question of the internal fascist threat in France was the decisive factor in the difference between the attitudes of the French Socialists and the Socialist International. When Cachin and Thorez came to Brussels, on the day following the cantonal elections in France, they were armed not only with the successful unity of action pact in France but with the moral support of the French Socialists as well. The complete change in attitude of the latter was epitomized by the change in Blum's attitude. Anything but naive in regard to Communist tactics and certainly not liable to forget past Communist injuries, Blum had become a virtual apologist for the new Comintern policy. Once he had decided that the move was not merely a temporary maneuver he could overlook all of the other distasteful aspects of an alliance with the Communists because of his fear of the Right. This same element of course did not exist for the International and also did not exist for its Scandinavian, English, Dutch and Belgian sections, which were those most opposed to international unity of action. For them the unreliability and undesirability of joining with the Communists remained unadulterated.[7] If the fact that the French Socialists were effected to a greater extent than others by the purely military aspects of Nazi Germany also played a part in the difference of attitudes, this factor was certainly of less importance in October of 1934 than the effect of the internal fascist threat.

The suspicions of the I.O.S. leaders were expressed frankly by Vandervelde at the opening of the meeting:

> I will not hide from you the fact that the letter (from the Comintern) provoked diverse reactions among the representatives of the I.O.S. The situation varies greatly from country to country as you know. There are those places such as Austria, France and Spain where the idea of international collaboration meets with sympathy; on the other hand, there are other countries where the psychology of the parties is very different, notably the Scandinavian countries, Holland and England. In the latter the fact that the two Internationals attempted a rapprochement twelve years ago at the conference of Berlin, and what has passed since, have created a sort of scorn, and they see in the present step what they have always called the maneuver of the **front unique**.[8]

Furthermore what could the Comintern expect from such a quickly arranged meeting? Vandervelde pointed out that he and Adler could not speak for the I.O.S. but could merely report to it what had taken place at this meeting. And he held out little hope for an agreement on the international level:

> Your letter was directed at the events in Spain. At the present moment the strike in Spain is about to finish. Caballero, a member of our Executive, has been arrested. Even before the arrival of your letter we gave the moral support of the International to the Spanish workers. In this regard, although we will make inquiries, we do not believe that it will be possible to create anything like common action for the events in Spain in the countries where such an agreement doesn't already exist.
>
> ... I will add in my personal capacity, not speaking as president of the International, that I am convinced that the great question will be in what sort of manner the cooperation of the democracies of Europe with the Soviet Union can be organized.[9]

The principal aim of Vandervelde and Adler was to extract from the Communist delegates exactly what they were seeking. There were two possibilities. Either the Comintern merely wanted common action for the limited objective of aid to the Spanish workers, or it sought a more general and more permanent rapport between the two Internationals. In either case the approach used by the Communists was perplexing. If "real" and permanent unity of action was sought, the Comintern and the whole world knew that the I.O.S. was in favor of it. It had in fact published an appeal to that effect that very morning.[10] Why this suddenness and urgency on the part of the Comintern? Permanent bases for unity of action could not be established overnight.

Cachin retreated to the other position. He declared that permanent unity of action was not the primary concern. He and Thorez had been charged primarily to seek the support of the IInd International on the specific question of a common means of aiding the Spanish workers.[11] He admitted the truth of Vandervelde's statement that the situation was grave in Spain, but added that the Comintern did not consider all hope for the strikers was yet lost. The situation was no less serious for the Socialists than it was for the Communists, he argued, both parties being threatened with extinction in Spain. He then outlined the specific proposals of the Comintern:

> 1. To organize common manifestations and meetings under the slogan: **Down with the Lerroux government! Everything for the defense of the Spanish workers and peasants battling against reaction!**

2. To organize a common plan of trade union organizations in such a way as not to permit the transport of troops or munitions to the Lerroux government.

3. To organize common interventions of the two parliamentary factions, Socialist and Communist, in each country, demanding the convocation of parliament to protest against the barbarous persecution of which the Spanish people are now the victims. Also to organize interventions in the Communist and Socialist municipalities toward the same objective.

4. To coordinate the supply of immediate material aid for the Spanish proletariat ...[12]

This program, with its proposals for joint parliamentary and trade union action, obviously involved considerably more than the "limited objective" suggested by Cachin and its accomplishment would have required a comprehensive understanding between the Internationals. Yet Cachin apparently refused to consider that fact to be vital:

We think that if, without waiting for the conditions and guarantees which are necessary -- we fully understand the need for these -- for a fuller and more complete action, we could make it understood from now on that, rising above all differences and for this special purpose, we attest to the world that the two Internationals are ready to enter into battle for the defense of our Spanish comrades -- we think, I say, that this would constitute an important and historic act, a great event that would give great confidence not only to the Spanish proletariat, but to the international proletariat as well.[13]

However Cachin's argument included a flaw upon which Adler was quick to seize. He had stated that because of the Spanish crisis it was necessary not only that the national sections of the Internationals act vigorously by common manifestations and protest meetings, but that in France and other countries bordering on Spain the Internationals ensure that their national sections bring direct aid to the Spanish workers. If that were the sole aim of the Comintern in soliciting the support of the I.O.S. its concern would appear to be quite meaningless. For, as Adler pointed out, there were but three countries either bordering on or directly opposite to Spain. Two of these, Italy and Portugal, were excluded because of the fascist regimes in power. The third was France, and there unity of action already existed. Why could the French pact not serve as the basis for common action in relation to Spain? Furthermore in the countries not bordering on Spain two types of difficulties presented themselves. Because of "fascist" regimes, or for other obvious reasons, unity of action between Socialists and Communists was precluded in the Soviet Union, Austria, Poland, Germany, Latvia and Estonia. That left Great Britain, Denmark, Sweden and Holland, in which the Socialists had already manifested in favor of their Spanish comrades, but where the problems of common action were especially acute.[14]

The logic of Adler's argument was irrefutable; the Communists were forced to return to a discussion of the broader issues involved in the relations between the parties. It was at this point that Thorez introduced the history of developments in France as an argument in favor of the possibility of international unity of action, and it was also at this point, perhaps, that the larger purpose of the Communists became apparent. Thorez claimed of the French experience:

> We have had the good fortune to be the first to realize common action and we take great satisfaction in stating the happy repercussions of it. In France Socialist and Communist workers consider that there are no serious obstacles to the organization of common action. They believe, precisely because they have achieved common action, that all that is at one time or another invoked against the united front, maneuver or whatever, is not important when such serious events solicit our attention.[15]

He continued that a delay in getting started would shake the faith of both Socialist and Communist workers whose hopes had been so high when it was announced that there would be a meeting of the two Internationals.[16] His most significant statement was that this would discourage the formation of united fronts in other countries such as England and Belgium. This immediately raised the larger question and Vandervelde interrupted him. In the ensuing dialogue it became clear that the Communists were pleading the case for unity of action in general and not merely for a limited objective:

> **Vandervelde** - You know very well, Thorez, that in Belgium as in these other countries the disproportion is such...
>
> **Thorez** - I would like to reply frankly to that objection by saying that there can be a great danger for the international working class in persisting in such an objection to the **front unique**; one cannot say that one working class party, even when it is not yet quantitatively as important as another which is organized into a great party, is a negligible quantity. You well know that our little Communist party of Austria fought and still fights,

that our little Communist party of England fights also, that our little Belgian Communist party fights equally effectively; there is even an agreement at this very moment between the Jeunesses Communistes and the Jeunes Gardes Socialistes (in Belgium).

Vandervelde - Our Jeunes Gardes Socialistes have adjourned for three months precisely because there are difficulties in this ...

Thorez - We fear on behalf of the workers that objection against the **front unique** coming from those who lead a part of the working class and who believe that they have maintained sufficient influence to be able, by their own forces alone, to oppose a sufficient barrier to fascism; we consider that dangerous. The experience in Austria is significant in this regard. And even in France, we have been able to verify last Sunday and the Sunday before that, that where there exists sometimes in the Parti Socialiste still a tendency to slow down common action and not to apply fully the dispositions of the pact (this is a reference to the cantonal elections) -- that neither of us has advanced, while the bourgeois parties have gained ... While wherever we have struck blows together we have advanced together...

Moreover it cannot be said that the Comintern has not formulated a response in time to permit the organization of common action. You know this, and I tell you very frankly, our desire is to organize a common action immediately; but if we must discuss, we will discuss. We have become accustomed to discussing very frankly with our Socialist comrades in France; and if you say to us 'you should have accepted our former offers' we reply, perhaps you should have accepted the proposals of the German Communist party in July of 1932 and in January of 1933, perhaps the Social-democrats should have accepted the proposals for unity of action made at that time by our party. But where will that get us? ...[17]

Having opened the door to the larger question the two Socialist leaders revealed the source of their difficulty concerning the Communist proposals. The question was much larger, Adler said, than that of whether there should be a common meeting this week or not. It involved an action of such importance to the future of the working class that it could not be taken lightly:

> We must not lose sight of the fact that your offer to conclude a pact now recalls to the Socialists of all countries the memory

of similar cases where the intention to improvise pacts of circumstance in this manner gave the impression of being maneuvers. And our parties are on guard against maneuvers. You know the story of your Comintern congresses, you know all that.[18]

Vandervelde concurred in this although conceding that it was "evident that what had happened in France was an event the importance of which could not be exaggerated".[19] Cachin protested vigorously against this line of argument. He was "pained" at the suggestion of maneuvers. The French experience was decisive in this, and it had been accomplished not merely by the P.C.F. alone but in the name of the Comintern "which recommends the united front to all". In view of the loyal attitude in France the existence of a maneuver shouldn't be even considered. He concluded with an argument which had previously always come from the Socialist rather than the Communist side:

> Of that which happened twelve years ago you may think what you will, but let me tell you that events are no longer the same. We are in a Europe that is two-thirds fascist; if tomorrow fascism becomes established in Spain, what force, what power will it not acquire, and to what extent will not fascism in France draw encouragement from it? ... The danger is there; the fire is in our houses; the working class is menaced everywhere in the gravest manner; ...[20]

Adler was quite evidently impressed by the intensity of the assertions by the two Communists and the lengths to which they were apparently prepared to go in order to make the new position of the Comintern carry conviction.[21] Like Blum after Ivry he found himself faced with the realization that this was not merely another Communist propaganda move, but that they really wanted some form of unity of action, whatever the motivation for it. Like Blum also the question then became that of determining what this underlying motivation was. But here the similarity between the attitudes of the I.O.S. leaders and the Parti Socialiste leaders ceased. In both cases, that is on both the national and international plane, the respective leaders considered that there were two possible interpretations of the Communist move; (1) that it was merely the implementation of Soviet foreign policy, or (2) that the Comintern had really come to regard the spread of fascism as being so dangerous that it must alter its attitude toward the IInd International in order to oppose successful resistance to fascism within those nations in which it was a serious threat. However whereas the French leaders were willing to accept unity of action even though they believed it to be based on the former, the leaders of the International were not interested unless the latter interpretation were true. A second revealing bit of dialogue transpired at Brussels in relation to this question:

Adler - But the problem remains and, in conversation, I freely confess to you ... we do not know at this moment, is this really a change of course at Moscow, or is it merely a maneuver on a grand scale? ...

Thorez - Neither one nor the other, but simply an international will for union.

Adler - That is a phrase, but for us who know all about that it is a big question. Is it true that they now consider at Moscow that the situation in the countries where democratic liberties and parliamentarism are still in force demands another attitude than that which the Comintern has had through all these past years? Do they really consider that it is now no longer necessary to say of us 'these are the Social-fascists, the traitors of the proletariat who defend the bourgeois'? Is it really that or is it a maneuver which we don't yet understand in full detail? The answer to this is the real basis of decision for us.

Cachin - It is formally understood, not only by our agreement with the Parti Socialiste but in a proposal of the Comintern written black on white, that from the day that an accord is made for common action all criticism of the parties whoever they are will be abstained from ... You have there, in the affirmation of the International, in the pact realized in France ... assurances which must, it seems to me, give you every satisfaction from this time on.

Thorez - I tell you very frankly citizen Adler that there is no new course nor maneuver in grand style on the part of Moscow. There is not and there will not be any change in the policy of the Comintern.

Very gently each time that the Parti Socialiste said 'we can create the united front in France because the Communists have changed their policy' we replied, 'No the Communists have not changed their policy but the workers, Socialist and Communist, want the united front'. And perhaps because we have a strong Communist party in France, that wish, raised by us, was decisive in the realization of the united front.[22]

As Vandervelde had declared at the outset, nothing definite could emerge from this meeting. The most that the Socialist leaders could do was report what had transpired to the Executive of the I.O.S. and see that it was discussed at the next meeting of that body in November. However, he declared, there was nothing to prevent other national parties within the I.O.S. from doing what the French had done.

Finally, in his concluding speech, Adler exposed the essence of the Socialist dilemma to the Communist delegates:

> Out preoccupation is to know whether actually, as you say, the French experience is characteristic and valid for all countries. Or whether the situation in France is, from the point of view of the foreign policy of the Soviet Union, a special case, while the other countries are to be treated in the previous manner. If the experience of France is characteristic then there would really be hope for us all. But if we see that in other countries, such as Austria, other things are done, then it is to be feared that this is only a maneuver. You understand that for us, as officials of the I.O.S., it is essential to know whether the French example is characteristic or not. If so we say that it represents a change of course for Moscow. You are not pleased to regard it thus. We hope that the resolutions of your next congress will give us the opportunity of enlightening ourselves.[23]

He closed with the expression of the hope that the meeting had been a step in the direction of the end desired by each, but that if tomorrow's Communist press should say "There are some in the Socialist party who want unity and some traitors who don't want it" any value of the meeting would be lost.

Upon adjournment the Socialists promised an answer to the Communist delegates after the meeting of the Executive in Paris in November. The I.O.S. Executive met from the 12th to the 16th of November. In addition to Bräcke, Blum and Longuet, the regular S.F.I.O. delegation to the International, Auriol, Salomon Grumbach and Zyromski also attended this meeting. On the 17th it issued its answer to Cachin and Thorez. International accord was rejected, but the I.O.S. released its national sections to make agreements on the national level as they wished. The ban (voted on 18 and 19 March 1933) forbidding local pacts until the Comintern had responded to the overtures of the I.O.S. for common defense was now lifted, and each section was "free to act in the fullness of its autonomy".[24]

This decision of the I.O.S. was greeted with considerable disappointment by several of its national delegations, including the French. Immediately after notification of the decision seven of these delegation published a statement called "A Declaration of Seven Socialist Parties" in which the International was urged to repeat with insistence the offer made to the Comintern in February of 1933 and to ask the Comintern if it was ready to seek, "with full equality of the rights of all the affiliated parties", the conditions of common action on the international plane.[25] Thus the leaders of the French Socialist party were much more favorably disposed to common action on the international level than was the I.O.S. itself. Vandervelde and Adler, like Blum, believed that the action of the Communists in France was dictated, primarily at least, by the exigencies of Soviet foreign policy. But, faced with problems with which Blum was not, unless the **front unique** were instituted uniformly and not just in France and perhaps Spain they weren't prepared to be convinced either as to its sincerity or its value.[26]

* * *

Several points about the Brussels discussion deserve particular emphasis. First the fact that the Comintern had initiated it meant that the experimental period in France, if such it was, had proved successful from the Comintern point of view and was now to be applied on the international plane. The statements by Thorez and Cachin that they were empowered to seek unity of action only for the limited purpose of bringing aid to the Spanish Marxists are not particularly meaningful in the view of the type of unity of action that was proposed. It might as well have been argued that unity of action in France was also for the "limited purpose" of defense against fascism. By seeking a common trade union plan and common parliamentary action as well as the organization of common manifestations the Communist proposals contained the principal elements of the unity of action that had been achieved in France. It must be assumed that the Comintern was intent upon exploring the possibilities of reasonably permanent and comprehensive common action.

The second significant aspect was the type of argument used by the Communists. The argument that international unity of action must be established because "Europe is two-thirds Fascist" and because, as demonstrated in France, "In unity there is strength and in disunity helplessness" involved a complete about face for the Comintern. It involved, indeed, adoption of the position long since held by the Socialists against which the Comintern had always opposed the line that fascism was merely the result of Socialist blundering and betrayal the remedy for which was to turn away from Socialdemocracy toward the IIIrd International. We have already seen, of course, this identical turning on the part of the P.C.F. in France. Now it was applied for the first time on the international level. Here again was an indication of the end sought by the Comintern, beyond that of mere temporary aid to Spain.

A final clue to the intentions of the Comintern is found in the meekness of Thorez and Cachin in their discussion with the I.O.S. leaders. The elaborate professions of good faith and the attitude of outraged righteousness at the suggestion of a maneuver call to mind the behavior of these same two men at the meeting with the leaders of the Parti Socialiste on July 14th in Paris. Now, as then, it was clear that the Communists were prepared to make elaborate concessions, so anxious were they that their project succeed.

On the Socialist side is found of course that same deepseated suspicion of a maneuver that had so tortured Blum. The dramatic change in Comintern attitude, which the Communists absurdly denied, succeeded in perplexing the I.O.S. leaders even three months after its occurrence in France. Nevertheless Vandervelde, as the French Socialists had done, exhibited a sincere and unequivocal desire for unity of action if a satisfactory basis for it could be found.

If both the Comintern and the I.O.S. sincerely wished unity of action the reasons for their failure to achieve it require explanation. It is submitted that one need not search too far for this explanation. Just as the sole obstacle to unity of action for the French Socialist leaders, after Ivry at least, had been their fear of a maneuver, so was this the sole obstacle for the I.O.S. But the leaders of the International, for the very reason that this was an international and not a national organization, could not be faced with the one factor which overbalanced this fear in the minds of the French, the threat of fascism within the nation. For the Communists the explanation is slightly more complicated but no less obvious. Unity of action in France was a price which the Comintern was willing to pay in the interests of securing a French ally for the Soviet Union. It was also willing to pay this price with the I.O.S. to the extent necessary to further its policy in Spain and perhaps elsewhere as the occasions arose. But when the I.O.S. identified itself and its policies with those of its sections in which, because of the absence of an internal fascist threat, there was no hope of national unity of action being established and which represented countries not vitally concerned in the security of the Soviet Union (England, the Scandinavian countries, Holland, etc.) the gain for the Comintern was not worth the cost. Dmitrov, at the VIIth World Congress of the Comintern in 1935, was to include the creation of international proletarian unity of action as one of the goals of the IIIrd International, but after Brussels there were no further overt attempts on the part of that body to establish it.[27]

NOTES

1. See Vandervelde, L'ALTERNATIVE, **op. cit.**, p. 269; also his introductory statement to the XXX Congrès National of the Parti Socialiste at Paris in 1933, COMPTE RENDU DU XXX CONGRÈS NATIONAL, **op. cit.**, p. 214.
2. Report of the French delegation to the I.O.S., RAPPORT ADMINISTRATIF AU XXXII CONGRES NATIONAL, **op. cit.**, p. 491.
3. L'HUMANITÉ, 11 October 1934.
4. According to an unsigned Communist article Lenin had said of the 1922 Conference:

    "The representatives of the IInd International and the II½ International need a **front unique** because they hope to weaken us by means of exaggerated concessions on our part. They hope to penetrate without paying into our locals. They hope, by the united front tactic, to demonstrate to the workers that the reformist tactic is proper and that the revolutionary tactic is false. **As for us we need** the **front unique** because we hope to be able to prove the contrary to the workers ... In order to aid these masses to fight against capital, in order to aid them to understand the 'subtle mechanism' of two fronts in all the international economy and politic, we have adopted the tactic of united front and we will apply it to the end."

    "En guise de post-face - Pour le Front unique de lutte du proletariat international", Bureau d'éditions, Paris 1935, p. 33.
5. See statement by Vandervelde at the Brussels meeting. FRONT UNIQUE INTERNATIONAL, Bureau d'éditions, Paris, 1935, p. 27.
6. The text of this letter is not available as it was altered in the course of the meeting. The altered text was published in LE POPULAIRE 19 October 1934.
7. The Swedish and Swiss Social-democrats and the Parti Ouvrier Belge had already refused unity of action. The Paris correspondent of a Swiss Social-democrat paper wrote of the happenings in France:

"The Soviet Union which bends all its efforts to incorporate itself in the community of nations and wants to have forgotten the antagonism so strongly underlined formerly by its relations in regard to western capitalism and western democracy has every interest in adapting the Communist parties to these tendencies." VOLKSRECHT, 19 July 1934.

8. The writer has reproduced the account of this meeting in considerable detail because of his conviction that, standing by itself, it is one of the most revealing presentations of the new Comintern approach to unity of action and the traditional Socialist caution toward dealing with the Communists that is to be found in any of the documents relating to the history of Socialist-Communist relations.

The stenographic account which is the principal source of information upon this meeting is contained in a pamphlet, FRONT UNIQUE INTERNATIONAL - À L'AIDE DES HÉROIQUES COMBATTANTS D'ESPAGNE, Textes et Documents, Bureau d'éditions, Paris, 1935. Since this is a Communist publication it has been checked in so far as is possible against the Socialist version appearing in the form of general comments in LE POPULAIRE of 19 October 1934 and the report of Severac to the XXXII Congrès National of the Parti Socialist. To the extent that this afforded a comparison the Communist version, when stripped of its editorialisation, has proved accurate. It is submitted that, in view of the ease of refutation and the absence of any such refutation by the Socialists, the reproduction of the actual discussion is in all probability quite accurate.

9. FRONT UNIQUE INTERNATIONAL, **op. cit.**, p. 27.

10. Printed in the organ of the C.G.T., LE PEUPLE, 15 October 1934.

11. "The mandate which the Comintern confided in us is much less to treat the whole problem of the **front unique** between the two internationals then to pose the specific question of immediate action in favor of our Spanish comrades." Cachin, FRONT UNIQUE INTERNATIONAL, **op. cit.**, p. 28.

12. L'HUMANITÉ, 13 October 1934. cf. appeal for unity of action made by the P.C.F. to the Parti Socialiste, LE POPULAIRE, 27 June 1934.

13. FRONT UNIQUE INTERNATIONAL, **op. cit.**, p. 29.

14. cf. Bela Kun, "Contre le front unique tout argument est bon", C.B., 15 September 1934, p. 1003, in which he lists the arguments made by the national sections of the I.O.S. against the front unique and attempts to refute them.
15. FRONT UNIQUE INTERNATIONAL, **op. cit.**, p. 31.
16. On the 13th at Bulliers there was a rally at which the appeal of the Comintern was announced. The foremost of the Paris Socialist leaders, Zyromski, spoke in favor of the projected international unity of action declaring it to be both "possible and necessary". BATAILLE SOCIALISTE, 15 October 1934.
17. FRONT UNIQUE INTERNATIONAL, **op. cit.**, p. 33.
18. FRONT UNIQUE INTERNATIONAL, **op. cit.**, p. 33. The Socialist leaders rejected Thorez' invitation to speak at a joint rally in Paris in favor of the Spanish workers. Vandervelde said that whereas personally they would do so, as officials of the I.O.S. they could not.
19. **Ibid.**, p. 34.
20. FRONT UNIQUE INTERNATIONAL, **op. cit.**, p. 34.
21. At this point in the discussion it was agreed that the response prepared by the I.O.S. prior to the meeting was unnecessarily harsh, and the delegates turned to a rephrasing of it. Adler was willing to concede the need for leaving the door open for future discussions.
22. FRONT UNIQUE INTERNATIONAL, **op. cit.**, p. 35.
23. **Ibid.**
24. RAPPORT ADMINISTRATIF AU XXXII CONGRÈS NATIONAL, **op. cit.**, p. 103. After the close of the meeting there were two joint sessions between the I.O.S. and the Fédération Syndicative Internationale, represented respectively by de Brouckere and Jouhaux, at which the policy on unity was declared to have remained unchanged. The only positive result of these meetings was the sending of a telegram to Karl Seitz, imprisoned in Vienna.
25. Blum, Bräcke and Longuet signed this for France. The other parties were those of Switzerland, Spain, Italy, the Polish Bund, the Russian Social-democrats (represented by Dan) and Austria.

    As the chief protagonist within the Parti Socialiste of common action Zyromski was particularly bitter at the I.O.S. decision. He declared in LE POPULAIRE of 27 November:

"Basically this means - and this is serious - that the I.O.S. renounces being the motor center and animator of international action.

"This powerlessness, stated and admitted, is merely the extension of its former weaknesses, which we have often denounced."

26. As Vandervelde told a reporter from LE POPULAIRE, it was difficult for the IInd International to accept the sincerity of this movement by the Comintern in view of the internal conditions in the U.S.S.R.:

"It is unfortunately conceivable that the Comintern fight with us in France and Spain and elsewhere in defense of democratic liberties while in the U.S.S.R. the same liberties do not exist." LE POPULAIRE, 11 November 1934.

27. VIIe CONGRÈS MONDIALE. Editions en Langues Etrangères, Moscow, 1939, Compte rendu abrégé, p. 132.

CHAPTER NINE

THE DORIOT INCIDENT

In search for those factors which bore upon the decision of the French Communists to alter their tactics so drastically in the summer of 1934, the story of Jacques Doriot cannot be omitted. The history of Doriot's relationship to the party and of his separation from it raises the provocative query as to whether or not it was in fact Doriot's influence that provided the final impetus for this change. Despite the apparent impossibility of initiating policy changes within the Comintern from the national or local level the circumstances surrounding the career of Doriot suggest a strong possibility of an exception in this case.

Unlike any of the other leaders of the P.C.F. Doriot's position within the Comintern and the P.C.F. was based more upon the party's need for him than upon his need for the party. He was a self-made rather than a party-made leader. His strength derived from the personal following that he had created among the workers of St. Denis and the Paris-Nord area, and these workers, in turn, appeared to be the primary object of his loyalty.[1] As a result, from his earliest association with the party he could and did display an attitude of independence to an extent unmatched by any of the other leaders of the French party.

Doriot's formal association with the revolutionary Socialism began in 1916 when, at the age of 18, he joined the Jeunesses Socialistes and the Parti Socialiste at St. Denis.[2] Later in that year he was conscripted and served in the infantry for the duration of the war, after which he was posted to a colonial regiment in Hungary. It was there that he was exposed to revolution for the first time. He is also reputed to have been present in Fiume at the time of d'Annunzio's coup. Upon returning to France he opposed the scission with the Parti Socialiste, a point of some significance perhaps, but remained with his St. Denis section when it elected to adhere to the IIIrd International (prior to Tours).

The beginning of his career with the Comintern dates from June 1921 when he attended the 3rd Congress of the International as a representative of the French Youth Movement. Apparently attracting the attention of the leaders of the Comintern, he remained in Moscow fourteen months at this time working on the commission for latin countries under Trotsky.[3] He returned to France for the P.C.F. congress in 1922 and then was sent on a Comintern mission for six months in Germany. When he returned from Germany he was made secretary general of the Jeunesses Communistes. Jailed for a few months in the winter of 1923-24, upon his release he had already acquired a not inconsiderable reputation with the workers and within the party itself. In 1925 he was again sent on a mission for the Comintern, this time to China.[4] Forceful, energetic and capable of brilliant oratory he had so established himself at party meetings and manifestations that upon his return to France in 1926 he was, at 28, one of the leading figures of the party.[5]

From 1927 on the fissures began to appear that are inevitable in any relationship between a local leader who wishes to retain some independence and the Comintern. Doriot had risen rapidly within the party hierarchy, becoming a member of the Bureau politique of the P.C.F., leader of its parliamentary faction, and ultimately member of the Executive of the Comintern. But Doriot had on frequent occasions taken a rather strong stand against the policies of the Comintern, for instance, as we have seen, over the electoral tactic in 1928. In the course of these disagreements with Comintern policies he asserted a degree of independence which would have undoubtedly brought expulsion to a less important figure. The size of his popular following in the Paris suburbs as well as in all of France, the need for his oratorical talents in the Chamber, and the fact that Doriot never pushed his rebellions to the breaking point prevented an open rift in the period from 1928-1933.[6]

It is difficult if not impossible to determine the exact nature of Doriot's political philosophy, if indeed he possessed one.[7] The direction which his chronic deviation from the party line assumed revealed more of a tactical inclination than a positive doctrine. Nor did Doriot ever attempt to justify his divergence, as did the Neos and to some extent Bergery, in terms of a positive doctrine. The essence of Doriot's position between 1928 and his expulsion in 1934 may best be summarized perhaps by saying that whenever the interests of the Comintern were in conflict with the political interests of the workers in France he sided with the latter -- a somewhat remarkable role to adopt and still survive as a member of the Comintern Executive.

The question of personal ambition is always raised in connection with men of the temperament and in the position of Doriot.[8] It is certainly beyond the scope of this study to attempt to analyze the extent to which he was motivated and influenced by personal ambition rather than by a more selfless cause. Such ambition was without question present in abundance -- this was of course the line which the Communists later took to smear him -- but his career also presented abundant evidence of a consistent and sincere desire to advance the cause of the French (and particularly the St. Denis) worker whether or not, at any given time, this end was in harmony with the Comintern line. The position that he took in late 1933, and which he intensified after the Feburary riots, was the logical outgrowth of this attitude.

Doriot's effect upon the policies of the proletarian parties, to the extent that it existed, occurred during the winter of 1933-34 and continued through the following spring. During that period he gradually developed into the "man of tomorrow" for much of the extreme Left in France.[9] By taking a position that sought to combine the interests of revolutionary proletarianism with the principles of local autonomy he attracted the allegiance, or at least the sympathy, of large numbers of Socialists and Communists alike who also sought to attain that somewhat elusive combination. There were two basic elements to Doriot's appeal: (1) that the proletarian forces could not afford disunity during this period of crisis, and (2) that the policies of the proletarian political groups should be dictated by the interests of the French workers rather than by external considerations, i.e. those of the Comintern. Using this simple but timely appeal and treading the fine line between what is considered militant (and national) Socialism and what is considered fascism Doriot presented for many an extremely attractive alternative to either the blind intransigence of the Communists or the confused inactivity of the Socialists.

Doriot's call for unity of action of the proletarian parties gained him popularity not only among the lower echelons of all of the workers' parties, but from the leadership of the P.U.P. and the Parti Socialiste as well.[10] In contrast to Bergery, Doriot was not seeking a sweeping alliance of all of the factions of the Left in a campaign against the "200 families", but rather a much more permanent and fundamental return to the unity of the Marxist parties that had been created in 1905.[11] This was a program which the Socialists, for instance, could applaud at the same time as they denounced the "Frontism" of Bergery.[12]

The real significance of the Doriot dissidence in 1934, however, was the dilemma which he posed for the Comintern. In effect he placed the tactic of **front unique en bas** between himself and the party. Furthermore, he gave such publicity to the choice he was forcing upon the Comintern that it could neither avoid making this choice nor conceal the nature of it. The serious nature of this dilemma, from the point of view of the Comintern, cannot be exaggerated. The International and French leaders both feared, and with considerable justification, that if Doriot were to be separated from the party he would in all probability take an important part of his following with him, including virtually the entire St. Denis faction and a good share from the parent Paris-Nord region. Such a loss from this region which was qualitatively as well as quantitatively perhaps the most important in France would be a serious and perhaps even a mortal blow to the enfeebled French party.

It is unfortunate, from a historical point of view, that Doriot himself solved this problem for the Comintern. In May and June of 1934 he compounded his venal sin of disagreement with the mortal one of open attack and his expulsion thereupon became inevitable. Although he had started his protestations much earlier, and in the days of the countermanifestations following the February riots had been outspoken in his demands for unity, at that time he had, nevertheless, remained sufficiently within the fold to act as the leader of the all Communist demonstration of February 9th. However on May 5th, two weeks before the opening of the Socialist congress at Toulouse, he launched a full scale attack against the policies of the P.C.F. in what had become his personal organ, L'EMANCIPATION. He pointed to the "revolutionary helplessness of the IIIrd International in the largest countries of Europe".[13] He called for a party founded on a democratic basis within the general framework of Socialist doctrine.[14] He repeated his most effective appeal for an "alliance of the revolutionary dynamism of the Communists with the formidable political experience possessed by Social-democracy". But he despaired of the possibility of either party's capacity to accomplish the desired end in their present form:

> In order to orient this action (i.e. the defense against fascism), in order to wage it properly, a revolutionary party is indispensable. But alas it is a fact that none such exists; neither the Socialist party, past treason, nor the P.C.F. whose notorious incapacity has been placed in full relief, can assume this role.[15]

On the 16th the Executive of the Comintern published an edict signed by Dmitrov, Heckert, Kuusinen, MacIlhone, Manuilski and Piatnitski in which it declared:

> The Executive Committee of the Comintern has exhausted all means of saving Doriot for the party and preventing his isolation from the working masses. It is clear to the Comintern that Doriot speaks and writes on the **front unique** not in the interest of its realization but simply in order to be able, under the cover of phrases about the **front unique**, to prepare a scission in the party. The Comintern does not believe that Doriot, who destroys the united front within the party can be honestly and sincerely in favor of a **front unique** of the working class.[16]

The extent of the rift between Doriot and the Comintern could no longer be concealed; the open battle was on. There followed further attempts by the International to induce Doriot to abandon his position, hurried consultations between the Executive and the leaders of the P.C.F., almost feverish attempts to dissuade Doriot before he had gone too far.[17] However Doriot remained adamant. He ignored an order to go to Moscow to discuss the dispute and the end was in sight. By mid-June Thorez and the other labor leaders of the P.C.F. had turned against him openly and at the national conference at Ivry in the last week of June he was expelled.[18]

Thus the problem of the disposition of Doriot himself was solved. As an expellee he became merely another name on the P.C.F.'s large list of enemies against whom it could and did unleash its unrestricted invective. However he had already performed one service to the cause of proletarian unity by showing the Socialists, and everyone else, that there existed within the P.C.F. a sizable body of opinion favoring united action or perhaps even greater unity, and that all that stood in its way was the restraining hand of Moscow. A Socialist delegate to the National Congress at Toulouse declared that the Doriot incident revealed beyond doubt that the Comintern was opposed to any kind of unity of action with the Socialists.[19] However the question as to what to do about Doriot himself was but a part of the dilemma which he had placed before the Comintern, for it was in turn inextricably linked to the greater question of party policy concerning the **front unique en bas.** It is to the extent that Doriot influenced the Comintern in its decision concerning this greater question that his dissidence was of real importance.

Since the documents and publications of the P.C.F. and the writings of Doriot himself shed little light upon this question we are, to a considerable extent, reduced to conjecture. In this conjecture, however, certain significant facts demand attention. The first of these was the extreme reluctance of the Comintern to expel Doriot even after he began to attack it openly. Secondly, up until his exclusion neither the Comintern nor any of its national sections had abandoned the **front unique en bas.** Finally, the expulsion of Doriot and the change of policy of the P.C.F. were announced simultaneously at Ivry. The almost inescapable inference from this is that the Communist leaders sought to compensate those within the P.C.F. who would be most restless over the expulsion of Doriot by undertaking at least a partial adoption of the position which he had advocated and which had found such a widespread response among them.

It should be noted that when Doriot and Thorez were ordered to Moscow in May Thorez did go, and he returned to France fully instructed as to the future course of the P.C.F. in relation to Doriot.[20] It has become a common experience to see the Comintern expel someone and at the same time adopt the course which the expellee had advocated. However what transpired between Thorez and the Executive Committee at that time in relation to the change of tactics in France, if anything, remains a mystery which constitutes the missing link in the history of the origins of unity of action and hence of the Popular Front as well. It is submitted that in all probability, because of the above-mentioned factors and because of the chronology of events surrounding Doriot's expulsion, the decision to abandon the **front unique en bas** was made at the same time as the decision to expel Doriot, that is in May, and that the two decisions were considered by the Comintern to be inseparable.

In order to place the effect of the Doriot incident in its proper perspective it is of course necessary to bear in mind at all times the larger factors such as the effect of the rearmament of Germany upon the Soviet Union and the effect of the February émeute upon the French Communists. The significant point, however, is that the position taken by Doriot was based on a recognition of these factors whereas the **front unique en bas** tactic of the Comintern was the product of an analysis made in 1928 and never changed. The absence of any need for discussion at national conferences and the like for a party organized along the lines of the Communist party means that such an organization can change its tactics as soon as it decides upon the need for a change. Yet the Communists did not change their tactics after the accession of Hitler nor after the February émeute. They did not change them, in fact, until faced with the unavoidable choice of either doing so or losing all the strength that Doriot could lead out of the party. Thus whereas it would be an exaggeration to suggest that the dissidence of Doriot by itself led the P.C.F. onto the path of united action, the available evidence would certainly indicate that it was the dilemma posed by the position he assumed that gave the party its final impetus in that direction.

After the P.C.F. adopted the policy of unity of action with the Socialists Doriot's position lost much of its significance. He still maintained absolute control of the St. Denis section, but the Parti Populaire Francais which he attempted to create 18 months later never achieved much more than a local following.[21] However his influence upon the development of united action had not quite ended. After his expulsion he waged a steady and bitter campaign against the P.C.F. in L'EMANCIPATION.[22] Because of his years of intimate association with the hierarchy of both the national party and the Comintern he could give the sting and bite of fact to questions upon which the Socialists and others could only conjecture.[23] The principal theme of his attacks was that the change in line by the P.C.F. was merely a Comintern maneuver and although, as we have seen, the Socialist leaders were in little need of cautioning on this point, his denunciations came at a time when the most difficult problem facing the P.C.F. was to overcome Socialist suspicion on this point. He was rewarded to the extent of causing the P.C.F. infinite bother in its negotiations with the Socialists, and by forcing Thorez, Duclos and other of the leaders to expend a considerable amount of thought and effort to distinguish between what he had been expelled for and what they had done immediately after his expulsion.[24]

An epilogue was written to the story of the relations between Doriot and the P.C.F. in the course of the negotiations for organic unity between all of the proletarian groups that took place in late 1935. The P.C.F. flatly refused to permit the inclusion of the Doriot-Barbé group in the Commission on Unification. Finally, after agreement with Doriot and Barbé on the one hand and the P.C.F. on the other, the Commission held a meeting on October 28th, at which neither disputant was present and asked the St. Denis dissidents to represent themselves by someone other than either Doriot or Barbé. This proposal was accepted and Dutilleul and Marschall were appointed in their place. But the P.C.F. then announced that these two having had the same attitude as Doriot, the Communist delegation would not participate alongside of them in the Commission. Finally the Commission reconvened on November 5th and passed a resolution demanding that the St. Denis faction withdraw altogether.[25] Thus the Communists were successful in preventing Doriot and his followers from participating in the plans for a unity which they had been the first among the Communists to champion.

In this discussion of the Doriot incident I have tried to avoid the dangerous pitfall of making too much of the effect of a single factor upon the course of historical events. On the other hand the role of Doriot in shaping the policies of the Comintern in France in 1934 has been totally ignored, or, in my opinion, badly under-estimated. In the little that has been written about him and in the popular conception about him in France today Doriot is dismissed as but another ambitious and intelligent "strong man" who sought personal glorification first with the extreme Left, then independently, and finally with the extreme Right.[26] There is undoubtedly considerable truth in such an appraisal of him, but it does not go far enough. Whatever his motivations Doriot possessed both the power within the P.C.F. and the popularity with the French workers as a whole to bring tremendous pressure upon the former to abandon its increasingly unpopular tactics. To dismiss him on the grounds of his personal ambition is to ignore entirely the significance of his rupture with the P.C.F. His brief period of extreme popularity following the February riots was a function of the challenge of domestic fascism, the effect of which upon French workers whether Communist, Socialist or non-party was seriously under-estimated by the Communists leaders. Perhaps the greatest single result of the Doriot incident was its revelation to the Communists of the extent to which this domestic fascist threat, in 1934 at least, dominated the thinking of the French Left.

NOTES

1. In the 1932 legislative elections only Doriot and Clamamus of all the Communist candidates were elected on the first ballot. As the total popular vote of the P.C.F. dropped from 1,068,000 in 1928 to 796,000 in 1932 (see LE TEMPS, 15 May 1932) and all of the Communist candidates but himself lost ground, Doriot became the most powerful member of the party's parliamentary group. His great debating ability and flair for impassioned oratory retained that post for him until the time of his voluntary resignation in 1933.

2. Born of peasant parents at Bresle (l'Oise) in 1898 Doriot is reputed to have been greatly affected by hearing Jaurès speak at Greil in 1914 a few months before the latter's assassination. See the comprehensive but overly sympathetic biography of Doriot, Drieu la Rochelle, DORIOT OU LA VIE D'UN OUVRIER FRANCAIS, Paris, 1937.

3. Whatever the dialectical name for Doriot's subsequent deviation it can hardly have been called Trotskyism, yet Doriot's association with Trotsky at this time was apparently sufficient grounds for the application of that label in 1934:

   "The party lays bare the Social-democrat and Trotskyist contents of the platform openly defended by comrade Doriot to the applause of all the enemies of Communism.

   "The Party, in its vigorous fight against the Trotskyist Doriot-Barbé group, has assimilated still more completely the principles of Leninism. It understands better what Stalin said in 1924 apropos of the conceptions of the counter-revolutionary Trotsky who today is rejoined by comrade Doriot."
   C.B., 15 June 1934, p. 714.

4. According to Drieu la Rochelle, **op. cit.**, p. 27, Doriot's initial rebellion against the Comintern dated from the China experience.

5. See Walter, **op. cit.**, p. 265.

6. For instance after his strong disagreement with the decision of the Central Committee and the Executive over the change of electoral tactics in 1928, Doriot was the soul of meekness:

   "It was declared that our point of view was not correct. Although not convinced, from that moment on we considered the discussion closed and we turned to the application of the tactic decided upon.

   "Under these conditions the discussion here can have only one aim; that of convincing us."

   Speech of Doriot at the IXth Plenum, CLASSE CONTRE CLASS, **op. cit.**, p. 70.

   For a discussion of Doriot's habit of attacking and then withdrawing "his apologies scarcely less wounding than the original offense" see Dingle, RUSSIA'S WORK IN FRANCE, Robert Hale Ltd., London 1938.

7. Doriot published four brochures: LA FRANCE NE SÉRA PAS UN PAYS D'ESCLAVES, Nevers, Impr. Chassaing, 1936; LE FRONT DE LA LIBERTÉ FACE AU COMMUNISME, Lagny, Impr. Grevin et fils, 1937; LA FRANCE AVEC NOUS, Lagny, 1937; and L'EXPERIENCE SOVIETIQUE ET LE COMMUNISME FRANCAIS, Paris, 1937. These, along with his writings in L'ÉMANCIPATION and his statements at Communist meetings etc., constituted the sum of his political expression. In none of these does he attempt any exposition of a positive political doctrine other than the desire for reunification of the proletarian parties.

8. Walter, for instance, who takes the side of the P.C.F. in the Doriot dispute, asserts that he was greatly influenced and impressed by the success of Hitler's methods, and attributes most of his defiance of the Comintern to Doriot's ambition for personal power, **op. cit.**, p. 266.

9. A phenomenon which extracted a violent response from the Communist leaders. Duclos wrote:

   "Now Doriot is presented as a sort of banner by the leaders of the Parti Socialiste. They seem to think at LE POPULAIRE that the anti-Communist attacks of Doriot will stop the flow of Socialist workers toward the Communist party, toward the Comintern."

   C.B., 15 June 1934, p. 718.

10. Since Doriot's unitarian position coincided with that of the P.U.P. it was natural that he should receive the support of the latter. The Communists were forced to admit this in a resolution passed by the Central Committee in October of 1934:

    "Moreover the Bureau Politique is persuaded that the pupist workers will not approve the support accorded by Paul Louis to the scissionist Doriot ... the **front unique** is not served by favoring the disorganizing and anti-unitarian enterprises of the Doriot-Barbé group and of their Trotskyist and other allies."

    "Pour l'unite d'action", C.B., 1 October 1934, p. 1173.

11. "A single class, a single C.G.T., a single party ... unity of action is nothing. In order to be able to act it is necessary that the working class be organized into a single party."

    Doriot, L'ÉMANCIPATION, 10 September 1934.

    Compare with a statement by A. Ferry, secretary of Bergery's Jeunesses Frontistes:

    "We wish to create a revolutionary party of the French people destined, not to assure a vague control over a machine that no longer functions, but to seize power. No reform can be undertaken without that. It cannot be a question of the dictatorship of the proletariat, since that represents only a fourth of the population. If power were given to it as the Marxists wish that would be to throw the rest of the country to fascism."

    Interview in NOTRE TEMPS, 14 July 1935.

12. Doriot's position on unity was almost indistinguishable from that of the Center and left wing of the Parti Socialiste:

    "The bases of fusion? Nothing simpler; one can even take the texts of 1905 while still taking into account the Russian revolution and the war. The danger for the revolutionists of finding themselves in a single party with the reformists only exists in the diseased imagination of the Communists. Unity will resolve all the problems and bring the working class to power."

    L'ÉMANCIPATION, 15 September 1934.

    Whereas Bergery sought a "reconciliation francaise":

    "The reconciliation of the working class, the peasant class and of that majority of the bourgeoisie who have remained faithful to its traditions of work, intelligence and honesty."

    Bergery radio speech 24 April 1936, printed in LA FLECHE, 2 May 1936.

Thus, roughly speaking, Bergery took the position favoring a Popular Front as advocated by the Communists and Doriot aimed at the organic unity sought by the Socialists.

13. L'ÉMANCIPATION, 5 May 1934.

14. Attacking the retention of the **front unique en bas** tactic after the **émeute,** Doriot sent a protest memorandum to the Executive Committee of the Comintern, simultaneously distributing copies of the memorandum with the P.C.F. In this he described what had prompted the St. Denis department of the party to initiate this protest:

    "The events of February 6-12, in which (the St. Denis department) participated, showed them that the tactic of the party contained fundamental defects and that it offended the feelings of the Socialist workers as well as the unorganized workers.... They believed that the democratic regime should not become an empty word."

    Doriot, LETTRE OUVERTE À L'INTERNATIONALE, Lagny, 1934, preface, p. 2.

15. L'ÉMANCIPATION, 5 May 1934.

16. "L'International a parlé", C.B., 1 June 1934, p. 643.

17. An ultimatum was delivered by the Bureau politique in late May:

    "The Bureau politique demands that Comrade Doriot:

    (1) Approve and comply with the document of the Comintern.

    (2) Cease immediately the battle against the Central Committee in all its forms (meetings, articles, press, factional work within the party, mass and municipal organizations etc.)

    (3) Publish the document of the Executive Committee in L'ÉMANCIPATION.

    (4) Make a declaration published in L'ÉMANCIPATION and L'HUMANITÉ indicating that he accepts the order to cease all battle against the Central Committee and that under its direction he will undertake the battle against fascism and for the **front unique** of action prevented until now by his scissionist work.

    (5) Guarantee the appearance of L'ÉMANCIPATION under the control of the regional committee of Paris-Nord as is provided in the basic statutes of the party."

    "Documents du P.C.F.", C.B., 1 June 1934, p. 656.

18. In the order expelling him the Comintern revealed the extent to which he had disrupted the activities of the P.C.F.:

    "Breaking with the most elementary discipline Doriot edited and published factums hostile to the party and to the Comintern. He has transformed the Communist paper L'ÉMANCIPATION into a sheet of gossip and calumnies against the party and its militants. He has disorganized the activity of the department of St. Denis and of its cells. He has made it difficult and even impossible for the workers faithful to the Comintern to be present in the assemblies of the party and to express their attachment to Communism."

    "Documents du P.C.F.", C.B., 1 August 1934, p. 925.

19. Vielle (Gironde):

    "I saw in LE POPULAIRE of yesterday the decision of the Comintern against Doriot.

    The Comintern thus condemned the line of loyal action with the Parti Socialiste."

    COMPTE RENDU DU XXXI CONGRÈS NATIONAL, **op. cit.**, p. 269.

20. Walter, **op. cit**, p. 270.

21. The Parti Populaire Français was inaugurated June 28, 1936. Doriot described it as "the militants of St. Denis plus a few friends from outside." Doriot, LA FRANCE SÉRA AVEC NOUS, **op. cit.**, p. 5.

22. Aided by Barbé, one time treasurer of the P.C.F. who had also been expelled, Doriot published a series of articles in L'ÉMANCIPATION revealing the source of funds for the P.C.F., the extent of Moscow control, the nature of Communist tactics, etc.

23. The obvious delight of the Socialists at these attacks drew a heated response from the P.C.F.:

    "The Parti Socialiste speaks of non-aggression pacts of a loyal **front unique.** It complains of maneuvers directed against it.

    "Did LE POPULAIRE make a demonstration of loyalty in reproducing the calomnies against our party by the scissionist Doriot?"

    Thorez, "l'Organization du front unique de lutte", C.B., 1 July 1934, p. 775.

24. See Cachin and Thorez, DU FRONT UNIQUE AU FRONT POPULAIRE, pamphlet, Bureau d'éditions, Paris, 1935; and Borkenau, HISTORY OF THE COMINTERN, Faber, 1938, p. 387.

25. Report of the Socialist delegation to the Commission on Unification, RAPPORT ADMINISTRATIF AU XXXIII CONGRÈS NATIONAL, Librairie Populaire, 1936, pp. 171-181.

26. Thus implementing the Communist campaign to smear him. See Romier, "Le scissioniste Doriot contre le Communisme", C.B., 15 November 1934, p. 1338.

    Doriot, it must be admitted, subsequently invited much of the criticism against himself by the non-Communist Left. It was his political misfortune perhaps rather than his fault that through his attacks on the Comintern he gained a popularity with certain Rightist factions and was lauded in their organs (notably Henry de Kerillis' L'ECHO DE PARIS) which served as a kiss of death for him with many of those with whom he had been most popular upon splitting from the P.C.F. However, he tended toward fascist inclinations increasingly in the late thirties, and by the outbreak of war in 1939 had long since left all of his friends of the Left behind.

PART THREE

THE CRUCIAL CONGRESSES

"I firmly believe that in the case of an invasion of the national soil by an aggressor, for example by Hitler Germany, all the proletarians of this country -- and the accent of my statement, Thorez fully understood it, was upon the words, 'all the proletarians without distinction' -- will rise up with the rest of the country."
> Blum, at the Congress of Mulhouse, June, 1935.

"We have worked, according to Blum, to render the front unique inevitable, and we have, in fact, rendered it inevitable."
> Thorez, at the VIIth World Congress of the Comintern,
> July, 1935

"What is it that brought us victory before, at the time of the great battles of Boulangism and the Dreyfus affair? Indissoluble union of all the forces of the Left. If the rally which we have realized is maintained and consolidated; if the proletarians of the cities and of the country, the civil servants, the savants, artists, young and old, men and women, remain closely united ... the democracy which is said to be agonizing ... will become again the great hope of the world."
> Ferdinand Herold, speaking in the name of the Ligue des Droits
> de l'Homme at the Rassemblement Populaire, July 14, 1935.

CHAPTER TEN

MULHOUSE, JUNE 1935

In the spring of 1935 events other than the persistent Communist pressure were forcing the Socialists to abandon their desire for proletarian unity and accept the Popular Front instead. The domestic policy of the Socialists, including that part of it concerned with the defense against internal fascism, was being molded to a growing extent by the ominous developments in international affairs, and these in turn necessitated consideration of the factors leading to a favorable balance of power in Europe more than those involved in the class struggle within France. German rearmament had become the dominant external influence upon the foreign policies of both France and the Soviet Union, and in its attempts to counter this threat the French government had forsaken the dubious safeguards of collective security for its pre-war faith in power and alliances as the best means of national security. As an answer to Hitler's violation of the Versailles Treaty (and also to the loss of the Saar) French policy was to maintain friendly relations with Italy, raise the strength of its own military forces, and engage in alliances with those nations, such as the Soviet Union, which were in a position to be of some military value against the IIIrd Reich. The first meant turning its back upon Abyssinia, the second increasing military expenditures and raising the term of conscription, and the third joining in common cause with bolshevism if and when such an agreement could be reached. By June of 1935 all three of these had been accomplished. The Rome accords were signed in March and the Stresa Pact in April; rearmament, which can be said to have dated from Doumergue's premiership, was implemented by the institution of the much contested **service de deux ans**;[1] and France and Russia had come to terms.

In the face of this growing international tension the Socialist plea for the retention of the class struggle, for the pacifism consistent with Socialist traditions, had the same lack of conviction for Socialist and non-Socialist alike that it had had twenty years earlier. Moreover the Socialists were now raising this cry alone, for the P.C.F. no longer favored anti-militarism or national insurrection in case of war. After May the Communists deserted Blum in his fight against the two year conscription. Also even Auriol, Blum and Paul Faure found it difficult to escape the logic of the argument that the external threat of fascism was, in 1935, at least as great a danger as domestic fascism, and it was impossible to deny that all of the military and diplomatic policies of the government were directed at protecting France from Hitler.

After the signing of the Franco-Soviet Pact there was no confusion or complication whatsoever in the attitude of the French Communists. The defense of the Soviet Union against the German threat had become their sole guiding principle.[2] Thus the Popular Front, to the great extent that it was a Communist device at this stage, was also directed at this objective. Its program now included, as one of its unexpressed but most important clauses, the creation of a militarily powerful France.[3] Radical and Communist found considerable agreement on this, and as Blum sought to invoke the principles of Jaurès he found himself and his party without support. In view of developments abroad and the about face of the Communists in France, the reaffirmation of exclusively proletarian and revolutionary doctrines which the Socialists had made at Toulouse a year before was becoming increasingly difficult to maintain. Thus in the spring of 1935 the Parti Socialiste was engaged in a rearguard action to defend its pacifist traditions, an action against which all elements both to the Right and Left of the party were now united, and an action for which a large number of its own leaders were becoming increasingly unenthusiastic.

Despite the tremendous if not decisive influence of external events upon the relationships of the parties of the Left, however, the negotiations between the P.C.F. and the Parti Socialiste concerning the latter's adherence to the Popular Front still were carried on almost exclusively in terms of domestic issues and the internal battle against fascism. The relative merits of organic unity of the proletariat and a Popular Front of all anti-fascist forces were argued in terms of the agreement best suited to the survival of the proletariat in the face of the Rightist onslaught. The question of which arrangement would affect most favorably the ability and determination of France to resist German aggression, although it became uppermost in Communist aims after the Franco-Soviet Pact and also was an important consideration of the Socialist leaders, was never an explicit part of the negotiations.

It had become evident shortly after the initial Communist proposals for the Popular Front, that the Parti Socialiste was less interested in such a front than in the extension of the bonds of unity of action to organic unity of the proletariat parties.[4] The desire for unification of the proletariat combined both the traditional position of the Socialists and that which they had reaffirmed at Toulouse as a corollary to turning away from the Radicals and other middle class allies. On the other hand the combined tactic of a united front with the Socialists and an anti-fascist Popular Front with the rest of the forces of the Left was infinitely better suited to the desires of the Communists. It gave them a maximum of positive influence and security with a minimum of loss of independence of action. As the role of the P.C.F. tended to become increasingly that of assuring a French ally for the Soviet Union, the importance to it of the Popular Front rather than organic unity of the two parties grew accordingly. For the Popular Front, unlike organic unity, held substantial promise of putting a sympathetic government in power, a government in which the Communists would not participate but one which could be depended upon to carry out the policies of the P.C.F. in foreign relations at least.

In the struggle over the question of whether or not organic unity was preferable to the Popular Front, the Pupists sided with the Parti-Socialiste. The use of their leaders, Paul Louis and Juncker, as a convenient third party for the initiation of unity negotiations was of considerable value to the Socialists. Throughout the period from the time of Thorez' initiation of the Popular Front until the congress of the Parti Socialiste at Mulhouse, the Socialists and the P.U.P., both of whom had rejected collaboration with nonproletarians, worked together for the extension of the united front to organic unity.[5]

Answering a letter from the Bureau Politique of the P.C.F. on November 25th, 1934, Blum declared, with the approval of the C.A.P., that the Pact of Unity of 1905 should be used as a starting point for consideration of the bases of organic unity. Blum's letter constituted an exhaustive recounting of the differences in approach to the question of unity that existed between the two parties, the exigencies of Socialist tradition concerning the question of unity, and all the arguments in favor of the type of proletarian unity that had been created at Amsterdam thirty years before.[6] On the 10th of December in a letter to the Parti Socialiste asking for a list of immediate claims and grievances to be included in a program of joint action, the Bureau Politique appended a rejection of the principles of the 1905 Pact:

> Realizing the lesson of events, we think that organic unity of the working class must be undertaken under conditions that will give the maximum of guarantees concerning the accomplishment of the historic mission of the proletariat.
>
> We cannot forget that the Charter of 1905 ended in tragedy in the month of August 1914. Furthermore we cannot forget that the Revolution of October 1917 enriched the experience of the working class with an example of tremendous importance. The proletariat has the duty of realizing the principles and methods which made the force and the grandeur of the party, under the guidance of which the Russian proletariat achieved victory, and which have served as the bases for the foundation of the Comintern.
>
> The events of the past twenty years and in particular the experience of the Russian Revolution clearly demonstrate that the program of the Comintern is that which can serve as the basis for a single party of the proletariat capable of leading the exploited classes to victory.[7]

Severac commented to the C.A.P. that the fundamental divergence on the question of the basis of unity as indicated by this letter boded ill for the future of the unity negotiations. Moreover despite Communist lip-service to the cause of organic unity, there was a growing conviction among the leaders of the Parti Socialiste that the P.C.F. had no intention of carrying unity of action to the point of organic unity.[8] If this were so, and if all that the P.C.F. sought was a limited and temporary alliance hardly dissimilar to that which it was now seeking with the Radicals, there was indeed a conflict of views between the parties on this question. However, determined to explore any possibility for such unity, the Socialists exhibited an eagerness in these negotiations comparable to that which the Communists had shown in July when the question was unity of action. On the 21st the C.A.P. replied:

> We are not ignorant of the difficulties; but we continue to believe that they are not insurmountable and that there is no more urgent problem than that of unity.
>
> We continue to believe also that there is no better basis for discussion of organic unity than this unity pact of 1905 which, until 1920, had been our common charter.
>
> It contains nothing that a Socialist or Communist cannot accept, nothing he cannot repudiate without ceasing to be either a Socialist or Communist.

It appears to us moreover that the principles which you have demanded in your letter in no way contradict those proclaimed in the 1905 Pact.[9]

The Socialists were unwilling that the P.C.F. should evade discussion of organic unity on the pretext that no common ground for such discussion could be found, and they urged that meetings be arranged in any case to explore the possibilities of such a common ground. But the Bureau Politique, by constantly repeating its unacceptable counter-proposals, succeeded in postponing any such meetings in late 1934 or early 1935.[10]

When the Conseil National of the Parti Socialiste convened on March 3rd, 1935, it received another letter from the Bureau Politique complaining bitterly that the unity of action undertaken in July was not being carried out in all places, notably at St. Denis. Again the P.C.F. made what was apparently an affirmation of its desire for eventual organic unity:

> The common battle against fascism and the capitalist regime must end in the unification of the working class. That is the goal pursued unswervingly by the Communist party since the French workers movement found itself divided by the refusal of the minority to bow before the decisions freely taken at the Congress of Tours in 1920.
>
> The moment has come to go further on the path of unity of action.[11]

But the only basis upon which the P.C.F. would consider such unity was still the bolshevik program, and the emphasis again was upon broadening the scope of unity of action rather than extending unity of action to organic unity. In addition the goals which the P.C.F. proposed in this letter, (1) the organization of immediate action, (2) the "study of conditions" for the unification of the entire working class, (3) a campaign for the unity of the international working class movements, also neatly skirted the question of an immediate plan for organic unity.

After a vigorous debate within the Conseil National the C.A.P. informed the Bureau Politique that although many deceptions had been noticed by the federations of the Parti Socialiste in the manner in which the Communists applied the principles of unity of action, the C.A.P. was agreed that the advantages of continuation of unity of action outweighed the disadvantages. It objected vehemently however to some of the articles in the CAHIERS DU BOLCHEVISME and the INTERNATIONAL COMMUNISTE that had been written since the Communist undertaking to cease criticism of the Parti Socialiste.[12]

At this meeting a resolution, proposed by Lebas and voted unanimously, outlined the Socialist approach to the method of defending against fascism:

> The Conseil National recognizes that the political circumstances which justified the unity of action with the P.C.F. still exist, and as a result it must continue.
>
> It can only regret that efforts made by its delegates for the elaboration of a common program of immediate claims has foundered.
>
> That check, of which it must take account, fixes the limitations of common action already traced by the pact.
>
> However the party will make every effort to extend unity of action and give it a character of claims common to the two working parties.
>
> The Conseil National ... is persuaded that the surest means of succeeding (in checking fascism) is to do everything to arrive at organic unity.
>
> Without disregarding the difficulties which the Parti Socialiste will have to surmount on the route leading to it, the Conseil National invites all those who wish to engage themselves with it and charges the C.A.P. to constitute a special Commission whose mandate will be to invite the workers parties, the P.C.F. and the P.U.P., to work with the Parti Socialiste in the constitution of a single party of workers predicated on the following bases:
>
> (1) Organization of the proletariat in a class party for the conquest of power and the socialization of the means of production and exchange, that is to say, the transformation of the capitalist society into a collectivist or Communist society.
>
> (2) Action of the party determined by the party itself gathered in national assemblies, after consultation with its local or departmental groups.[13]

This resolution came as the culmination of a long series of communications between the parties as to the course of development of the united front. The wide disparity between their respective attitudes reflected the fundamental difference in their ultimate aims. The P.C.F. wanted to rally everyone around the questions of immediate claims. It cared little whether these claims were completely consistent with the interests of the proletariat at all times, so long as they served as an effective rallying point for as broad as possible a segment of the anti-fascist forces.[14] The Socialists on the other hand were seeking a long range or permanent program for unity of action, or more, between the parties, based solely on the class aspects of Socialist and, they believed, Communist doctrines.

On the 13th of March Blum wrote to the Central Committee of the P.C.F., declaring the intention of the Parti Socialiste to go further in unity of action. The following day the C.A.P. issued invitations to the P.C.F. and the P.U.P. asking them to designate a delegation to a Commission on Unification. The P.U.P. accepted immediately.[15] The P.C.F. however delayed its response, and on March 23rd sent a counter-proposal including a request that the Parti Socialiste wage a joint campaign with it against the two year conscription, for the defense of the native populations of North Africa, and against the high cost of living. Its only reference to the problem of organic unity was that the two parties, Communist and Socialist, discuss it alone, i.e. not including the P.U.P.[16]

The C.A.P. chose to regard this reply as containing nothing constituting a Communist refusal to participate in a meeting to discuss unification and charged Severac to repeat the invitation.[17] The P.C.F. answered on the 4th of April, its response again containing counter-proposals and again an equivocal reply to the invitation. It complained that it had expected that the unification session would discuss international accord, etc., and repeated its suggestion that the two major parties handle the question of unity alone.[18]

The first meeting of the Unification Commission was held on April 11th. The P.C.F. didn't attend. In its absence the P.U.P. and Socialist delegations resolved:

> The delegates present have declared unanimously that no task is more urgent than the realization of the unity of the proletariat on the political plane.
>
> They undertake no prepare in all loyalty that reunification and to spare no effort that it be achieved quickly.[19]

At the second meeting, on the 18th, the P.C.F. and also some independent Socialists and Communists took part. The meeting produced nothing more than a decision to establish a subcommittee to study the problem. Thus the matter ended. Communist resistance had again been successful in thwarting positive steps toward organic unity.

Against this background of the breakdown of negotiations for organic unity and the increasingly critical international situation the XXXIInd National Congress of the Parti Socialiste opened at the Salle des Fêtes of the Fédération of the Haut-Rhin, Mulhouse, on June 9th. At this congress the I.O.S. was represented by de Brouckère and Adler. Also present were representatives of the Spanish Socialist party, the Parti Ouvrier Belge, and the Social-democratic parties of Czecho-slovakia and Hungary. Several questions of the utmost importance to Socialists throughout Europe lay before this congress.[20]

Each of these questions was implicit rather than expressed; the decisions facing the French Socialists dealt ostensibly with the lesser sphere of immediate domestic policy. Each question, also implicitly, was dominated to a considerable extent by international developments. The unexpressed influence of the worsening international situation when translated into immediate issues presented three major problems for the Socialists.

First, did the threat of a rearming and aggressive Germany require that French and other Socialists forego their pacifist traditions and support all measures leading to national security?

Secondly, faced with the change in the Comintern position on national defense, should the Socialists accept the Popular Front as the only available means of combatting both internal and foreign fascism, in place of the apparently unattainable organic unity of the proletarian parties?

Finally, should the Socialists abandon the revolutionary and non-participatory approach to the problems of securing power and accept a coalition with Republican and Communist which would place them in a position to secure an immediate share of power, albeit at the price of doctrinal purity?

Ostensibly the party was faced at Mulhouse with questions of an internal nature; domestic fascism and the economic crisis. The danger of fascism within France in June of 1935 was not a very serious one despite the continued activities of the various leagues, but the myth value of such a danger lingered on. At Mulhouse this myth persisted, and it established, to a larger degree, the nature of the issues that were argued. But many of the same men who, in face of the much more convincing fascist threat in the spring of 1934, had demanded that the party assert its proletarian character in order to combat internal fascism, now saw that the real danger lay elsewhere.

The Rapport Moral referred only to the internal question:

> Since our last National Congress an event of considerable importance to the life of our groups and the general activity of our party has been produced from the abrupt change of attitude of the P.C.F.
>
> The C.A.P. nominated at Toulouse, from its first meeting on, has been approached with proposals for common action by the Communist party.
>
> The latter has tried to give the false impression ... that our party, after long years of resistance and refusal, has finally ceded to Communist pressure and given a belated adherence to the front unique.
>
> The truth is quite different and there is not a militant who could not bear witness to it.
>
> If the Socialists have very legitimately refused common action, it is because the Communist party has never hidden its desire to 'pluck the tailfeathers' and remove the kernel from our organization; that its campaigns of disparagement and insults and the maintenance of its candidates on the second ballot have made any rapprochement impossible until now.
>
> By modifying its tactic in regard to our party (i.e. by suspending criticism), the P.C.F. accepted the conditions which we have demanded for a long time.
>
> The result is known. A pact of unity was signed. The Parti Socialiste has applied it loyally.[21]

Immediately following the reading of the Rapport Moral the nature of the internal division in the party became apparent. The left wing led by Zyromski and Pivert demanded that the Socialists continue to press for organic unity. This faction had won its battle at Toulouse in 1934 to the extent of seeing the party adopt a revolutionary Socialist position in regard to the crisis. It considered organic unity to be the only consistent means of extending unity of action. The logic of this position suffered somewhat from the fact that the principal other proletarian party, the P.C.F., now rejected organic unity in favor of the Popular Front. Nevertheless Zyromski and Pivert still pressed for it as the only truly Socialist course of action.[22] They castigated severely the inactivity of the C.A.P. which had been charged at Toulouse with the mission of carrying out a revolutionary policy, and, they alleged, had failed in this mission through timidity and negligence, if not worse. Zyromski called for the rejection of the Rapport Moral as not being strong enough, as failing to exhort the party sufficiently to take the initiative in unity of action:

> I have reread the brochure of Severac on unity of action and organic unity (the Administrative report of the C.A.P.) and I say again, No Severac we are not in agreement; because you with a sort of complaisance and perhaps even with a sort of nostalgia, you envisage a unity of action which would be watered down, which would be narrowed, and which would be limited to the organization in common of occasional manifestations. That is a beginning; but for that enlargement of unity of action, that junction of the working forces of this country for a common and positive action which must lead inevitably to organic unity one senses your apprehension and scorn.... That we should be vigilant, that we must protect the framework and the integrity of our party, that we must denounce a certain number of maneuvers of which I am aware, I agree with you. But, you see, and this is the basic reason of our disagreement ... you have not sensed in this movement both its necessity and its power, and worry, distrust and uneasiness have predominated with you over initiative, spirit and audacity.[23]

The first step in the program of revolutionary defense against the fascists, they argued, was a remodelling of the defensive structure of the party along more vigorous and active lines. It was intolerable that the proletariat offer no effective resistance to the raids of the Croix de Feu and other Rightist para-military organizations upon their headquarters. Label an active defense putchism, insurrectionism, bolshevism or blanquism, declared Zyromski, nevertheless it was this type of action that was in the "true spirit of revolutionary Socialism and the most authentic Marxism".[24]

The Zyromski-Pivert proposals for self-defense were rejected by the majority of the party.[25] But the defeat of the left wing was sealed by Paul Faure's defense of the Rapport Moral, and in making this defense he introduced indirectly the suggestion that the Popular Front method was the one that should be followed by the Socialists.

First there must be no armed or violent action by the Socialists:

> Speaking in my own name I repeat to you that I will never accept for my part, the organization of an armed retort, of going like burglars to the headquarters of the Croix de Feu and of using their methods, because on the day we do that our party is lost.

Secondly in defending against criticism that he had not been sufficiently active against the fascists he stated:

> In the face of the fascist insurrection the center of resistance, the rallying point, the sole force capable of saving democracy, the republic and the proletariat are the large municipalities which constitute it. Around these must be formed provisionary governments joining the Socialists, Communists, Republicans, all those who want to break fascism.[26]

In effect this suggestion was a capitulation to the point of view urged by the Comintern, an acceptance of the Popular Front in place of relying on the combined strength of the purely proletarian forces.

Each of the opposing factions within the party found itself placed in a peculiar position by the turn of events. Zyromski and Pivert, as left wing Socialists, were committed to that policy most closely related to the revolutionary aspects of Socialism. This meant the rejection of any attempts to modify party policy in order to attract the support of the more moderate parties. It also meant a strict adherence to social pacifism, the rejection of war whatever the circumstances. As a result it had been they, through the years, who had sought closer ties with the P.C.F. and who now were pressing hardest for organic unity of the proletariat. But these positions were no longer compatible with one another now that the line of the P.C.F. had shifted so drastically. The Communists now professed to stand for a brand of social and political reform so watered down that even the Radicals could accept its overall program. Furthermore since the signing of the Franco-Soviet pact the P.C.F. was no longer opposed to national defene and militarism, quite the contrary. Thus Zyromski and Pivert, in their fight for organic unity in order to combat war and in order to create a powerful and unified revolutionary party, were in fact seeking support from an ally that had ceased to exist. Supported on the question of absolute pacifism only by the Trotskyists (led by Molinier) this faction was reduced to an almost single-handed crusade to retain the principles of revolutionary Socialism in regard to the growing international crisis.[27]

Defeated in their arguments for improved means of internal self-defense they turned to a vehement denunciation of war whatever the cause. Each delivered a pronouncement against the Rome accords. Pivert added a final plea for the only course that lay open to this faction in view of the Communist change:

> Organic unity despite the words of Stalin! Unity and the battle against war, at any price, by insurrection. The government of the Soviets sees the situation from its point of view. We have the duty of seeing it from our own, and we don't accept the confusion of the interests of the international proletariat with a provisional system of alliances which are, in any case, extremely fragile.... Unify yourselves, create a great revolutionary party and at the interior of your united organizations fight against war by all means, and since we must consider Soviet Russia as a target for international capitalism, defend Soviet Russia! But defend it not by letting ourselves be enlisted by our General Staff in order to go to fight the German proletariat; defend it by the only means which remains to us, by the conquest of power in our country and by the international revolution.[28]

However, the attitude of the rest of the party was steadily and surely tending toward the position now advocated by the Communists -- the Popular Front and all of its implications in domestic and foreign policy. Blum revealed his resignation to the demands of national security by defending the parliamentary support given by the Socialists to the Rome accords, although he qualified it with the statement that had the Italian Socialist leader Nenni requested otherwise it would not have been given.[29] As to the question of the party's attitude toward war, Blum's contribution must have recalled the manner in which the party had pulled away from Jaurès' position in 1914:

> But this attitude of prevention, of absolute desperate prevention against war, as I said one day speaking with Jaurès, is not enough. It doesn't suffice when war is a fact. We have seen it; all parties of the International have seen it, in 1914. And we notice now that it doesn't suffice when war, without being a fact, nevertheless assumes the aspect of something approaching, whose menace seems to weigh heavily, to cast a shadow, over the world; at

these moments it no longer suffices to say 'everything to prevent war'. We are obliged to say something more and that is what has happened in recent times, where we now find ourselves in the presence of the problem posed by the rearmament of Hitler, and by the undeniably serious character of the menace which this rearmament causes to weigh upon France and upon Europe.[30]

In addition Blum supported the Franco-Soviet pact,[31] and the conclusions which he drew from it were very similar to those of the P.C.F.:

I explain that by saying that in the state of facts as it exists at present, even before the assistance pact and the Stalin communiqué' -- it was impossible to conceive otherwise than that the defeat of France by Hitler would release him for Soviet Russia. And that, as a result, there would be no difference between the attitudes of Socialist and Communist workers.[32]

Blum held not only that the new Communist position created a greater identity of interests between Communist and Socialist, but also that there had been developments within the Radical party which made the Communist project for a broad front which would include the Radicals, no longer intolerable to the Parti Socialiste. Like the turnabout on the question of national defense this position was the utter rejection of Toulouse, and Blum had to proceed carefully indeed in his explanation of the difference between the Radical party of June 1935 and that of May 1934. He pointed to the 75 or 80 Radical deputies who had voted against the full powers demanded by Flandin and Bouisson and a majority of whom abstained in the vote of full powers to Laval. In their attitude, he said, there was something new to be noticed. It was not merely that they sought a union of the Left and a cartel government, that was neither new nor peculiar to them. It was rather that after three years of deception and disillusionment they seemed to understand why the Socialists and Radicals had never until now been able to reach an understanding. He cited an article by Daladier on the true meaning of the budgetary deficit and a statement by Jean Zay at a meeting of the Delegations des Gauches, as evidences that for the first time certain elements within the Radical party understood the divergences between Socialist and Radical over the methods of relieving the crisis.

The tendency of a considerable faction of the Radicals to adopt a firmer attitude toward the National Union government, and the success of the meetings of the Delegations des Gauches, in the convocation of which the Socialists had played a nominal role but the P.C.F. had provided the real initiative, seemed to have done much to swing Blum more or less wholeheartedly, by the time of the Mulhouse Congress, over to the Popular Front as envisaged by the Communists. Blum gave full credit to the Communist initiative:

> ... in this initiative they have played a still greater role than ourselves! In the meetings of the delegates of the Left no one has pressed more ardently for the constitution of a government in which the Radical party would take the initiative and the responsibility than they ... [33]

But the creation of a Popular Front for defense against fascism and the establishment of a program for a Popular Front government were two entirely different things for many of the leaders of the party. Whereas several of the moderate leaders such as Severac, and even Paul Faure, were willing to accept the defensive Popular Front in place of organic unity, about which they were decidedly unenthusiastic, they were still wary of a government comprised only of Socialists and Radicals from which the Communists would hold themselves aloof in a position to attack policies and perhaps to monopolize the leadership of proletarian interests. Thus Severac interrupted Blum's speech with a reminder that the Communists would not participate in this government they were so anxious to see formed. Blum answered this with a further eulogy of the good faith of the Communists:

> I am going to say that, Severac. Moreover Thorez said it himself in the Chamber in addressing Herriot on the day when Flandin was overthrown. He repeated it in all our meetings, where the forcefulness, the clarity and the energy of his words made a great impression on Radicals of all nuances.[34]

Blum interpreted the Communist position on participation as envisaging that neither the Socialists nor the Communists should take part in the projected government. Not only had they not pressed the Socialists to decide to participate, but in all the private conversations between Blum and Thorez, the latter had expressed his hope that they would not do so. A difficulty arose, however, from the fact that the Communists in their dealings with the Radicals, had made it difficult for the Socialists not to participate. When the P.C.F. urged the Radicals to take power and promised that they would support all the "useful measures" that the latter proposed, and that as a result, with Communist and Socialist backing, they would constitute the most powerful government France had ever known, the Radicals replied: "yes, but will the Socialists come with us?"[35] Blum concluded his analysis with the statement:

> The Communists didn't wish our participation but, less accustomed to these debates than ourselves, taking part in them for the first time ... they pressed for a solution which, to the Radical way of thinking, necessarily implied Socialist participation.[36]

But for all of Blum's arguments in favor of the Popular Front he made one qualification at the end of his speech which, since it can hardly be ascribed to naivete or a belief in the possibility of organic unity as well as the Popular Front, must have been an attempt to appease certain of the uneasy elements in the party:

> I have always feared one thing about the Popular Front; that it might become, finally, a means of avoiding organic unity. I only want the Popular Front with the organic unity of the two workers parties (very strong applause) as a core, a pillar, a center.[37]

By taking this position which called for both the Popular Front and organic unity instead of a choice between the two, Blum solved the problem of how to lead the party away from its resolutions for proletarian unity, made at Toulouse, to the immediate initiation of the Popular Front. For the question now became merely which was to be applied first, and in view of the attitude of the P.C.F. there could be but one answer to that.

Thus when the congress passed to the discussion of "the Battle for Power and Against the Crisis", the debates inevitably narrowed to the question of whether the party would, as its next immediate step, accept the way of the Popular Front or renounce it in favor of a revolutionary approach to the seizure of power. Severac opened the debate with the proposition that the taking of power was a fundamental tenet of the Parti Socialiste, but, he added, the means of defeating fascism and arriving at power was not by arms but by mass action, by broadening the mass base of the party. Zyromski raged against this, but again he was virtually alone. Zyromski was offering illegal revolutionary action as a means to power at a time when the Socialists were being offered a much more plausible and less painful means by the Popular Front.[38] Despite the fact that he could cite the resolutions reached at Toulouse to support him in his plea for the retention of the revolutionary characteristics of party policy, he could make no appreciable impression upon the congress. Secondly his assertion that substantial progress was being made toward organic unity, that the search for the necessary points of juncture between Soviet Communism and Social-democracy was bearing fruit, and that good faith, tenacity and "the desire for unity with a rage" were all that were necessary to its achievement, was not very convincing in view of the delaying tactics of the P.C.F.[39]

There were other voices in the party advocating organic unity, but unlike Zyromski most of these made the exceedingly tenuous identification of organic unity with the Popular Front against fascism. Vieux (Loire), among others, apparently failed to see the clear distinction which the Communists had drawn between the Popular Front (combined with the united front and the question of organic unity. He marked the broad limits which the P.C.F. had laid down for the anti-fascist front:

> The Communists have gone further than ourselves. They had advocated, ever since they took the initiative for a delegation of the Left, going as far as Bonnevay in order to fight against fascism and disarm it.

But he failed to recognize the obstacles which they had placed in the path of organic unity:

> And are we ready, comrades, to take power? The taking of power is premature if we envisage it alone. We must first ... realize organic unity. Under the circumstances it can be realized rapidly. Three years ago if one had spoken of unity of action with the Communists we would have laughed. Now today not only do we hold meetings and manifestations with the Communists but from all evidences we are approaching organic unity. Once unity is realized the conquest will be a question of days.[40]

However for each delegate who retained the plea for organic unity there were several who, in one form or another, saw the advantages of the Popular Front. Jules Moch demanded the streamlining of party organization so that the party could respond more quickly to the requirements of cooperative action. Dupont argued that the party must beware of alienating the small landowners above all, for it was this group who, in Germany, regarded Hitler as a barrier between themselves and the Socialists who were going to deprive them of their property. If the Parti Socialiste could not join with them it must at least prevent their going over to fascism. Even the planists, notably Maurice Paz and Briche (Jura), found they could reiterate the demand for more attention to the plan of the C.G.T. without incurring the denunciation of planism that had been a feature of the Toulouse congress.[41]

Of the leaders of the party it was Vincent Auriol who presented the most direct plea for the Popular Front method. He disagreed with the advocacy of absolutes in the question of the taking of power by the Socialists. The time was not ripe for assumption of power by the Socialists alone. It was a delusion to believe that they should be satisfied with nothing less than total power and that while awaiting this they should be content with "reforms to palliate the present evils". The crises, economic and political, demanded that the party act, and there was only one way in which it could act effectively.

> Therefore we must mobilize all of the popular masses who suffer from the crisis and who are at the same time attached to liberty; the peasants, townsmen, intellectuals, all the parties, all workers' organizations, all conscripts, all veterans. It is that mobilization which responds to the spirit of the masses.

Around whom should they mobilize?

> Around the great political and economic organizations of the working class, the C.G.T., C.G.T.U., the P.C.F., the Parti Socialiste. But without excluding anyone! Marching with all those who wish combat, accepting all the anti-fascist organizations, even those young Radicals who are tired of the inertia and the defection of their chiefs and who, in the countryside -- for that also counts -- comprise the peasant masses and the middle classes, for in reality the parliamentary division of the Radical party is but the reflection of the parliamentary situation of the country; those who are with us on the second ballot are with us in parliament; those who are against us in parliament are with the National Union throughout the country.[42]

It was Auriol who set the pattern for the establishment of the Popular Front at this time as a necessary immediate step and one having priority over organic unity, which was a long range development that could not be rushed:

> 'But', they tell me, 'first we must realize organic unity'. But if that is really one of the conditions of success, believe me such organic unity will be facilitated by the movement itself,

it will be forged by common action; even if it does depend upon the will of Moscow, the Russian leaders themselves will be imprssed by that force which united itself spontaneously in the face of the danger which menaces Moscow itself, all the forces of labor and of peace.[43]

It should be noted that Auriol, despite his immense prestige within the party, had traditionally represented a position noticeably more conservative than that of Blum, and under other circumstances, when the consensus of party opinion (and Blum's opinion) was oriented more toward the revolutionary aspects of Socialism, had not always been able to rally substantial support. This had been demonstrated at Toulouse. But at Mulhouse his position was fully in harmony with the temper of the party and it was apparently his leadership, even more than Blum's, that crystallized this sentiment in the direction of the Popular Front.

The position of Lebas, who had submitted the motion that was ultimately to be adopted by the congress, was substantially that of Auriol. Fascism would find the Socialists and all the workers of France in its path. February 12th had demonstrated that beyond question. Despite earlier disagreements there was no lack of unity of action. It was the masses themselves who had risen in the defense against fascism, and it was these masses, "Socialist and Republican", that still provided the effective answer to the fascist threat.[44] Zyromski launched a final attack arguing that if the masses were to provide a barrier to fascism and also to assume power they must be prepared for the insurrection, that is to say armed. Lebas countered this with the assertion that it wasn't the policy of Socialism to arm the proletarian at least until after power had been attained by mass action.

Argument about the ways and means of assuming power continued. The party would not accept the Van Zeeland type of coalition. It wouldn't revolt; it wouldn't arm. It would work for unity in the antifascist struggle and rely on proletarian pressure without armed insurrection. The left wing accused Lebas, Severac and Paul Faure of immobilism, of the timidity of a "chien crêvé". The latter retorted:

> General armament of the people? If it is for tomorrow when we have power, in order to assure the defense of this country, we must without doubt find something other than that. If it is for the immediate conquest of power I believe that it is simply a formula of the congress, nothing more. In reality tell me

> seriously what progress you will make in the general armament of the proletariat that you advocate, from the revolutionary point of view. Here you express your formula, but elsewhere when you buy a machine gun the fascists will buy four! When you have an airplane the fascists will have 15 of them, because you possess neither the material means nor the legal conditions to organize that propaganda .... There is the great illusion.[45]

Universal suffrage, Paul Faure argued, is the means to power. No one says that it is the only means, but it exists and should be taken advantage of:

> Universal suffrage? But then tell me: at Marseilles, at Mulhouse, at Lille, at Roubaix -- I should have to name hundreds -- local political power has been won. Why do you wish to reject the hypothesis when it is generalised for the whole country?[46]

When the time for a vote came the congress charged a commission from the C.A.P. to study further the plans for unification.[47] But the real struggle centered about "the battle for power and against the crisis". Five motions were submitted. Reynard (extreme left wing) moved that a delegation be sent to the IIIrd International to discuss unity and that the party delegates to the IInd International be authorized to charge it to do the same; that there be no alliance with the bourgeois parties whatever the pretext, even for the defense of the U.S.S.R.; and that there be a preparation for the insurrectional general strike, the armament of the proletariat, and a campaign for anti-militarism by all means.[48] The Trotskyist Molinier demanded colonial insurrection (over the protest of the colonial delegates themselves), the creation of groups of self-defense to act as a proletarian militia, and that the party return to the line of Leninism and bolshevism. There could be no rapport with the Radicals:

> The committee of unity of anti-fascist action contains leading members of the Radical party. And yet at the same time this same Radical party is in power and imprisons those who fight against war as soldiers, René Gerin and others! Let us therefore comprehend something of this anti-fascist battle! We also demand 'Rupture with the Radical party'.[49]

The motion of Auriol, Paz and Moch was withdrawn in favor of a separate motion for immediate action, to be submitted later by Auriol. The fourth motion, that of Zyromski and the faction of the **Bataille Socialiste**, called for the party to adhere to its revolutionary tradition. Finally came the motion of Lebas. It too called for the retention of the principles of revolutionary (and reformist) action. But it deemed "a **coup de force** prepared secretly and undertaken by assorted combat formations" to be "puerile and perilous" for the party. It was necessary to employ the multiple forms of direct action of the working class on the economic terrain. It asserted that in the battle against fascism the agreements reached between the Socialists and the P.C.F. had had the happiest results. They must be maintained and extended. In contrast to Zyromski's call for no participation and no coalition governments, it moved to incorporate the decision of the C.A.P. in November 1934 to the effect that no limitations would be placed in advance to the support the party would give, in view of the crisis and the fascist menace.

Lebas' motion was voted by 2,025 votes to 777 for Zyromski's, with that of Molinier getting 105 and that of Reynard 83.[50] However this motion which had consumed most of the time of the congress did not have the importance upon succeeding affairs that Auriol's uncontested motion did. When the question of the method that would be used by the party to achieve power had been settled in favor of the Lebas motion, Auriol submitted a motion calling for immediate action, the expansion of the regional organizations of the Popular Front, and joint anti-fascist action in all Socialist departments and municipalities. With the exception of the abstention of two delegations (those of the Rhône and the Action Socialiste), this was adopted unanimously. Thus the Parti Socialiste committed itself to the Popular Front almost casually, while contesting bitterly the question of the means of taking power, an issue that was no longer pertinent had the delegates then realized the full significance of the Popular Front.[51]

All of the party leaders with the exception of the two from the Fédération de la Seine had advocated a course of action that would make the party's adherence to the Popular Front inevitable. The spirit of the resolutions taken a year before at Toulouse had been reversed. Stress was no longer laid upon the pure proletarian policy of the party, but rather upon the use of all means "without rejecting anyone" to combat fascism. In addition a closer coordination with the P.C.F. was demanded, not because the P.C.F. stood for an extreme degree of revolutionary Socialism, for it no longer did, but merely as one important means of extending the anti-fascist front. With this attitude it was inevitable that the party withdraw from its earlier repudiation of the Radicals and join in a Popular Front which included all anti-fascist forces. The P.C.F., by taking this line itself, had given the Parti Socialiste the choice of following or else standing alone. Zyromski and Pivert preferred that it stand alone rather than compromise with the Radicals, but everyone else of importance within the party was in favor of accepting the broad anti-fascist front proposed by the Communists, some because they saw in this the only means by which any effective unity of action with the Communists could be attained, others for the directly opposite reason that they wished a rapport with the Radicals in spite of the fact that the Communists had taken the leadership in this direction. All were quite evidently influenced by the growing need for a united Left that could make its strength felt immediately upon the course of French foreign policy.

The decisions at Mulhouse virtually obliterated the effects of the Toulouse congress, and the attitude of the Parti Socialiste was more or less that which it had been before February 6th in regard to the Radicals. From Mulhouse on it was evident that support of the Popular Front would have priority over the attempt at organic unity in the Parti Socialiste as well as in the P.C.F.

The congress closed on June 12th. On the 15th the Central Committee of the P.C.F. sent the following letter to the C.A.P.:

> Dear Comrades,
> It is with great joy that we learn of the Vincent Auriol resolution, voted by a quasi-majority, Trotskyists excepted, by your Congress of Mulhouse.
> ... We find there (i.e. in the Auriol resolution) the idea which guided our Communist party when, November 24th 1934, we proposed to your National Council the formation of a **Popular Front of work, peace and liberty.**
> ... With a view to responding to the men of February 6th, we propose that there be a joint intervention of the Socialist parliamentary group and the Communist faction, along with the Radical group and other groups of the left, to send a delegation to the president of the Council with the demand:
> (1) That measures be taken against the agitations of Colonel de la Rocque, chief of the Croix de Feu, who is ... menacing the labor population of our country;
> (2) that discussion of the report of the commission on the 6th of February be undertaken;
> (3) that the fascist leagues be disarmed and dissolved.[52]

It also invited the Parti Socialiste to participate with it in the rally of "Peace and Liberty" to be held on the 14th of July. It declared that the trade unions and other anti-fascist organizations must also be persuaded to join this rally. The letter concluded:

> We have noticed also that the Mulhouse Congress occupied itself with the question of mass self-defense the creation of which we proposed in our letter of November 24th, and it seems to us necessary that our two parties should study immediately the organization of a veritable **popular defense** grouping the forces of various groups wanting peace and liberty.[53]

On the 17th of June, at the Palais de la Mutualite, the Amsterdam-Pleyel group held a preliminary meeting at which the delegations of the various parties were informed of the developments of the preparatory commission, and those who hadn't officially taken a position were invited to send an observer. Preparations for the Rassemblement populaire, the rally of the People's Front, on July 14th, were underway.[54]

The P.C.F. then had found in the Mulhouse resolutions the complete acceptance of the Popular Front by the Socialists. Apparently this was all that had been lacking for it to push ahead with its plans for the giant rally encompassing all anti-fascist sympathizers. Working through the Amsterdam-Pleyel "Comite National de Lutte" it pressed the Parti Socialiste to translate its Mulhouse resolution into action within a week of the Mulhouse Congress. Since a large segment of the Radical party had already pledged its support to the rally, the decision of the Parti Socialiste at Mulhouse changed the Popular Front from project to accomplished fact. Again the combination of Communist pressure and the pressure of political developments had made the Socialists turn from the course which they claimed to be that of 'true Socialism" and fall in with Communist plans.

NOTES

1. An elaborate exposition of the Communist opposition to the **service de deux ans** which three months later was to cause them considerable embarrassment, was contained in Thorez, "L,organization de la Paix et Liberté", C.B., 1 January 1935, p. 26.

2. See L'HUMANITÉ 17, 18 and 19 May 1935, in which under the slogan "Stalin is right", anti-militarism was abandoned by the P.C.F. Péri made an elaborate attempt to reconcile Communist anti-militarism with Stalin's declaration approving French military measures in L'HUMANITÉ May 21, 1935; despite Stalin's statement, actually it was not until Ercoli's report to the VIIth World Congress, 18 August 1935, that official International sanction was given to the abandonment of anti-militarism and agitation in favor of an increase of French military power.

3. See Dmitrov, "La lutte pour le front unique", C.B., 1 December 1934, p. 1373.

4. In a letter from the C.A.P. to the Bureau Politique on 27 November 1934 the Socialists declared:

    "In our opinion a common program is the natural extension of our unity of action of yesterday and today, since it would trace the plan for a new phase of the battle against fascism... It would contribute to the organic unity which is what we wish next, in the sense that it would permit the delimitation of common zones of action and of thought." LE POPULAIRE, 28 November 1934.

5. Although small the P.U.P. was by no means of negligible importance. Its parliamentary group, under the leadership of Sellier, consisted of 9 deputies, only one less than the P.C.F. itself. Joining the Union Socialiste-Communiste in 1930 it polled 300,000 votes according to the Socialists, in the 1932 elections (although LE TEMPS of May 9, 1932 credited it with but 78,000 on the first ballot.)

6. The P.C.F. letter, after listing the specific measures which it proposed as a basis for unity of action, concluded:

"... We hope that the Conseil National will adopt the program proposed by us ... we wish that together we might be able to prepare the success of trade union unity and that we might advance along the way toward the single party of the working class."

Blum's reply said, in part:

"The Conseil National feels that in submitting your project directly to it you intended in a sense to make an appeal to it, to obtain from the whole of the Parti Socialiste 'the adoption of the bases of the program proposed by the P.C.F.'. After a prolonged debate the Conseil National is inclined to the opinion of our delegates to the Commission of coordination and of the C.A.P. They believe that if a **common program** of action should be established between the two parties -- and we continue to wish for it wholeheartedly -- it is in the direction traced by the Socialist project that study must be resumed."

Both letters were reproduced in the Communist brochure LA CONFÉRENCE NATIONALE D'IVRY AUX ASSISES DE LA PAIX ET LIBERTÉ, **op. cit.**, pp. 21, 24.

7. Correspondence between the Parti Socialiste and the P.C.F. on the subject of organic unity; compiled in RAPPORT ADMINISTRATIF AU XXXII CONGRÈS NATIONAL, Librairie Populaire, 1935, pp. 89-90.

8. Severac, J.B., DE L'UNITÉ D'ACTION À L'UNITÉ ORGANIQUE, Paris, Societé d'éditions "Nouveau Promethée, 1936, p. 17.

9. LE POPULAIRE, 21 December 1934.

10. See pamphlet, LA FUSION DU PARTI SOCIALISTE ET DU PARTI COMMUNISTE EST ELLE POSSIBLE ET SOUHAITABLE?, Imprimerie Union, Paris, 1937.

11. Correspondence on organic unity etc., **op. cit.**, p. 99. Compare this with the letter of 24 November in which the P.C.F. also dangled the bait of organic unity before the Parti Socialiste in order to get the latter to cooperate in the broadening of unity of action;

"Immediate action opens the way to the realization of organic unity and all those who wish it ... will certainly be with us in support of the program (i.e. that program outlined by the P.C.F.) which has as its goal the defense of the workers. There is the secret of the consolidation and enlargement of unity of action. There is the way leading to organic unity." L'HUMANITÉ, 25 November 1934.

12. In two of the more flagrant disturbances of the tranquillity that was supposed to exist between the parties as a result of the unity of action pact, the Socialists struck back. The first of these arose from the denial, by M. Marty, that there had been seven Socialist parties that signed the declaration in October to the International, Marty refusing to recognize the existence of the Russian Social-democratic party led by Dan. Blum indignantly replied:

    "The fact that Soviet legality forbids to this party (the mensheviks) all forms of organization and all forms of activity, hasn't resulted in the abolition of it. It will always exist. Obviously Marty is convinced that it no longer exists in Russia, and it no longer corresponds to any kind of reality. But we have the right to distinguish between Marty's opinion and our own; it is absolutely necessary that the mensheviks possess the liberty of organization and of action which they don't enjoy in Russia." LE POPULAIRE, 20 November 1934.

    And at the time of the terror following Kirov's assassination Blum published the menshevik protest in LE POPULAIRE, with the following comment:

    "Our readers will find below an important and serious declaration which the foreign delegation of the Social-democratic (menshevik) party has asked LE POPULAIRE to publish.

    "It is unnecessary to say that the request of our menshevik friends has placed a delicate decision before the leadership of POPULAIRE. But for my part I do not believe that the most trusting and loyal practice of unity of action should lead me to haggle about the hospitality of LE POPULAIRE to a party which is fraternally linked to our international action and which joined its signature with ours when we asked the Executive of the International to seek unity of action." LE POPULAIRE, 30 December 1934.

13. Compte rendu sténographique du Conseil National, LE POPULAIRE, 4 March 1935.

14. Speaking to an "Information Assembly" composed of both Communists and Socialists on December 20th Thorez declared:

    "We have already worked well, we have obtained appreciable results, but we still remain weak and it does no good to delude ourselves. There still remain hundreds of thousands or millions of proletarians and petty bourgeoisie who remain outside of the great unitary current. There are still entire regions of the country which escape the influence of the front unique.

If we don't take care they may well spring out from the fascist Vendees against our victorious proletarian march." L'HUMANITÉ, 21 December 1934.

15. The Parti Socialiste nominated its delegation on March 6th to include: Auriol, Blum, Bräcke, Paul Faure (or Severac), Frossard, Lebas, Longuet, and Zyromski. The P.U.P. delegated Bachelet, Boissery, duteil, Gaudeaux, Juncker, Garchery, Letrange and Paul Louis.

16. Communist pressure to eliminate the P.U.P. from the unity discussions stemmed principally from the support and favor with which the latter looked on Doriot's plans. See "Documents du P.C.F. - Pour l'unité d'action", C.B., 1 October 1934, p. 1173.

    Also the P.U.P. after the Communist switch to the support of national defense, was firmly and absolutely opposed to the P.C.F. on three major grounds. The P.U.P. pronounced unequivocally against national defense whatever the circumstances, insisted upon absolute trade union autonomy, and demanded democratic methods within the proposed unified party. RAPPORT ADMINISTRATIF AU XXXIII CONGRÈS NATIONAL, **op. cit.**, p. 96.

17. On April 3rd the C.A.P. had written to the P.U.P.:

    "Although the P.C.F. has not yet advised us of its decisions on this point, but convinced that it will not be long in designating its delegates, we have fixed the first meeting of the Unification Commission for Tuesday 11 April at 2100, etc. ..." Correspondence on organic unity, etc., **op. cit** , p. 107. By the same courier it sent a letter to the P.C.F. notifying it of the acceptance by the P.U.P. and the date of the meeting.

18. L'HUMANITÉ, 4 April 1935.

19. RAPPORTS DE LA COMMISSION D'UNIFICATION, published in an untitled brochure by the Parti Socialiste, éditions de la Liberté, Paris 1937, p. 19.

20. On the 6th and 7th of May the Bureau of the Executive of the I.O.S. met at Brussels, with Blum representing the Parti Socialiste. The meeting produced a resolution which revealed the indecision and vagueness of the I.O.S. concerning the proper course for Socialists in face of the increasing international tension:

    "We salute the cooperation of the European democracies with the Soviet Union to prevent war. We do not wish an entente against the German people nor against any other people; what we wish is to guarantee the maintenance of peace for all by an action to which all peoples are called to cooperate in a perfect equality of rights." RAPPORTS AU XXXIII CONGRÈS NATIONAL DES DÉLÉGUES À L'INTERNATIONALE OUVRIÉRE SOCIALISTE, Librairie Populaire, Paris, 1936, p. 270.

21. Rapport Moral, prepared by Paul Faure and accepted at the Conseil National of March 3rd. RAPPORT MORAL AU XXXII CONGRÈS NATIONAL, Librairie Populaire, Paris 1935, p. 3.

22. In a pamphlet which he wrote in 1936 Zyromski described briefly his theories on unification and the history of his unsuccessful struggle toward that end. SUR LE CHEMIN DE L'UNITÉ, Editions "Nouveau Prométhée", Paris, 1936, pp. 6-9.

23. Compte rendu sténographique du XXXII Congrès National, **op. cit** , p. 16.

24. Pivert declared:

    "I ask you to visit the site of L'HUMANITÉ or of the P.C.F., then to visit the site of rue Victor-Massé. You will see the difference, comrades. You will see that one doesn't enter the P.C.F. or L'HUMANITÉ as if it were a mill. All we wanted to do is to put in order the headquarters at rue Victor-Massé; we wanted to take a certain number of practical precautions. However, the comrades who were charged with studying the means to protect the site of the party, to make proposals, have been ordered to pass to another type of activity." **Ibid.**, pp. 18. 27.

25. Lebas attempted to placate Zyromski and at the same time to avoid a discussion of self-defense by reminding Zyromski that no one prevented him from taking what steps for self-defense he wished in the Paris region. When Zyromski protested Lebas cautioned him against discussing matters of self-defense in what amounted to a public congress.

    At this a voice from the rear cried: "Alors c'est l'action clandestine!" Compte rendu sténographique du XXXII Congrès National, **op. cit.**, p. 38.

26. **Ibid.**, p. 84.

27. SUR LE CHEMIN DE L'UNITÉ, **op. cit.**, p. 11.

28. COMPTE RENDU DU XXXII CONGRÈS NATIONAL, **op. cit.**, p. 195.

29. At the end of the congress a telegram was received from Nenni which undermined Blum's argument:

    "Address Congress; fraternal salutations. Italian Socialist party always stands against fascist dictatorship. Ardently wish that Congress deliberations reinforce popular action against fascism and war whose menace grows in East Africa in the name of so-called civilization. Amitiés. P. Nenni."
    RAPPORT ADMINISTRATIF AU XXXII CONGRÈS NATIONAL, **op. cit.**, p. 306.

30. COMPTE RENDU DU XXXII CONGRÈS NATIONAL, **op. cit.**, p. 215; at this speech the Trotskyist Molinier screamed, "We will kill ourselves", **Ibid.**

    For a description of Jaurès' anti-militarist campaign immediately before his death see Brogan, THE DEVELOPMENT OF MODERN FRANCE, Hamish Hamilton, London, 1949, pp. 527-529, and Zevaes, HISTOIRE DU SOCIALISME ET DU COMMUNISME EN FRANCE, **op. cit** , pp. 328 ff. Also Weinstein, Harold R., JEAN JAURÈS - A STUDY OF PATRIOTISM IN THE FRENCH SOCIALIST MOVEMENT, Columbia University Press, New York, 1936.

31. Blum concluded this argument with a statement revealing his satisfaction at the effects caused by the change in attitude of the P.C.F. It was perhaps from this moment on that the cause of those against the Popular Front was doomed:

    "I think that we must welcome, whatever are our thoughts about the Stalin communiqué, the interpretations which have been given to it in France, and which come so near to the position voluntarily taken by many of us, both as a consequence of unity of action, and as one of the conditions which will render organic unity easier." **Op. cit.**, p. 216.

32. COMPTE RENDU DU XXXII CONGRÈS NATIONAL, **op. cit.**, p. 215. cf. Cachin at the VIIth World Congress of the Comintern:

    "What would the French workers say if, by misfortune, we hesitated to adopt a tactic imposed by events and if by this we put Hitlerian fascism in power in Paris? And what would the workers of the Soviet Union say if, by a policy of sectarianism, we procured the support of French fascism for Hitler; for, do not doubt it for a moment comrades, the French fascists on the morrow of their victory -- if it ever took place -would be at the side of Hitler preparing a war against the Soviet Union."
    VIIe CONGRÈS MONDIALE, **op. cit.**, p. 90.

Justifying the Socialist vote in favor of the Franco-Soviet Pact Longuet later said in the Chamber:

"The (Socialist) party is above all an instrument of peace; that is why it has welcomed the adhesion to all men who make peace their essential objective.

"It denies the fatal Hitlerian theory of the localization of conflict, a theory to which it opposes the theses of Litvinov of the indivisibilty of peace." JOURNAL OFFICIEL, 13 February 1936, p. 372.

33. COMPTE RENDU DU XXXII CONGRÈS NATIONAL, **op. cit.**, p. 224.

34. COMPTE RENDU DU XXXII CONGRÈS NATIONAL, **op. cit.**, p. 224.

35. Radical inquiries about a government of the Left were received by the Parti Socialiste on June 5th. The Radicals posed three questions:

(1) What sort of a majority group did the Socialists envisage; a strict Cartel or a majority comprising such men as Bonnevay?

(2) Were they in favor of full powers being granted to this government?

(3) Would such a government be established with a view toward deflation or devaluation?

Printed in L'ERE Nouvelle, 5 June 1935, and LE POPULAIRE, 6 June 1935.

36. COMPTE RENDU DU XXXII CONGRÈS NATIONAL, **op. cit.**, p. 226.

37. **Ibid.**, p. 227.

38. Zyromski:

"We would cease to be Marxists, to be Socialists, we would cease to be revolutionaries, if at the present time we should give any importance to that eventuality of which the reports of our comrades Paul Faure and Severac speak, to that eventuality of the accession to Socialism by the normal game of electoral and parliamentary growth.

"Whether we wish it or not comrades, in spite of the fact that we do not favor systematic violence, although we wish a revolution accomplished in joy, calm and peace, we know that we cannot at the present moment economize on the proletarian revolution." COMPTE RENDU DU XXXII CONGRÈS NATIONAL, **op. cit.**, p. 251-252.

39. This phrase "we must desire unity with a rage" was borrowed from the veteran Socialist leader Vaillant, whose use of it at the time of unification in 1905 can hardly have supported Zyromski's position at Mulhouse.

40. COMPTE RENDU DU XXXII CONGRÈS NATIONAL, **op. cit.**, p. 265.

41. In fact quite the contrary. When Briche complained that "there have not been specific indications as to the method to be applied, not only between the trade union movement and our own, but between all the organizations of the anti-fascist movement", Lebas admitted this deficiency and recalled how often Blum had regretted that the C.G.T. and the party had different organs. COMPTE RENDU DU XXXII CONGRÈS NATIONAL, **op. cit.**, p. 329.

42. COMPTE RENDU DU XXXII CONGRÈS NATIONAL, **op. cit.**, pp. 409-410.

43. **Ibid.**, p. 414, cf. Dmitrov's statement on the priority of the front unique as against the Popular Front. VIIe CONGRÈS MONDIALE, **op. cit.**, p. 135; and Thorez' similar statement, C.B., 1 January 1935, p. 33.

44. This was the position taken by Lebas in his motion at Toulouse advocating caution in dealing with the P.C.F. Even at that time he had been successful in opposing Zyromski's extremism, but by a smaller margin and upon a motion which made a much milder appeal for moderation and cooperation with all forces of the Left. The extent of the difference between Lebas' success at Mulhouse and at Toulouse is perhaps the best measure of the changed temper of the party.

45. COMPTE RENDU DU XXXII CONGRÈS NATIONAL, **op. cit.**, p. 443.

46. COMPTE RENDU DU XXXII CONGRÈS NATIONAL, **op. cit.**, p. 443.

47. Severac moved:

"I have put the comrades of the Commission on resolutions au courant of the status of the work of the Commission on unification of the proletarian parties, the P.C.F., the Parti Socialiste, the P.U.P. and some other political formations which take part with us in the class struggle.

"The commission proposes to you to charge Bräcke, Blum, Auriol,

Zyromski and Paul Faure to examine closely the texts proposed by the P.C.F. and the P.U.P. and eventually to prepare one for our own party."

This was adopted without discussion. **Ibid.**, p. 444.

48. The Left extremists had been unable to combine their motions into a single motion, each having taken a different position on the question of the unity of the parties.

49. At which Lebas remarked: "Then we should move toward bolshevism. What is that boy doing here?" **op. cit.**, p. 537.

50. The Lebas motion stated in part:

    "In this battle against fascism, which is one of the pressing tasks of the Parti Socialiste, the accords reached between it and the P.C.F. have had the happiest results. Like the Conseil National of March 3rd, the Congress of Mulhouse registers satisfaction with them and decides to continue this action despite the disavowal which has just been inflicted by the Secretary General of the Comintern upon the opposition of the two workers' parties to the militarist policy of the French government.

    "Just as the vigor of common action depends to a large extent upon the strength of the Parti Socialiste, so does future unity ... demand that the front unique of which so much is said first be made a living and fertile reality within our own ranks, our own sections, federations, Conseils, national congresses, etc."

    COMPTE RENDU DU XXXII CONGRÈS NATIONAL, **op. cit.**, p. 556.

51. The Auriol resolution voted 12 June:

    "By reason of the miseries accruing to the laboring masses and the dangers which menace public liberties, the Congress is resolved to take the immediate measures which impose themselves.

    "It decides to intensify its own means of propaganda and give a mandate to the C.A.P. to establish, to this effect, a plan inspired with the most modern processes and methods.

    "It decides to pursue, with even greater persistence, the realization of organic unity of the working class, since it is around a united party that the rally of the workers masses, of the peasant masses, and of the threatened or ruined middle classes will derive all its spirit and all its effectiveness.

    "... In this effort the party intends to abdicate nothing; neither its independence, nor its program, nor its discipline, to which its militants and its officers always remain subordinate.

"... For this action it makes an appeal to the Communist party as well as to other proletarian parties and the great trade-union organizations, the workers and the peasants. In accord with them it will devote itself to grouping all the anti-fascist organizations and all the elements of democracy which arose spontaneously on the morrow of the 6th of February.

"Consequently the Congress gives a mandate to the C.A.P., while accelerating the work of the unification commission, to convoke without delay a meeting comprising, alongside of the delegates of the political and economic organizations of the workers and peasant class, the representatives of all the principal groupings having already testified to their resolution to fight against fascism and the crisis." LE POPULAIRE, 13 June 1935.

52. LA CONFÉRENCE NATIONALE D'IVRY AUX ASSISES DE LA PAIX ET LIBERTÉ, **op. cit** , p. 29.
53. **Ibid.**
54. See Cogniot, Georges, PAIX ET LIBERTÉ, Éditions du Mouvement Amsterdam, Discours prononcé au Congrès Populaire du Grand Paris, le 28 Juin 1936.

CHAPTER ELEVEN

THE NEW FACE OF THE COMMUNIST PARTY

There being, of course, no such candid and comprehensive source of reliable material upon the development of Communist thought as is afforded in the case of the Socialists by their national congresses, one can only trace such development by deduction from the official bulletins, the party press, the reports of meetings and congresses, speeches and the like. However, due to their conviction that a positive position of one kind or another must always be maintained before the public, the Communists leave themselves extremely exposed to a day to day comparison and analysis of their tactical development. Moreover in addition to these sources there are the tactical instruments of the P.C.F., transmitted usually through the CAHIERS DU BOLCHEVISME, by which the party informs its affiliates and subsections of all the ramifications of and provides the explanations and dialectical ammunition for the changes in line and tactics as they are decided in Paris, or in Moscow. Finally there is much to be gained from a study of the national and international congresses for, despite the staging and pre-planning of these events, there is an inevitable element of thought revelation in the exposition of a new line. Examined by means of these sources in the eighteen months between the national conference at Ivry (June 1934) and the national conference at Villeurbanne (January 1936), the new character of the P.C.F. and the tactical thought of the Communist leaders that lay behind it gradually took form.

In general there were three separate aspects to this development which, although they overlapped to some extent, were nevertheless distinct enough to warrant separate consideration: (1) the change in line, that is the overt change in official attitude toward all aspects of internal and foreign policy; (2) the less public change in tactics, consisting of the tactical reorganization by the party in order to implement the new policies; and (3) the influence of the French experience with the front unique and the front populaire upon the policies of the International itself -- revealed most strikingly at the VIIth World Congress.

The Change in Line

The first aspect, the change in line, was the most sensational and at the same time the least significant since it represented little beyond the official and public declarations of the party leaders. No very profound research was required by the French Socialist, Radical or Rightist who wished to present a rather remarkable and damning picture of the complete about face made by the P.C.F. in this period.[1] It will perhaps suffice to list the course taken by some of the more important changes.

The Class Struggle. Prior to Ivry it had been an inviolable part of Communist doctrine; the "battle of classes, three words, express all there is to Communist policy".[2] At Ivry this was modified but not completely altered; "class against class is nothing more than a 'tactic' which has not been revised, those who think that it has are mistaken".[3] Then, a year later, it was declared that a "tactic" not having the firmness of an essential principle is modifiable and is now modified into the new tactic of the Popular Front.[4] Finally Duclos declared that it was necessary to make certain indispensable alliances between classes.[5] In their propaganda for the rassemblement the Communists declared that it excluded only the "200 families" (the basis for winning over the Radicals);[6] and in the Villeurbanne manifesto it was declared that the union aimed at by the P.C.F. excluded no one.[7]

Bourgeois democracy. In 1933 and through the spring of 1934 bourgeois democracy led to fascism; as late as June 1934 it was declared that fascism would arise armed out of bourgeois-democracy.[8] then, at Ivry, it was resolved that the Communists would defend democratic liberties.[9] Finally, in the Front Francais sought by the Communists in 1936, Duclos called for union within the framework of the bourgeois-democratic state.[10]

Nation. From the position that the proletarians have no country, in early 1934,[11] the P.C.F. changed first to "Communists must establish their fatherland by rendering France Communist" at Ivry,[12] and finally to "the Communists are patriots of present day France" at Villeurbanne.[13]

National defense. The Communists remained fierce enemies of national defense through 1934[14] Then they undertook the reconciliation of anti-militarism with the Stalin declaration approving the military measures taken by France.[15] Finally they became enthusiastic supporters of an increase in French military power.[16]

Chauvinism. In early 1934 they deplored the chauvinism of the anti-fascists;[17] in 1935-36 they supported an all-out battle against international fascism with a chauvinistic attitude far surpassing anything they had condemned.[18]

Radicals. In May 1933, "All that is national must draw Daladier and Hitler together. The enemy for both of them is revolutionary internationalism".[19] In May 1936, "The Radicals will not desert the cause in the face of the Fascist Leagues. Their spokesmen, Daladier, Marc Rucart, Pierre Cot and Gaston Marin fight side by side with us".[20]

League of Nations. In October 1933, "We must not tire of pointing out that the comedy of Geneva has lasted twelve years during which time the Hendersons, MacDonalds, Boncours and others have piped their peaceful tune on the banks of Lac Leman".[21] In June 1936, "We must support the League of Nations in its struggle in favor of peace".[22]

These were but some of the many abrupt changes which came as corollaries to the major turning. All aspects of the line in France were necessarily affected by it. The Communist attitude toward the Saar plebescite, toward the return of Alsace-Lorraine, toward the sanctity of the Versailles Treaty underwent similar reversals.[23] Instead of denouncing Catholicism as the "opium of the people", the P.C.F. in 1936 was seeking an alliance with the Catholic leaders.[24] Startling as these many changes in line were, however, they all followed fairly consistently from the basic shift in the attitude of the Comintern toward class collaboration in France. Once the Socialists were convinced that they had correctly analyzed the underlying motives of this shifting they were no longer taken by surprise as the succession of incidental changes unfolded. It was rather in the realm of tactical reorganization that the innovations of the P.C.F. gave the Socialists some cause for concern and also some clue as to the breadth of the Communist experiment in France.

The Change in Tactics.

The tactical reorganization of the P.C.F. may be divided into two phases, that which was required for its new policy in regard to the Socialists, and that which was required in order to win the Radicals to the Popular Front. The first is expressed by a fairly simple formula: "Achieve organic unity with the Socialists wherever it would affaord an opportunity for the expansion of Communist influence without loss of political independence. Avoid it and be content with unity of action wherever there is substantial danger that unity might mean the loss of freedom of action to respond immediately and absolutely to the orders of the Comintern". Thus the Communists sought the organic unity of the trade union confederations by which means they hoped to broaden their influence considerably, but rejected fusion of the parties themselves (despite their protestations to the Socialists to the contrary) because such fusion would inevitably terminate their primary function, that of serving Comintern ends. This same policy was carried out with all of the Communist affiliates. The Fédération Sportive du Travail (Communist) initiated a meeting with the Union des Societés Sportives et Gymnique du Travail (Socialist and independent) at which it was decided to convoke a fusion congress in December (of 1934). From this a single Fédération Sportive et Gymnique du Travail emerged.[25] At the same time, however, the Jeunesses Communistes were ordered to seek fuller collaboration with the Jeunesses Socialistes but to avoid organic unity. The merging of the sporting associations was an attempt to bring the youth of the two parties closer together as a more effective and maneuverable body; but the youth organizations themselves being too closely linked to the parties and thus to the political independence of the parties were not allowed by the Communists to establish organic unity. Pursuant to the same tactical formula the Amsterdam-Pleyel committees were instructed to seek the collaboration of the Socialist Comité de Vigilance des Intellectuels and the Radical Ligue des Droits de l'Homme, whereas the individual trade unions within the C.G.T.U. were to seek organic unity with their corresponding unions within the C.G.T.[26]

This simultaneous attempt to achieve trade union unity and resist unity of the parties themselves faced impressive obstacles. It was not remarkable that the Socialist leaders failed to see why the opportunities for trade union unity were so great when political unity was impossible, particularly in view of the Communist insistence upon the political role of the unions themselves. Furthermore, Jouhaux and the other leaders of the C.G.T. were anxious for trade union unity only under certain limited conditions. It was as clear to them as it was to the Communists that the greatest advantages of such unity lay with the latter, and while Jouhaux, in much the same manner as Blum, had always hoped for eventual reunification of the confederations, like Blum also he had learned over a long period time the need for caution and safeguards.[27] Jouhaux imposed three conditions as pre-requisites for the discussion of trade union fusion. One was that any projected united federation be entirely independent of party control and have no direct political affiliation. Secondly he insisted that any steps taken by the C.G.T. in the direction of unity be in accordance with the procedures of the Fédération Syndicale Internationale and be submitted for the approval of the organization. Finally he made a series of particular demands as to the joint program upon which such unity could be based.[28]

In acceding to these conditions the Communists revealed the extent to which they were willing to compromise their doctrines in order to achieve trade union unity. Piatnitski, speaking for the International, went to great lengths to explain how the acceptance of trade union independence was proper in certain special cases.[29] He asserted that unions, since they were waging a constant war against the bourgeoisie, could not be neutral politically, but that in France it was not a question of neutrality but rather of the independence of trade unions from party politics. In France, he argued, there were two large trade union confederations, each of which followed one party, and the P.C.F. sought the unification of these two confederations. But the Communists could not accept unification under the Parti Socialiste and the converse was true of the Socialists. He circumvented Lenin's writings by saying that even the truest affirmation could not be turned into dogma, and that therefore Lenin's postulate of the impossibility of trade union neutrality and political independence, while true as a general principle, would become dogma if it were applied blindly in France without taking into account the concrete situation in which the battle for trade union unity was being waged in France. The question of leadership of the trade union movement was not a question of a declaration or a dogma, but rather of the proper policy and tactics that would permit the leadership of the Communist party to conquer the masses. Unity of the trade union movement would assure to the P.C.F. the best possibility of exercising its influence over larger masses than was possible at present. Therefore the French Communists acted correctly in not making the question of unity depend on the independence of trade union movement. He qualified this, however, with the statement that political independence of the trade unions did not mean that the Communists would or should abstain from pursuing their own policies within the unions:

The French Communists, wanting to take a big step toward

trade union unity, have accepted the formula of independence, but that doesn't mean in any sense that they renounce the task of influencing by all possible means the activity of these united trade unions through their factions within them. This is why the Communists don't place as a condition to unity previous recognition of the Communist party in the united trade unions; but by their work in these trade unions they will dictate themselves to convincing the majority of the members of the value of Communist leadership.[30]

In order to meet the objections of the C.G.T. as to the impossibility of reaching a program for organic unity satisfactory to the two confederations, the Communists pointed to the experience in Spain where, they claimed, by the use of a minimum program such as the 40 hour week, the freedom to strike, salary increases, social insurance and the like such a basis had been found. Piatnitski, however, recognized that a different tactic was demanded in France because of the "hostility of the bureaucracy of the C.G.T." to trade union unity. In 1934 he, like the local C.G.T.U. leaders, accused the C.G.T. of being prepared to accept unity only on the condition that the C.G.T.U. enter into the C.G.T. as constituted, more or less in the same manner as an individual member. However this was not a reason for the C.G.T.U. to abandon its attempts at unity in France, Piatnitski argued, for in that country more than anywhere else large masses of workers and civil servants, comprising an important part of the C.G.T. and the autonomous confederations, were beginning to enter into the large **front unique** despite and against the trade union bureaucracy. The extent of this tendency to unite could not fail to exercise pressure on the reformist leadership in spite of its opposition to unity and its plan for the unconditional entrance of the C.G.T.U. into the C.G.T.

Thus the pressure of the C.G.T.U. upon the C.G.T. continued. The former passed a resolution declaring its willingness to set up a joint commission for the preparation of the bases for unity. Jouhaux had no objection to this and the C.G.T. passed a similar resolution but then qualified it with the declaration that any subscription to such a commission could only be made with the approval of the F.S.I.[31] This stipulation automatically imposed a delay which thwarted the Communist designs for immediate action in that direction. The C.G.T.U. then proposed that the question of unity be put to a vote of the joint members of the two confederations, the balloting to be handled by a joint committee, declaring that **"Whatever the result of the C.G.T.U. declares in advance that it would bow before the**

majority. What does the C.G.T. think of that?"[32] This was to a considerable extent a propaganda move as the Communists wanted to secure the credit for initiating a vote that was certain to favor union, but it was also consistent with the other pressure that they were putting on the C.G.T. for organic unity.

In conjuction with the campaign for organic unity of the trade unions the Communists also revealed the extent of their opposition to organic unity of the parties themselves, an attitude which they usually tried to conceal from the Socialists. A single party of the working class was acceptable to them only on the following bases; the non-collaboration of classes, absolute hostility to national defense, and the co-existence of illegal with legal agitation.[33] Many Socialists and some Communists, after the signing of the unity of action pact, favored running a joint candidate for the two parties in many of the departments for the cantonal elections in October of 1934. This, however, was rejected unequivocally by the Communist leadership. The only time when Communists wouldn't put up candidates on the first ballot was when they didn't have the strength to support them. According to Duclos no argument could militate in favor of such an arrangement. "The P.C.F. is not the Parti Socialiste. If there were no difference between them, there would not be any difference in their programs, their means, their ends."[34]

Thus while the P.C.F. was negotiating with the Parti Socialiste in presumed seriousness over the possibilities of organic unity its writers were declaring in the CAHIERS DU BOLCHEVISME that:

> One thing is sure: the co-existence of Marxists and revisionists in a single party has, in all countries, at the decisive moment brought victory to the latter. In Germany the revolutionary Left was submerged by the opportunists become chauvinists, the same as in France... The dogma of unity prevented the Lefts from breaking with the party ... if French Marxism revealed itself at the moment of war to be incapable of opposing resistance to the policy of the party, it was because it had already been greatly undermined by a prolonged collaboration with the revisionists in a single party.[35]

According to the Communists the experience of the 1914-1918 war had proved beyond question that organic unity with the "opportunists" always permitted the latter at the decisive moment to deviate the revolutionary movement from its proper course. Organic unity of the proletariat, in order to be useful and durable, could only be made on the basis of the principles of revolutionary Marxism, of Communism, thus:

> **Communists are for the unity of battle of the working class.** But this unity can only be and will only be forged **by the battle against the theory and the tactic of a class understanding with the bourgeoisie,** an understanding which constitutes the basis of the policy of every Social-Democratic party.
>
> **Communists are for the grouping of all the workers in a single proletarian revolutionary party,** whose program and tactic have as an aim to fight not in words but in deeds for the dictatorship of the proletariat and for the Soviets, in short on the basis of the **program and tactic of the Comintern.**
>
> Communists are always against organic unity without principles, preached by Doriot, because the unification of the Communist party -- whose policy is that of the battle for the proletarian dictatorship -- with the Social-Democratic party -- whose policy always goes back in one form or another to collaboration with the bourgeoisie -- would have no other effect than to consolidate the bourgeoisie and weaken the proletariat.[36]

In support of this thesis another Communist, Albert Vassart, wrote that there could be no middle line on the question of party principles. There could be no arithmetic mean, no synthesis of two doctrines disagreeing on such fundamentals as use of parliamentary means against the overthrow of parliament, peaceful against revolutionary means of acquiring power:

> The victory of the Russian workers and peasants in 1917 was possible because, at the head of the revolting masses, was a party forged by Lenin over a period of many years. This party was capable of developing its action under the most terrible conditions of repression ... capable also of maintaining its unity, its political homogeneity in suppressing without hesitation all the elements which were unworthy of belonging to the party. Lenin, who was the principal organizer of the party, always affirmed that the triumph of the October revolution was due above all to the solidarity, to the capacity for action of the Bolshevik party.
>
> 'It is certain that the whole world now sees that the bolsheviks would not have been able to maintain themselves in power not two years and a half, but two months and a half, without the

truly inflexible discipline of iron of our party (La maladie infantile du communisme, p. 13)'.[37]

This then was the new face that the P.C.F. presented to the Socialists from late 1934 until the establishment of the Popular Front (and afterward). In one major respect at least, the desire for trade union unity, it was a radically different face from that which they had known since before the signing of the unity of action pact. However on the issue which most concerned the Socialists, that of political reunification, there was little if any change. Certainly the Communist attitude toward the Socialists demonstrated no change comparable in scope to that with which they now confronted the Radicals.

The tactical changes made by the Communists in order to win the support of the Radicals for the Popular Front constituted the principal changes made after Ivry. These stretched over all aspects of the relations between the P.C.F. and those groups from which the Radicals drew most of their political strength. Their examination is perhaps best approached by dividing the whole tactical change into its component parts.

1. **The General Campaign.** The full scale campaign, as we have seen, was not launched until October of 1934, however mention of the need not to alienate the middle classes was made at Ivry and continued through the intervening months. In many respects this campaign was similar to the **front unique en bas** formerly used against the Socialists, that is it consisted of the attempt to separate the Radical rank and file from their leaders. There were apparently two reasons for the decision to use this tactic rather than to attempt a rapport with the leaders themselves. First the Communist leaders recognized, in late 1934 and early 1935 at least, that there was little hope of winning the support of Radical leaders of the Herriot type, whose emotional antipathy to bolshevism was as unshaken as ever.[38] Secondly the serious split within the Radical party over the question of support of the National Union government made the success of this tactic much more possible than it had been in the case of the Socialists. Thus the factions within the Radical party that sympathized with the Ligue des Droits de l'Homme, or with Daladier, or with the group that had formed the Parti-Radical Socialiste Camille Pelletan, were the original targets of the Communists. Duclos declared:

We are sure that the Radical workers, whatever may be the attitude of the ministers who are members of their party, are in the main with us in defending the immediate salary claims, the abrogation of the decree-laws, etc...

We are sure that the Communist and Socialist workers who fight together for the defense of democratic liberties in order to check the plans of Doumergue and Marchandeau, are approved of by an imposing portion of the Radical workers in spite of all that certain of their leaders have said.[39]

In his instructions to the party Thorez outlined its task as being that of showing the middle classes a way other than that of Herriot. It could not be true, he argued, that the middle classes were guided and influenced solely by MM. Doumergue, Marin, Flandin, and Herriot. The Communists must increase their agitation to win to the cause of the Popular Front those who were not yet ready for Communism or the institution of Soviets. Here again, as he had done with the I.O.S. leaders at Brussels, Thorez used the argument that the establishment of a fascist dictatorship in France would be a calamity not only for the workers in France but for the international proletariat as well coming after the progress of the fascist wave in Germany, Italy, Austria and Spain. He appended the somewhat significant warning to his own militants that it would also constitute an extremely grave menace to the Soviet Union.

In the main, however, the general campaign was based on an attempt to identify the interests of the "middle classes" with those of the Communists, to minimize the differences and emphasize the common interest -- the defense against fascism within France.[40] To this end the P.C.F. leaders demanded that all other facets of activity be subordinated. There was no room for theoretical discussion. At any price, meaning apparently the complete renunciation of party doctrines if necessary, the support of the middle class groups must be enlisted.

2. **The campaign for the peasants and intellectuals.** In an article entitled "Pour l'alliance avec les classes moyennes" Thorez declared that "More important than theoretical discussion is the mobilization of thousands and thousands of peasants".[41] Originally the Communists hoped to accomplish this through the C.G.T. which had a much larger rural following than either the C.G.T.U. or the P.C.F. itself. However it was the Radical party that had the greatest influence over the small peasant and the agricultural workers, and, after October, the campaign to enlist these groups was directed primarily through that party. Similarly the simplest means of approaching the estimated 4,000 intellectuals grouped around Alain, Rivet, Gerome and Langevin was through the Radicals.

Thus the party militants were instructed to broaden their base among the peasants by cooperating with all of the non-Communist peasant organizations. Their strongest foothold among the peasants was the Confédération Générale des Paysannes Travailleurs, and all of the Communist organizations, industrial as well as agricultural, were ordered to rally in defense of its claims and aid in the distribution of its organ, LA VOIX PAYSANNE. However they were not to ignore the millions of peasants grouped in agricultural organizations under bourgeois leadership. In such cases, the instructions stated, they must not refuse to join these organizations but must work within them to create an internal opposition, an internal committe of peasant workers following the program of the C.G.P.T.

> The Communists in the core of the C.G.P.T. and other trade union and cooperative organizations must collaborate with the catholic, Socialist and non-party peasant-worker.[42]

At the end of October and the beginning of November, 1934, the C.G.P.T. organized between 30 and 40 departmental congresses in order to consolidate the special peasant grievances in each region and inaugurate a plan of action for meetings, demonstrations and the like from November to May 1935. Cooperatives and agricultural associations of all political tendencies were invited to these congresses. Also included were other groups having peasants and agricultural workers in their ranks, such as anti-fascist committees, Socialist sections, etc. Duclos informed the Communists that they must not lose sight of the fact that there were three million agricultural workers in France and that Lenin had said that this was the group, in the country, upon which the Communists must rely:

> All the pro-fascist forces must disappear. This requires the assembling of ... all those who belong to the diverse workers and peasant organizations as well as the Radical workers who, if they wish to survive, have no other solution than that of taking their place in the Front Populaire ...[43]

3. **The electoral tactic.** The most immediate and effective way of wooing Radical favor was still by means of electoral support. In preparation for the cantonal elections of October 7 and 14, 1934, Duclos indicated the change in the P.C.F. tactics in that respect. Obviously, because of the unity of action pact with the Socialists, the Communists had to return to the 1924 tactic of withdrawal on the second ballot where this would insure Socialist victory over a rightist candidate.[44] But the question also arose of what Communist

policy should be where neither a Socialist nor Communist candidate could be successful. Suppose, said Duclos, that Chiappe were to be the candidate in the 3rd Arrondissement (of which, according to him, there was some possibility), would the P.C.F. by maintaining its candidate on the second ballot see that enemy elected? On the contrary, in such a case it would do everything in its power to defeat him:

> Good, they say, that is an exceptional case, one can even in such a situation vote for a Radical, but can one go further? Thus is posed the question of what we will do in regard to Radical candidates.

In his answer to this Duclos called attention to the fact that the National Union government was having a difficult time keeping the Radicals in it, and that the Radicals were not happy and were split among themselves:

> In these conditions if a Radical candidate makes a declaration against the National Union government, against the decree-laws and against the fascist bands we can vote for him, in order on the one hand to beat fascism and on the other to prevent the masses that follow the Radical party from being unknowingly driven to fascism.[45]

Thus even before the inauguration of the Popular Front the Communists had made significant modifications of their electoral line and had given a substantial sugar-coating to the pill which they were trying to force upon the Radicals.

4. **National defense and anti-militarism.** There remained but one major obstacle to a rapprochement between the Radicals and the Communists. But it was an obstacle of primary importance.

Despite all of the changes in the P.C.F. line which made an accord between Radical and Communist possible, and despite the Communist pronouncement that it "loved" France, the P.C.F. remained opposed to national defense through 1934 and the first four months of 1935. Three days after he had launched the Popular Front in the Chamber, Thorez made the statement, "Thus it is that in effect we are the adversaries of the lie of national defense".[46] The position of national defense in Radical doctrine, always strong, had grown immeasurably in importance through 1933-34. It seemed impossible that Radical and Communist could come together in a movement dedicated primarily to the fight against fascism with this absolute conflict of ideas on one of the most important aspects of this fight. Furthermore, Communist opposition to national defense had long been one of the principal sources of Radical antagonism toward the P.C.F.[47] Such opposition smacked of sabotage to the Radicals, of part of the bolshevik attempt to undermine and betray the French nation. Thus when the P.C.F. retained the rejection of national defense in its program for a united anti-fascist front the Radicals for the most part regarded this as a hopeless contradiction in terms. An editorial in L'ÈRE NOUVELLE in August declared:

> Abandon national defense? But is that not the surest way of making France a prey to the fascism that one would combat inside it?
>
> Battle against the government? But is that not asking the Radicals to deny their chiefs and to blame them themselves?
>
> Surely the proposals and the offers of the Communists are hardly serious, and all that one can say is that it is not by demagogic or revolutionary policy that fascism is fought.[48]

In May of 1935 this barrier was finally removed. The anachronism of a French Communist party dedicated to the undermining of national defense at the same time as the Soviet Union was seeking a military alliance with France was ended by the signing of the Franco-Soviet Pact.[49] Overnight the P.C.F. completely altered its position. The pact itself was signed May 2nd. From the 13th to the 15th Laval visited Stalin in Moscow to discuss implementation of its terms. At this time Stalin issued a statement approving the military measures being taken by France, a communiqué to that effect being broadcast from Moscow on the 17th:

> The representatives of the Soviet Union and of France have been able to assure that their constant efforts in all diplomatic undertakings have been directed toward the same end; the maintenance of peace in the organization of collective security.
>
> They have been in full agreement in recognizing, in the present state of the international situation, the obligations which impose themselves upon States sincerely attached to the safeguards of peace.... The primary duty incumbent upon them, in this same interest of maintaining the peace, is not to let their means of national defense become weakened in any way. In this regard M. Stalin understands and fully approves the policy of national

defense undertaken by France in order to maintain its armed forces up to the level which security demands.[50]

Nothing more was needed for the P.C.F. On the 17th of May L'HUMANITÉ published an article by Vaillant-Couturier asserting that the French Army must be an ally of the Soviet Union. On the 23rd Cachin wrote:

> We must not forget for an instant that we French Communists have a double duty. Lest I should astound our Socialist allies I will say that the first of these duties is to defend the Soviet Union. For if Hitlerian fascism succeeded in its aim of crushing the Soviets, fascism would be the master of Europe, and it is enough that Germany and the center of the Continent should be enslaved temporarily by it, as a result of a bad policy condemned by history.[51]

With the switch on the question of national defense the last vestige of the old Communist line had disappeared. To the extent that the Radicals were willing to accept this change at face value they could find no grounds for disagreement with the methods by which the Communists now proposed to combat the fascist threat. Furthermore as the Communists eased the path for the Radicals to join the Popular Front many of the latter were finding it increasingly difficult to remain within a National Union coalition which appeared to be drifting steadily farther to the Right. By May of 1935 a large proportion of Radical sympathy was in favor of adhering to the movement, and there remained but the need for official sanction.

The Impact on the International.

The larger significance of the French Communists' experience with unity of action and the Popular Front was revealed at the VIIth World Congress of the Comintern which convened in Moscow in July of 1935. At this congress it became apparent that what had been taking place in France during the preceding year had been largely in the nature of an experiment the results of which would provide the International with a guide for its future policy on the international level as well as in its various national sections. It is significant in this respect that the congress had originally been scheduled for the summer of 1934, but in May of that year had been postponed for twelve months. It is also significant that at the time of the postponement the order of business of the congress, a year away, had been established, and that the principal subject on the agenda, which was delegated to the foremost member of the Executive, Dmitrov, was the report on the fascist offensive and the tasks of the Comintern in the battle for unity of the working class.[52] Here was the first evidence that the Comintern was using the P.C.F. and the French political arena as a proving ground to determine the feasibility of the combined United Front-Popular Front tactic, and that it was withholding judgment upon that tactic until it had had a chance to observe the results in France.

The Rassemblement Populaire was only a week old, a month had passed since the Socialist congress at Mulhouse, and the signing of the unity of action pact was almost exactly a year old when this congress, the first in seven years, opened on July 20. It was devoted almost entirely to the analysis of the arguments for and against unity of action as a result of which the French delegates played an important role and the discussion of the French experience dominated the congress.[53]

There is perhaps an art to the interpretation of the speeches and reports at a Comintern congress. Since such congresses are designed not for discussion but in order to issue instructions to the party and reveal indirectly the new line of Comintern thought each sentence, almost each word, has some specific purpose. The particular vocabulary that is used; the choice of personalities; significant omissions; changed emphasis -- all these factors are supposed to provide a cue to the initiated as to what their future course of behavior must be. Some of the instructing is not done in such an indirect manner of course. But in order to maintain the fiction of a congress most of the exposition of a new line is done indirectly through the medium of key speeches by the favored leaders of the moment. Thus at the VIIth World Congress Pieck, Ercoli, and above all Dmitrov were to make the three most significant reports for the International.[54]

Pieck's opening report established the general limits within which subsequent discussion was to be contained. Examining this report in the light of its function as a keynote speech one finds several significant revelations.

First it immediately became obvious that the Comintern was prepared to credit the French with having initiated the United Front-Popular Front tactic and also of having demonstrated its proper application. Pieck referred to the decisive role of the French several times during his report:

> The fight of the French proletariat has shown the workers how

the proletariat must act in capitalist countries in order to repulse the attacks of fascism and to fit itself for the conquest of the dictatorship of the proletariat, for Socialism. The united front agreement between the Socialists and Communists in France ... has pointed the way to be followed by the Left Social-democrats of all countries.[55]

Secondly Pieck's report indicated that the Comintern intended to apply the United Front-Popular Front tactic throughout the party and that the method of application was to be based on the French experience. He stated repeatedly that "the success of the French proletariat was of the greatest international importance":[56]

... The French party did not let itself be lulled by the theory of lesser evil and by talk of formal democracy as was the case in Germany, but at the first fascist rally flocked into the streets to oppose fascism without distinction as to party in the tremendous political demonstration of February 9th and the political general strike of February 12th, 1934. In this way the French proletariat **repulsed the first big attack of the fascists.** The French proletariat, by establishing a fighting united front in the February days, proved strikingly what a tremendous force the proletariat is when it is united and does not evade the struggle but takes a prompt stand against its enemy.[57]

And he declared later:

The work of our French party which has known how to arouse and to organize, against fascist barbarism, the will to resist in the most profound depths of the French people, must be an example for all our parties.[58]

Pieck also cast some light on the future positive steps to be taken by the national Communist parties. Predicting that they were on the eve of great battles in France and that both camps were now preparing for these battles, he postulated that the victory or defeat of the Popular Front would be of immense import to the entire international workers movement. In this connection he made what was perhaps the most important statement in his report:

We are entering a period of liquidation of the scission in the working class; we are thus creating in its midst the forces capable of overthrowing fascism and installing the dictatorship of the proletariat.

The way in which we must undertake this is by the creation of a united proletarian front, trade union unity, and the popular front of all the workers.[59]

A final revelation in the Pieck report was the attitude of the Comintern toward organic unity. He declared, as the French Communists had been doing, that there must be a single revolutionary party. But like the position previously revealed by the P.C.F. leaders, this single party was only acceptable to the Communists if based on the Communist concept of a revolutionary party. Here was the condition that made organic unity impossible. For the French Socialists who were watching this congress for indications as to what the future course of the Comintern would be, this statement should have (but didn't) caused them to resign any hope for such unity. By giving full credit to the French for the initiation of the Popular Front concept, Pieck's report also throws some significant light on the relations between the French party and the Comintern in the period between the émeute in Paris and the turning in the line of the P.C.F. at Ivry. It has been suggested that the Comintern, frustrated in all its attempts to secure a substantial following in France by the usual means, increasingly mindful of the need for a French ally as the German threat grew more serious and considerably intimidated by the unexpected extent of rightist strength in France as manifested by the émeute and subsequent events, was frightened out of continuing that tactic which it had applied since 1928; that, uncertain as to what to substitute for this tactic and desperate in its fear of having France become dominated by the Right it wavered during the spring of 1934 and finally released the P.C.F. to follow, in opportunist fashion, any policy that seemed most likely to insure its survival and at the same time to prevent the Right from gaining complete control of the government; finally, that once this was done the P.C.F. responded inevitably to the demand from within its own ranks as well as from the rest of the Left for united action against the rightist threat. Certainly the admission, if true, that the concept of the Popular Front originated with the French would tend to corroborate this hypothesis.

Subsequent speeches by Cachin and Thorez also lent support to the theory that international developments, i.e. the rearmament of Germany, forced the Comintern to give the P.C.F. its head; that internal developments, i.e. the show of strength by the French Right, forced the P.C.F. to enter upon a course of collaboration rather than sabotage of party relationships, and that the success of this formula had shown the Communists a new way to accomplish their ends both in France and elsewhere.

Cachin's function apparently was to recite the glories as well as the potentialities of the Popular Front. Speaking at the second session, on the 27th of July, he began with a salute to Henri Barbusse and Romain Rolland, both present at the congress, as being the initiators of the idea of a Popular Front at the Peace Congress in Amsterdam in 1932.[60] He implied that there had been a steady development of the concept from that time until its successful consummation in July of 1935.[61] This of course was ridiculous. As we have seen, the P.C.F. had no intention of joining in unity of action with the Socialists, much less the Radicals, in the period between the Amsterdam congress and the turning at Ivry. Cachin omitted mention of the Ivry conference entirely and made no distinction between the policies of the P.C.F. before and after it.[62] This was obviously all part of the P.C.F. fiction that there had been no change at Ivry but merely a perfectly consistent extension of past policies.

Although Cachin's contribution was principally a recounting of the origins of the new tactic in France, he too supplied some evidence of the motivation behind the Comintern's decision to change. The French Communists, he said, fully realized along with the whole of the Comintern that the world had arrived at the second cycle of revolutions and wars. It was precisely for that reason and because they were experiencing an extremely clear sensation of danger that the Communists must tear the largest possible section of the masses away from capitalism:

> We are doing this in order to place on the side of the proletariat the largest number of popular forces; we wish to rescue them from the influence of finance capital which prepares, along with fascism, war.[63]

Actually Thorez' intervention was considerably more revealing than that of Cachin in that his version of the origins of the Popular Front dealt with the internal political pressures. He claimed that there had been and still was a real danger of fascism in France and that it was when the Right tried to use the Stavisky scandal to overthrow the Radical party which was in power that the Communists decided to join the latter in common defense.[64]

Thorez also outlined the basic technique used by the P.C.F. Simply stated it was the defense of all the claims and all the liberties of everyone in France except the undefined "fascists". In the economic sphere this was translated into a simple slogan -- make the rich pay wherever the economic crisis required sacrifice. Quite obviously by this approach an appeal could be made to all the elements of French society which did not consider themselves to be among the "200 families". He appended that in addition the P.C.F. had found it useful to wage this campaign in the name of French revolutionary traditions in order to attract non-party and non-Marxist support.[65]

One statement by Thorez, it is submitted, definitely established the fact that the concept of the Popular Front originated in France rather than in the Comintern:

> When the Central Committee conceived of the idea of the Popular Front and prepared the program for it, in October 1934, we could not foresee how rapid its success would be.[66]

While this claim in no way proves that the P.C.F. leaders invented the new tactic it does tend to prove that concept was first established in some one of the groups of the Left in France rather than in the Comintern.[67] It is inconceivable that Thorez would have usurped credit for it otherwise. In view of the success of the Popular Front from the Communist point of view it is unusual enough that he did not credit the Executive Committee with its initiation in any case.

Thorez was candid in his admission that the Radicals were the principal objective of the Popular Front campaign. He admitted that once the **front unique** had been established with the Socialists all the efforts of the French militants were directed toward the Radicals. The P.C.F. waged a campaign by posters, the press, at meetings and in the Chamber of Deputies. On the eve of each of the two congresses of the Radical party since Ivry (at Nantes in October of 1934 and at Lyon in March of 1935) the Communists organized large meetings at which representatives of the Central Committee explained the Communist concept of the Popular Front, addressing themselves particularly to the Radical delegates.

Another significant revelation by Thorez concerned the decision taken by the P.C.F. in regard to participation should the Popular Front become a government. He asserted that there could be no question of the P.C.F. participating in parliamentary coalitions like that of Brandler in Saxe in 1923, nor in the coalition governments like those in Belgium, Czechoslovakia and Spain. Nor was the "labor government" concept as practised in England acceptable to the P.C.F. He admitted that since the P.C.F. was still a small minority party in France it could not hope for the immediate establishment of Soviets. Therefore it must not consider the installation of Soviets as the immediate goal at this time.[68] The clear but unexpressed conclusion from this statement was that the P.C.F. would not participate in any such government, but nevertheless would support it and would withdraw from its former intransigent position of absolute insistence upon the installation of Soviets.

In closing Thorez recognised that the Socialists had found the new policies of the P.C.F. to be too mild. The Socialists said that the **prélevement** upon capital was not sufficient and that there must be socialization of the banks and large industries. In his answer to this Thorez revealed nothing new in so far as the French Socialists were concerned, but his statements effectively underlined once again that the single aim of the Communists at this time was to achieve power whatever the doctrinal cost:

> We replied very quietly; we Communists are for socialization, we are for outright expropriation of the capitalist expropriators, but we consider that in order to socialize it is necessary to fulfill one condition, a very small condition, to possess power, to take power.
>
> Nevertheless we Communists do not propose that you Socialists adopt our fundamental program. We propose to reach an agreement with you about that which it is possible to do together today.[69]

Implicit in this admission perhaps was the simple answer to the whole question of the motivation behind the Communist change. The theory of "total power tomorrow" had given way to that of "whatever power possible today" in order to safeguard the Soviet Union. Such power must be attained at any cost, and the important factor was not by what means but how soon.

The speeches of the French delegates and the reports of Pieck and other Comintern leaders were but preliminaries to the two reports submitted by Dmitrov. Dmitrov was at the height of his favor with Stalin and his words were generally interpreted as representing the opinion of Stalin himself.[70] An examination of his two reports reveals the recognition of the complete failure of the old (i.e. 1928) policy of the Comintern, the decision to scrap it, and the embarkation on a new course the nature of which had been indicated by the developments in France.

Dmitrov began with what must be regarded as the official analysis of the fascist offensive. According to this analysis the spearhead of that offensive was German Nazism. It drew its strength from appeals to the most urgent needs of all levels of society. The Communists had always under-estimated the strength and danger of fascism; for years they had relied on the advanced state of Socialism among the German proletariat, saying that "Germany is not Italy" and the like. Now it had arrived in Germany and there was great danger of its success elsewhere. There was but one course of action that could ensure the prevention of this success:

> The first thing that must be done ... is to form a united front, to establish unity of action of the workers in every factory, in every district, in every region, in every country, all over the world. Unity of action of the proletariat on a national and international scale is the mighty weapon which renders the working class capable not only of successful defense but also of successful counter-attack against fascism, against the class enemy.[71]

This postulate also embraced united action of the IInd and IIIrd Internationals in order to oppose fascism on an international scale.

Step by step as Dmitrov elaborated the new tactic the parallel with the developments in France became more apparent. The signing of unity of action pacts between Socialists and Communists, he said, was but the first step. These must be implemented by committees elected from all parties which could include in the mass movement the unorganized workers "and on this basis create the necessary wide and active rank and file ... and train hundreds of thousands of non-party bolsheviks".[72] Joint action of the organized workers was the starting point but taken alone it failed to exploit situations such as that in France where the combined total of organized workers, Socialist and Communist, was only one million and the total number of workers was eleven million:

> The creation of non-partisan class bodies is the best form for carrying out, extending and strengthening the united front among the rank and file of the masses. Such bodies would also be the best bulwark against any attempt of the opponents of the united front to disrupt the established unity of the working class.[73]

But the **front unique** was only one aspect of the double tactic which must be used against fascism. In addition there must be a wide People's Front. Here again France had shown the way. As had been done in France in regard to Herriot the Comintern prescribed doing wherever a moderate party was partially composed of bourgeois elements and partially of petty bourgeoisie:

> Under certain conditions we can and must try to draw these parties and organizations or certain sections of them to the side of the anti-fascist People's Front despite their bourgeois leadership. Such for instance is the situation today in France with the Radical party.... But regardless of whether or not there is any chance of attracting these parties and organizations as a whole to the People's Front, our tactic must **under all circumstances** be directed toward drawing the small peasants, artisans, handicrafters, etc., among their members into the anti-fascist Popular Front.[74]

The manner in which this tactic was to be applied varied from organization to organization and country to country. There were certain key questions in each country which were determinative and these must be completely understood before the choice of alternative courses of action was made. This then was the essence of the Popular Front as incorporated into the policy of the International based on the experience in France. Communist parties must seek to enroll the heterogeneous liberal and moderate parties and other groups in the anti-fascist struggle. Failing in this they must try to draw the elements sympathetic to the Popular Front away from their parties. The decisive factor was the extent to which elements hostile to the Popular Front controlled the liberal and moderate political groups.

Based upon these criteria the special tasks for the P.C.F., according to Dmitrov, were: (1) the creation of a united front not only in the political but in the economic field as well; (2) the establishment of trade union unity; (3) the enrollment of the peasants and the petty bourgeoisie in the anti-fascist front; (4) the consolidation and strengthening of the anti-fascist organizations; (5) the attainment of the disbanding of the fascist organizations; (6) the purge from the police and army of all conspirators preparing a fascist coup; (7) the initiation of a campaign against the reactionary cliques within the Catholic Church; (8) the neutralization of fascistic elements in the army. Dmitrov declared that by thus solidifying all the elements which comprised the lower and lower middle classes it would strike at the Achilles Heel of fascism which was its heterogeneous social basis. This solidification must begin with trade union unity for that was the initial source of strength of a united class movement. From there it must expand to all sympathetic forces within the nation.

In order to facilitate the enlistment of all of these divergent elements Dmitrov enlarged upon the statements of Thorez as to the Communist position on nationalism:

> We are the irreconcilable opponents, on principle, of bourgeois nationalism in all its forms. But we **are not supporters of national nihilism** and should never act as such. The task of educating the workers and all working people in the spirit of proletarian internationalism is one of the fundamental tasks of every Communist party. But anyone who thinks that this permits him, or perhaps even compels him, to sneer at all the national sentiments of the wide masses is far from being a genuine bolshevik, and has understood nothing of the training of Lenin and Stalin on the national question.[75]

Dmitrov also gave the closing speech of the World Congress on the 20th of August. In this he summarized the changes in Communist position declaring that the congress had laid the foundations for such a wide mobilization of the forces of all toilers against capitalism as had never before existed in the history of the working class struggle. The congress had set as the task of the international proletariat that of consolidating its forces both politically and organizationally. The most significant change revealed by Dmitrov was that the Communist parties were to put an end "to the isolation to which they had been reduced by the Social-democratic policy of class collaboration with the bourgeois".[76] They were charged with "rallying the working people around the working class in a broad People's Front against the offensive of capital and reaction, against fascism and the threat of war in each individual country and in the internationnal arena".[77] He paid a final tribute to the part played by the French in the new developments and, for what it is worth, gave them full credit for the initiative in the Popular Front:

> We have not invented this task. It has been prompted by the experience of the world labor movement itself, above all the experience of the proletariat in France. The great merit of the P.C.F. is that it grasped the need of the **hour**, that it paid no heed to the sectarians who tried to hold back the party and hamper the realization of the united front of struggle against fascism, but acted boldly and in bolshevik fashion and, by its pact with the Socialist party providing for joint action, prepared the united front of the proletariat as the basis for the anti-fasicst People's Front now in the making. By this action, which accords with the vital interest of all the working people, the French

> workers, both Communist and Social, have once more advanced the French labor movement to first place, to a leading position in capitalist Europe, and have shown that they are worthy successors of the Communards, worthy heirs to the glorious legacy of the Paris Commune.
>
> It is the great service of the P.C.F. and the French proletariat that by their fighting against fascism in a united popular front they helped to prepare the decisions of our Congress which are of such tremendous importance for the workers of all countries.[78]

He also let it be known that the Comintern had indeed made a tactical change -- thus admitting what Thorez had hitherto attempted to deny for the French party:

> ... Our congress acting in the spirit and guided by the method of **living Marxism-Leninism** has reshaped the tactical lines of the Comintern to meet the changed world situation.[79]

Following this closing speech the resolutions on the various reports were voted. The resolution on Dmitrov's report called for trade union unity both nationally and internationally, prescribed that the forms of the **front unique** would vary according to the concrete situations and the character of the workers' organizations, and established the principle of an anti-imperialist Popular Front in the colonies. Its key paragraph was the following:

> Without renouncing for an instant their independent work of Communist propaganda, of organization and of mobilization of the masses, Communists must try, in order to facilitate for the workers the road to unity of action, to **realize common action with the Social-democratic parties, reformist trade unions and other organizations of workers against the class enemies of the proletariat on the basis of accords of brief or long duration.**[80]

Despite the sensational nature of the changes in line at this congress, which produced the fundamental revision of doctrinal emphasis from anti-Socialism to anti-fascism, not very much was said that was new to the French leaders. After the congress they returned to Paris to resume their campaign for the Popular Front in exactly the same manner as they had been doing for many months. At Moscow they had been the actors rather than the spectators -- they had been there more to teach than to learn.

But there had been one new concept introduced at this congress which was also new to the French. This was Dmitrov's assertion, partly by implication but mainly by direct statement, that the Comintern could and in fact must adjust and adapt its policies to the changing world situation. At first glance there is nothing particularly startling about this. The world had seen many overall reversals and thousands of minor ones in the relatively short history of the Comintern. No one who was at all conversant with this history had any doubt that the Comintern would in the future, as it had in the past, change its position whenever and wherever to do so was to its advantage. However until the VIIth World Congress such changes in line, however contradictory, had always been carefully fitted into the doctrines of the founding fathers -- frequently, of course, through miracles of logical contortions and distortions. This was based on the principle that the teachings of Marx, Engels, and Lenin were sacred, that they defined the limits of the policies of the party and that these limits could not be transcended -- or at least that all policies, however much opposed to these teachings, must be explained in terms of them. Now Dmitrov had relieved the party of the necessity for this sometimes onerous rationalization. This congress had provided "**a new tactical orientation for the Comintern**".[81] In effect, in the names of Marx and Lenin themselves he repudiated their doctrines:

> We would not be revolutionary Marxists, Leninists, worthy pupils of Marx, Engels, Lenin and Stalin if we did not suitably **reconstitute** our policies and tactics in accordance with the changing situation and the changes in the world labor movement.[82]

He declared the Communists to be the enemies of all cut and dried schemes. Thus he substituted the concept which came to be called "living bolshevism" for the former worship of doctrinaire orthodoxy. Due respect was of course still paid to the old theories -- that required but simple ritual -- but under the new formula the Comintern had the "duty" to respond to events. In effect of course this relieved Stalin of the last obstacle to the use of the Comintern as a freely maneuverable tool. He need no longer search for a means of circumventing or rationalizing the writings of Marx, Engels and Lenin. Schumpeter points significantly to the approximate coincidence in time between Stalin's ultimate victory over Kamenev and Zinoviev and the complete subjugation of the Comintern to the interests of Soviet foreign policy.[83] Certainly the VIIth World Congress released the Comintern for use in that manner, for if the dedication of that body to the World Revolution had not terminated, it had at least been suspended while Stalin put international Communism to more immediate tactical use. The voices of the dead authors of the World Revolution were, and were to be, drowned out by the fanfare welcoming the arrival of the "living bolshevism" of Stalin. For the time being "living bolshevism" meant anti-fascism, but according to Dmitrov's hypothesis it could change to whatever was demanded by changing circumstances.

The effect of this change upon the position of the P.C.F. was considerable. Its immediate result of course was that the leaders, who for a year had been denying any change in line despite the obvious absurdity of such denials, could now wear their new face openly. The propriety of change was in itself now part of Comintern doctrine. At their Villeurbanne Conference in January of 1936 it was proclaimed:

> The International changes its tactic. Do you believe that Stalin and Dmitrov are bureaucrats who do not see facts ... ? The bolsheviks are living. Read Dmitrov, read Stalin, their interviews with the proletariat. He is not on the moon, Comrade Stalin, he has his feet on the ground. Communists adapt their tactics to the situation, without losing sight of the final goal. There it is, our whole secret.[84]

But the effect of this change reached further than that. Now that the year-old policy of the P.C.F. had become the declared policy of Comintern as well, the French Communists were infinitely strengthened in their dealings with both the Parti Socialiste and the Radicals. Despite the fact that all could recognize that this turning was merely a move to aid in the defense of the Soviet Union,[85] it also dispelled any lingering doubts concerning a maneuver. Thus many of the objections of the I.O.S. were also removed. Popular Frontism was the new face of the Communist party, and of the whole Communist party. And the non-Communist Left in France seemed prepared to believe that, at least as long as the Hitler threat existed, Popular Frontism was here to stay.

NOTES

1. Among the more comprehensive of the summations of the Communist changes were Georges Izard, OÚ VA LE COMMUNISME?, Grasset, Paris, 1936; Chastanet, LA RÉPUBLIQUE DES CRABES, Alsatia, Paris (no date); Legendre, POUR LUTTER CONTRE LE FRONT POPULAIRE, Imprimerie Réunies, Senlis, 1937, also his MENSONGES COMMUNISTES, centre de propaganda républicaine, Paris, 1938; see also Paul-Boncour's ENTRE DEUX GUERRES, Librairie Plon, Paris, 1945, pp. 68, 69.
2. "Classe contre classe", speech by Thorez, L'HUMANITÉ, 5 December 1932.
3. Report of Duclos to the Ivry Conference, C.B., 1 July 1934, p. 790.
4. L'HUMANITÉ, 26 June 1935.
5. L'HUMANITÉ, 30 November 1935, see also Thorez, POUR LA CAUSE DU PEUPLE, Report to the Central Committee, 17 October 1935, Paris, Imprimerie Centrale, 1936.
6. Thorez, FRONT POPULAIRE EN MARCHE, Speech in the Chamber of Deputies, 13 November 1934, Bureau d'Editions, Paris, 1934.
7. Thorez, L'UNION DE LA NATION FRANCAISE, Report to the 8th National Conference at Villeurbanne, Publications revolutionnaires, Paris 1936, p. 11.
8. L'HUMANITÉ, 19 June 1934.
9. C.B., 1 July 1934, p. 774, and Thorez, PAR L'UNITÉ D'ACTION NOUS VAINCRONS LE FASCISME, Report to the Ivry Conference, Bureau d'éditions, Paris 1934.
10. L'HUMANITÉ, 15 August 1936.
11. Thorez, Dewez, Ramette, LES COMMUNISTES CONTRE LE GUERRE, speeches in the Chamber of Deputies, 15 June 1934, Imprimerie d'art Voltaire, Paris, 1934.

12. PAR L'UNITÉ D'ACTION NOUS VAINCRONS LE FASCISME, op. cit., p. 3.
13. Duclos report to the Villeurbanne Conference, L'HUMANITÉ, 28 January 1936.
14. A. Mortier, "Le Service de deux ans et la lutte contre la guerre", C.B. 15 July-1 August 1934, p. 880.
15. See Article by Gabriel Péri in L'HUMANITÉ, 21 May 1935.
16. COMPTE RENDU DU VIIIe CONFÉRENCE NATIONALE, VILLEURBANNE 22-25 JANUARY 1936, Comite Populaire du propagande, Paris, 1937.
17. Speech of Racamond at the "Anti-fascist Congress", Salle Pleyel, L'HUMANITÉ, 5 June 1935.
18. Speech by Duclos at the Velodrome d'Hiver, L'HUMANITÉ, 9 August 1936.
19. L'HUMANITÉ, 21 May 1933.
20. Ibid., 3 May 1936.
21. L'HUMANITÉ, 4 October 1933.
22. Ibid., 15 June 1936.
23. In his attack on the P.C.F. after his expulsion Doriot recounted how as the Soviet Union became more worried about Germany's rearmament the position of the P.C.F. changed from that favoring return of the Saar to Germany, non-inclusion of Alsace-Lorraine in France proper, and the denunciation of the Versailles Treaty to the exact opposite in each case. Doriot, L'EXPERIENCE SOVIÈTIQUE ET LE COMMUNISME FRANCAIS, op. cit., pp. 27 ff.
24. Walter, op. cit., pp. 293-302.
25. The common program upon which this was based was:
    (1) Defense of the claims of workers in sports.
    (2) Battle against the attempts at "fascisation" and militarization of sport.
    (3) Organic independence of the workers sport movement.
    (4) Battle for the International unity of workers sport.
    V. Michaut, "La lutte pour l'unité de la jeunesse", C.B., 15 December 1934, p. 1472.

26. As of September 1st, 1934, Piatnitski claimed, there were already 166 united trade unions: 105 among the railroad workers, 27 among the tobacco workers, 12 among the tram workers, 3 among the miners, etc.

    "Les problèmes du mouvement syndical international" (shortened text of his report to a joint meeting of the committees of the International Syndicale Rouge) - C.B., 1 November 1934, p. 1275.

27. cf. Jouhaux, LA C.G.T.: CE QU'ELLE EST? CE QU'ELLE VEUT, Collection, Problèmes et documents, Gallimard, Paris, 1937, PASSIM.

28. An excellent discussion of the C.G.T. prerequisites for unification is contained in a thesis submitted at Lyon in 1938, Veillard, Raymond, LE PLAN DE LA C.G.T., pp. 202-222, available at the Bibliothèque St. Geneviève in Paris.

29. cf. statement of Dmitrov at the VIIth World Congress to the effect that Communists "no longer insist on the independence of Red trade unions at all costs". VIIe CONGRÈS MONDIALE, **op.cit.**, p. 514.

30. C.B., 1 November 1934, pp. 1283-4.

31. LE PEUPLE, 9 November 1934; commenting on the resolution of the C.G.T.U., the Communists declared:

    "Agreed on its bases the two C.C.N.'s decided to launch an appeal in common to all the unions to organize their fusion immediately. They decided to constitute a two-party commission in order to direct and control the fusion at all echelons of the trade union movement and to organize the inter-confederal congress of unity. This congress will decide about the statutes, about proportional representation, about the program, about the leadership of the thus unified C.G.T. and about its international affiliation."

    C.B., 15 November 1934, p. 1322.

32. C.B., 15 November 1934, p. 1326.

33. Report of the meeting of the Commission on unification, November 15, 1935. LE POPULAIRE, 17 November 1935.

34. Duclos, C.B., 1 October 1934, p. 1117. It is worth noting that the Socialists had the same attitude toward the first ballot at this time. However, at their Congres extraordinaire at Boulogne-sur-Seine 1 and 2 February 1936 they introduced a substantial modification:

The federations are obliged to present candidates on the first ballot in all districts.

"However the Congress recognizes the exceptional situation arising from the fact that at this very moment the party is doing everything in its power to realize organic unity. It therefore authorizes those federations which judge it necessary to negotiate for the choice of a single candidate on the first ballot with the corresponding organizations of the proletarian parties that participate with it in the Commission on Unification."
RAPPORT ADMINISTRATIF AU XXXIII CONGRÈS NATIONAL, **op. cit.**, p. 32.

35. Romier, "Le scissioniste Doriot contre le Communisme", C.B., 15 November 1934, p. 1341.
36. **Ibid.**, p. 1342.
37. C.B., 15 December 1934, p. 1454.
38. See for instance statements in the organ of the moderate wing of the Radical party in October of 1934:

    "If the Parti Socialiste has joined its actions with those of the P.C.F. it is in order to wage the class battle in a more active manner, to create by speculating on the discontentment and the general difficulties, a continuous agitation, a condition favorable to the brutal conquest of power. In this program where are the democratic liberties and what becomes of them? The Common Front knows liberty only for the needs of its propaganda and the facilitation of its undertakings. This goal attained ... adieu to liberty." Georges Ricou, L'ÈRE NOUVELLE, 15 October 1934.

    "Any conversation between the Radical-Socialists and the Common Front is impossible; it is even unimaginable." L'ÈRE NOUVELLE, 9 October 1934.

39. CONTRE L'UNION NATIONALE, EN AVANT POUR LE FRONT POPULAIRE, Bureau d'editions, Paris 1935, p. 17.
40. Duclos, L'UNITÉ POUR LE VICTOIRE, speech at the joint Socialist and Communist meeting at the Salle de la Mutualité, 2 December 1935. Bourges, Imprimerie ouvrière du Centre, 1936, p. 7.
41. C.B., 15 November 1934, p. 1314.
42. Waldeck-Rochet, "Le travail des communistes a la campagne", C.B., 15 October 1934, p. 1228.

43. Duclos, C.B., 15 November 1934, p. 1313.
44. Thus for the municipal elections of 5 and 12 May 1935, the P.C.F. and the Parti Socialiste issued a joint manifesto through the Committee of coordination:

    "The enemies of the people did not win the victories they expected last Sunday. Next Sunday the popular forces must realize their unity of action to beat reaction.

    "The P.C.F. and the Parti Socialiste have decided to do everything to check the men of February 6th.

    "Everywhere the Socialist and Communist candidates will desist in favor of the most successful among them." LE POPULAIRE, 7 May 1935.
45. Duclos, C.B., 15 August 1934, pp. 937-8.
46. JOURNAL OFFICIEL, 16 November 1934, p. 2342.
47. Émile Roche wrote in RÉPUBLIQUE of October 4th, 1934: "On the subject of national defense we can only be deeply divided with the members of the Common Front".
48. L'ÈRE NOUVELLE, 23 August 1934.
49. For an excellent history of the Franco-Soviet negotiations starting in 1933 and leading to the pact in 1935 see Beloff, FOREIGN Policy of Soviet Russia (issued under the auspices of the Royal Institute of International Affairs) Oxford University Press, 1947, Volume I, pp. 141-143, and 148-151.
50. LE TEMPS, 17 May 1935.

    L'HUMANITÉ, 23 May 1935.
51. Speaking at the VIIth World Congress, Cachin described the Franco-Soviet Pact as having been approved by worker, peasant, Communist, Socialist and democrat in France as a step toward peace:

    "Comrades, the day when the announcement of Stalin's declaration was received in France it produced, as you can imagine, a tremendous splash. Socialist chiefs could be heard complaining, while invoking the purity of their doctrine and their anti-war and pacifist intransigence, of words that, they said, seemd to disavow their attitude and that of the P.C.F.

    "... the intervention of Stalin has received an excellent welcome in our country. Not unanimous certainly. For there are the Hitlerians, then there are the neo-fascists and naturally the

Trotskyists with their small and suspicious group. Finally there is Doriot." VIIe CONGRÈS MONDIALE, **op. cit.**, p. 91.

52. The postponement was officially announced after the meeting of the Praesidium of 5 September 1934. The order of business, however, had been determined as early as the 28 May meeting of this body. It included:
    I. The account of the activity of the Executive Committee of the Comintern (Reporter - Pieck).
    II. The offensive of fascism and the tasks of the Comintern in the battle for unity of the workers class against it (Reporter - Dmitrov).
    III. The preparation of the imperialist war and the tasks of the Comintern (Reporter - Ercoli).
    IV. The account of the building of Socialism in the Soviet Union (Reporter - Manuilski).
    V. Election of the directing organs of the Comintern.

    Printed in C.B., 1 October 1934, p. 1115.

53. Cachin, Thorez and André Marty spoke for the P.C.F. Barbusse and Rolland, symbolizing the initiation of the idea of the Popular Front, were also present.

    Marty's contribution, in the discussion following Ercoli's report, consisted of an explanation of the new position of the P.C.F. in regard to the question of national defense as a result of the Franco-Soviet pact. In direct contradiction to the previous line of the P.C.F. it was now campaigning against disobedience and desertion and was urging the workers to respond to mobilization even in the case of a "reactionary war". Marty repeated the warning of the Radical deputy Marc Rucart, made at the July 14th rally, to the effect that the forces of the Popular Front must beware lest the Army become the tool of minority factions. VIIe CONGRÈS MONDIALE, **op. cit.**, p. 431.

54. Just as Manuilski had represented the anti-Socialist line of the Comintern after 1928 so now did the favor with which Dmitrov was regarded indicate the change of emphasis toward anti-fascism. As the "hero" of the Reichstag affair trials Dmitrov was the most clear-cut symbol available to Stalin through which to present the new line.

55. VIIe CONGRÈS MONDIALE, **op. cit.**, p. 46.

56. **Ibid.**, pp. 45, 46.

57. VIIe CONGRÈS MONDIALE, **op. cit.**, p. 45.
58. **Ibid.**, p. 108 (Pieck's concluding speech to the opening session).
59. **Ibid.**, p. 113.
60. This had become the constant claim of the French Communists. See Cogniot, Georges, PAIX ET LIBERTÉ, Editions du mouvement Amsterdam-Pleyel (Speech by Cogniot to the Congrès Populaire du Grand Paris, 28 June 1936), Paris, 1936, p. 4.
61. Bulletin of June 1936 of the Comité Amsterdam-Pleyel:

    "Just as in the 1932-34 period thousands of workers, peasants, intellectuals, little people of all kinds found their rallying point at Amsterdam-Pleyel, so in 1936 in order to insure the victory of the program in the preparation of which we collaborated, at the base of which we put our signature, there are millions who in this way seek the path to the **Great Unity**." Paris, 1936.
62. Cachin said:

    "I want simply to give you two dates: that of the beginning, when we entered seriously into the idea of the front unique, into the idea of the Popular Front - this was after the Congress at Amsterdam in August 1932.

    "That was our beginning, our entry into the game, and then here is our date of arrival; July 14th, 1935, which saw the massive realization of the double tactic of front unique and front populaire." VIIe CONGRÈS MONDIALE, **op. cit.**, p. 87.
63. VIIe CONGRÈS MONDIALE, **op. cit.**, p. 90.
64. Here again Thorez felt constrained to explain away the participation of the Communists on February 6th, using the same argument that it had been in the nature of a counter-manifestation. That the need for this explanation still existed demonstrates how, in their under-estimation of the real fear of fascism in the ranks of the French Left, they had put themselves in an extremely embarrassing position in relation to their subsequent drive for leadership of the anti-fascist campaign.
65. He claimed that Engels had authorized the use of revolutionary traditions for political advancement -- thus the exaltation of the memories of 1789, 1793 and 1871.
66. VIIe CONGRÈS MONDIALE, **op. cit.**, p. 200.
67. Guy Jerram, whose period of greatest activity coincided with the birth of the Popular Front, claims that the idea originated

within the A.R.A.C., whose members were both Socialists and Communists as well as non-party, and not within the P.C.F. itself. Interview with Jerram, 15 November 1949.

68. This was an attempt to avoid the paradox of the Communist position in France which Bergery, for one, never tired of pointing out:

"What does the Communist Party think?

"If one looks to the external manifestations of the party for a response to the questions raised, one becomes perplexed indeed.

"For while the militants continue to shout for 'Soviets everywhere' within a party which tolerates neither indiscipline nor fantasy, L'Humanite passes from 'class against class' (1933) to front unique (1934), from front unique to a 'reconciliation francaise against the 200 families' (1935), from this reconciliation to 'National Union' (last week), finally from 'National Union' to 'France to the French' (L'HUMANITÉ of the day before yesterday).

"We are neither for National Union nor Soviets everywhere ... But we can understand the holding of one or the other of these theses.

"The only thing that escapes us ... since at least 70 to 80% of the population reject, rightly or wrongly, the Soviet system ... is how one can expect to achieve Soviets everywhere and National Union simultaneously." LA FLÈCHE, 4 July 1936.

69. VIIe CONGRÈS MONDIALE, **op. cit**, p. 206. At the meeting of the Central Committee of the P.C.F. June 1st and 2nd 1935, the report of the Bureau Politique to the committee recounted how the enemy of the **front unique** had shifted from the Social-democrats to the fascists, and concluded:

"Even though we believe that only Soviets will assure the well being of the masses, we say that there is a limit to the oppression and exploitation of capital, and that even parliamentary means may be used if those elected and their Governments take into account the will of the people."

Rapport du comité central, see brochure LA CONFÉRENCE NATIONALE D'IVRY, Bureau d'éditions, Paris, 1936, p. 24.

70. cf. Deutscher, **op. cit.**, p. 420.
71. VIIe CONGRÈS MONDIALE, **op. cit.**, p. 132.
72. VIIe CONGRÈS MONDIALE, **op. cit.**, p. 137.
73. **Ibid.**, p. 138.

74. **Ibid.**, p. 139. Dmitrov had previously warned against the dangers of a rigid application of a set formula to all countries:

"It is particularly necessary to avoid the application in a schematic way of the tactic of **front unique**, without taking into account the relationship of the force of classes and of concrete conditions existing in each country, France, for example, to a country where the conditions are otherwise, at times even radically different, for example England. Transporting the experience acquired in one country of political and organizational action, without critical analysis, to all other countries, has often led to failures which have cost the working class dearly."

C.B., 1 December 1934, p. 1378.

75. VIIe CONGRÈS MONDIALE, **op. cit.**, p. 169.
76. VIIe CONGRÈS MONDIALE, **op. cit.**, p. 511.
77. **Ibid.**
78. VIIe CONGRÈS MONDIALE, **op. cit.**, p. 511. In the CAHIERS DU BOLSHEVISME in December 1934 had appeared an article by Dmitrov entitled "La lutte pour le front unique". This article revealed that, as of that date at least, the Comintern Executive had accepted the progress made by the P.C.F. as a pattern for the initial steps:

"In France the **front unique** has developed rapidly in the course of the last few months; the P.C.F. and the Parti Socialiste have concluded a pact of common battle against fascism and the bourgeois offensive; the working class, grouping itself into a **front unique** and starting to unite itself into joint unions, is repulsing successfully the provocative stories of fascism.

"All this is only the first step. In spite of the resistance of the leadership of the IInd International and of certain Social-democratic parties to the **front unique**, we must go further, we must enlarge and strengthen the **front unique** in the masses. The **front unique** means above all **the broad mobilization and union of the masses from below**, around single organisms of battle created by the masses themselves. The immediate task of the **front unique** at this moment is to create **elected organisms of the front unique at the base** principally in the shops and factories. A no less important task ... is to unite the trade union organizations of the working class." C.B., 1 December 1934, p. 1375.

Dmitrov at this time asserted that there were two principal difficulties: (1) easy discouragement and the inability to comprehend that this must be done from the base, (2) the tendency to compromise the class battle in order to fit it into the Social-democratic pattern, instead of working simultaneously for the **front unique** and direct Communist aims.

"Always while fighting for the creation of the **front unique** Communists must not lose for an instant the revolutionary perspective, they must know how to link the **front unique** with the strategic task, the battle for the victory of the proletariat revolution, for the dictatorship of the proletariat."

Ibid., p. 1377.

79. VIIe CONGRÈS MONDIALE, **op. cit.**, p. 515.

80. VIIe CONGRÈS MONDIALE, **op. cit.**, p. 532. In an article appearing in the CAHIERS DU BOLCHEVISME of 1 January 1935, entitled "L'Organization du Front Populaire du Travail, de la aix et de la Liberté", Thorez had laid down this same rule:

"It is said that we must conquer the majority of the working class first and then turn toward the middle classes. That is not right. We must carry on the two tasks at once. Our party, having given meaning to the workers class by its tactic of **Front unique** can and must do more in order to win the middle classes, above all the peasants."

C.B., 1 January 1935, p. 33.

81. VIIe CONGRÈS MONDIALE, **op. cit.**, p. 515.

82. **Ibid.**, p. 179.

83. Schumpeter, CAPITALISM, SOCIALISM AND DEMOCRACY, Harper & Brothers, New York, 1947, pp. 360-361.

84. Thorez, L'UNION DE LA NATIONAL FRANCAISE, **op. cit.**, p. 8.

85. An argument which that faction of the Radical party that opposed the Popular Front constantly used:

"We have asked the P.C.F. and notably M. Thorez a question.

" 'You advocate the formation of a French Front'. The idea is excellent. But of what is it a question? Around what program of action does it suit you for us to unite?"

"No response. But the manifestations of recent days have shown us where they wish to lead us. Everything would indicate that they wished to lead us to war -- to a 'preventive war' of course.

"Well we won't march. I won't march."

Jean Piot, L'OEUVRE, 5 September 1936.

CHAPTER TWELVE

CONCLUSION

In this work we have not been concerned with the factors that brought the parties of the Popular Front to power but rather with those factors which brought them together. Thus the Rassemblement populaire of July 14th, 1935, and its immediate aftermath constitute the logical point at which to end this study. The decision on the part of both the Radicals and Socialists to participate in the rally marked the significant formal change in policy for the two parties, and what followed was largely a question of implementation of this new policy. Perhaps the rally itself and the events leading up to it deserve final brief consideration.

We have seen that the Popular Front was the creation of the P.C.F. and that the Socialist decision to adhere to it was made by the party as a whole at Mulhouse only a month before the rally. We have also seen the internal schism that was growing in the Radical party over the question of support of the National Union government. The Radicals on the other hand were won over bit by bit between the beginning of the year and the time of the rally. Split internally and under consistent Communist pressure the various factions within the party began to drift in groups to the support of the Popular Front. When the P.C.F. held a large manifestation at Bulliers on January 18th the Ligue des Droits de L'Homme was in official attendance. Its president Victor Basch declared the allegiance of the Ligue to the movement.[1] Four days later, also at Bulliers, the Communists issued a second appeal at a manifestation in commemoration of Lenin's death. Again large numbers of Radicals were present. Communist pressure never relaxed. On the 10th of February a demonstration was held in the Place de la République to celebrate the anniversary of the previous year's activities. L'HUMANITÉ claimed the next day that "everyone" had been present; "Communists, Socialists, unionists, pacifists, Radicals, non-party anti-fascists, men, women and children showed ... the same enthusiasm and anger, thus accumulating an explosive force which, by organizing itself, would soon become irresistible".² Only the C.G.T. remained officially absent.

On May 10th Daladier published an article in PETIT PROVENCAL in which he declared:

> Reds against Whites. The old slogan of our fathers resounds again in our dear and great country. This evening due to the far-sighted efforts of the Republicans in the largest portion of our cities it is not hideous dictatorship but liberty which again will take possession of the Hotels de Ville.³

A week later the Communist about face on the question of national defense removed the final barrier to cooperation by the Radicals. At its meeting of June 19th the Executive Committee of the Radical party decided to join the anti-fascist rally and circulated a letter to that effect to the presidents of its federations:

> All of Republican France, parties and groupings of the Left intermingled, must rise on the 14th of July against the growing menace of fascism, for work and peace.⁴

On the 25th Daladier attended a meeting of the P.C.F. at the Mutualité bringing the greetings of the Radical party to the proletariat, vowing undying hatred of the parties of the 200 families and unreserved support of the Popular Front. This marked the successful culmination of the Communist campaign. A final minor but psychologically important concession to the Radicals was that the Marseillaise and the tricolor should share honors with the International and the red flag at the rally.

Thus on the 14th of July with Thorez, Daladier and Blum marching under the tricolor and the red flag, all three with arms raised and fists clenched, the expression of anti-fascist sentiment was consolidated into an impressive display of the strength of the combined Left Republican and proletarian forces of France. An estimated 500,000 manifestants demonstrated in Paris with 2,400,000 more in the provinces. The patriotic demonstrations of the Right in the west of Paris seemed pale by comparison, and the "fascist threat" an absurdity in view of the relative size and enthusiasm of the respective forces.

But the defense against fascism was the cord that bound the parties together. At the rally the speakers representing both the Socialist and Radical parties made this absolutely clear. In his speech on behalf of the Parti Socialiste Paul Faure exclaimed:

No, no, that shame inflicted on other neighboring countries will be spared us; abolished liberties, suppressed universal suffrage, trade union rights destroyed, all the conquests and all the hopes of democracy annihilated.[5]

And certainly the Radicals could only justify their presence in company with the bolshevik in the name of anti-fascism. The president of the Radical federation of the Seine, Ernest Perney, went out of his way to point this out:

All those who serve it (the Republic) intend to safeguard that liberty which it has won so difficultly. But they also know that this minumum of liberty will only be saved if the menace of the new dictatorships, which manifest themselves more strongly each day, are definitely crushed.

That is the real reason why at this time the Parti Radical-Socialiste, profoundly attached to its own doctrine, owes it to itself to be present at this rally with all those who wish to defend the Nation and liberty against all such undertakings whatever mask they wear.

Our presence here signifies ... that we intend to withhold nothing, that we will remain faithful to a great and noble tradition of union and of Republican defense.[6]

But the emphasis for the Communist speakers was different. Duclos speaking for the P.C.F. and Racamond speaking for the C.G.T.U. stressed the economic and other positive gains that could be realized by a political force such as that gathered together at the rally.[7] Here was the first real sign of the ending of one phase and the beginning of another. At this Popular Front rally, which the Communists had called and to which they had secured the adhesion of the Radicals and Socialists in the name of the anti-fascist struggle, the seeds were sown for the next big step on the Communist agenda -- the transformation of an essentially negative and defensive force into a political coalition capable of taking and exercising governmental power. Neither the Socialists nor the Radicals fully understood what was taking place. We have seen how at Mulhouse the former accepted adhesion to the Popular Front almost casually and, after having accepted it, continued with a long and heated debate over the various Socialist theories of taking power. A similar situation existed within the Radical party, which had adhered to the July 14th rally with all its implications despite the complete absence of a common positive ground for action with the Communists, purely because of the common defensive cause which they shared. But in each case once the parties had decided to adhere to this rally there was no turning back. There was considerable truth in Cachin's statement at the VIIth World Congress that "July 14th marked the date of arrival".[8] For that date unquestionably marked the successful culmination of the twelve month campaign of the P.C.F. From that time on it was inevitable that the three parties proceed to the formation of a platform, however heterogeneous, however paradoxical, however unrevolutionary that platform might be, that would serve as the basis for a Popular Front government. And a Popular Front government would be the crowning achievement of the P.C.F., for such a government would be an absolute guarantee of French aid for the Soviet Union in case of German aggression.

Following the July 14th rally and through the remainder of 1935 and the early months of 1936, events transpired as the Communists intended that they should. Those goals which the Communists sought as part of their overall plan were accomplished -- those in which they had no interest or opposed failed. Thus an electoral program was established. Through the National Committee of the Popular Front the Communists prevailed upon the Socialists and Radicals to proceed with its creation. The Socialists, hesitant and reluctant as ever to create or participate in a "super-party", were caught in the dynamism of the Popular Front movement and could do nothing else.[9] The Radicals were seduced by Communist consent to, in fact Communist initiation of, a program so mild that it contained nothing to which they could object -- in fact a program which was virtually that of the Cahiers de Huyghens.[10]

The other major successful attainment of the Communists was that of trade union unity. The campaign for this, which had begun in September of 1934, had been accelerated after the rally and particularly after the instructions laid down at the VIIth World Congress. Principally because of the willingness of the C.G.T.U. to accede to most of Jouhaux's conditions for such unity, by the end of September 1935 merely the official formalities were lacking to make it an accomplished fact. On the 28th of January 1936 a joint confederal congress declared the fusion to be operative at the base of the two C.G.T.s, and on March 2nd, at the Congress of Toulouse, the union was consummated. But both parties had long since recognized its de facto existence.[11]

Finally there was the question of organic unity, to which, of course, the Communists were unalterably opposed. The naivete with which the Socialists allowed themselves to continue to hope for this impossible eventuality is, in retrospect, both incredible and pitiful. Negotiations toward this end contined throughout the period between the rally and the elections in May of 1936, but, in view of the constant barriers placed in its path by the Communists, the retention of faith in its ultimate success on the part of the Socialists defies reasonable explanation. At last realization of this fact seemed to dawn upon the Socialist leaders, and by the time of the elections the issue was to all intents and purposes dead.[12]

Thus, gradually, in the ten months between the rally and the elections the "anti-fascist front" became the "super-party" - a "super-party" in which the Communists were, only in the most literal sense, silent partners. Subsequent political developments helped to assure this new coalition's success at the polls. An attack upon Blum's person by members of the Action Francaise in February did much to discredit the Right in the eyes of the French voter. Then on March 7th the armies of the IIIrd Reich occupied the Rhineland, and as the symbol of anti-fascism the Popular Front enjoyed greatly enhanced prestige. Finally, it must be remembered, the Radicals and Socialists together had commanded a majority in 1932 so that with the added strength afforded by Communist support electoral victory in 1936 was not to be unexpected. In May the victory came, and, taking the Popular Front parties as a whole, it was indeed impressive. With a comfortable majority in the Chamber and a sweeping electoral mandate behind it the Popular Front embarked upon its new role -- that of providing a government for France.

The difficulties inherent in this new role, the realization of the difference between cooperation against a common enemy and cooperation in the administration of a government, the rediscovery of the latent incompatibilities that had lain dormant during the pre-election months -- all are questions far beyond the scope of this study. The story of the genesis of the Popular Front and of the effect of the Popular Front concept upon the parties which comprised it, ended, to all intents and purposes, with the rally on July 14th.

It should be unnecessary to state, in conclusion, that despite all of the many and varied factors that contributed to the ultimate establishment of the Popular Front the decisive factor in its genesis was the twofold threat presented by events in Germany -- the coming of Hitler and the subsequent rearming of the IIIrd Reich. Before the arrival of Hitler the French Socialists and Communists had been increasingly at each others' throats, and the entente between the Socialists and Radicals was well on its way toward being destroyed by the mutual inability to find a common denominator of economic theory. The mere accession to power of the Nazis did not substantially alter the position of either the Radicals or the Communists but it did serve to shake the faith of the French Socialist leaders in their ability to stand alone. It also gave rise to the abortive movements within each party that were based solely on the threat of internal fascism and the need for party cooperation in order to avoid it. However Doriot, Bergery, and Renaudel and Déat sowed their seeds of class collaboration too early -- after the arrival of Hitler but before the conviction within the Kremlin and within the minds of the majority of Radicals that Nazi Germany constituted a serious military threat to the Soviet Union and France respectively. Thus the ground was not yet sufficiently fertile. Even the Parti Socialiste with its hyper-sensitive almost neurotic fear of fascism within France was not yet prepared to make unreserved doctrinal sacrifices for the sake of allies. Yet the dissidents in each case succeeded at least in introducing a new line of thought into the introspection that was going on within each of their parties. The concept that the best means of opposing internal fascism were party cooperation within the Left, class collaboration between the Left and Center, and the avoidance of anything that might serve to drive potential allies toward the Right, was at least articulated if not immediately accepted.

There remained the need for the second aspect of the threat occasioned by the advent of Hitler before the tendency toward disunity which had been partially halted by his arrival could be stopped completely and then put into reverse. This came about as the Communists began to realize that Hitler would follow the course of Bismarck rather than Rapallo in his relations with the Soviet Union. From that time on, and the date for this must be placed some time in the early spring of 1934, the story of the genesis of the Popular Front in France is the story of how the bolsheviks used the fears of both the Socialists and the Radicals to lead these two parties toward the ends desired by the Comintern. From the P.C.F. turning at Ivry in June of 1934 until the formation of a Popular Front party and its electoral success in May of 1936, the Communists provided both the initiative and the direction for the successive steps leading to the establishment of a Popular Front government. Where the desires of the Socialists conflicted with Communist plans these desires were frustrated at every turn. The Socialist decision to return to a program consistent with the ancient theories of revolutionary proletarianism, made at Toulouse, was rendered meaningless by the Communist campaign for broad class and party alliances -- with the result that the Socialists were forced to abandon it at Mulhouse. The Socialist desire for organic unity of the proletarian parties was blocked by the Communists, although the bait of such unity was constantly dangled before the Socialists, and conversely the Socialists were forced to accept that broad political alliance which they were very much disposed to avoid. Moreover they were forced to transform this alliance into a positive political coalition with a program which was neither of their own choosing nor to their liking.

The question arises as to why and how the P.C.F. with less than one quarter of the strength of the Parti Socialiste and infinitely less influence on French political affairs, was able so to maneuver the Socialists at will. Unlike the Radicals the susceptibility of the Socialists may not be explained in terms of the rising nationalism which spread throughout France, as the military threat created by a rearming Germany became more acute and more apparent. On the contrary the Socialists made a desperate last stand against this tendency toward nationalism as it engulfed the Radicals and as it, for quite different reasons, received the enthusiastic support of the Communists. There is only one explanation of Socialist behavior throughout this period and it is the explanation which they themselves were prepared to admit. The Socialists were blinded by their irrational fear of a fascist coup in France -- and they were blinded to such an extent as to be unable to resist any projects of the Communists made in the name of anti-fascism. Communist realization of this, combined with a more accurate appraisal of the limited extent of any such danger, made the Communists the tactical masters of the Parti Socialiste from Ivry on. Parenthetically the best illustration of the extent to which this was true was the failure of the Communists in their dealings with the I.O.S. at the Brussels meeting, since the latter were largely free of the confused emotionalism that beset the French Socialist party.

This brings us to the evaluation of the Paris **émeute** and its effect upon the three parties. With the historical perspective which we now have, limited though it may be, it is obvious that the Paris riots marked the end rather than the beginning of whatever potential fascist threat there may have been in France. The tremendous display of strength by the Left in the ensuing week settled this conclusively. Furthermore the source of a fascist threat, or at least that which the Socialists considered to be the source, the leagues of the extreme Right, were in fact so feeble. As we suggested in the discussion of the **émeute** the Communists appeared to have been aware of this whereas the Socialists clearly were not, and were thrown into a panic which clouded their judgment and colored their actions from that time forward. What became the useful fascist myth for the Communists was no myth for the majority of the Socialist leaders and particularly for that man who more than anyone else was responsible for the shaping of Socialist policy.

Leon Blum had had unsurpassed experience in dealing with the Communists and he was, of course, a man of good common sense as well as brilliant intellect. He had tasted of Communist untrustworthiness early and often in his political career. Moreover his integrity and essential humanitarianism rebelled violently against the tenets and methods of bolshevism. Finally he was among the first clearly to detect the reason for the P.C.F.'s change at Ivry -- clearly to interrelate the exigencies of Soviet foreign policy with the strange behavior of the French Communists. Yet it is primarily upon Blum's shoulders that the blame must fall for the subsequent miscalculations and clouded judgment that were ultimately to cost the Socialists so dearly. Shaken to the core by the success of Hitler, a possibility for which he had been totally unprepared, Blum read into the **émeute** in the Place de la Concorde a danger all out of proportion of the facts -- and the effect of this upon him was permanent. Because of his irrational exaggeration of the extent of the fascist threat in France, after Ivry Blum was an invaluable asset to the Communists in their campaign to enlist the support of the Socialists toward their own ends. It is at least probable that without this attitude on the part of Blum the Popular Front would never have materialized. Except for the traditional left wing within the Parti Socialiste it was Blum who was the chief protagonist for acceptance of the unity of action pact with the P.C.F. When, at Mulhouse, Communist plans for the Popular Front did not coincide with those of the left wing of the Parti Socialiste, Blum was again a champion of the Communist position. He had become the principal apologist for the P.C.F. position within the Socialist party, and, of course, the Communists couldn't have had a better friend at court. Step by step, with Blum's encouragement or at least with his approval, the Socialists gave in to the various Communist proposals until the final shape of the Popular Front was almost exactly that wished by the latter.

A final word about the effect of the creation of a Popular Front upon the position of the P.C.F. in France. We have discussed at considerable length in the course of the thesis, the interaction of the Communist experience in France and the policies of the Comintern upon one another. But in addition there were most important effects upon the status and position of the P.C.F. within the French political scene. The presence of the P.C.F. in the antifascist Popular Front not only served to resuscitate that party in the very tangible terms of seats in the Chamber, votes, and enlarged party membership, but it also had a much more permanent and sinister result. For the first time in its existence the P.C.F. was now clothed with an aspect of respectability. The French Communist was no longer the man with the knife in his teeth but rather an enthusiastic ally in the struggle against what was considered to be a more immediate and more dangerous enemy. The P.C.F. used this new respectability to create the organization in France that was ultimately to undermine the Parti Socialiste. For fifteen years Blum had been able to defend successfully against the various Communist attempts to accomplish that goal -- more than that, he had been instrumental in reducing the P.C.F. to the position of impotency which it had reached in 1932-33. But, by the act of constructing the Popular Front itself, the Socialists threw away all they had gained -- the Communists were raised from the status of despised foreign agents to that of partners. It was a lot more difficult to reduce them to their original status than it had been to keep them there. This was indeed a high price to pay for an ally against a fascist threat which a more rational appraisal would have revealed not to have been terribly serious. After 1935 not only was a substantial Communist party in France to stay, but it had acquired the trade union foothold that was ultimately to give it ascendancy and finally complete control of the C.G.T.

In this study the Radicals have played a substantially less important part than the two proletarian parties. This arose in part from the fact that their participation in unity of action started at a much later date. Another reason for this is the impossibility of drawing general or useful conclusions from the behavior or thought of the members and leaders of the Radical party during this period. By the time of the Popular Front the Parti Radical had become to a great extent a party of individuals rather than of doctrine, and the devotion to rather vague liberal principles that served as their common denominator meant that a careful study of the reasons for Radical participation in the Popular Front would have required the separate evaluation of the widely diverging political opinions of many very small factions and even individuals within the party. In contrast to the complexity afforded by the wide range of opinion within this loose coalition, however, there was a certain simplicity to the manner in which the party as a whole responded to the anti-fascist appeal once the barrier of disagreement on national defense had been removed by the Communist turning. But the Radicals were as quick to be disenchanted as they had been to become seduced, and as between themselves and either the Socialists or the Communists it is hard to see any far-reaching effects arising from their relatively brief alliance.

Beginning in 1934, at least, Hitler represented a growing threat to the security of France, to the security of the Soviet Union and to the political philosophies of the Left in general. Despite the extreme over-simplification involved in explaining the development of the Popular Front in these terms alone, there can be little doubt that the reason for its development in France and not elsewhere stems from the peculiar degree to which the French Left was affected by all aspects of this threat simultaneously. The foreign policy of the Soviet Union, the domestic fears of the French Socialists, and the devotion to the nation and to republican ideals so prevalent among the Radicals, were all found to be pointing in the same direction. Their combined effect was finally sufficient to bridge the tremendous gaps, both emotional and doctrinal, that separated the widely different parties of the French Left. Considering the extent of the previous rifts and antipathies the fact of the creation of such unity was remarkable indeed. It provided at least one striking example of the ultimate choice that would be made by the non-Communist French Left if pushed far enough and if not given the opportunity to avoid making a definite choice.

NOTES

1. According to the Communist report Basch said:
   "We inaugurate, this evening, fraternal and regular collaboration of the Ligue des Droits de l'Homme with all the united anti-fascist organizations, to which we bring the support of our 2,440 sections, our 180,00 members." L'HUMANITÉ, 19 January 1935.
2. L'HUMANITÉ, 11 February 1935.
3. "Rassemblement des républicains", PETIT PROVENCAL, 10 May 1935.
4. LA CONFÉRENCE NATIONALE AU ASSIZES DE LA PAIX ET LIBERTÉ, **op. cit.** p. 39.
5. RASSEMBLEMENT POPULAIRE, 14 JUILLET 1935 (Pamphlet compiling the speeches at the rally) Comité National du Rassemblement populaire, Paris, 1935, p. 12.
6. RASSEMBLEMENT POPULAIRE, 14 JUILLET 1935, **op.cit.**, p. 11.
7. The latter stated:
   "Give work to the millions of unemployed, guarantee the salaries of civil servants and employees in the public services, that is how to combat the disastrous effects of the crisis in the middle classes. Nothing can separate us on this ground. On the contrary everything tends in the direction of our solid and continued unity. The C.G.T.U. vows that it is ready to contribute complete loyalty to the elaboration of a program of claims and of action which, when put into execution, will guarantee work and bread for the masses."
   Ibid., p. 10.
   It is also significant in this connection that the Communists had gradually been substituting the slogan "Work, Peace and Bread" for that of "Peace, Bread and Liberty", the former relating more directly to a positive program than the latter, which had served as the anti-fascist slogan.
8. VIIe CONGRES MONDIALE, **op. cit.**, p. 87.

9. At their Conseil National of 16-17 November 1935, the Parti Socialiste expressed its fears concerning the development of the Popular Front into a super-party in its mandate to the parliamentary group:

"At the same time in the application of the decisions of the Congress of Mulhouse and in accordance with the declarations of the C.A.P., the Conseil National states that this movement must be considered as a temporary liaison of parties, groupings and organizations with a view to a common battle against the measures of the present government, against fascism and for peace, and it will not therefore, without risking losing its power, be transformed into a sort of super-party with regular subscriptions and permanent cadres."
RAPPORT ADMINISTRATIF AU XXXIII CONGRÈS NATIONAL, **op. cit.**, p. 38.

As a result of Socialist insistence the preamble to the statutes of the Popular Front stated in part:

"The Rassemblement Populaire is neither a party nor a super-party; it is a center of liaison between the organizations and groupings which, quite while maintaining their autonomy, have united for a common action with a view to proceeding to the coordination of the anti-fascist forces of this country."
STATUTS DU RASSEMBLEMENT POPULAIRE, 3 January 1936, Comité National du Rassemblement Populaire, Paris, 1936, p. 1.

10. As early as June 5th, 1935, the P.C.F. representatives to the Délégation des Gauches made the following statement:

"The Communist party, whose fundamental program includes the socialization of the means of production and exchange ... believes that it is possible at the present moment to apply a policy of positive action based on a broad popular front.

"The Communist party, renewing its former declaration concerning its eventual attitude in regard to a government of the Left, affirms that it is disposed to support in the Chamber and before the country all real measures to ensure the safeguarding of the franc, the energetic repression of speculation, the protection of the interests of the laboring population, the defense of democratic liberties, disarmament and dissolution of the fascist leagues, and the maintenance of peace." L'HUMANITÉ, 6 June 1935.

cf. the comparison of the Cahiers de Huyghens and the program of the Popular Front, **supra** Chapter IV, pp. 116-118.

11. Speaking to the Congrès extraordinaire of the Parti Socialiste at Boulogne-sur-Seine 1-2 February 1936, Blum declared:

   "... At this very moment there is in the act of being accomplished a great event ... that is trade union unity.

   "This has, in reality, already happened. Unity of the trade unions, although not yet realized had, since September or October, already arrived at such a stage of its development that success could be considered as achieved."
   RAPPORT ADMINISTRATIF AU XXXIII CONGRÈS NATIONAL, **op. cit** , p. 127.

12. On May 29th, 1935, the Communists had made a counter-proposal to the Socialist platform, entitled "Charte d'unification de la classe ouvrière de France" the patently unacceptable conditions of which they absolutely refused to modify. Finally in February of 1936 Blum declared:

   "I don't consider that the Communist program can serve as a basis for unification. A unification is a fusion of parties and not the absorption of one by the other. I believe the Charter of Unity of May 29th to be in reality the charter of a Communist party, and not a charter for the ... fusion of all proletarian parties existing today."
   RAPPORT ADMINISTRATIF AU XXXIII CONGRÈS NATIONAL, **op. cit.**, p. 126.

BIBLIOGRAPHY

At the time of this study, the experience of the Popular Front was too recent to have received careful historical treatment prior to this attempt to do so. Therefore there was in effect no problem of defending the material herein presented against other works in the field. The nearest approach to a careful study of this event was in Walter's HISTOIRE DU PARTI COMMUNISTE FRANCAIS, which carried the history of the French party through the period with which this thesis deals. Walter's work is well documented and I shall make no attempt to discount its importance. But Walter was concerned only with the Communist side of the developments leading up to the Popular Front and, outside of his book there has been no work that has tried to make a detailed and documented study of even one side of the Popular Front. General studies of the history of the French extreme Left such as Zevaes' HISTOIRE DU SOCIALISME ET COMMUNISME EN FRANCE DE 1871 a 1947, Dolleans' HISTOIRE DU SOCIALISME EN FRANCE DE LA REVOLUTION Ã NOS JOURS, 1789-1936, cover too extensive a period to permit a detailed analysis of this experience. There remain only the prejudiced accounts written in the heat of the period itself, and these of course are many. The vast majority of them are in pamphlet form and a large percentage are either official propaganda pieces or personal exposés by the personalities who played some political role in sympathy or antipathy with the development of the Popular Front. Properly evaluated these are of course of considerable value as material revealing the positions of the various factions at the time -- but by definition they fail even to attempt to present an objective account of this event.

If the secondary sources are necessarily and understandably thin for a subject as recent as this then was, the primary sources offered a wide range of untapped material. Broken down into general groupings the following are the principal categories of primary sources which have been used in this thesis:

1. The press and other organs of the main parties -- L'HUMANITE, LE POPULAIRE, L'ÈRE NOUVELLE, etc. -- which, despite their

distortions for purposes of propaganda, nevertheless serve as bulletins for the official business of their respective parties and offer a day to day basis for comparison and the observation of development. In this category also fall the regional organs of the three parties. These, along with the CAHIERS DU BOLSHEVISME of the P.C.F., were examined in detail throughout the 1933-35 period. The last named publication was an excellent source of Communist Central Committee reports, party documents, and official rationalizations of Communist maneuvers and the like, since its main function was to serve as a clearing house for that sort of information. Moreover being designed more for Communist consumption than to serve as a propaganda organ, it did not devote quite so much of its space to the calumnies, gross distortions of fact, etc., which are such a prominent feature of L'HUMANITÉ.

2. The factional party press -- L'OEUVRE, VIE SOCIALISTE, BATAILLE SOCIALISTE, L'EMANCIPATION, L'APPEL, LA FLECHE, LE FRONT, etc. - which served to present the divergent points of view within the parties. In this connection also the neutral and hostile press was consulted on all occasions where the problems extended beyond internal party affairs.

3. The reports of the Congresses, committee meetings, conferences, etc. of the three parties and their splinter groups. I have been particularly fortunate in securing access to virtually the entire official compilation of Socialist reports, the reports of their parliamentary group (made to the Commission Administrative Permanent), the reports of the Socialist delegations to the I.O.S., the administrative and moral reports to their national congresses, the reports of the Socialist delegations to the Commission on Unification between the three proletarian parties and to the Committees of Coordination of the unity of action pact etc. In addition I have been able to consult the stenographic records of the national congresses and the meetings of the Conseil National and the C.A.P. of the Parti Socialiste. Finally this same source also yielded the complete file of correspondence between the Parti Socialiste and both the P.C.F. and the P.U.P. on the subject of unity of action and organic unity, some of which was also published in LE POPULAIRE.

Obviously no such direct access existed in the case of the P.C.F., yet because of the peculiar Communist penchant for publication of all of its meeting reports, however minute, I believe that I have been able to gain almost as complete a coverage there as in the case of the Socialists. Through L'HUMANITÉ, VIE OUVRIÈRE, the CAHIERS DU BOLCHEVISME, the regional Communist organs, or the myriad of party pamphlets that issued from the Bureau d'éditions or the Publications Revolutionnaires during this period, sooner or later almost all of the reports came to light.

The reports of the various meetings and conferences within the Radical party are the weak link in this coverage, both because the Radicals held substantially fewer meetings and because they devoted considerably less money and effort to the propagandization of those which they did hold. Aside from the reports of the national congresses themselves and occasional reports of the meetings of the Executive Committee of the Radical party, which are available, I have had to be content with the accounts and reports reprinted in the Radical press. For the part played by the Radicals in the meetings of the Délégations des Gauches, the Comité National du Rassemblement Populaire and other meetings in which the Socialists also took part, I have had to rely principally on the Socialist version.

4. The reports and statistics published by the French government itself. Although some of the reports were destroyed during the German occupation there is still of course a complete file of the JOURNAL OFFICIEL DE LA RÉPUBLIQUE as well as most of the relevant official government reports such as that of the Commission d'enquête charged to investigate the causes of and facts surrounding the events of the week of February 6th to 12th, 1934. From the former a complete record of the reports and debates in the Chambre des Députés is available.

5. Finally one of the most important primary sources was the publication of the stenographic accounts of private discussions between the officials of the different parties during this period -- for example the account of the meeting between the I.O.S. leaders and the Communist delegation at Brussels, the discussion which took place over the Cahiers de Huyghens between the Socialist and Radical delegations, that which took place between the Communist and Socialist delegations on July 14th, 1934, the day before the Socialists met to consider the P.C.F. offer for unity of action and several others: which for the political purposes of one side or the other were ultimately released either through the press or in pamphlet form.

Beyond these specific categories lie the immense number of miscellaneous primary sources which fill in the background for this thesis. The numerous pamphlets attacking or defending the Popular Front, the writings of the participants either in the form of memoir or active argument, the trade union organs, the statistical information on everything from party membership and election results to unemployment figures and the state of national finances, and not least important certainly the personal recollections of the veterans of the Popular Front days most of whom were still living, of course, and many of whom were still playing prominent roles in French political affairs.

The extensive party reports of congresses, meetings, inter-party conferences and the like, mentioned above, constitute the most important source of material for this thesis. They appear in footnotes throughout the text where cited and it seemed preferable to treat them in a general way in this bibliography rather than to present an exhaustive and repetitious listing of the individual reports themselves. Thus the bibliography included below contains only those pamphlets, speeches, writings, etc., **other** than the official reports of the party congresses, etc., which have made some direct contribution of material to this thesis. I have also listed the most useful secondary sources including several recent doctorate theses submitted to various French universities, which have also been of value in providing background or incidental material.

PRIMARY SOURCES.
1. **Newspapers and Periodicals.**
    L'AMI DU PEUPLE (Socialist).
    L'APPEL (Neo-Socialist).
    L'AUBE (Catholic Socialist).
    BATAILLE SOCIALISTE (Socialist-left wing).
    COMBAT MARXISTE.
    CORRESPONDANCE INTERNATIONALE (Communist).
    CORRESPONDANT.
    LE CRI DES JEUNES (Communist).
    LE CRI DU PEUPLE (Communist).
    LE CRI DU PEUPLE D'AUVERGNE (Communist).
    L'ECHO DE PARIS (Catholic).
    L'EMANCIPATION NATIONALE (Doriot's organ).
    L'ERE NOUVELLE (Radical).
    Newspapers
    L'ETINCELLE (Communist).
    L'ETUDIANT SOCIALISTE (Socialist).
    FIGARO.
    LA FLÈCHE (Frontist).
    LA FRANCE RADICALE (Radical).

LE FRONT (bi-weekly of the Union of Socialist Radicals).
L'HUMANITÉ (official Communist organ).
L'INTRANSIGEANT.
LA JEUNE RÉPUBLIQUE (bi-weekly of the Jeunesse Radicales).
JOURNAL DE LA DEMOCRATIC (Radical-Socialiste) 1868-1944; became LA DÉPÊCHE DU MIDI in November, 1947.
JOURNAL OFFICIEL DE LA RÉPUBLIQUE FRANÇAISE.
JOURNAL DE TOULOUSE.
LE LIBERTAIRE.
LA LIBERTÉ.
LA LUTTE OUVRIÈRE (Trotskyist).
LE MONDE.
LE MUTILÉ.
L'OEUVRE (Radical).
L'ORDRE (Moderate Republican).
PAIX ET LIBERTÉ (bi-weekly of the Amsterdam-Pleyel Movement).
LE PETIT BLEU.
LA PETITE DEMOCRATE (bi-weekly of the P.D.P.).
PEUPLE (C.G.T daily).
LE POPULAIRE (Socialist daily).
QUOTIDIEN.
REGARDS (illustrated bi-weekly of the P.C.F.).
LA RÉPUBLIQUE (Moderate Radical daily).
RÉPUBLIQUE DE L'OISE (Radical).
LE REVEIL DU COMBATTANT (Communist).
REVOLUTION (bi-weekly of the J.S.R.).
ROUGE MIDI (Communist).
SEMEUR (Communist).
SEPT (Catholic Socialist bi-weekly).
LE TEMPS.
TERRE NOUVELLE (Christian monthly).
TRAVAILLEUR DE LA BANLIEUR-SUD (Communist).
TRAVAILLEUR DU CENTRE QUEST (Communist).
TRAVAILLEUR DU 18eme (Communist).
TRAVAILLEUR DU SUD-OUEST (Communist).
LA VAGUE (bi-weekly of the Gauche Revolutionnaire).
VIE OUVRIERE (organ of the C.G.T.U.).
VIE SOCIALISTE (Socialist right wing - became Renaudel's organ).
VOIX DE L'EST (Communist).
VOIX DU PEUPLE DE LYONS (Communist).
VOLKSRECHT (Swiss Social-democratic daily).
VU.

Periodicals
BULLETIN COMMUNISTE (Communist until 1924).
CAHIERS DU BOLCHEVISME (Communist).
LE DOCUMENT (Catholic monthly, moderate).
ESPRIT.
L'INTERNATIONALE COMMUNISTE (Communist).
MON CAMARADE (Communist).
LA NOUVELLE RÉVUE SOCIALISTE (Socialist).
REVUE DES DEUX MONDES.
LA RÉVUE D'ECONOMIE POLITIQUE.
LA REVUE DE PARIS.
LA RÉVUE POLITIQUE ET PARLEMENTAIRE.
LA RÉVUE DES VIVANTS.
SEPT (bi-weekly of the Catholic-Socialists).

2. **Socialist publications.**

   Alter, Victor,
   COMMENT RÉALISER LE SOCIALISME?, Valois, 1932.

   Auriol, Vincent,
   UN BILAN (Conference by Auriol). Paris, Parti Socialiste, Librairie Populaire, 1936.

   LE GOUVERNEMENT DU FRONT POPULAIRE, UN BILAN, UN PROGRAMME DES ACTES - speech by Auriol in chamber 19 June 1936. Paris, Imprimerie l'Emancipatrice, 1936.

   HIER ET DEMAIN. AGONIE D'UNE LEGISLATURE. Paris, Librairie Populaire, 1933.

   LAS STABILIZATION ET LE PARTI SOCIALISTE. Paris, Librairie Populaire, 1933.

   Benda, Julien,
   PRECISION (1930-1937). Paris Editions de la Nouvelle Revue francaise, 1937.

   Blum, Leon,
   BOLCHEVISME AND SOCIALISME (8th ed.) Paris, Librairie Populaire, 1936.

   JEAN JAURÈS, Conference given 16 Feb. 1933 at Theâtre des Ambassadeurs. Lomoges, Impr. Nouvelle. Paris, Librairie populaire, 1936.

   POUR LA VIEILLE MAISON. Invervention at Congres of Tours (1920) Librairie Populaire, 1936.

LA QUESTION D'ESPAGNE. Speech pronounced at the Chamber 26 Jan. 1939. Paris, Imprimerie La Renaissance, Librairie Populaire, 1939.

RADICALISME ET SOCIÀLISME, Librairie Populaire, 1938.

LE SOCIALISME À VU CLAIR. Paris, Imprimerie F. Beroud, Librairie Populaire, 1936.

LE SOCIALISME DEVANT LA CRISE (4th ed.). Paris, Imprimerie F. Beroud, 1936.

LÉON BLUM EN ACTION POUR LA PAIX: UNE SCÉANCE HISTORIQUE A LA CHAMBRE DES DEPUTÉS. Limoges, Imprimerie nouvelle, Paris, Librairie Populaire, 1936.

LES RADICAUX ET NOUS 1931-1934. Courbevoie, Librairie Populaire, 1935.

RADICALISME ET SOCIALISME. Imprimerie F. Beroud, Paris, 1938.

LES COMMUNISTES ET NOUS. Paris, Imprimerie F. Beroud, 1936.

L'EXERCICE DU POUVOIR (Discours prononcés de mai 1936 a mai 1937) Editions de la Nouvelle Revue francaises, 1937.

LA JEUNESSE ET LE SOCIALISME - conférence prononcee le 30 juin 1934 (Maison de la Mutualité). Paris, Imprimerie F. Beroud 1937.

LA MÉTHODE SOCIALISTE, CONFERENCE PRONONNCÉ LORS DE L'OUVERTURE DES COURS DE L'ECOLE SOCIALISTE, 10 November, 1931. Paris, Editions de la liberte, 1945.

LE PROBLEME DE L'UNITÉ. Paris, Editions de la liberté, 1945.

PROLETARIAT EN DEUIL. ROGER SALENGRO. Declaration by Blum. Paris, Imprimerie Dodeman, 1936.

LE SOCIALISME DANS LA BATAILLE ELECTORALE (conference by Paul Faure). Paris, Parti Socialiste, Librairie Populaire, 1936.

Bourgin, Hubert,
    DE JAURÈS À LÉON BLUM. Ecole Normale et Politique; Mesnil-sur-l'Estree, Imprimerie Firmin-Didot, Paris, 1938.

LES COMMUNISTES ET NOUS (collection of texts). Paris, Parti Socialist, Librairie Populaire, 1936.

Compère-Morel,
   SOCIALISME ET BOLCHEVISME - POURQUOI NOUS N'AVONS PAS ADHERÉ À INTERNATIONALE DITE COMMUNISTE DES BOLCHEVISTES RUSSES. Paris, editions P.S. S.F.I.O., 1921.

Déat, Marcel,
   PS, S.F.I.O. - RAPPORT DU GROUPE SOCIALISTE AU PARLEMENT, rapport du groupe au Congrès national extraordinaire. Avignon, 16 and 17 April, 1933.

   LE FRONT POPULAIRE au tournant. Paris, Imprimerie Dubois et Bauer, 1937.

   PERSPECTIVES SOCIALISTES, Paris, Librairie Valois, 1930.

Dunois, Amedée,
   QUESTIONS DIVERSES. Paris, Parti Socialiste, Librairie Populaire, 1936.

Dupuy, Xavier,
   POUR L'UNION SOCIALE ET NATIONALE. Paris, Les presses modernes, 1936.

   ELECTIONS LÉGISLATIVES DE 1936. PROGRAMME DU PARTI SOCIALISTE. Librairie populaire 1936.

   L'EXECUTION DU PLAN DU TRAVAIL PAR HENRI DE MAN ET L'EQUIPE DU BUREAU D'ETUDES SOCIALISTES, Antwerp, de Sikkel, Paris, Alcan, 1935.

Fargues, Paul,
   SOCIALISME ET COMMUNISME. Cahors, Imprimerie A. Coulesant, Paris, 1937.

Fauchère, Germaine,
   L'ACTION PARLEMENTAIRE (2 volumes). Paris, Parti Socialiste, Librairie Populaire, 1936.

Feretti,
   CE QU'EST LE PARTI SOCIALISTE. Paris, Librairie Populaire, 1933.

Fontanier, Henry,
   LE PROBLEME DE LA PAIX. Paris, Parti Socialiste, Librairie Populaire, 1936.

Frossard, L.O.,
   DE JAURÈS À LÉNINE. NOTES ET SOUVENIRS D'UN MILITANT. Paris, editions de la Nouvelle revue Socialiste 1930.

Gernez, Raymond,
   L'UNITÉ EST-ELLE POSSIBLE? Paris, Roger Roux, imprimeur, 1946.

   LE GOUVERNEMENT À DIRECTION SOCIALISTE. SES REALIZATIONS. Limoges, Imprimerie nouvelle, 1937.

Guesde, Jules,
   LA DOCTRINE SOCIALISTE, DOUBLE REPONSE À MM. DE MUN ET PAUL DESCHANEL, Bar-le-duc, imprimerie Comte-Jacquet, Paris 1938.

Guy-Grand, Déat, Marcel, Perroux, Francois, Morin, Gaston, Rosentock-Franck, L., Bouvier-Ajam, M., Joffre, Alphonse:
   "Le Corporatisme" - CAHIER SPECIAL DES ARCHIVES DE PHILOSOPHIE DU DROIT ET DE SOCIOLOGIE JURIDIQUE, Sirey, 1938.

Jaurès, Jean, and Guesde, Jules,
   LES DEUX METHODES: CONFERENCE PAR JEAN JAURÈS ET JULES GUESDE, LILLE 1900. Paris, editions de la Liberte, 1945.

Lebas, J.,
   CRITIQUE SOCIALISTE DU P.C., ORGANIZATION, TACTIQUE, DOCTRINE. Lille, Imprimerie ouvriere, 1920.

de Man, Henri,
   APRES COUP. Editions de la Toison d'Or, Brussels, 1941.

   AU DELA DE MARXISME. Paris, Alcan, 1927, 1929.

   CAVALIER SEUL. Brussels, Editions du Cheval Aile, 1948.

   L'ÉDITION DU PLAN DU TRAVAIL. Editions "De Sikkel" Antwerp, 1935.

   LA JOIE AU TRAVAIL, ENQUÊTE BASÉE SUR DES TEMOIGNAGES D'OUVRIERS ET D'EMPLOYES. Nouvel edition, 1935, Alcan, Paris.

   LE PLAN DU TRAVAIL, Brussels, Labor, 1934.

   PSYCHOLOGIE DU SOCIALISME, Iena, 1926.

   LE SOCIALISME CONSTRUCTIF, Paris, Alcan, 1933.

Man, Hendrik de,
   DIE SOZIALISTISCHE IDEE. Iena, E. Diederieks (Leipzig, 1933).

Moch, Jules,
   ARGUMENTS ET DOCUMENTS, Paris, Parti Socialiste, Librairie Populaire, 1936.

   LE P.S. ET LE SITUATION FINANCIÈRE. Paris, Librairie Populaire, 1933.

   POUR MARCHER AU POUVOIR. Paris, Société d'editions "Nouveau Promethee", 1935.

   LE PROGRAMME AGRICOLE DU PARTI SOCIALISTE. Paris, Librairie Populaire, 1933.

   LE PROGRAMME IMMÉDIATE DU PARTI SOCIALISTE. Paris, Librairie Populaire, 1933.

Modiano, Hélene,
   LES MUNITIONAIRES CONTRE LA NATION. Paris, Parti Socialiste, Librairie Populaire, 1936.

   LES MILITAIRES CONTRE LA NATION. Paris, Librairie Populaire, 1936.

Modiano, René,
   LES MAITRES SECRETS DE LA PRESSE, Paris, Parti Socialiste, Librairie Populaire, 1936.

Monnet et Polleau,
   LE PARTI SOCIALISTE ET L'AGRICULTURE. Paris, Parti Socialiste, Librairie Populaire, 1936.

Montagnon, B., Adrien Marquet, Marcel Déat,
   NEO-SOCIALISME?   ORDRE-AUTORITE-NATION.   Paris, Grasset (1933).

Naville, Claude,
   ANDRÉ GIDE ET LE COMMUNISME, suivis d'etudes et fragments avec une preface de Pierre Naville, Paris, Librairie du Travail, 1936.

Osmin, Léon,
   FIGURES DE JADIS. LES PIONNIERS OBSCUR DU SOCIALISME. Lettres prefaces de Blum, Paul Faure, Bräcke, Severac, Zyromski, and many others. Paris (no date).

PARTI SOCIALISTE EN PRESENCE DES DECRETS-LOIS. Paris, Imprimerie F. Beroud, Secr. Gen. du Parti Soc. S.F.I.O. (1939).

LE PARTI SOCIALISTE ET LES ELECTIONS CANTONALES. Librairie Populairie, Paris, 1937.

Paul, Marion,
SOCIALISME ET NATION. Paris, Imprimerie du Centaure, 1933.

Paz, Maurice,
LE SIX FEVRIER. CAUSES, PHYSIONOMIE, SIGNIFICATION ET CONSEQUENCES. Editions du P.S., S.F.I.O., Paris, Librairie Populaire, 1936.

Paul Faure,
LE SOCIALISME DANS LA BATAILLE ELECTORALE. (Conference by Paul Faure). Paris, Parti Socialiste, Librairie Populaire, 1936.

Picard et Marceau-Pivert,
L'ARMÉE PRÉTORIENNE DES TRUSTS. Paris, Parti Socialiste, Librairie Populaire, 1936.

Pierson, J.,
LA THÉORIE DU SALAIRE CHEZ LES SOCIALISTES FRANCAIS. Paris, Librairie du Recueil Sirey, 1936.

Marceau-Pivert, Lucien Herard, René Modiano,
4 discours et une programme (Conseil national and Montrouge) 14 Feb. 1937 (Conseil National Puteaux 18 Apr. 1937). De l'Éxercice à la conquête de pouvoir. Paris, Imprimerie industrielle at artistique (sans date).

Marceau-Pivert,
TENDRE LA MAIN AUX CATHOLIQUES? - Reponse et reflexions d'un socialiste - 3rd ed. Paris, Imprimerie F. Beroud, Librairie Populaire du Parti Socialiste S.F.I.O., 1938.

LE PROGRAMME DU PARTI. Paris, Parti Socialiste, Librairie Populaire, 1936.

PROGRAMME DU PARTI SOCIALISTE. Paris, Librairie Populaire, 1933.

RADICAUX ET SOCIALISTES (1932-1936). Limoges, Imprimerie nouvelle, Paris, Librairie Populaire, 1936 (no author).

Sellier, Henri and Poggioli, Antonin,
PARTI SOCIALISTE - PROGRAMME MUNICIPAL POUR

LES ELECTIONS DE 1935 - Paris Union des elues municipaux socialistes, 1935.

Severac, J.B.,
DE L'UNITÉ D'ACTION À L'UNITÉ ORGANIQUE. Paris, Société d'editions "Nouveau Prometheé" 1934.

LE PARTI SOCIALISTE. SES PRINCIPLES ET SES TACTICS. Paris, Librairie Populaire, 1936.

Suarez, Georges,
LA GRANDE PEUR DU 6 FÉBRIER AU PALAIS BOURBON. Paris, B. Grasset, 1934.

POUR UN PARTI CENTRAL. Paris, éditions Denoel et Steele, 1936.

"Que veut, que peut - le front commun", LE DOCUMENT. July, 1938.

V.D.,
LA FUSION DU PARTI SOCIALISTE ET DU P.C. EST ELLE POSSIBLE ET SOUHAITABLE? Paris, Imprimerie Union, 1937.

Weill-Raynal, Etienne,
CONTRE LE DÉFLATION BUDGETAIRE POUR UNE POLITIQUE FINANCIERE SOCIALISTE. Limoges Imprimerie nouvelle, Paris, Librairie Populaire, 1936.

LA POLITIQUE DE DÉFLATION. Paris, Parti Socialiste, Librairie Populaire, 1936.

RADICAUX ET SOCIALISTES. Paris, Parti Socialiste, Librairie Populaire, 1936.

Zyromski, Jean,
SUR LE CHIMIN DE L'UNITÉ. Paris, Editions "Nouveau Promethee" 1936.

3. Communist publications.

AU PAS DE CHARGE, CAMARADES! Resolutions of the C.C. of the federation of J.C.s (April 1931). Bureau d'éditions, Paris, 1931.

Bewer, O.,
L'INTERNATIONALE COMMUNISTE ET SES SECTIONS, APRÉS LE VIe CONGRÈS. Paris, Imprimerie centrale, 5 Rue Erard; Bureau d'éditions, 132 Fauborg St. - Denis, 1932.

LE MANUEL DU MILITANT. Paris, Imprimerie centrale, 5 Rue Erard; Bureau d'éditions, 132 Faubourg St. - Denis, 1932.

Bonté,
LES DEUX GRANDS MISISONS DU P.C.F.: UNION DU FRONT POPULAIRE ET PARTI UNIQUE DE LA CLASSE ouvrière (Report of the Plenary meeting of the C.C. at Montreuil). bureau d'éditions, Paris, 1937.

LE P.C. ET L'UNITÉ POLITIQUE. Editions de la Liberté, Paris, 1937.

Boukharine, N.,
A.B.C. DU COMMUNISME, Paris, Librairie de L'HUMANITÉ, 1925.

Cachin, Marcel, et Thorez, Maurice,
DU FRONT UNIQUE AU FRONT POPULAIRE. Speeches before the Chambre des Deputes, Bureau d'éditions, Paris, 1935.

OUI, NOUS ORGANISERONS LE FRONT UNIQUE DE LA CLASSE OUVRIÈRE! Speech to the VIIth World Congress of the Comintern. Bureau d'éditions, Paris, 1935.

CLASSE CONTRE CLASSE, LA QUESTION FRANCAISE AU IXe EXECUTIF ET AU VIe CONGRÈS DE L'I.C. Courbevoie, La cootypographie, Société ouvriere d'imprimerie, 11 Rue de Metz, Paris, 1929.

Cogniot, G.,
PAIX ET LIBERTÉ. Discours prononcé au Congrès populaire 28 June 1936, Paris, Amsterdam-Pleyel, 1936.

VIe CONFERENCE NATIONAL DU P.C.F. (St. - Denis, 31 March-7 April, 1929). Manifesto, theses, resolutions - Paris, 1929.

CONTRE LA GUERRE ET LE FASCISME: L'UNITÉ. Resolutions et Decisions. Paris, Imprimerie l'Emancipatrice, Bureau d'editions, 1935 (31 jan. 1936).

LE COUP DE MAIN FASCISTE ET LA RIPOSTE REPUBLICAINE (Textes et documents). Saigon, Imprimerie de l'Union Ngrujen-VanCua, 1934.

Davanne, Henri,
LA POLITIQUE DE L'INTERNATIONAL COMMUNISTE ET LE MOUVEMENT OUVRIER EN FRANCE. Paris, Parti ouvrier et paysan, 1930.

DEUX ANS D'ACTIVITÉ AUX SERVICE DU PEUPLE - reports of the Central COmmittee for the IXth C.N. at Arles 25-29 Dec. 1937. Paris, Imprimerie I.C.C., 1938.

DEUX TACTIQUES. Paris Imprimerie Centrale: Bureau d'éditions, 1932.

Dmitrov, Georges,
    AU SEUIL DE 1937: L'AVENIRE DU FRONT POPULAIRE. Paris, Bureau d'editions, 1938.

    POUR L'UNITÉ DE LA CLASSE OUVRIÈRE CONTRE LE FASCISME: II. Paris, Imprimerie l'Emancipatrice; Bureau d'éditions, 1935 (31 Jan. 1936).

    THE UNITED FRONT. London, Lawrence & Wishart, 1938.

LES DOSSIERS DE L'AGITATEUR. - RIPOSTES ET ATTAQUES CONTRE LE PARTI SOCIALISTE. Paris, agit-prop. centrale du P.C.F. (sans date).

Duclos, Jacques,
    AN EVANT POUR LE FRONT UNIQUE D'ACTION ANTI-FASCISTE. Bureau d'éditions, 1930.

    FAIRE L'UNITÉ - Report to the National Conference of the P.C.F. at Arles 25 to 29 Dec. 1937.

    RETOUR AU PROGRAMME - Report to meeting of C.C. 22 July 1937. Paris, Imprimerie Central du Croissant, 1938.

    L'UNITÉ POUR LA VICTOIRE (speech at joint socialist and communist meeting 2 Dec. 1935, Salle de la Mutualité). Bourges, Imprimerie ouvriere du Centre, 1936.

L'ECOLE ÉLÉMENTAIRE DU P.C.F. Paris, Imprimerie la Produtrice: Section National d'éducation du P.C.F. 120 rue Lafayette. Dec. 1937.

Elections legislatives de 1936. DOCUMENTATION DES CANDIDATS DU P.C. (S.L.) 1936.

Ferrat, A.,
    HISTOIRE DU P.C.F. Paris, Bureau d'éditions, 1931.

    LETTRE OUVERTE AUX MEMBRES DU P.C. Paris, l'Auteur, 1936.

Frachon, Benoit,
    L'UNION POUR LA DÉFENSE DU PAIN (Discours prononce au VIIIe C.N. du P.C., VIlleurbanne, 22-25 Jan. 1936). Paris, Imprimerie centrale de la Bourse, 1936.

LE GOUVERNEMENT DU FRONT POPULAIRE ET LA PAIX. Paris, Société d'editions internationals, 1936.

Hervé, Pierre,
LA LIBÉRATION TRAHIE, Paris, Grasset, 1945.

Kuusinen, O.,
LA POSITION DE L'I.C. devant la crise, la guerre et le fascisme. Paris, Imprimerie francaise: Bureau d'editions, 1934 (18 Apr. 1935).

Lenine,
QUE FAIRE. Paris, 1925.

Lenine, V.I.,
LA MALADIE INFANTILE DU COMMUNISME. Paris, Imprimerie centrale, 1930.

Manouilski,
LE VIIe CONGRÈS EST LE CONGRÈS DE L'UNITÉ. Paris, Imprimerie Emancipatrice, Bureau d'éditions, 1936.

Marecot, D.,
LETTRES À UN CAMARADE SOCIALISTE, 1935. Paris, Centre de diffusion du livre et de la presse, 1935.

Marty, André,
DU PAIN AUX TRAVAILLEURS ET NON DES HONNEURS A DOUMERGUE! Speech at the municipal Conseil of Paris on the attribution of Doumergue's name to a street in Paris. Compte rendu de la séance du lundi 19 novembre 1934. (Extraits du Bulletin municipal officiel du 21 Nov. 33). Paris, Publications revolutionnaires, 1934.

LA POLITIQUE MUNICIPALE COMMUNISTE. LES PILLARDS DE PARIS (Discours prononce au Conseil Municipal de Paris, 31 Dec. 1934).

L'UNION POUR LIBÉRER L'HUMANITÉ. DES PAGES IMMORTELLES D'HÉROISME (Discours prononce au VII C.N. du P.C., VIlleurbanne, 22-25 January 1936). Paris, Publications Revolutionnaires, 1936.

Marx, Karl,
LES LUTTES DE CLASSE EN FRANCE suivi de: LES JOURNÉES DE JUIN 1848, by Friedrich Engels. LA LEÇON DES BARRICADES (Bibliotheque Marxiste) 1935, Editions Sociales.

P.C.F. (Region Paris-Ouest) VIIe CONFÉRENCE REGIONALE 1938. Paris, Imprimerie D.M.F. 1938.

COMPTE-RENDU DU VIII C.N. OF P.C.F. - VILLEURBANNE 22-25 JAN. 1936. Comité populaire du propagande, 1937.

LE CONGRÈS D'ARLES, IXTH CONGRÈS DU P.C.F., 25-29 DEC. 1937; preface by Bonté. Paris, Imprimerie J.E.P. 1938.

LE P.C.F. DEVANT L'I.C. Preface by Bureau Politique of P.C.F., Paris, 1931.

PARTI COMMUNISTE DE FRANCE; QUATRE ANS DE LA LUTTE POUR L'UNITÉ (VIIIe C.N.). Paris, Imprimerie centrale 1938.

Paul, Marcel, Grésa, et Berlioz.
LES ÉLUS COMMUNISTES CONTRE LES DECRETS LOIS (Discours prononces au conseil general de la Seine et au Conseil principal de Paris 1935). Publication du Comité Populaire de propagande, 1936.

Piatnitsky, O.,
LE TRAVAIL D'ORGANISATION DES PARTIS COMMUNISTES DANS LES PAYS CAPITALISTES. Paris, Imprimerie centrale, Bureau d'éditions, 1928.

Rappaport, Ch.,
PRÉCIS DE COMMUNISME. Paris, Bureau d'éditions du Parti Communiste, 1935.

REPORT OF THE 7th WORLD CONGRESS OF THE COMMUNIST INTERNATIONAL. London, Modern Books, 1936.

RESOLUTIONS ADOPTÉES PAR LA CONFÉRENCE NATIONALE DU P.C.F. 9-10-11-12 MARS 1930. bourges, Imprimerie ouvriere du centre, 1931.

Rosmer,
LE MOUVEMENT OUVRIER PENDANT LA GUERRE. Paris, Librairie du Travail, 1935.

VIIe CONGRES MONDIALE,
Compte-rendu abrégé Editions en Langues étrangères, Moscow, 1939.

STATUS DU P.C.F.
(adopted at Congress of Lille, June, 1936). Paris, Publications revolutionnaires, 1936.

STATUTS DU P.C.F., ADOPTÉS AU CONGRÈS DE LILLE, 1936.
Proposition de modifications. Paris, Publications révolutionnaires, 1936.

THESES AND DECISIONS OF THE THIRTEENTH PLENUM OF THE E.C.C.I. London, Modern Books, 1934.

THÈSES, MANIFESTES ET RESOLUTIONS ADOPTÉS PAR LES 1er, 2eme, 3eme et 4eme CONGRES DE L'I.C. (1919-1923). Textes complèts (Bibliothèque Communiste) 1934 Paris, Librairie du Travail, 1936.

THÈSES ET RESOLUTIONS DU VIe CONGRÈS DE L'I.C. Paris (sans date).

THÈSES, RESOLUTIONS ET DECISIONS ADOPTÉES À LA 10e SESSION PLENIERE DU C.E. DE L'I.C. JULY 1929. Paris, 1930.

Thorez, Maurice,
FRONT POPULAIRE EN MARCHE. Discours CHAMBRE DES DEPUTÉS, le 13 Nov. 1934. Bureau d'editions, Paris, 1935.

UN AN DE FRONT POPULAIRE. L'UNITÉ OUVRIÈRE - Report to assembly of militants of the Paris region, 9 June 1937 at Mutualité - Paris, Imprimerie centrale du Croissant, 1938.

LA FRANCE DU FRONT POPULAIRE ET SA MISSION DANS LE MONDE - Report and speech of Thorez to 9th C.N. of P.C.F., Arles 25-29 Dec. 1937. Paris, Imprimerie Centrale du Croissant, 1938.

Thorez, Gitton, Duclos,
L'ACTION DU PROLETARIAT ET LE FRONT UNIQUE. Rapports to the C.C. of July 1933. Paris, 1933.

Thorez, Maurice,
L'UNION DE LA NATION FRANCAISE - Report to VIIIe C.N. Paris, Publications revolutionnaires, 1936.

LE P.C., SES LUTTES, SES MÉRITES, SES PROGRÈS (Discours prononcé Salle Wagram le 26 décembre 1935). Paris, Imprimerie centrale de la Bourse, 1936.

PAR L'UNITÉ D'ACTION NOUS VAINCRONS LE FASCISME - Report of the C.C. at the National conference (Ivry, 23, 24, 25 and 26 June 1934).

POUR LA CAUSE DU PEUPLE - Report to C.C. 17 Oct. 1935. Paris, Imprimerie centrale, 1936.

POUR LA VICTOIRE DU PEUPLE - FIDELITÉ AU PROGRÈS DU FRONT POPULAIRE. Paris, Imprimerie centrale des Croissant, 1936.

LA SITUATION EN FRANCE ET L'ACTION COMMUNISTE. Report to C.C. on the work of the XIth Plenum of the C.E. of the I.C. and the tasks of the P.C.F. 27 June 1931.

"La Tactique unitaire des communistes", L'HUMANITÉ 13 Feb. 1935.

TOUT POUR LE FRONT POPULAIRE. TOUT PAR LE FRONT POPULAIRE - Report to C.N. 22 Jan. 1937. Paris, Imprimerie centrale, 1937.

Thorez, Dewez, Ramette,
LES COMMUNISTES CONTRE LA GUERRE. Speeches in Chamber 15 June 1934. Paris, Imprimerie d'art Voltaire: 16 Nov. 1934.

Thorez et Frachon,
LE COMMUNISME VIT IL VAINCRA. Program and tactic of the P.C. Paris, Imprimerie centrale, Bureau d'éditions, 1931.

Trotsky, Léon,
"La France à un tournannt" en guise de preface a DÉFENSE DU TERRORISME, Paris, 1936.

OU VA LA FRANCE? Recueil d'article oct. 1934-jul 1936. Paris, Librairie du travail 1936.

TWELFTH PLENUM OF THE EXECUTIVE COMMITTEE OF THE COMMUNIST INTERNATIONAL. Theses and Resolutions. London, Modern Books, 1932.

4. Radical publications.

Berthod, Aimé,
POURQUOI ET COMMENT NOUS RESTONS ANTICLERICAUX. Paris, Parti Republicain radical et radical-socialiste 1927.

Bonnet, G.,
LE PARTI RADICAL DEVANT LES PROBLÈMES DU TEMPS PRESENT. Paris, 1936.

Bourgeois, Léon,
LA SOLIDARITÉ. Paris, Parti Républicain radical et radical-socialiste.

Cartier, Raymond,
HISTOIRE DU RADICALISME. Paris, Centre de Propagande du Républicains nationaux, 1939.

Castel, Leon,
 L'OEUVRE DU GROUPE PARLEMENTAIRE DU PARTI RADICAL ET RADICAL-SOCIALISTE. Paris, Parti Republicain radical et radical-socialiste.

Daladier, Édouard,
 AVANT LA BATAILLE. Discours prononcé à Orange le 8 janvier 1928. Paris, éditions du Parti radical-socialiste.

ENTENTE INTERNATIONAL DES PARTIS RADICAUX ET DES PARTIS DEMOCRATIQUES SIMILAIRES. Compte rendu du congrès de Karlsrhe. Paris, A. Goulhot et fils, 1927.

Fabius de Champville, LE COMITÉ EXECUTIF DU PARTI RADICAL ET RADICAL-SOCIALISTE (1897-1907). Paris, Républicain radical et radical-socialiste.

Fabius de Champville, G.,
 LE RADICALISME, SES PRINCIPES, SON PROGRAMME, 1936, F. deLaunay, Paris, 1936.

Girod, Genéral,
 LA DÉFENSE NATIONALE ET LE PARTI RADICAL-SOCIALISTE. Paris, Parti Républicain radical et radical-socialiste.

Herriot, Edouard,
 POURQUOI JE SUIS RADICAL-SOCIALISTE. Paris, Editions de France, 1928.

Jammy-Schmidt,
 LES GRANDES THÈSES RADICALES. DE CONDORCÂT À EDOUARD HERRIOT. Preface by Herriot. Paris, éditions des partiques, 1921.

 IDÉES ET IMAGES RADICALES. Barleduc, Imprimerie Comte-Jacquet, 1934.

Lambert, Charles,
 LA POLITIQUE SOCIALE DU PARTI RADICAL. Paris, Parti Republicain radical et radical-socialiste.

Morin, L.,
 EDOUARD HERRIOT, HOMME POLITIQUE FRANCAIS, 1872. L'Anniversaire de la naissance de M. Edouard Herriot, Troyes, 1936.

Parti Radical et Radical-socialiste, Congrès comptes rendus - Paris, e Comité Executif 1933, 1934, 1935.

Parti republicain radical et radical-socialiste - DÉCLARATION DU PARTI VOTÉE PAR LE CONGRÈS DE PARIS 29 Oct. 1927. Paris, Comite Executiv 1927.

5. **Miscellaneous pamphlets, books and reports.**

Belin, René,
LA REVOLUTION SYNDICALE DE 1936. COLLECTION LE TRAVAIL ET LA VIE. Paris, Maison du Livre Francais, 1937.

Bénard, Charles,
LE FRONT POPULAIRE PAYSAN. Paris, Fédération National Catholique, 1936.

LE "PROGRAMME" DU FRONT POPULAIRE, 1936, Paris, Fédération National Catholique, 1936.

Bergery, Gaston,
L'ECONOMIE FRONTISTE, LES CRISES, LES CAUSES DE LA CRISE. LIBERALISME - MARXISME. (Rapport soumis aux Assises nationales de Dec. 1938) Paris, Imprimerie J.E.P. 1939.

Berlioz, J.,
LA BANQUEROUTE FRAUDULEUX DES GAUCHES. Paris, Publications revolutionnaires, 1933.

BILAN DU COMMUNISME. Paris, Librairie technique et économique, 1937.

Bonnevay, Laurent,
LES JOURNÉES SANGLANTES DE FEVRIER 1934 , Paris, Flammarion, 1935.

Bourgin, Georges,
NOTES BIBLIOGRAPHIQUES SUR L'HISTOIRE SOCIALE DE LA FRANCE. Leiden, E.J. Brill, 1937.

CRISE POLITIQUE FRANCAISE. Compte rendus integral des debats parlementaires des 29 et 31 mai, Documents politiques, juin- août 1935.

C.G.T.: CONGRÈS CONFEDERAL D'UNITÉ À TOULOUSE, from 2 to 5 mars 1936. Compte-rendu sténographique et débats. C.G.T., 211 Rue Lafayette, Paris, 1936.

C.G.T. 1935, CONGRÈS CONFEDERAL DE PARIS. RAPPORT MORAL ET FINANCIER. Compte rendu des debats du XXIXth C.N. corporatif (XXIInd de la C.G.T.), held at Palais de la

Mutulité, from 24-27 September, 1935. C.G.T., 211 Rue Lafayette, Paris, 1936.

C.G.T. Federation des ouvriers en metaux et similaires de France: Congrès d'unité tenu à Paris, les 25, 26 et 27 novembre 1936. Compte-rendu, Versailles, Imprimerie "La Gutenberg" 1937.

Catois, Gustave,
    COMMENT BARRER LA ROUTE AU FASCISME? Rapport adopte au Congres National de Strasbourg (August, 1927), Société Internationale Fédération nationale de libres penseurs de France et des colonies, Section français de la libre pensée internationale 1927.

Cherau, Gaston,
    CONCORDE! LE 6 FEVRIER 1934. Paris, éditions Deusel et Steele, 1934.

COMMISISON D'ENQUÊTE CHARGÉE DE RECHERCHES LES CAUSES ET LES ORIGINES DES ÉVÉNEMENTS DU 6 FEB. 1934 ET JOURS SUIVANTS, AINSI QUE TOUTES LES RESPONSIBILITES ENCOURISES. Paris, Imprimerie de la Chambre des Deputes, 1934. Rapport general par marc Rucart.

LE COMPLOT COMMUNISTE DEVANT LE SÉNAT. Speeches of Gautherot, Blum, Clamamus (2 Feb. 1937), some commentaries; Fortenay-aux-Roses, Imprimerie Louis Bellenand et fils, 1937.

COMPLOT (le) COMMUNO-SOCIALISTE. L'INSURRECTION ARMÉE, DANS L'UNITÉ D'ACTION. Preface; de la Rocque, Paris, 1935.

CONTRE LE FASCISME LE FRONT COMMUN. Manifeste, Paris, Front Commun, 1938.

Déat and Violette,
    UNE EXPERIENCE COMMENCE (A brochure of the Union Républicains Socialistes, 1936).

Delion, Marcel
    LE P.C.F., LA IIIe INTERNATIONALE ET L'U.R.S.S. Paris, Centre du propagande des républicains nationaux, 1936.

Doriot,
    L'EXPÉRIENCE SOVIÉTIQUE ET LE COMMUNISME FRANCAIS, Paris, 1937.

    LA FRANCE AVEC NOUS, Lagny, 1937.

LA FRANCE NE SERA PAS UN PAYS D'ESCLAVE. Nevers, Imprimerie Chassaing, 1936.

LE FRONT DE LA LIBERTÉ FACE AU COMMUNISME. Lagny, Imprimerie Emmanuel Grevin et fils, 1937.

Doumergue, Gaston,
DISCOURS À LA NATION FRANCAISE. Paris, Denoel et Steele, 1934. Radio speeches from 24 March to 4 Oct. 1934.

LE FRONT POPULAIRE NOUS A TROMPÉS - Faits, Figures, Preuves. Paris, Imprimerie commercial, 1937.

FRONT UNIQUE INTERNATIONAL. A L'AIDE DES HÉROIQUES COMBATTANTS D'ESPAGNE. Textes et documents. Bureau d'editions, Paris, 1935.

14 JUILLET 1935. Ed. par le Comité National du rassemblement populaire, Paris, Imprimerie central du Croissant, 1935. Speeches, impressions, etc.

Feugère, Fernand,
INTERVENTIONS ET VOTES INDIVIDUELS DES DEPUTÉS DU FRONT POPULAIRE. Moulins, Grepin-LeBlond, 1936.

Flandin, Pierre-Etienne,
Discours. LE MINISTÈRE FLANDIN, NOVEMBRE 1934-mai 1935. Editions de la nouvelle Revue française, Paris, 1937.

LE FRONT POPULAIRE NOUS CONDUIRE À LA CATASTROPHE. Lagny, Imprimerie Emmanuel Grèvin et fils, 1937.

Gautherot, Gustave,
LA POLITIQUE GÉNÉRALE DE LA FÉDÉRATION RÉPUBLICAINE DE FRANCE. Rapport presente au Congrès National de Nice 13 April 1935. Paris, Imprimerie de la Fédération républicaine 1935.

Hoog, Georges,
JEUNS RÉPUBLICAINS ET RASSEMBLEMENT POPULAIRE. Paris, la jeune république, oct.-nov., 1936 (Cahiers de la democratie, 41-42).

Izard, G.,
OU VA LE COMMUNISME? Paris, Grasset, 1936.

Jacoby, Jean,
LE FRONT POPULAIRE EN FRANCE ET LES ÉGAREMENTS DU SOCIALISME MODERNE. St. - Armand, Imprimerie R. Bussiere, 1937.

Jouhaux,
    COLLECTION: PROBLÈMES ET DOCUMENTS. LA C.G.T., CE QU'ELLE EST? CE QU'ELLE VEUT. Paris, Gallimard, 1937.

Lachapelle, Georges,
    ELECTIONS LEGISLATIVES 26 avril et 3 mai 1936. Official results; edited by LE TEMPS, 1936.

Legendre, Jean,
    BOBARDS ELECTORAUX. Paris, Imprimerie du centre de propagande des républicains nationaux (no date).

    LE FRONT COMMON. Centre de propagande Républicain, Paris, 1935.

    MENSONGES COMMUNISTES. Paris, Imprimerie du centre de propagande republicainn, 1938.

    POUR LUTTER CONTRE LE FRONT POPULAIRE. Senlis, Imprimerie reunies, 1937.

    Lettres a Brigitte. Paris, Imprimerie F. Beroud, Paris 1936, LIbrairie Populaire, 4th ed., 1937.

    LETTRES AUX MEMBRES DU P.C.: Signette, Delafarde, Monatte Rosmer - Courbevoie (s.d..

Lhomme, Jean,
    LE PROBLÈME DES CLASSES. Doctrines et faits. Paris, Recueil Serez, 1938.

Massa, E.H.,
    LA DECADENCE SOCIALISTE. Paris, Jouve et Cie, 1926.

Maublanc, René,
    LE PACIFISME ET LES INTELLECTUELS, (STRATEGIE ET TACTIQUE DE LA LUTTE CONTRE LA GUERRE ET LE FASCISME). Publications du Comité mondial de Pacifisme, Paris, 1936.

Maulion, Paul,
    MAY 1936-AOÛT 1938 DU FRONT POPULAIRE AU SALUT PUBLIC Mesnil, Firmin-Didot, 1938.

Meunevee, R.,
    LA CHUTE DU CABINET DALADIER, Documents politiques, 1933.

Robbe, Fernand,
    ET MAINTENANT? - APRÈS 12 MOIS DE GOUVERNEMENT DE FRONT POPULAIRE. Paris, S.E.D.A., 1937.

Sabiani, Simon,
   COLERE DU PEUPLE (preface by Doriot). Lagny, Imprimerie E. Grevin et fils, 1937.

Serge, Jean,
   FRANCE, '36, LE FRONT POPULAIRE FOURRIER DU COMMUNISME. Paris, editions C.E.A., 1943.

Soustanau-Lacau, Georges,
   MEMOIRES D'UN FRANÇAIS REBELLE, 1914-48. Paris, R. Laffont, 1948.

Spartacus,
   "Le P.C. est il francais?" "La France soldat de l'U.R.S.S." RÉPUBLIQUE MODERNE, Aug. 1946, pp. 11-14; July, pp. 10-12; May, 1946, pp. 12-15.

STATUS DU RASSEMBLEMENT POPULAIRE (3 January 1936) Comité National du Rassemblement, Paris, 1936.

Thomé, Georges,
   MEMOIRE PRESENTÉ LE 8 DEC. 1934 A LA COMMISSION D'ENQUÊTE SUR LES AFFAIRES STAVISKY. Paris, Saintes Imprimerie de l'independant, 1935.

LE TROISIEME FORCE, MOUVEMENT D'EVEIL ET DE GROUPEMENT DES FORCES COMBATTANTS POUR LA CONQUÊTE DU NOUVEAU STATUT SOCIAL ET INTERNATIONAL, Paris, Imprimerie Parisiennes réunies, 1932.

UN AN DE FRONT POPULAIRE À DIRECTION SOCIALISTE. Marseilles, Imprimerie St. Lazare, Paris, centre de Propagande des Républicains nationaux, 1937.

Vandervelde, Emile,
   L'ALTERNATIVE. Paris, L'Eglantine, 1933.

Vigneau, Albert and Orland, Vivienne,
   FRANC-MAÇONNERIE ET FRONT POPULAIRE. Paris, Imprimerie La Technique du Livre, 1936.

Wissant, André de,
   LA FRANCE À LA RECHERCHE D'UNE MYSTIQUE. Interviews of de la Rocque, H. de Kerilli, Marcel Déat, President Flandin, J.B. Severac, Bordeaux, Messageries Hachettes, 1936.

Ybarnegaray,
   LE GRAND SOIR DES HONNÊTES GENS. 6 FEVRIER 1934. Paris, éditions des Ambassadeurs, 1934.

SECONDARY SOURCES.

6. Theses.

Baudouin, Francis,
   L'EXPERIENCE SOCIAL FRANÇAISE (Thèse, Paris) 1939.

Finet, P.,
   LES SEMAINES SOCIALES DE FRANCE. Thèse, Grenoble, 1933.

Fourchy,
   LES DOCTRINES DU PARTI SOCIALISTE FRANÇAIS. These, Nancy, 1929.

Gaucher, Francois,
   CONTRIBUTION À L'HISTOIRE DU SOCIALISME FRANCAIS (1905-1933). Thesis for doctorate Université de Paris -- Faculté de droit. Paris, Les Presses modernes, 1934.

Hoebaux, Jean,
   LE NÉO-SOCIALISME EN FRANCE ENTRE 1930 et 1940. Doctorat en Droit Thèse. Paris, Faculté de Droit, 1947.

Jean, Robert,
   LE COMMUNISME DEVANT LA LOI PENALE. Thesis for doctorate, Besançon, Imprimerie Millot frères, 1930.

Maurice, J.,
   LE PARTI RADICAL (Thèse, Paris, 1929).

Roux, Marie-Laetitia,
   LE SOCIALISME DE M. HENRI DE MAN, Doctorate thesis. Paris, Librairie Technique et economique, 1937.

Spire, Alfred,
   LE DECLIN DU MARXISME DANS LES TENDENCES SOCIALISTE DE LA FRANCE CONTEMPORAINE - Thèse pour le doctorate presente par A. Spire 1937, Nancy, Imprimerie A. Tollard, 1937.

Tisne, A.,
   L'UNITÉ SYNDICALE. Thèse, Toulouse, 1935.

Veillard, Raymond,
   LE PLAN DE LA C.G.T. Thèse, Lyon, 1938.

7. Books and pamphlets constituting secondary sources.

Aftalion, A.,
   LES FONDEMENTS DU SOCIALISME, étude critique. Paris, Riviere, 1923.

Alain,
   LES ELÉMENTS D'UNE DOCTRINE RADICAL. Paris, Gallimard, 1929.

Akron, Robert,
   LA FIN DE L'APRÈS-GUERRE. Paris, Gallimard, Dec. 1938.

Arqué, Georges, et Dantun, Yves,
   UNE EMEUTE - ÉTUDE HISTORIQUE SUR LE 6 FEBRIER. Editions des documents du siecle, Paris 1934.

Bardoux, Jacques,
   LES SOVIETS CONTRE LA FRANCE, Flammarion Paris, 1936.

   J'ACCUSE MOSCOW, Flammarion, Paris, 1937.

de la Batut, Guy,
   GUIDE DU PARIS REVOLUTIONNAIRE. Paris, éditions sociales internationales, 1937.

Baumont, Maurice,
   FAILLITÉ DE LA PAIX, 1918-1939, Paris, 1945.

Beloff,
   THE FOREIGN POLICY OF SOVIET RUSSIA. Issued under the auspices of the Royal Institute of International Affairs, Oxford University Press, 1947.

Berdiaeff, Nicolas,
   PROBLÈME DU COMMUNISME, Paris-Bruges, Imprimerie editions Desdee, De Brouwer et Cie, 1933 (13 Avril).

Bernoville, Gaetan,
   LA FARCE DE LA MAIN TENDUE, DU FRENTE POPULAR AU FRONT POPULAIRE. Paris, Grasset (1937).

Blum, Léon,
   LÉON BLUM BEFORE HIS JUDGES, London, Routledge 1943.

Bois, E.J.,
   TRUTH ON THE TRAGEDY OF FRANCE. London, Hodder & Stoughton, 1941.

Boissonet, J.,
   LA MISÈRE PAR LA SUPERABONDANCE. KARL MARX PÈRE DE LA CRISE MONDIALE. Paris, Recueil Sirez 1938.

Borkenau, F.,
   THE COMMUNIST INTERNATIONAL. London, Faber, 1938.

Brogan, D.A.,
 THE DEVELOPMENT OF MODERN FRANCE. London, Hamilton, 1940.

Bussière, Dr. Francis,
 SOUS LE REGNE DES FOSSOYEURS D'EMPIRE. St. Amand, Cher, Imrimerie de R. BUssiere, 1943.

Cameron, E.R.,
 PROLOGUE TO APPEASEMENT, 1933-36. University of Pennsylvania, Philadelphia, 1942.

Carrere, P.,
 PROFILE, Paris, 1935.

Caruilleau, Robert,
 DU BLOC NATIONAL AU FRONT POPULAIRE. Paris, Spes, 1939.

Chalouveine, Marc,
 HISTORIQUE DU 6 FEV. 1934. Paris, Figuiere, 1935.

Chastanet, J.L.,
 LA RÉPUBLIQUE DES CRABES. SIX MOIS DE FRONT POPULAIRE. Paris, Alsatia s.d.

Corcos, Fernand,
 CATECHISME DES PARTIS POLITIQUES. Paris, Editions Montaigne, 1932.

Cot, Pierre,
 LE PROCÈS DE LA RÉPUBLIQUE. New York Editions de la Maison Française, 1944.

Curtius, E.R.,
 THE CIVILIZATION OF FRANCE, translated by O. Wyon, London, 1932.

Debu Bridel, Jacques,
 L'AGONIE DE LA TROISIÈME REPUBLIQUE, 1929-39. Paris, Editions du Bateau ivre (1948).

Delbos, Yvon,
 L'EXPERIENCE ROUGE. Paris, 1936.

Deutscher, O.,
 STALIN. London, Oxford Univeristy Press, 1949.

Dingle, Reginald,
 RUSSIA'S WORK IN FRANCE. London, Robert Hale, Ltd., 1938.

RUSSIA'S WORK IN SPAIN. London, published by Spanish Press Services, Ltd., Victory House, 99 Regent St., W.1. and printed by the Echo Press Ltd., Loughborough 1937.

Dollèans, Edouard,
 HISTOIRE DU MOUVEMENT OUVRIER, 1871-1936, Librairie Armand Colin, Paris, 1939.

Drieu La Rochelle,
 AVEC DORIOT. UNE CAMPAGNE D'EMANCIPATION NATIONAL 1937. Paris, editions de la Nouvelle Revue Française.

Einzig, Paul,
 FRANCE'S CRISIS. London, Macmillan, 1934.

Fabry, Jean,
 FEVRIER 1934-JUIN 1940. DE LA PLACE DE LA CONCORDE AU COURS DE L'INTENDANCE. Paris, Editions de France, 1942.

Fajon,
 LES GRANDS PROBLÈMES DE LA POLITIQUE CONTEMPORAINE. duc, Imprimerie Comte-Jacquet, 1938.

Ferle, T.,
 LE COMMUNISME EN FRANCE, Paris, Imprimerie Maison de la Bonne Presse, 1937.

Ferré, Louise-Marie,
 LES CLASSES SOCIALES DANS LA FRANCE CONTEMPORAINE. Paris, chez l'auteur, 1936.

Florinsky, Michael,
 WORLD REVOLUTION AND THE U.S.S.R. London, 1933.

LE FRONT POPULAIRE ET LE CONTROLE DES CHANGES. Paris, SAociete d'etudes et d'information economique, 1937.

Germain-Martin,
 CONTRIBUTION À L'HISTOIRE DE L'ÉVOLUTION SOCIALE DE LA FRANCE. Paris, éditions Domat-Montchretien, 1937.

Germain-Martin, Louis,
 LA POLITIQUE ECONOMIQUE DE LA FRANCE DE 1930 A JUIN 1935. Paris, Fourant, 1947.

Goguel, François,
 LA POLITIQUE DES PARTIS SOUS LA IIIe REPUBLIQUE. Paris, Editions du Seuil, 1946.

Gouttenoire de Toury, Fernand,
    LE FRONT POPULAIRE RUINÉ PAR SES CHEFS. Paris, Sorlot, 1939.

Hauck, Henry,
    HISTOIRE DU SOCIALISME, CONFÉRENCE DU 19 DEC. 1944 (S.1,1945) (Ecole du Propagandiste. Fédération socialiste de la Seine cours No. 1.) Paris, 1948.

Herriot, Philippe,
    LE 6 FEVRIER. Paris, Flammarion, 1934.

Hill, Norman L., Stoke, Harold W.,
    THE BACKGROUND OF EUROPEAN GOVERNMENTS. N.Y., Farrar & Rinehart, 1935.

Historicus,
    "Stalin on Revolution", FOREIGN AFFAIRS QUARTERLY, Jan. 1949.

Kranz, Herbert,
    DANS LES COULISSES DES MINISTÈRES ET DE L'ETAT-MAJOR, 1930-1940. Paris, Les documents contemporains, 1942.

Labin, Suzanne,
    STALIN'S RUSSIA. Victor Gollancz, Ltd. London, 1949.

Levine, Louis,
    SYNDICALISM IN FRANCE. New York, Columbia University Press, 1914.

Levy, Louis,
    LA FRANCE EST UNE DEMOCRATIE. Victor Gollancz, Ltd. London, 1943.

Lombard, Paul,
    FRONT POPULAIRE. Paris, Editions de France, 1936.

    QUATORZE MOIS DE DÉMENSE, L'EXPÉRIENCE LÉON BLUM. Paris, les éditions de France.

Massevy, Raymond,
    HISTOIRE DE LA FRANCE, 1914-1939. Editions Correa, 1945.

Maxe, J.,
    DE ZIMMERWALD AU BOLCHEVISME. Paris, Editions Bossard, 1920.

Maynard, Sir John,
    RUSSIA IN FLUX. Victor Gollancz, Ltd. London, 1946.

Millet, Raymond,
   JOUHAUX ET LA C.G.T. Paris, Denoel et Steele, 1937.

   Arbellot, Simon, LIGUES ET GROUPEMENTS, DE L'EXTRÊME DROÎTE A L'EXTRÊME GAUCHE. Paris, edition du Temps, 1935.

   LA REVOLUTION DE 193, LE COMMUNISME OU QUOI? Paris, Grasset, 1936.

Paul, Louis,
   HISTOIRE DU SOCIALISME EN FRANCE DE LA REVOLUTION À NOS JOURS. 3rd edition. Librairie des Sciences politiques et sociales, paris, 1937.

Paul Boncour, J.,
   ENTRE DEUX GUERRES. Paris, Librairie Plon, 1945.

Peel, George,
   THE ECONOMIC POLICY OF FRANCE. London, Macmillan, 1937.

Pickles, D.,
   THE FRENCH POLITICAL SCENE. London, 1938.

Reybaud, E.,
   ENQUÊTE SUR LES PARTIS ET GROUPEMENTS FANCAIS. Marseilles, éditions Rebo, 1930.

Rossi, A.,
   PHYSIOLOGIE DU PARTI COMMUNISTE FRANÇAIS. Paris, Editions Self, 1948.

Schumpeter, J.A.,
   CAPITALISM, SOCIALISM AND DEMOCRACY. Harper Bros., New York, 1942.

Siegfried, André,
   TABLEAU DES PARTIS EN FRANCE. Paris, Grasset, 1930.

Spire, Alfred,
   INVENTAIRE DES SOCIALISTES FRANCAIS CONTEMPORAIN. Paris, Librairie de Medicis, 1945.

Symposium sur le communisme francais - ESPRIT (Feb. 1946, pp. 164-270).

Thibaudet, A.,
   LES IDÉES POLITIQUES DE LA FRANCE. Paris, Stock, 1932.

   LA RÉPUBLIQUE DES PROFESSEURS. Paris, Grasset, 1927.

Thiebault, Marcel,
 EN LISANT M. LÉON BLUM, UN HOMME, UNE POLITIQUE, UN PARTI. Paris, Nouvelle Revue française, 1937.

Thorez,
 DU CONGRÈS DE TOURS AU FRONT POPULAIRE 1920-1935. Paris, Imprimerie Centrale, 1935.

Tonnelat, Ernest,
 CHARLES ANDLER, SA VIE ET SON OEUVRE. Publications de la Faculté des lettres de Strasbourg, Paris, Les Belles-Lettres, 1937.

Vaucher, Paul,
 POST-WAR FRANCE. Home University Library. London, 1934.

Vichniac, Max,
 LÉON BLUM, Paris, Flammarion, 1937.

Vincent, Charles,
 THE POPULAR FRONT IN FRANCE. A SHORT HISTORY OF THE FRENCH WORKING CLASS FROM 1934 to 1938. London, Independent Labor Party, 1938.

Walter, Gerard.
 HISTOIRE DU PARTI COMMUNISTE FRANÇAIS. Paris, Aimery Somogy, editeur, 1948.

Warren, Edouard de.,
 LA POLITIQUE DES MODERÉS. Paris, 114 Champs d'Elysées, 1929.

Weinstein, Harold R.,
 JEAN JAURÈS. A STUDY OF PATRIOTISM IN THE FRENCH SOCIALIST MOVEMENT. New York, Columbia University Press, 1936.

Werth, A.,
 FRANCE IN FERMENT, London, Jarrolds Publishers Ltd., 1935.

Zévaès,
 LA FUSILLADE DE FOURMIES, Paris, Mellottée, 1936.

 LES GRANDS MANIFESTES DU SOCIALISME FRANCAIS DANS LE XIXe SIECLE. Paris, Societe nouvelle d'Imprimerie, 1938.

LE SOCIALISME EN FRANCE DEPUIS 1904. Paris, Bibliothèque Charpentier, October, 1934.

Zirnheld, M.J., CINQUANTE ANS DE SYNDICALISME CHRÉTIEN. Paris, Editions 'Spes', 1937.

INDEX

Adler, Friedrich, pp. 32, 51, 166 169-176, 181n, 205
Alain, Émile Chartier, pp. 239
Amsterdam-Pleyel, Mouvement de, pp. 34-36, 39, 40, 44n, 46n, 48n, 115, 130, 132, 138, 139, 143n, 144n, 145n, 152, 219, 233, 262n
Association Républicaine des Anciens Combattants (l'A.R.A.C.), pp. iv, 34, 39, 42n, 100, 119n, 262n, 263n
Auriol, Vincent, pp. 79, 91n, 130, 175, 199, 214-218, 228n

Barbé, pp. 189, 195n
Barbusse, Henri, pp. 34, 247
Basch, Victor, pp. 266, 276n
Bauer, Otto, pp. 32
Bergery, Gaston, pp. 41, 48n, 57, 67, 70n, 83, 97, 143n, 148, 184, 185, 193n, 263n, 271
Blum, Léon, pp. 1, 4, 11, 15, 16, 26n, 27n, 28n, 30, 32, 33, 38, 46n, 50, 55, 58, 60, 61, 63, 65, 71n, 73n, 79, 80, 82, 97, 102, 103, 111, 120n, 125n, 129-131, 133-135, 137, 149-151,153, 162n, 163n, 166-168, 173, 175-177, 197, 199, 200, 204, 209-212, 215, 225n, 234, 267, 273, 278n
Bonardi, pp. 129
Bonnafous, Max, pp. 55, 56
Bonnaure, pp. 129
Bourgeois, Léon, pp. 1
Bräcke, A.M.D., pp. 62, 136-138, 165n, 175
Bukharin, N., pp. 10
Buré, Émile, pp. 77

Cachin, Marcel, pp. 3, 8, 167-170, 173, 174, 176, 177, 225n, 243, 246, 247, 260n, 262n, 269
C.A.P. (Permanent Administrative Commission of the Parti Socialiste) pp. 37, 43n, 109, 113, 115, 131, 132, 146, 149, 151, 161n, 200-204, 207, 216, 223n, 228n
Caillaux, Joseph, pp. 79, 142n
Cayrel, pp. 64
Challaye, Fellicien, pp. 43n
Chaumeis, André, pp. 90n
Chautemps, Camille, pp. 83, 142n
Chiappe, Jean, pp. 45n, 85-87, 92n, 93n, 133, 241
Clamamus, pp. 191n
Clemenceau, Georges, pp. 2
Compère-Morel, A., pp. 50, 72n, 94n
Congrès Extraordinaire (Parti Socialiste) Avignon, April 1933, pp. 59-61, 63
VI. Congrès Mondiale (Parti Communiste) Moscow, 1928, pp. 7, 11, 12, 17, 33, 45n
VII. Congrès Mondiale (Parti Communiste) Moscow, July-August 1935, pp. iii, 154, 167, 178n 243, 244, 254, 258n, 260n, 269
XXX. Congrès National (Parti Socialiste) Paris, July 14-17, 1933, pp. 45n, 61-63, 69n, 71n, 72n, 73n, 89n
XXXI. Congrès National (Parti Socialiste) Toulouse, May 20-24, 1934, pp. 124n, 125n, 132, 138-140, 143n, 144n, 145n, 149, 153, 166, 186, 210, 218

XXXII. Congrès National (Parti Sociliste) Mulhouse, June 9- , 1935,
    pp. 167, 200, 205, 206, 215, 218, 219, 268, 272, 273
Constant, Lucien, pp. 66, 74n, 115
Cot, Pierre, pp. 135, 232
Croix de Feu, pp. 35

Daladier, Édouard, pp. 58, 63, 82, 83, 102, 112, 125n, 128, 129,
    133-135, 210, 267
Dandicol, Jean Renaud, pp. 5
Darnar, Pierre, pp. 84, 92n
deBrouckère, pp. 205
deJouvenel, Henry, pp. 95
de la Rocque, Colonel Francois, pp. 35, 45n
de Man, Henri, pp. 48, 51, 52, 55, 56, 66, 68n, 71n
de Tinguy du Pouët, pp. 106
Déat, Marcel, pp. 26n, 49-57, 59, 64, 65, 69n, 71n, 97, 148, 271
Deixonne, PP. 137
Dengel, pp. 9
Deschizeaux, pp. 64
Doriot, Jacques, pp. 8-10, 53-55, 57, 64, 67, 69n, 70n, 97, 100,
    103, 107, 116, 117, 120n, 183-190, 191n-196n, 257n, 271
Dormoy, Marx, pp. 138, 151, 152, 162n
Doumergue, Gaston, pp. 97, 109, 110, 128, 129, 239
Dmitrov, Georges, pp. 178, 244, 249-255, 258n, 261n, 264n
Dreyfus, Alfred, pp. 2, 197
Duclos, Jacques, pp. 36, 39, 100, 108, 153, 154, 159, 163n, 189,
    192n, 231, 236, 238, 240, 241, 268
Dutilleul, pp. 189

Emeute of 6 February 1934, pp. 86-88, 92n, 96-103, 105, 107, 109-112,
    118n-122n, 128, 131, 133, 140, 143n, 149, 150, 167, 188, 194n,
    246, 272, 273

Farinet, Emile, pp. 110, 119n, 138, 149
Faure, Paul, pp. 27n, 34, 38, 43n, 59-62, 65, 66, 70, 73n, 78, 79, 85,
    89n, 90n, 105-107, 115, 116, 121n, 130, 132, 138, 146, 149, 151,
    163n, 208, 215, 216, 267
Faure, Petrus, pp. 104, 105
Ferrat, André, pp. 16
Flandin, Pierre Etienne, pp. 63, 71n, 210, 239
Front unique en bas, pp. 7, 17, 18, 20n, 28n, 31, 35, 37, 40, 65, 98,
    99, 114, 115, 125n, 146, 172, 176, 179n, 181n, 186-188, 193n, 194n,
    235, 238, 248, 250, 253, 264n, 265n
Frossard, Ludovic Oscar, pp. 1, 16, 21n, 61, 69n, 115, 134, 135, 144n,
    149, 151
Frot, Camille, PP. 135, 137

Garat, pp. 129
Gibarti, Louis, pp. 44n
Gide, André, pp. 34
Gitton, Marcel, pp. 113, 126n
Grumbach, Jacques, pp. 71n, 73n, 137, 149
Guesde, Jules, pp. 4, 19n, 52

Herold, Fernand, pp. 197
Herriot, Édouard, pp. 79-82, 91n, 97, 129, 130, 142n, 238, 239, 249
Hitler, Adolf, pp. 14, 17, 18, 30, 31, 33, 37, 38, 40, 49, 54-56, 63,
    83, 87, 88, 101, 126n, 150, 188, 198, 199, 209, 210, 270, 271, 273, 275
Huyghens, Cahiers de, pp. 54, 59, 79, 80-82, 91n, 269

Ivry, National Conference of Parti Communiste, June, 1934, pp. 42n, 146,
    149, 153, 173, 177, 187, 188, 230, 231, 238, 246, 247, 271, 273

Jaurès, Jean, pp. 4, 49, 50, 58, 63, 64, 209
Jerram, Guy, pp. 119n, 262n
Jouhaux, Léon, pp. 5, 104, 105, 112, 121n, 122n, 123n, 181n, 233-235
Just, pp. 138, 145n, 149

Kahn, Émile, pp. 53
Kamenev, pp. 254
Kun, Bela, pp. 42n, 181n
Kuusinen, O., pp. 40

Langevin, Paul, pp. 48n, 239
Laval, Pierre, pp. 210, 242
Lafont, pp. 64
Lazurick, pp. 39
Lebas, Jean-Baptiste, pp. 79, 145n, 149, 157, 163n, 203, 215, 217, 224n,
    227n, 228n
Lecache, Bernard, pp. 48n
Legendre, Jean, pp. 95
Lenin, V.I., pp. 6, 7, 21n, 112
Lerroux y Garcia, Alejandro, pp. 169, 170
Longuet, Jean, pp. 4, 69n, 107, 175, 226n

Manuilski, pp. 13, 28n
Marin, Gaston, pp. 232, 239
Marquet, Adrien, pp. 50, 56, 58, 59, 62, 69n, 70n, 73n, 74n, 107
Marschall, pp. 189
Marty, André, pp. 99, 261n
Marty, Michel, pp. 125n, 222n
Moch, Jules, pp. 137, 213, 216
Molinier, pp. 216, 225n
Monmousseau, Gaston, pp. 5, 8
Monnet, Georges, pp. 48n
Montagnon, Barthélemy, pp. 50, 54, 62, 71n, 72n
Mornet, Gaston, pp. 45n
Mussolini, B. pp. 14

Naegelen, pp. 136, 137
Nenni, P., pp. 209, 225n

Parti Unitaire (or de l'Unité) Proletarienne, pp. 42n, 104, 105, 131,
    193n, 200, 204, 220n, 223n
Paul-Boncour, Joseph, pp. 65, 82
Paul, Louis, pp. 131, 143n, 223
Paz, Maurice, pp. 136, 214, 216

Peri, Gabriel, pp. 220n
Perney, Ernest, pp. 268
Piatnitski, Jossif Arnovitch, pp. 13, 14, 234, 235, 258n
Pieck, Wilhelm, pp. 244-246
Pivert, Marceau, pp. 16, 57, 60, 110, 115, 121, 149, 206-209, 218, 224n
Poincaré, Raymond, pp. 10, 77
Popular Front, The, pp. ii, iii, 6, 7, 45n, 74n, 80, 81, 111, 120n,
    148, 154, 156-159, 194n, 198-200, 205, 207, 208, 211-215, 217, 225n,
    231, 233, 238, 241, 243, 244, 246-248, 250-253, 255, 266-268, 270,
    273-275

Racamond, Julien, pp. 268
Ramette, pp. 70n, 122n, 123
Renaud, Jean, pp. 8-10, 53, 54, 70n
Renaudel, Pierre, pp. 3, 16, 28n, 30, 50, 53, 54, 62, 63, 65, 69n, 70n,
    72n, 79, 85, 133, 143n, 271
Renoult, René, pp. 79
Ricou, Georges, pp. 259n
Rivet, Paul, pp. 239
Roche, Émile, pp. 260n
Rolland, Romain, pp. 34, 247
Rosenfeld, pp. 37, 46n
Rucart, Marc, pp. 92n, 232, 261n

Salengro, Roger, pp. 53
Sarraut, Maurice Albert, pp. 79, 83, 90n
Schuller, pp. 10, 22n
Sémard, Pierre, pp. 5, 8
Sembat, Marcel, pp. 19n
Severac, J.B., pp. 59, 61, 115, 116, 130, 137, 149, 201, 204, 207,
    211, 212, 227n
Siegfried, André, pp. 26n
Spinasse, pp. 53
Stalin, Joseph, pp. 242, 255, 260n
Stavisky, Alexandre, pp. 84, 85, 87, 92n, 93n, 128, 129, 247

Tardieu, André, pp. 63, 71n, 85, 90n, 94n, 108, 109
Thorez, Maurice, pp. 8, 10, 25n, 35, 38, 39, 42n, 65, 97, 114, 125n,
    127n, 146, 148, 153, 154, 156, 159, 162n, 163n, 164n, 167, 168, 171,
    172, 174, 176, 177, 187, 189, 197, 211, 222n, 239, 241, 246-249, 253,
    262n, 265n, 267
Togliatti (Ercoli), pp. 10, 244
Tours, Congrès de, pp. 1, 2, 4, 6, 15, 17, 19n, 108, 140, 149, 153, 202
Trotsky, Léon, pp. 184, 191n, 209, 216, 218, 261n
Twenty-one Conditions, The, pp. 4, 6, 19n, 20n

Vaillant-Couturier, Paul, pp. 243
Vandervelde, Émile, pp. 32-34, 51, 61, 166, 168, 169, 171, 172-174,
    176, 177, 181n, 182n
Vassart, Albert, pp. 237
Vielle, pp. 138
Villeurbanne (National Conference of Parti Communiste, 22-25 January
    1936), pp. 230, 231, 255
Viviani, René, pp. 19

Weill, Georges, pp. 154, 157, 163n

Zay, Jean, pp. 210
Zevaes, Gustave, pp. 19n
Zetkin, Clara, pp. 6
Zinoviev, pp. 254
Zyromski, Jean, pp. 38, 57, 59, 61, 115, 145n, 149, 152, 165n, 175, 181n, 206-208, 212, 215-218, 226n

End

ABOUT THE AUTHOR

Karl G. Harr, Jr., a magna cum laude, Phi Betta Kappa, graduate (and, later, Trustee) of Princeton University and a graduate of the Yale Law School, earned his Doctor of Philosophy degree as a Rhodes Scholar at Oxford University.

Following practice of law in New York City, he entered government service, first as Deputy Assistant Secretary of Defense for International Security Affairs, and then as Special Assistant to President Eisenhower. In the latter capacity, he was the President's principal adviser concerning the coordination of national security operations, was Vice Chairman of the Operations Coordinating Board and was required to attend all meetings of the Cabinet, National Security Council and National Aeronautics and Space Council. He was also a member of the President's Committee on Information Activities Abroad, a top level group set up to evaluate the effect of our national security operations.

Dr. Harr continues his concern with international relations by serving as Chairman of the Board of The Experiment in International Living, and as a member of the Boards of Freedom House and the Dwight D. Eisenhower World Affairs Institute.

Currently, Karl Harr is President of the Aerospace Industries Association of America, Inc. He and his wife, Patricia, reside in Chevy Chase, Maryland. They have four grown children and two grandchildren.